EMERGENCY SUBSTITUTES

For	You Can Use
1 square unsweetened chocolate	3 tablespoons unsweetened cocoa powder, plus 1 tablespoon butter or margarine
2 tablespoons flour (for thickening)	1 tablespoon cornstarch
1 cup sifted cake flour	⅞ cup sifted all-purpose flour (1 cup less 2 tablespoons)
1 cup buttermilk	1 tablespoon vinegar plus sweet milk to make 1 cup
1 egg	2 egg yolks (for custards)
¼ cup chopped onion	1 tablespoon instant minced onion, rehydrated
1 cup sweet milk	½ cup evaporated milk plus ½ cup water

EMERGENCY BAKING DISH SUBSTITUTES WHEN NECESSARY

When the recipe calls for a:

- 4 cup baking pan or dish, use:
    - 9-inch pie plate
    - 1-quart soufflé dish
- 6 cup baking pan or dish, use:
    - 9x1½-inch layer cake
    - 8x4x3-inch loaf pan
    - 10-inch pie plate
- 8 cup baking pan or dish, use:
    - 8x8x2-inch pan or dish
    - 11x7x1½-inch pan
    - 9x5x3-inch loaf pan

When using the shallow dishes, a time and temperature adjustment may be necessary.

Family Circle

RECIPES AMERICA LOVES BEST

Compiled by Nika Hazelton
with the Food Editors of Family Circle Magazine

Times
BOOKS

Published by TIMES BOOKS, a division of
Quadrangle/The New York Times Book Co., Inc.
Three Park Avenue, New York, NY 10016

Published simultaneously in Canada by
Fitzhenry & Whiteside, Ltd., Toronto

Library of Congress Catalog Card Number 81-84898
ISBN 0-8129-1008-7

Manufactured in the United States of America

10 9 8 7 6 5 4 3 2 1

Special Project Staff

Food Editor - Jean Hewitt
Senior Associate Food Editor - Jane O'Keefe
Art Director - Joseph Taveroni
Senior Art Associate - Walter Skibitsky
Production Manager - Kathy Reilly
Type Supervisor - Wendy Hylfelt

Project Management - Annabelle Arenz
John Jaxheimer

Photographs by - Bill McGinn
Rudy Muller
George Nordhausen
Gordon E. Smith

Library of Congress Cataloging in Publication Data
Main entry under title:

Family circle recipes America loves best.

Includes index.
1. Cookery. I. Hazleton, Nika. II. Family Circle
(Mount Morris, Ill.)
TX715.F1918   1982   641.5   81-84898
ISBN 0-8129-1008-7   AACR2

Foreword

Each year, Family Circle publishes hundreds of marvelous recipes in articles that are pored-over and saved by many of our 18 million readers. Now, as we celebrate our first 50 years of publication, we have undertaken the giant task of analyzing our storehouse of food information, and reviewing the interests and concerns of our readers as reflected in letters we've received over the years.

The result is very special. I am proud to present FAMILY CIRCLE'S RECIPES AMERICA LOVES BEST, a collection of over 500 of your all-time favorites: the finest in American cooking, special treats for everyone.

Making the selections wasn't easy, but we're sure you'll find many recipes that will please you, your family, your pocketbook. You'll be tempted by sections on appetizers and beverages; soups and sandwiches; vegetables and salads; meat, poultry, fish; breads, eggs, cheese; pasta and desserts—and more. There's even a "QUICK AND EASY" chapter for today's busy homemaker. Delicious, economical winners, all. And the color photographs look good enough to eat!

Every single dish was triple-tested in our kitchen to ensure perfect results in yours. We checked out all the ingredients, measurements, temperatures, timings. We checked supermarket shelves to make sure the ingredients were easily available. We're proud of our 50-year association with supermarkets. Together we have significantly improved the country's knowledge and appreciation of food.

I want to give special thanks to three gifted women who compiled and edited this book. Jean Hewitt, Family Circle's Food Editor since 1975, has written nine cookbooks, including the award-winning NEW YORK TIMES NATURAL FOODS COOKBOOK. Her unerring judgment in choosing the best recipes was a terrific help. Jane O'Keefe, our Senior Associate Food Editor, was a major contributor to the *first* FAMILY CIRCLE COOKBOOK, which sold over half a million copies. Jane knows exactly how to create menus that have irresistible appeal, with recipes that are easily understood even by novice cooks. Nika Hazelton has written 23 cookbooks (among them AMERICAN HOME COOKING) and is also a columnist for the *National Review*. She brought her versatility and years of experience to the project.

Our trio of top cooking pros succeeded admirably in making this collection a fitting commemorative to the world's largest-selling women's magazine and its golden anniversary. FAMILY CIRCLE'S RECIPES AMERICA LOVES BEST is a truly appetite-whetting book, one you will cherish and use often. With Family Circle's unmatched food know-how behind it, you are guaranteed pleasure both in the preparation and it the serving.

Enjoy!

Arthur Hettich
Editor-In-Chief

Family Circle

RECIPES AMERICA LOVES BEST

Contents

Stuffed Edam Cheese with Crisp Vegetables (page 16)

Appetizers and Beverages

Tasty morsels to pique the appetite before a meal,
and drinks for all occasions.

GOLDEN CHICKEN NUGGETS

These make-aheads will disappear fast at your next get-together.
Bake at 400° for 10 minutes.
Makes 4 to 5 dozen nuggets.

- 4 whole chicken breasts (about 12 ounces each)
- ½ cup packaged bread crumbs
- ¼ cup grated Parmesan cheese
- 1 teaspoon leaf thyme, crumbled
- 1 teaspoon leaf basil, crumbled
- 1 teaspoon salt
- ½ cup (1 stick), butter or margarine melted

1. Bone and halve chicken breasts; remove skin. Cut each breast half into 6 to 8 pieces, about 1½ inches square.
2. Combine bread crumbs, cheese, thyme, basil and salt on wax paper.
3. Dip chicken nuggets in melted butter, then in crumb mixture. Place in single layer on foil-lined cookie sheets.
4. Bake in a hot oven (400°) for 10 minutes.

GREEK APPETIZER MEATBALLS

The secret ingredient is ouzo, which imparts a delicate, elusive flavor.
Makes 32 meatballs.

- 1 pound ground round
- ½ cup soft bread crumbs (1 slice)
- 1 teaspoon salt
  Dash ground cinnamon
- 1 medium-size onion, grated
- 2 tablespoons chopped parsley
- 2 tablespoons chopped fresh mint
  OR: 1 teaspoon dried mint
- 1 egg
- ¼ cup Greek ouzo or any other anise-flavored liqueur
  Flour
- 2 tablespoons olive or vegetable oil

1. Combine beef, bread crumbs, salt, cinnamon, onion, parsley, mint, egg and ouzo in a large bowl; mix lightly with a fork, just until combined.
2. Shape meat mixture into small balls about the size of a quarter. Roll meatballs in flour to coat evenly; place in a single layer on a cookie sheet; refrigerate 1 hour.
3. Heat oil in a large skillet; add meatballs. Cook over medium-high heat, tossing and turning often, until evenly browned and cooked through, about 10 minutes.

> **Easy onions:** When a recipe calls for a small amount of grated or minced onion, cut a slice off the top of an onion, then cross-hatch the onion with a paring knife in very thin straight-down cuts, first one way, then the other, cutting about ⅛-inch deep. Slice off this portion of the onion to use, and wrap the rest to use another time.

TINY PANCAKES WITH SOUR CREAM AND RED CAVIAR

Makes 6 dozen.

- 1 container (16 ounces) frozen pancake batter, defrosted
- 1 container (8 ounces) dairy sour cream
- 1 jar (4¼ ounces) red salmon or red lumpfish caviar

1. Heat griddle; grease lightly. Pour approximately 1 teaspoon pancake batter for each pancake onto griddle; turn once. Place on a cookie sheet. Keep warm between sheets of paper toweling in a slow oven while baking the remaining pancakes.
2. To serve: Top with a dollop of sour cream and red caviar. Serve warm.

> **These tiny pancakes are a perfect finger food. They may be made ahead and warmed in the oven. To eat: Take a warm pancake, spread it neatly with sour cream, add a dab of caviar, then fold it and enjoy!**

BITE-SIZE FRANKWICHES

A miniature frank in a bun.
Bake at 400° for 10 minutes.
Makes 40 appetizers.

- 1 package (11 ounces) refrigerated baking powder biscuits
- 2 jars (6 ounces each) cocktail-size frankfurters
  Spicy brown mustard

1. Cut each biscuit into quarters. Place on an ungreased cookie sheet, point up.
2. Separate the top of each biscuit quarter slightly and place a frankfurter in the center. Secure each with a wooden pick.
3. Bake in a hot oven (400°) for 10 minutes, or until biscuits are golden brown. Serve hot with a dollop of mustard.

PERUVIAN PUFFS

The simple, savory filling may be made hours ahead.
Makes 30 appetizers.

- ½ cup grated Parmesan cheese
- ½ cup mayonnaise or salad dressing
- 1½ teaspoons anchovy paste
- 1 teaspoon minced onion
- 1 container (3⅓ ounces) cocktail-size pastry shells (croutelettes), about 30
  OR: tiny toast cups
- 1 jar (2¾ ounces) tiny cocktail shrimp, drained
  Parsley sprigs

1. Combine the Parmesan cheese, mayonnaise, anchovy paste and onion in a small bowl.
2. Spoon mixture evenly into cocktail-size pastry shells. Place on a jelly-roll pan.
3. Run under broiler, about 4 inches from heat, until tops are bubbly and beginning to brown, about 1 minute. Garnish with tiny cocktail shrimp and parsley sprigs.

> **To make your own tiny toast cups for hors d'oeuvres: Cut out 2-inch rounds from thin-sliced white bread. Press with rolling pin to compact slightly. Brush both sides with melted butter. Press firmly into miniature muffin-pan cups. Toast in a moderate oven (350°) for 15 minutes. Cool on wire racks.**

'ONO 'ONO SPARERIBS

Delicious is the word for these golden glazed ribs.
Makes about 36 appetizers.

- 4 to 5 pounds lean spareribs
- 2 teaspoons salt
  Tangy Barbecue Glaze
  (*recipe follows*)

1. Have butcher crack bones into 3- to

4-inch lengths. Place ribs in a large sauce-pan. Sprinkle in salt; add water to cover. Bring to boiling; lower heat; cover. Simmer 30 minutes or until ribs are almost tender.
2. Drain ribs; cut into 1-rib pieces. Put in a shallow glass dish; pour Tangy Barbecue Glaze over. Let ribs marinate for several hours or overnight in refrigerator.
3. Drain ribs, reserving glaze. Place ribs on grill, about 6 inches from grayed coals, or in broiler with tops about 4 inches from heat. Grill or broil about 20 minutes, turning often and brushing generously with reserved glaze, until ribs are browned and evenly glazed.

TANGY BARBECUE GLAZE
Makes about 2½ cups.

 1 large onion, finely chopped (1 cup)
 2 cloves garlic, finely chopped
 2 tablespoons vegetable oil
 1 cup chili sauce

 ½ cup lemon juice
 ⅓ cup molasses
 3 tablespoons Dijon-style mustard
 1 tablespoon Worcestershire sauce
 ¼ cup dark rum

Sauté onion and garlic in oil in a medium-size saucepan until tender, about 5 minutes. Stir in chili sauce, lemon juice, molasses, mustard and Worcestershire; bring to boiling; cover; lower heat. Simmer 20 minutes. Remove from heat; stir in rum.

> **For succulent, juicy spareribs, whether for a main dish or an appetizer, it is best to precook them to get rid of some of the fat. You can simmer them in water or bake on a rack in the oven. Precooking allows the ribs to be glazed on the grill or under the broiler without excessive charring and drying.**

From left to right: Tiny Pancakes with Sour Cream and Red Caviar; Peruvian Puffs; Boursin Stuffed Mushrooms (page 11); Bite-size Frankwiches; Cherry Tomatoes Stuffed with Avocado Egg Salad (page 11)

BEEF TERIYAKI

The sherry-soy marinade adds flavor and tenderizes.

Makes about 36 appetizers.

    1 top round steak (about
        1½ pounds), cut 1 inch thick
    ½ cup dry sherry
    ¾ cup soy sauce
    3 tablespoons bottled steak sauce
    2 tablespoons sugar
    2 cloves garlic, minced

1. Pierce steak all over deeply with a fork; place in shallow nonmetal dish.
2. Make marinade: Combine sherry, soy sauce, steak sauce, sugar and garlic in a small bowl. Pour about ⅓ over steak; cover. (Reserve remaining marinade for dipping.) Refrigerate several hours or overnight, turning steak several times.
3. Cut meat into long thin slices about ⅛ inch thick; thread accordion-style onto 8-inch bamboo skewers; brush with marinade.
4. Broil, 2 to 3 inches from heat, 1 minute; turn and broil 1 minute longer. Serve with reserved marinade for dipping.

> **Bamboo skewers won't burn if you soak them in water for an hour or so before threading the food to be broiled on them.**

IOWA BLUE CHEESE TART

Bake at 375° for 45 minutes.
Makes 12 servings.

    ½ package piecrust mix
    2 packages (3 ounces each) cream
        cheese
    4 ounces blue cheese
    2 tablespoons butter or margarine,
        softened
    ¼ cup heavy cream
    3 eggs
    ⅛ teaspoon cayenne
    ¼ teaspoon salt
    ⅛ teaspoon pepper
    1 teaspoon chopped chives

1. Prepare piecrust mix, following label directions for a single crust. Roll out to a 12-inch round; fit into a 9-inch fluted tart pan with a removable bottom or a 9-inch pie plate.
2. Preheat oven to moderate (375°).
3. Beat cream cheese in a medium-size bowl with electric mixer until softened. Crumble in blue cheese; beat until blended. Add butter, heavy cream, eggs, cayenne, salt and pepper; beat until light and smooth. Stir in chives. Pour into prepared pastry-lined pan.
4. Bake in preheated moderate oven (375°) for 45 minutes, or until tart is puffy and brown. Cool 5 minutes on wire rack. Loosen and remove side of pan. Garnish with additional chopped chives; serve in wedges with fresh fruit, if you wish.

FRIED BRIE

The melted warm inside of the Brie and the crunchy "fried" breaded outside make this an unusual treat.

Makes 12 servings.

    ½ pound Brie cheese
        Flour
    1 egg
    1 tablespoon water
    ½ cup packaged bread crumbs
    2 tablespoons butter or margarine
    1 loaf French bread

1. Remove and discard paper and plastic wrapping from cheese. Coat all surfaces with flour.
2. Beat egg with water in a pie plate until foamy. Dip cheese in egg, then in crumbs, coating well.
3. Heat butter in small skillet or flameproof stove-to-table casserole just until it foams. Put cheese in skillet; cover; cook

Iowa Blue Cheese Tart

over low heat about 5 minutes, or until golden brown on one side. Turn and cook, covered, on other side until golden.
4. Remove from heat; make a cut in the cheese so it will run. Serve at once while warm with bread that has been cut into small pieces. Pass around while warm—cheese firms as it cools.

SESAME CHICKEN WINGS
Miniature "drumsticks" in a cream and crumb coating "fry" with ease in the oven. Delicious hot or cold.
Bake at 375° for 40 minutes.
Makes about 36 appetizers.

3 pounds chicken wings (about 18)
2 tablespoons toasted sesame seeds
¾ cup packaged bread crumbs
1 teaspoon paprika
½ teaspoon salt
⅓ cup heavy cream

½ cup (1 stick) butter or margarine
Bottled duck sauce

1. Remove tips of chicken wings; freeze for making soup. Bend wing at the joint; cut into two sections.
2. Combine sesame seeds, bread crumbs, paprika and salt in a shallow dish.
3. Dip chicken pieces in cream, using a brush to coat completely; roll in crumb mixture. Refrigerate at least 1 hour to set the crumb coating.
4. Melt butter in a 13x9x2-inch pan in the oven while it preheats to moderate (375°). Remove pan from oven when butter is melted. Add chicken; turn to coat all over.
5. Bake in preheated moderate oven (375°) for 40 minutes, or until golden and tender. Serve with bottled duck sauce.

> **Nutty sesame seeds: Sesame seeds gain a wonderful nut-like flavor when toasted. Just sprinkle a thin layer of seeds in a skillet and shake or stir over low heat until they are a toasty golden color.**

Crispy Coconut Shrimp

CRISPY COCONUT SHRIMP

Makes about 24 appetizers.

    1 pound medium-size fresh shrimp
    ¼ cup flour
    ½ teaspoon salt
    ½ teaspoon dry mustard
    1 egg
    2 tablespoons heavy cream
    ¾ cup flaked coconut
    ⅓ cup packaged bread crumbs
      Chinese Mustard Sauce (*recipe follows*)
      Bottled duck sauce

1. Shell and devein shrimp, but leave tails with the shell on.
2. Combine flour, salt and dry mustard in one small bowl; beat egg and cream in second small bowl. Combine coconut and bread crumbs on a sheet of wax paper.
3. Dip shrimp in flour mixture, then in egg-cream mixture, and finally in coconut crumb mixture, coating well. Refrigerate in a single layer until ready to cook.
4. Pour oil into a medium-size saucepan to 2-inch depth. Heat to 350° on a deep-fat frying thermometer.

5. Fry shrimp, a few at a time, in hot oil for about 2 minutes or until golden brown. Remove with slotted spoon to paper toweling to drain. Keep warm in a very slow oven (250°) until all shrimp are cooked. Serve with Chinese Mustard Sauce and bottled duck sauce for dipping.

CHINESE MUSTARD SAUCE: Mix ⅓ cup dry mustard with 1 tablespoon honey, 2 teaspoons vinegar and ¼ cup cold water until well blended; refrigerate. Makes about ⅓ cup.

SPINACH-CHEESE PUFFS
(Spanakotiropetes)
Make these multilayered Greek pastries ahead of time; refrigerate until baking at serving time. To make their triangular shape, just fold like a flag.

Bake at 375° for 20 minutes.
Makes about 44 appetizers.

    2 eggs
    1 medium-size onion, quartered
    ½ pound feta cheese, crumbled or
      diced fine
    1 package (8 ounces) cream cheese

1 package (10 ounces) frozen chopped spinach, thawed
2 tablespoons chopped parsley
1 tablespoon snipped fresh dill
 OR: 1 teaspoon dillweed
 Dash pepper
24 sheets (about ¾ of a 1-pound package) phyllo or strudel pastry
1 cup (2 sticks) butter or margarine, melted

1. Combine eggs, onion and feta cheese in container of electric blender. Whirl until smooth; add cream cheese; whirl again a few seconds until smooth. Squeeze spinach with hands to remove as much liquid as possible. Add to cheese mixture with parsley, dill and pepper; blend just until combined. Refrigerate at least 1 hour.
2. Stack 2 leaves (22 x 16 inches each) of phyllo pastry on working surface; cover with plastic wrap to prevent drying. For each puff cut off a strip 2 inches wide and 16 inches long, cutting through both leaves; brush with melted butter or margarine.
3. Place a rounded teaspoon of filling on one end of strip. Fold one corner to opposite side, forming a triangle shape. Continue folding this way to the end of the strip. Repeat with remaining pastry and filling until all is used. Arrange the filled pastries on an ungreased jelly-roll pan.
4. Bake in moderate oven (375°) 20 minutes or until golden brown. Serve hot.

> **Phyllo or strudel leaves are tissue-thin pastry leaves that are used for many savory and sweet recipes of both Greek and German origin. When baked, they puff into unbelievably delicate shattery pastry. They are usually available frozen. When using the defrosted leaves, cover the leaves that are not being used with damp toweling or plastic wrap to keep them from drying.**

OYSTERS ROCKEFELLER

This dish was invented at Antoine's, the famous New Orleans restaurant, by Jules Alciatore in the 1850s. It is so rich that he named it after the wealthiest man in the country at the time.

Makes 6 servings.

6 tablespoons (¾ stick) butter or margarine
½ cup packaged bread crumbs
2 cups spinach leaves, washed and stemmed
½ cup parsley sprigs
½ cup diced celery
2 tablespoons diced onion
1 tablespoon Pernod liqueur
¼ teaspoon salt
3 drops liquid red-pepper seasoning
18 large oysters on the half shell (*see note*)
 Rock salt

1. Melt butter in a small saucepan; sauté bread crumbs for 1 minute, stirring often.
2. Combine butter mixture, spinach, parsley, celery, onion, Pernod, salt and red-pepper seasoning in container of electric blender. Cover and whirl at high speed, stopping blender to stir contents several times, until mixture is smooth. Pour into a small bowl; refrigerate until ready to use.
3. Arrange oysters in shells on a bed of rock salt in six individual heatproof dishes, placing 3 in each dish. (Rock salt steadies shells and retains heat.) Top each oyster with a tablespoonful of the spinach mixture, covering each oyster completely.
4. Broil 4 inches from heat, 3 minutes, or just until topping is lightly browned and heated through. Serve at once.

Note: If fresh oysters in the shell are not available, substitute canned oysters. Place well-drained oysters in small scallop shells or small, flame-proof serving dishes, and continue with recipe.

Sweet and Sour Pork Balls

SWEET AND SOUR PORK BALLS

Bake at 350° for 20 minutes.
Makes about 36 meatballs.

- 1 pound ground pork
- 1 can (8 ounces) water chestnuts, minced
- ½ cup minced green onions
- 1 teaspoon minced fresh gingerroot or preserved ginger
- ¾ teaspoon salt
- 1 tablespoon soy sauce
- 1 egg, lightly beaten
- ½ cup packaged bread crumbs
  Cornstarch
- 3 tablespoons vegetable oil
  Sweet and Sour Sauce
  (recipe follows)

1. Combine pork, water chestnuts, onion, ginger, salt, soy sauce, egg and bread crumbs in a large bowl; mix well. Shape into 36 balls. Roll in cornstarch to coat lightly, shaking off excess.

2. Brown in oil in a large skillet. Remove balls as they brown to a roasting pan; cover loosely with foil.

3. Bake in a moderate oven (350°) for 20 minutes, or until thoroughly cooked. Combine with Sweet and Sour Sauce, keep warm in a chafing dish.

SWEET AND SOUR SAUCE: Sauté ½ cup *each* cubed sweet green and sweet red pepper and 2 large, thinly sliced carrots, in 2 tablespoons vegetable oil in a large saucepan until tender, 3 minutes. Stir in 1 can (20 ounces) pineapple chunks in pineapple juice, ¼ cup vinegar, 1 tablespoon soy sauce, 2 tablespoons sugar, ½ cup beef broth and 2 teaspoons minced fresh ginger. Combine 2 tablespoons cornstarch with ⅓ cup water in a cup; stir into saucepan. Cook, stirring constantly, until mixture thickens and bubbles.

> **Freeze these ahead of time: Baked pork balls can be cooled, placed in a single layer on a jelly-roll pan and frozen just until firm, about 2 hours. Tumble them into a plastic freezer bag and store in the freezer for up to 2 weeks. You will find that they don't stick together, and hold their shape better. Defrost about 2 hours at room temperature.**

CHERRY TOMATOES STUFFED WITH AVOCADO EGG SALAD

Makes about 36 appetizers.

    1 large ripe avocado
    2 teaspoons lemon juice
    1 tablespoon mayonnaise
    4 hard-cooked eggs, peeled and very
        finely chopped
    1 small onion, finely chopped (¼ cup)
    ½ teaspoon salt
    ¼ teaspoon pepper
        About 36 cherry tomatoes, tops
            removed
        Parsley
        About 36 cocktail onions, drained

1. Halve and peel avocado; pit. Place avocado in a small bowl; sprinkle with lemon juice; mash. Stir in mayonnaise.

2. Add the eggs, onion, salt and pepper; blend well.

3. Scoop out cherry tomatoes and turn upside down on paper toweling to drain for several minutes. (A ¼ teaspoon measure is perfect for scooping out the tomatoes.)

4. Fill each tomato, using a pastry bag with no tip, or a small spoon.

5. Serve on a bed of parsley and garnish each tomato with a cocktail onion.

BOURSIN-STUFFED MUSHROOMS

They will keep their freshness for many hours so that you can make them ahead. Makes 3 dozen appetizers.

    36 small to medium-size mushrooms
     3 packages (5 ounces each) Boursin
        cheese with garlic and fines herbes,
        softened
        Parsley

1. Wipe mushrooms with a damp cloth; remove stems. (Use stems for soup.)

2. Spoon cheese into mushrooms. Garnish with parsley; refrigerate.

CHICKEN-FILLED PASTRY BOATS

A zesty chicken mixture fills these crisp make-ahead pastry shells.

Bake at 400° for 8 minutes.
Makes about 2 dozen.

    ½ package piecrust mix
    ¾ cup finely chopped cooked chicken
    2 tablespoons chopped green onions
    2 tablespoons chopped celery
    1½ teaspoons finely chopped canned
        hot chilies
    ½ teaspoon lime juice or lemon juice
    ½ teaspoon salt
    ¼ cup dairy sour cream
        Pitted black olives

1. Prepare piecrust mix, following label directions. Roll out pastry, half the amount at a time, to an ⅛-inch thickness on lightly floured surface.

2. Using 3-inch barquette pans or tiny tart pans, invert pans onto pastry and cut pastry ½-inch wider than pans. Press pastry into pans and trim even with edges. Arrange pans on cookie sheets. Prick pastry all over with a fork.

3. Bake in a hot oven (400°) for 8 minutes, or until golden. Cool pans on a wire rack, 5 minutes. Ease out of pans; cool completely.

4. Combine chicken, onion, celery, chilies, lime juice, salt and sour cream in a small bowl; toss to mix well; spoon into shells. Garnish with black olive wedges. Cover; refrigerate until serving time.

Make-ahead note: Pastry boats may be baked up to a week ahead. Store in covered containers with wax paper between layers. They may be recrisped just before filling by heating for 10 minutes in a moderate (350°) oven.

CHEESE AU POIVRE

A delicious herbed and peppered cream-cheese spread.

Makes 6 servings.

- 1 package (8 ounces) cream cheese, softened
- ½ cup (1 stick) butter or margarine, softened
- 1 tablespoon chopped chives
- 1 clove garlic, minced
- 1¼ teaspoons cracked black pepper
- ⅓ cup finely chopped parsley
  Pimiento

1. Blend cream cheese, butter, chives, garlic and 1 teaspoon of the cracked black pepper in a small bowl. Chill until firm enough to handle.

2. Shape into a ball on a piece of wax paper, using paper to help shape, if necessary; flatten slightly.

3. To decorate: Cut two ¾-inch wide pieces of wax paper; press onto cheese, forming an X. Place parsley on another piece of wax paper; carefully roll cheese ball in parsley, pressing in. Remove the wax paper strips. Sprinkle the remaining ¼ teaspoon cracked black pepper on strips where wax paper was removed. Decorate with pimiento. Keep refrigerated. Accompany cheese ball with Melba toast or assorted crackers.

EASY AND ELEGANT PÂTÉ

Makes about 10 servings.

- 1 medium-size onion, chopped (½ cup)
- 1 cup (2 sticks) butter or margarine
- 1½ pounds chicken livers
- ½ teaspoon salt
- ¼ teaspoon pepper
- ⅛ teaspoon ground nutmeg
- ½ cup heavy cream
- ½ cup brandy

1. Sauté onion in half the butter in a large skillet until tender, about 3 minutes. Add remaining butter and the chicken livers.

Sauté, stirring occasionally, until livers lose their pink color, about 10 minutes. Remove skillet from heat; add salt, pepper, nutmeg, cream and brandy.

2. Puree mixture, part at a time, in container of electric blender, including some liquid with the livers each time. Spoon pâté into a serving dish; refrigerate several hours or overnight. Serve with crisp crackers or Melba toast.

Blender tip: When pureeing solid food like chicken livers in the blender, it is important to puree in small batches with enough liquid (from the recipe) to get the food down into the blades of the blender, so it will do a proper job.

STUFFED CELERY PINWHEELS

Makes about 6 servings.

- 1 bunch celery
- 1 container (8 ounces) soft cream cheese
- 2 tablespoons milk
- 2 tablespoons very finely chopped pimiento
- ¼ teaspoon salt
  Dash liquid red-pepper seasoning

1. Pull off 6 to 8 of the unblemished stalks of celery. Wash under cold running water; pat dry on paper toweling.

2. Combine cheese, milk, pimiento, salt and red-pepper seasoning in a medium-size bowl; beat well.

3. "Butter" the inside curve of each stalk with the cream cheese mixture. Then reassemble the stalks, slightly overlapping and pressing tightly together. Wrap in foil or plastic wrap; refrigerate for about an hour for cheese to firm a bit.

4. Holding bunch firmly, cut into ¼-inch slices, so you can see the pink filling spiraling through the pale green of the celery.

SMOKED SALMON AND CHEESE CANAPÉS

Makes about 30 canapés.

- 1 container (8 ounces) whipped cream cheese
- ¼ pound smoked salmon
- 1 tablespoon lemon juice
- ¼ cup snipped dill
  Party pumpernickel bread
  Black or red lumpfish caviar
  Fresh dill sprigs

1. Spread cream cheese on wax paper to an 8- or 9-inch square. Chop salmon finely; spread evenly over cream cheese, pressing down slightly. Sprinkle with lemon juice. Roll up, jelly-roll fashion, scraping cheese from paper with small spatula as you roll. Roll in chopped dill. Wrap in foil. Chill several hours, or until firm enough to slice.
2. To serve: Slice with a thin-bladed sharp knife into ¼-inch-thick rounds. Arrange on thin slices of party pumpernickel bread. Garnish with caviar and dill.

> **Keeping canapés fresh:** Lightly dampen a clean towel; spread it smoothly on the bottom of a baking pan. Cut a sheet of wax paper or plastic wrap to fit over top of towel. Then line up canapés in a single layer. Cover top of pan with plastic wrap; refrigerate. The damp towel, separated from the canapés by the wax paper, will yield just enough moisture to keep them fresh, but not soggy.

BASIC DEVILED EGGS

Makes 12 egg halves.

- 6 hard-cooked eggs
- ¼ cup mayonnaise
- 1 teaspoon prepared mustard

1. Halve eggs, lengthwise or crosswise. Remove yolks from whites. Press yolks through a fine sieve into a small bowl. Stir in mayonnaise and mustard until well-blended.
2. Fit a pastry bag with a rosette tip; fill bag with yolk mixture. Pipe into egg whites. Or spoon yolk mixture into whites, mounding neatly. Keep refrigerated.

CURRIED EGGS: Add 1 teaspoon grated onion and 1 teaspoon curry powder to Basic Deviled Eggs.

PICKLED EGGS: Add 1 tablespoon well-drained pickle relish to Basic Deviled Eggs.

> **For never-fail hard-cooked eggs:** Put eggs in a large saucepan. Add cold water to cover eggs by 1 inch. Bring to boiling; lower heat at once, so water is barely simmering (or, remove pan from heat altogether). Let simmer (or stand) 14 minutes. Take to sink; drain, then run cold water into the pan until eggs are quite cool. Crack shells on countertop by rolling back and forth. Peel off shell. (If storing eggs for a few days, wait until just before peeling to crack shells.)

GARDEN ONION DIP

Makes 2 cups.

- 1 pint (2 cups) dairy sour cream
- 1 envelope dehydrated onion soup mix
- ¼ cup *each* finely diced radish, carrot, green pepper, celery

1. Combine sour cream, onion soup mix and diced vegetables in a medium-size bowl; blend well. Cover and refrigerate 1 hour or longer, until well chilled.
2. Stir dip before serving and spoon into a serving bowl. Garnish with additional diced radish, carrot and green pepper, if you wish.

> **Dipper tips:** Garden Onion Dip is good with potato or corn chips, cucumber sticks and broccoli flowerets.

Tex-Mex Dip

TEX-MEX DIP

Makes 16 appetizer servings.

3 medium-size ripe avocados
2 tablespoons lemon juice
½ teaspoon salt
¼ teaspoon pepper
1 cup (8 ounces) dairy sour cream
½ cup mayonnaise or salad dressing

1 package (1¼ ounces) taco seasoning mix
2 cans (10½ ounces each) plain or jalapeño bean dip
1 cup chopped green onions
3 medium-size tomatoes, cored, halved, seeded and coarsely chopped (2 cups)

2 cans (3½ ounces each) pitted black olives, drained and coarsely chopped
2 cups shredded sharp Cheddar cheese (8 ounces)
Large round tortilla chips

1. Peel, pit and mash avocados in a medium-size bowl with lemon juice, salt and pepper. Combine sour cream, mayonnaise and taco seasoning mix in a bowl.
2. To assemble: Spread bean dip on a large, shallow serving platter; top with seasoned avocado mixture; layer with sour-cream taco mixture. Sprinkle with chopped onions, tomatoes and olives; cover with shredded cheese. Serve chilled or at room temperature with round tortilla chips.

For happy, relaxed get-togethers with friends and family, dips and dunks make a good choice for openers. Choose a recipe that is not so stiff that it will break a cracker or chip. Crisp vegetables are excellent choices for stiffer dips.

CHILI CON QUESO PARTY DIP

Makes 8 cups.

1 can (15 ounces) chili con carne, without beans
2 jars (1 pound each) process cheese spread
1 pound sharp Cheddar cheese, shredded
2 tablespoons minced jalapeños or green chili peppers

1. Combine chili, cheeses and jalapeños in the top of a large double boiler. Heat over simmering water, stirring several times, until cheese melts and mixture is hot.
2. Pour into a chafing dish. Serve with corn chips or crackers.

CHILI-OLIVE DIP

Makes 1¾ cups.

¼ cup mayonnaise
1 can (4 ounces) chopped green chili peppers
½ cup drained pimiento-stuffed olives
1 cup (8 ounces) dairy sour cream
½ teaspoon salt
½ teaspoon chili powder

1. Place mayonnaise, chili peppers and olives in container of electric blender; cover and whirl until smooth.
2. Spoon sour cream into a small bowl and stir in mayonnaise mixture, salt and chili powder until well blended.
3. Cover; refrigerate about 1 hour.

CREAMY PARMESAN-HERB DIP

Serve this pale green, creamy dipping sauce in a scooped-out cauliflower and include the cauliflowerets among the dippers. Great as a pasta sauce, too.

Makes 2 cups.

2 very large cloves garlic
3 tablespoons lemon juice
2 eggs
½ cup grated Parmesan cheese
½ cup parsley sprigs
1 teaspoon leaf basil
1 teaspoon salt
½ teaspoon pepper
½ cup olive oil
½ cup vegetable oil

1. Whirl garlic, lemon juice, eggs, Parmesan cheese, parsley, basil, salt and pepper in container of electric blender, scraping side of blender often, until smooth.
2. Remove center of blender cover, or whole cover if blender has a solid cover. With blender running, pour oils in a thin stream very slowly into mixture, stopping once or twice to scrape down the thickening mixture from side of blender. Cover; refrigerate at least 2 hours.

STUFFED EDAM CHEESE WITH CRISP VEGETABLES

Makes about 3 cups.

    6 carrots, cut in thin diagonal pieces
    2 sweet green peppers, cut in strips
    2 stalks celery, cut in diagonal pieces
    1 medium-size zucchini, thinly sliced
    ¼ pound mushrooms, thickly sliced
    1 Dutch Edam cheese (about 2 pounds)
    2 tablespoons horseradish
    ½ cup undrained pickle relish
    1 cup (8 ounces) dairy sour cream
    6 slices bacon, crisp-fried and crumbled
        Parsley and dill sprigs

1. Prepare vegetables; wrap and chill.
2. Cut ½-inch off top of Edam; scoop out center with a sharp knife and then a spoon, leaving a shell about ½-inch thick; wrap and chill. Shred removed cheese; place in a medium-size bowl; stir in horseradish, pickle relish, sour cream and bacon; beat until blended; chill.
3. To serve: Allow dip to warm to room temperature before filling shell; garnish with parsley and dill. Serve with vegetables. Refill shell as needed.

For crisp, no-bother bacon, try the microwave way. Arrange bacon strips on paper toweling on a paper plate or Pyrex dish. Microwave. Paper toweling catches the fat, and the bacon keeps a nice straight shape.

POTTED SHRIMP BUTTER

Try this lemon-mace-flavored spread.
Makes about ¾ cup.

    1 package (7 ounces) frozen shelled and deveined shrimp
    ½ cup (1 stick) butter or margarine, softened
    1 clove garlic, minced
    2 tablespoons finely chopped parsley
    1 tablespoon finely chopped onion
    1 teaspoon grated lemon rind
    ⅛ teaspoon ground mace
    ½ teaspoon salt
    ⅛ teaspoon pepper

1. Cook the shrimp following label directions; drain; cool; chop finely.
2. Beat butter in a small bowl with electric mixer. Stir in shrimp, garlic, parsley, onion, lemon rind, mace, salt and pepper. Mix well; spoon into crock or serving bowl; cover. Refrigerate several hours. Allow to soften slightly before serving. Serve with crackers or Melba toast.

Snippable herbs: When using fresh herbs such as dill, chives, parsley, etc., hold them together in small bunches and snip with kitchen scissors. It is a lot faster this way, and you'll find the herbs will be light and fluffy, not bruised and wet as they often get when chopped.

MACADAMIA CHEDDAR BALLS

An easy make-ahead with two different cheeses plus crunchy macadamia nuts.
Makes about 5 dozen appetizers.

    1 package (8 ounces) cream cheese, softened
    ¼ cup (½ stick) butter or margarine, softened
    2½ cups extra sharp Cheddar cheese, shredded (10 ounces)
    ¼ cup finely chopped chutney
    1 cup chopped macadamia nuts or cashews
    ¼ cup chopped parsley

1. Beat cream cheese and butter in a large bowl with electric mixer until smooth. Beat in Cheddar cheese. Stir in chutney. Refrigerate overnight.
2. Shape into small balls (1 teaspoon each). Roll in nuts and parsley; refrigerate.

To soften butter in a hurry: Slice butter into a bowl, then beat with electric mixer, slowly at first, then increase speed until butter is soft and creamy.

HERBED CHEESE SPREAD

This savory, easy-to-make cottage-cheese spread goes well with any kind of cracker.
Makes 1¼ cups.

- 1 container (8 ounces) creamed cottage cheese
- 1 package (3 ounces) cream cheese, softened
- 1 tablespoon chopped parsley
- 1 tablespoon chopped chives
- ¼ teaspoon salt
- ¼ teaspoon leaf thyme, crumbled
- ¼ teaspoon leaf basil, crumbled
- ¼ teaspoon leaf savory, crumbled

Press cottage cheese through a food mill or large strainer into a medium-size bowl. Beat in cream cheese until smooth. Stir in parsley, chives, salt, thyme, basil and savory. Spoon into a serving dish; cover. Refrigerate several hours.

About dried herbs: Unless you plan to use a jar of dried herb within a short time, it is best to buy the leaf or unpowdered herb for good keeping quality. Label jars when you buy them, and try to replenish about every 6 months. Store them in a dark place in the kitchen where it isn't hot, and arrange alphabetically for convenience. When using the herb, crumble it with the fingers to release all the fragrant aroma and flavor. When substituting dried for fresh, use ⅓ less, since dried herbs have a more concentrated flavor than fresh. 1 tablespoon of fresh herb equals 1 teaspoon dried.

Keep your parsley dry: When finely chopping a small amount of parsley on a board or in a food processor, you will often find the parsley clumps and cannot be sprinkled freely. To prevent this, put the chopped parsley in a clean towel, then twist and squeeze out the liquid. Paper toweling can be used, but handle it gently!

BABA GHANOUSH

Almost every Middle Eastern country has a variation of this savory eggplant appetizer. We use it as a dip.
Makes 4 cups.

- 2 eggplants (about 1½ pounds each)
- 2 teaspoons salt
- ½ cup sesame paste (tahini)
- ¼ cup lemon juice
- 2 cloves garlic
- ¼ teaspoon pepper
- ¼ teaspoon ground cumin
- ¼ cup coarsely chopped parsley

1. Cut eggplants in half lengthwise; pierce skin with a fork in several places. Sprinkle cut sides with 1 teaspoon of the salt. Place, skin-side up, on wire racks over a jelly-roll pan. Broil, 6 inches from heat, about 10 minutes, or until skin is charred. Turn; broil an additional 10 minutes, or until tender. Remove from oven and turn eggplant skin-side up again. Allow to cool thoroughly.

2. Scoop eggplant pulp into container of electric blender. Add sesame paste, lemon juice, garlic, the remaining 1 teaspoon salt, pepper and cumin. Cover container; whirl just until mixture is smooth. Turn into bowl; stir in parsley. Cover. Refrigerate several hours. Sprinkle with additional parsley just before serving. Serve cold with toasted pita bread, sesame crackers or other "scoops."

OLD-FASHIONED HOT CHOCOLATE

Comforting and delicious on cold days.
Makes 4 servings.

    3 squares unsweetened chocolate
    ½ cup sugar
       Dash salt
    1 cup water
    3 cups milk

Combine chocolate, sugar, salt and water in a medium-size saucepan. Cook over low heat, stirring constantly, 5 minutes, or until chocolate is melted. Stir in milk slowly; heat just until piping hot. Beat with a rotary beater until foamy-topped. Serve with whipped cream or marshmallows, if you wish.

WASSAIL BOWL

Bake apples at 350° for 10 minutes.
Makes 12 four-ounce servings.

    2 red Delicious apples
    2 whole cloves
    2 whole allspice
    2 whole cardamom pods, crushed
    1 three-inch piece stick cinnamon
    1 quart ale
    ½ teaspoon ground ginger
    ½ teaspoon ground nutmeg
    1 cup sugar
    1½ cups dry sherry
    3 eggs, separated

1. Core apples; cut crosswise into ¼-inch-thick slices. Place slices in a shallow baking pan.
2. Bake in a moderate oven (350°) for 10 minutes or until apples are tender, but still firm enough to hold their shape; reserve.
3. Tie cloves, allspice, cardamom and cinnamon in a small piece of cheesecloth. Place in a kettle or Dutch oven with 1 cup of the ale, ginger and nutmeg. Heat very slowly for 20 minutes over low heat (do not allow to boil). Remove spice bag. Stir in remaining ale, ½ cup of the sugar and sherry. Heat slowly for 20 minutes.

4. Beat egg whites in a large bowl until foamy-white. Slowly beat in remaining ½ cup sugar until soft peaks form.
5. Beat egg yolks in a small bowl until light; fold into beaten whites. Slowly beat hot ale mixture into eggs until smooth.
6. Carefully pour the wassail into a heat-proof punch bowl; float baked apple slices on top. Serve in heatproof mugs.

MEXICAN HOT CHOCOLATE

Makes 6 servings.

    1 quart milk
    3 squares semisweet chocolate
    1 teaspoon ground cinnamon
    2 eggs
    6 three-inch pieces stick cinnamon

1. Heat milk in a large saucepan just to scalding. Stir in chocolate and cinnamon until chocolate melts, then beat with a rotary beater until smooth.
2. Beat eggs well in a small bowl; slowly beat in about 1 cup of the hot chocolate mixture, then beat back into remaining chocolate mixture in pan. Heat slowly, stirring constantly, 1 minute; beat again until frothy.
3. Ladle into heated mugs or glasses; place a cinnamon stick in each mug for a stirrer.

HOT MULLED CIDER

Makes 16 servings.

    9 whole cloves
    9 whole allspice
    4 two-inch pieces stick cinnamon,
        broken
    4 quarts apple cider
    1 cup firmly packed brown sugar
    2 lemons, thinly sliced

Tie cloves, allspice and cinnamon in cheesecloth; place in a large kettle with cider and sugar; simmer 5 minutes. Just before serving, remove spice bag. Serve in mugs and float a lemon slice in each.

Irish Coffee (page 21); Cappucino (page 21)

To make iced tea: Use half again as much tea as for regular brew. Steep 7 to 8 minutes. Strain out tea leaves or remove bags and store at room temperature to avoid clouding. To serve, pour over ice cubes in tall glasses. Garnish with lemon.

How to make a good pot of tea: Rinse a china or earthenware teapot with boiling water. Drain. Use fresh, good quality tea leaves and freshly drawn soft water. Measure 1 teaspoon loose tea or place 1 tea bag into the pot for each cup of boiling water. Take the pot to the kettle to pour the boiling water over the tea leaves. Let tea steep 3 to 5 minutes. Strain into cups if using loose tea and serve with sugar and lemon, or milk or cream.

DARJEELING PUNCH
Makes about 12 four-ounce servings.

    4 cups boiling water
    6 tea bags
    6 egg yolks
    ½ cup sugar
    1 tablespoon grated lemon rind
    2 cups rum, warmed

1. Pour boiling water over tea bags in a large heatproof bowl; let steep 3 to 5 minutes.
2. Beat egg yolks and sugar in a large bowl with electric mixer at high speed until light and fluffy. Beat in lemon rind.
3. Remove tea bags. Gradually add hot tea to egg yolk mixture; stir in rum.
4. Serve in warmed punch cups or small mugs. Sprinkle with additional grated lemon rind, if you wish.

About tea: All tea leaves come from the same plant. The most common tea available is the *Black* tea, a fermented blend of pekoe leaves from India and Sri Lanka. The other major kinds are the unfermented *Green,* from Japan, and the semifermented *Oolong* from Taiwan.

GLÖGG
(Swedish Christmas Punch)
Makes 8 servings.

    1 bottle (750 ml) dry red wine
   10 whole cardamom seeds
    3 strips fresh orange rind
    5 whole cloves
    1 piece (1½ inches) stick cinnamon
    1 can (4½ ounces) whole blanched almonds (1 cup)
    1 cup dark seedless raisins
    ½ pound sugar cubes
 1½ cups aquavit

1. Pour wine into a Dutch oven or kettle. Tie cardamom seeds, orange rind, cloves and cinnamon stick in several layers of cheesecloth; add to kettle. Cover.
2. Heat slowly to boiling; simmer 10 minutes. Add almonds, raisins and sugar cubes; stir vigorously. Simmer another 5 minutes, stirring often to dissolve sugar. Add aquavit; ladle while hot into mugs with a few almonds and raisins in each.

DOUBLE APPLE PUNCH
Makes 20 four-ounce servings.

    ⅔ cup firmly packed light brown sugar
    ¼ cup (½ stick) butter or margarine
    1 tablespoon grated orange rind
    1 tablespoon grated lemon rind
    ½ teaspoon ground cinnamon
    ¼ teaspoon ground nutmeg
    2 quarts apple cider
    ½ cup applejack (apple brandy)
      Cinnamon sticks

1. Combine brown sugar, butter, orange and lemon rinds, cinnamon, nutmeg and apple cider in a large saucepan. Heat slowly, stirring until mixture just comes to boiling, but do not boil.
2. Carefully pour into a heatproof punch bowl; stir in applejack. Garnish with orange or lemon slices, if you wish.
3. Serve in warmed punch cups or mugs with a cinnamon stick as a stirrer.

CAPPUCINO
Makes 18 four-ounce servings.

  3 three-inch pieces stick cinnamon
 12 whole cloves
  ½ cup instant espresso coffee
  6 cups boiling water
  ½ cup sugar
  3 cups light cream or half-and-half,
       warmed
  2 cups (1 pint) heavy cream
       Ground nutmeg

1. Tie cinnamon sticks and cloves in cheesecloth; drop into a large saucepan; stir in instant espresso coffee and boiling water; cover; steep 5 minutes.
2. Remove spice bag. Add sugar and light cream, stirring until sugar is dissolved. Heat 1 minute longer.
3. Beat heavy cream until soft peaks form.
4. Serve cappucino in demitasse cups; top each serving with a spoonful of whipped cream; sprinkle with nutmeg.

> **Espresso can be brewed in a regular coffee pot using a special espresso blend .**

CAFÉ BRÛLOT
Makes 8 servings.

  1 cup brandy
  5 lumps sugar
  4 cups very strong hot coffee
  1 three-inch piece stick cinnamon
  6 whole cloves
  1 piece vanilla bean
  3 strips fresh orange rind (no white)

1. Pour brandy over sugar lumps in a shallow dish. Let soak 15 minutes or until lumps are saturated. Remove 1 lump and reserve.
2. Pour coffee into chafing dish or metal bowl with a flame underneath it. Add cinnamon, cloves, vanilla bean and orange rind.

Stir well; add brandy and the 4 sugar lumps, stir gently.
3. Place the remaining brandy-soaked lump of sugar on a serving ladle and ignite carefully with a long match. Add, flaming, to the Café Brûlot and serve immediately.

IRISH COFFEE
Serve in Irish coffee goblets or in mugs.
Makes 8 servings.

  8 teaspoons sugar
  6 cups strong hot coffee
  8 jiggers Irish whiskey (1½ cups)
  ½ cup heavy cream, whipped

1. Heat each goblet or mug by putting a metal spoon in the empty goblet and pouring hot water onto the spoon and then into the goblet. Pour out water.
2. Put a teaspoon of sugar in each goblet. Add enough coffee to dissolve the sugar; stir. Add a jigger of Irish whiskey to each goblet, then fill goblet to within an inch of the brim with more coffee.
3. Slide a generous spoonful of whipped cream over the back of a teaspoon held over each goblet of coffee. Do not stir. Serve at once.

> **Coffee brewing hints:** Use your favorite coffee maker and a fresh batch of suitable grind coffee for the machine. Keep your coffee maker scrupulously clean by running a commercial cleaner through the pot or using a weak vinegar solution according to manufacturer's directions. Measure 2 level measuring tablespoons (1 standard coffee measure) coffee for each ¾ cup fresh water. Follow manufacturer's directions for brewing. Remove grounds as soon as coffee has brewed. Don't keep the pot of coffee warm for ever. Brew fresh batches.

OLD-FASHIONED LEMONADE

Makes 6 servings.

1½ cups sugar
1 cup water
Thin rind of 2 lemons, cut in strips (no white)
1 cup lemon juice
4 cups ice water

1. Gently boil sugar, the 1 cup water and lemon rind in a small saucepan 8 to 10 minutes, or until sugar is dissolved and mixture is syrupy; remove lemon rind; cool syrup to room temperature.

2. Pour syrup into a large pitcher; add lemon juice and ice water; stir well. Add plenty of ice cubes and stir well again. Serve in tall glasses with fresh mint, if you wish.

To make pink lemonade: Prepare lemonade as directed and mix in 3 tablespoons grenadine syrup.

To make old-fashioned limeade: Prepare as for Old-Fashioned Lemonade, substituting lime rind and lime juice for the lemon rind and lemon juice.

CHOCOLATE FROSTED

Makes 6 servings.

1 quart milk
¼ cup chocolate syrup
1 teaspoon vanilla
1 pint vanilla ice cream

Combine half each of the milk, chocolate syrup, vanilla and ice cream in container of electric blender; cover. Whirl until thick and smooth. Pour into 3 tall glasses. Repeat with remaining half of ingredients and 3 more glasses. If you do not have a blender, mix milk, syrup and vanilla in a large bowl, then beat in ice cream, a few spoonfuls at a time, with electric mixer.

VANILLA FROSTED

Makes 4 servings.

2¼ cups milk
½ pint vanilla ice cream
2 teaspoons vanilla

Combine milk, ice cream and vanilla in container of electric blender; cover; whirl until creamy smooth. (Or, combine all ingredients in a bowl and beat with electric mixer.) Pour into 4 tall glasses.

CHOCOLATE MALTED

Makes 1 serving.

1 tablespoon chocolate malted-milk drink powder
1 cup milk
2 tablespoons light cream or half-and-half
1 scoop chocolate ice cream

Combine chocolate malted-milk powder, milk and cream in container of electric blender; whirl 30 seconds. Put ice cream into a tall glass; pour in chocolate mixture.

BLACK-AND-WHITE SODA

Makes 1 serving.

2 tablespoons chocolate syrup
¼ cup milk
2 or 3 scoops vanilla ice cream
1 teaspoon vanilla
1 bottle (7 ounces) club soda, chilled
Whipped cream
Maraschino cherry

Combine chocolate syrup, milk, 1 scoop vanilla ice cream and vanilla in a tall glass. Stir vigorously with spoon to blend. Fill glass two-thirds full with club soda; stir. Add 1 or 2 more scoops of ice cream; fill glass with club soda. Garnish with whipped cream and cherry.

ORANGE EGG CREAM

This is especially good when the ice cream is just melted.

Makes about 4 cups or 2 servings.

- 2 cups orange juice
- ⅔ cup instant nonfat dry milk powder
- 2 eggs
- 1 pint vanilla ice cream

Combine orange juice, dry milk powder and eggs in container of electric blender. Cover; whirl until smooth. Add ice cream; whirl just until blended.

APRICOT-YOGURT FIZZ

The apricot-yogurt mixture can be blended ahead and refrigerated.

Makes about 3½ cups or 2 servings.

- 1 can (16 ounces) apricot halves, drained
- 1 container (8 ounces) plain yogurt
- 2 eggs
- ⅓ cup instant nonfat dry milk powder
- ½ cup club soda

Combine apricot halves, yogurt, eggs and dry milk powder in container of electric blender. Cover; whirl on medium speed until smooth. Pour into 2 glasses; add club soda; stir.

BANANA COW

Makes 4 servings.

- 2 medium-size bananas, peeled and cut into chunks
- 1 cup milk
- 2 tablespoons honey
- ¼ teaspoon vanilla
- 2 cups crushed ice
  Lime wedges

Combine bananas, milk, honey, vanilla and ice in container of electric blender; whirl until smooth. Pour into 4 ten-ounce highball glasses.

BUTTERMILK SWIRL

Thick and rich-tasting; why not try it for a satisfying breakfast?

Makes about 3 cups or 2 servings.

- 2 cups buttermilk
- 2 large bananas, peeled and cut into chunks
- ½ cup wheat germ
- 4 teaspoons honey
  Strawberry preserves or partially thawed frozen strawberries

1. Combine buttermilk, bananas, wheat germ and honey in container of electric blender. Whirl until smooth.
2. Pour a small amount into 2 glasses, alternating with some spoonfuls of preserves or frozen strawberries to swirl.

GUAVA FRUIT PUNCH

This is a pretty pink punch.

Makes 9 cups or 18 four-ounce punch-cup servings.

- 2 cans (7.1 ounces each) guava juice (about 2 cups)
- 1½ cups unsweetened pineapple juice
- 1 cup orange juice
- ¾ cup lemon juice
- ¼ cup sugar
- 3 tablespoons grenadine syrup
- 1 bottle (28 ounces) ginger ale, chilled
  Assorted fresh fruit for garnish

Combine guava, pineapple, orange and lemon juices, sugar and grenadine syrup in a 2½-quart container; stir until sugar is dissolved. (Can be prepared ahead to this point and refrigerated.) Just before serving, add ginger ale. Pour over an ice ring in a punch bowl. Garnish with skewers of assorted fresh fruit.

PINEAPPLE NOG

Tropical in taste, a refreshing way to start the day.

Makes about 4 cups or 2 servings.

  1 can (8 ounces) crushed pineapple in
    pineapple juice
  4 eggs
  ½ cup cream of coconut
  1 cup skim milk
  ⅛ teaspoon ground nutmeg

Combine pineapple, eggs, cream of coconut, milk and nutmeg in container of electric blender. Cover; whirl until smooth. Pour into 2 glasses; sprinkle each with additional nutmeg.

CHAMPAGNE PUNCH

Makes 25 four-ounce servings.

  ½ cup superfine granulated sugar
  1 cup Grand Marnier liqueur
  2 packages (10 ounces each) frozen
    peaches in quick-thaw pouch
  1 bottle (750 ml) chilled dry white wine
  2 bottles (750 ml) chilled
    Champagne (Brut)

Combine sugar and Grand Marnier in a punch bowl; stir until sugar dissolves. Place peach slices in punch bowl; pour in wine and champagne, stirring until peaches separate. Serve in punch cups with a peach slice in each.

Decorative cubes, rings and blocks: Half-fill an ice-cube tray, ring mold, metal mixing bowl or 9x5x3-inch loaf pan with water (plain or pastel-tinted). Partially freeze. Add maraschino cherries, citrus slices, pineapple chunks in decorative design. Freeze to anchor fruit; fill with ice water and freeze until firm. Use ice cubes to dress up fruit drinks; float ice ring or block in a punch bowl.

PIÑA COLADA

Smooth and mellow, one of the big favorites borrowed from the Caribbean.

Makes 4 servings.

  ⅔ cup light rum
  1 cup unsweetened pineapple juice
  ½ cup cream of coconut
  ¼ cup heavy cream
  2 cups crushed ice
    Fresh coconut (*optional*)
    Pineapple slices or sticks
    Fresh mint sprigs

Combine rum, pineapple juice, cream of coconut, cream and crushed ice in container of electric blender. Whirl until smooth. Pour over crushed ice in four 10-ounce highball glasses. Or, serve the drinks in a coconut half. Garnish with pineapple and mint; serve with straws.

PINEAPPLE MINT COOLER

Sparkling pineapple juice with the cool zip of mint.

Makes about 12 servings.

  4 cups unsweetened pineapple juice,
    chilled
  ½ cup lemon juice
  ¼ cup green crème de menthe
  1 bottle (28 ounces) lemon-lime
    carbonated beverage
    Canned or fresh pineapple slices

1. Combine pineapple and lemon juices and crème de menthe in a 2½-quart container; mix well. (Can be prepared ahead to this point.)
2. Add carbonated beverage just before serving. Serve over ice cubes in 8-ounce highball glasses or pour over an ice ring in a punch bowl. Garnish each serving with a quarter pineapple slice.

From bottom left, clockwise: Banana Cow (page 23); Mai Tai (page 27); Scorpion (page 27); Guava Fruit Punch (page 23); Piña Colada; Pineapple Mint Cooler

SYLLABUB

Makes 14 four-ounce servings.

    1 bottle (750 ml) Madeira or cream
        sherry (3⅓ cups)
    1 tablespoon grated lemon rind
    ⅓ cup lemon juice
    1½ cups sugar
    3 egg whites
    ½ cup heavy cream, whipped
    3 cups (1½ pints) light cream or half-
        and-half
        Shredded lemon rind
        Ground nutmeg

Combine Madeira, grated lemon rind, lemon juice and 1¼ cups of the sugar in a large punch bowl. Stir until sugar is dissolved. Beat egg whites with remaining ¼ cup sugar until meringue forms soft peaks. Fold whipped cream into egg white meringue. Stir in light cream; spoon meringue mixture on top. Sprinkle with shredded lemon rind and nutmeg.

PLANTATION EGGNOG

Makes 20 four-ounce servings.

    1 cup superfine granulated sugar
    9 eggs, separated
    2 cups bourbon
    ½ cup Cognac
    2 cups light cream or half-and-half
    3 cups heavy cream, whipped
        Grated nutmeg

Add ½ cup of the sugar to egg yolks in a medium-size bowl; beat with electric mixer until fluffy-thick. Stir in bourbon, cognac and light cream. Chill several hours, or until very cold. Beat egg whites in a large bowl until foamy. Beat in remaining ½ cup sugar, 1 tablespoon at a time, until meringue forms soft peaks. Fold beaten egg yolks, then whipped cream into meringue mixture; pour into a large punch bowl. Sprinkle with nutmeg. Ladle into punch cups.

The party bar: Remember that liquor stores now sell in new liter sizes, so keep these measurements in mind when shopping: One liter = 33.8 ounces, which yields a little more than a quart-size; 750 milliliters = 25.4 ounces which yields a little more than a fifth-size. Also, if serving wine with dinner, figure on fewer glasses to the bottle: 5 to 6 for a liter; 3 to 4 for 750 milliliters.

Whisky, gin, vodka (mixed drinks, highballs—1½ ounces): 22 servings per liter; 17 servings per 750 milliliters.

Table wines (red, white, rosé—4- to 5-ounce servings): 6 to 8 servings per liter; 5 to 6 servings per 750 milliliters.

Sherry (3-ounce servings): 11 servings per liter; 8 servings per 750 milliliters.

Champagne, sparkling wine (4- to 5-ounce servings): 6 to 8 servings per liter; 5 to 6 servings per 750 milliliters.

Note: As a general rule, allow two drinks per person for the first two hours, 1½ per person for the third hour and one drink per person after that. But it's always wise to have a little extra on hand!

QUICK COOLERS

Simple and refreshingly good on a warm summer evening.

Makes 1 serving.

Kir: Combine 6 ounces (¾ cup) chilled dry white wine with 1½ to 3 teaspoons crème de cassis in a wine glass; stir well.

Vermouth Cassis: Combine 4 ounces (½ cup) dry vermouth, 3 ice cubes and 1½ to 3 teaspoons crème de cassis in a large wine glass. Fill glass with club soda. Add a twist of lemon peel; stir.

Red Dubonnet Cooler: Combine 6 ounces (¾ cup) red Dubonnet and 3 ice cubes in a tall glass. Fill glass with club soda. Add a twist of orange peel and a dash of bitters; stir.

Wine Spritzer: Combine 6 ounces (¾ cup) dry red *or* white wine and 3 ice cubes in a large wine glass. Fill with club soda. Add a twist of lemon or lime peel; stir.

SUMMER SANGRIA

The perfect refreshment for a warm summer day.

Makes about 2 quarts.

  1 cup sugar
1½ cups water
  1 cup orange juice
  ½ cup brandy
  1 large orange, quartered
      and sliced
  1 lime, sliced
  1 cup honeydew melon balls
  1 bottle (750 ml) dry red
      or white wine, chilled

1. Combine sugar and water in a large pitcher; stir until sugar dissolves. Add orange juice, brandy, orange, lime and honeydew. Let stand 2 hours.
2. Add ice cubes and stir in chilled wine just before serving.

> **How to serve wine: Serve white wines slightly chilled (not ice cold), 1 to 2 hours in the refrigerator or ice bucket. Serve red wines at room temperature, 60-68 degrees. White wines are served before red, and dry before sweet. For glasses all you need is a stemmed clear glass with a large bowl that holds at least 8 ounces. Never fill the glass more than two-thirds full.**

SCORPION

Very exotic and a great favorite in Polynesian restaurants.

Makes 4 servings.

  1 cup dark rum
  ⅓ cup brandy

  1 cup orange juice
  ¾ cup lemon juice
  ¼ cup orgeat syrup (almond-
      flavored sugar syrup) or
      Amaretto liqueur
3½ cups crushed ice
      Gardenia (*optional*)

Combine rum, brandy, orange juice, lemon juice, orgeat and ice in container of electric blender, whirl 30 seconds. Serve over ice in a large footed champagne-type glass. Garnish each with a gardenia, if you wish.

> **Lemon, lime and orange dumbbells: Cut thinly-sliced fruit in small pyramid shapes; thread the pieces, points together, on long thin bamboo skewers. Use as stirrers for fruit drinks.**

MAI TAI

This has many versions throughout the islands, but it is considered the classic Hawaiian drink.

Makes 1 serving.

  3 tablespoons light rum
  2 tablespoons dark rum
  1 tablespoon Curaçao (orange liqueur)
  1 tablespoon fresh lime juice
  1 teaspoon sugar
  2 dashes aromatic bitters
      Fresh mint sprigs

Combine light and dark rums, Curaçao, lime juice, sugar and bitters in a cocktail shaker; shake well. Pour over crushed ice in a 6-ounce old-fashioned glass. Or, serve in a scooped-out small pineapple. Garnish with mint; serve with straws.

> **Lemon, lime and orange cartwheels: Slice thin; serrate edges with paring knife. Use to garnish fruit drinks, seafood or poultry platters.**

Won Ton Soup

Soups and Sandwiches

Hot and hearty or cool and light, soups are year-round favorites.
Add a sandwich and you will have a fine meal.

WON TON SOUP

Chinese mothers also have a special "cure-everything" soup.

Makes 6 servings.

    1 pound ground pork
    ½ cup chopped green onions
    1 egg
    2 tablespoons soy sauce
    2 teaspoons cornstarch
      Won Ton Wrappers (*recipe follows*)
    4 cans (13¾ ounces each) chicken broth
      OR: 7 cups Basic Chicken Broth
      (*page 36*)
    1 package (10 ounces) frozen peas
      and carrots
    3 cups fresh spinach leaves
    ⅓ cup dry sherry or white wine

1. Combine pork, green onions, egg, soy sauce and cornstarch in a bowl; mix.
2. Place about 1 slightly rounded teaspoonful pork filling on each won ton wrapper. Brush edges of wrapper with a little water to moisten. Bring one side of wrapper over filling; roll up as a cylinder, leaving about ½-inch of wrapper unrolled at the top. Pull the two ends of cylinder together to meet and overlap under filling, pinching firmly.
3. Place won tons in a single layer on cookie sheet as you work. Cover with plastic wrap to prevent drying.
4. Heat 3 to 4 quarts salted water to boiling in a large kettle; add half the won tons. After water returns to boiling, lower heat to moderate and cook won tons 5 minutes,

uncovered. Lift out to colander with slotted spoon. Repeat with remaining won tons.
5. Combine chicken broth and peas and carrots in a large saucepan; bring to boiling. Cook, covered, 5 minutes; add won tons and spinach; return to boiling. Stir in sherry and serve at once.
Note: To freeze won tons, place on cookie sheet in single layer and place in freezer. When won tons are frozen solid, transfer to plastic bags. To cook and serve: Follow Steps 4 and 5, increasing cooking time 5 minutes. Or, cook won tons following Step 4; plunge into cold water and drain; freeze as above. To cook, follow Step 5.

WON TON WRAPPERS
Makes 48 wrappers.

    3 cups sifted all-purpose flour
    1 teaspoon salt
    1 egg
    ⅔ cup water
      Cornstarch

1. Sift flour and salt into a large bowl. Make a well in center and add egg and water. Stir with a fork until dough holds together and leaves side of bowl clean. Turn out onto a lightly floured surface; knead until smooth and elastic, 4 to 5 minutes. Cover dough with a bowl and allow to rest 30 minutes.
2. Divide dough in half. On a lightly floured surface, roll out dough, half at a time, to a 21x14-inch rectangle. Dust lightly with cornstarch. Cut into 3½-inch squares. Stack squares on a plate (cornstarch will prevent them from sticking together).

BOOTHBAY CHOWDER

A hearty and savory blend of potatoes and clams.

Makes 8 servings.

      3 slices bacon
      1 large onion, chopped (1 cup)
      3 tablespoons flour
      1 teaspoon salt
    ¼ teaspoon pepper
      3 cups milk
      3 cans (about 6½ to 7 ounces each)
            minced clams
      1 bottle (8 ounces) clam juice
      1 cup water
      4 medium-size potatoes, pared and
            diced (about 3 cups)
      2 tablespoons chopped parsley

1. Cook bacon in a large heavy saucepan or Dutch oven until crisp. Remove with slotted spoon; drain on paper toweling; crumble; reserve. Add onion to bacon fat in saucepan; sauté until tender, about 3 minutes. Stir in flour, salt and pepper; cook 1 minute. Stir in milk until smooth. Cook, stirring constantly, until thickened and bubbly; lower heat to simmer.
2. Drain liquid from clams into a medium-size saucepan; reserve clams. Add bottled clam juice, water and potatoes. Simmer until potatoes are tender, about 15 minutes.
3. Add potatoes and their cooking liquid to the milk mixture; heat just until bubbly. Add clams; heat 1 minute more. Sprinkle with parsley and reserved bacon.

If you wish to substitute fresh clams for canned, buy the large chowder clams (you will need about 1 quart). Have them shucked and reserve the liquor. Strain and measure the liquor (you will need 1½ cups). If the measure is short, add bottled clam juice. Follow the recipe as for canned clams.

Boothbay Chowder

Iowa Corn Chowder

IOWA CORN CHOWDER

Old-fashioned goodness for late-night suppers, buffets and any of your formal and informal gatherings.

Makes 10 servings.

4 slices bacon, chopped
1 large onion, chopped (1 cup)
3 medium-size potatoes, pared and
  diced (1½ to 2 cups)
3 cups water
1 teaspoon salt
¼ teaspoon pepper
⅛ teaspoon leaf thyme, crumbled
1 package (10 ounces) frozen Fordhook
  lima beans
2 cans (12 ounces each) whole-kernel
  corn with peppers, undrained
1 tall can (13 ounces) evaporated milk
3 tablespoons flour
½ teaspoon paprika

1. Cook bacon in a large saucepan or Dutch oven until crisp. Add onion; sauté until tender, about 3 minutes.
2. Add potatoes, 2½ cups of the water, salt, pepper and thyme; cover. Simmer 10 minutes or until potatoes are almost tender. Add lima beans; cook 5 minutes more. Remove from heat.
3. Stir in corn with can liquid and evaporated milk. Blend flour with remaining ½ cup water; stir into chowder.
4. Cook, stirring constantly, over medium heat, until chowder thickens and bubbles, 1 minute. Ladle into a tureen or soup bowls; sprinkle with paprika. Good with crackers.

BLACK BEAN SOUP

A subtly flavored soup that is hearty enough to serve as a main course. You can freeze any leftovers in family-size portions.

Makes 10 servings.

1 pound dried black beans
4 cups water
2 large carrots, chopped (1 cup)
1 stalk celery, chopped (½ cup)
4 large onions, chopped (4 cups)
2 cloves garlic, crushed
3 tablespoons olive oil
½ teaspoon ground coriander
  Pinch ground cinnamon
1 thin strip of orange rind
¼ teaspoon cayenne
¼ pound salt pork, scored
5 cans (13¾ ounces each) beef broth
1 teaspoon salt (about)
1 teaspoon pepper (about)
½ cup chopped parsley
⅓ cup Madeira

1. Pick over and wash beans. Combine with the 4 cups water in a kettle or Dutch oven. Bring to boiling; cover; cook 2 minutes; remove from heat; let stand 1 hour.
2. Sauté carrots, celery, onions and garlic in olive oil in a large skillet, 10 minutes. Blend in coriander, cinnamon, orange rind and cayenne. Add to the beans along with salt pork and beef broth. Cover and simmer gently, 2½ to 3 hours, until beans are very soft. Remove and discard salt pork.
3. Puree beans and other kettle vegetables through a food mill or by whirling part at a time in container of electric blender.
4. Return puree to kettle, season with salt and pepper, add parsley, then stir in Madeira and simmer, uncovered, about 20 minutes longer. Taste for salt and pepper and add more if needed. Ladle into a tureen or soup bowls; garnish with chopped onions, sieved egg yolk and lemon slices, if you wish. Serve with warm crispy rolls.

> **Orange rind is often used in recipes for its elusive and delicate flavor. When using orange rind, take a vegetable parer and pare off the thin bright orange part of the rind that holds the flavorful oils. Be sure not to include any of the bitter white part. Store extra in the freezer.**

TOMATO AND ZUCCHINI SOUP

Makes 6 servings.

    1 medium-size onion, chopped (½ cup)
    2 tablespoons olive or vegetable oil
    2 small zucchini, finely diced
    4 cups tomato juice
    1 can (13¾ ounces) chicken broth
    3 tablespoons lime or lemon juice
    2 teaspoons Worcestershire sauce
    1 teaspoon salt
    1 teaspoon sugar
    ⅛ to ¼ teaspoon liquid red-pepper
        seasoning
    2 tablespoons chopped parsley
      Lime or lemon slices

1. Sauté onion in oil in large saucepan until tender, about 3 minutes. Stir in zucchini; sauté 2 minutes. Add tomato juice, chicken broth, lime juice, Worcestershire, salt, sugar and red-pepper seasoning.
2. Heat to boiling; lower heat; cover. Simmer 5 minutes. Stir in parsley. Ladle into soup bowls or mugs; garnish with lime or lemon slices.

ITALIAN BEAN SOUP

Add a salad and some crusty bread for a hearty lunch or supper.
Makes 10 servings.

    1 package (1 pound) dried white beans
        (Great Northern or small
        lima beans)
   10 cups water
    2 tablespoon olive oil
    1 clove garlic, minced
    1 large onion, chopped (1 cup)
    1 large carrot, diced
    1 stalk celery with top, chopped
    2 leeks, chopped
    ½ teaspoon leaf rosemary, crumbled
    1 canned green chili pepper,
        seeded and chopped
    1 leftover ham bone with some meat
    2 teaspoons salt (about)

    ½ teaspoon pepper (about)
      Grated Parmesan cheese
      Thinly sliced onion or leek

1. Pick over and wash beans; combine with 6 cups of the water in a kettle or Dutch oven. Bring to boiling; cover. Cook 2 minutes; remove from heat; let stand 1 hour.
2. Heat oil in a large skillet; add garlic, onion, carrot, celery, leeks, rosemary and chili pepper; sauté 5 minutes or until lightly browned. Stir into beans along with ham bone and remaining 4 cups water; cover.
3. Bring to boiling; lower heat, then simmer 2 hours. Remove ham bone, returning any meat to soup. Puree about half the beans through a sieve. Return puree to soup; taste; add salt and pepper; heat through. Serve in soup bowls; garnish with Parmesan cheese and onion or leek.

> **Leeks, that mild and delicious member of the onion family, grow in dark rich soil and are seldom perfectly clean. To clean leeks, trim root ends and any bruised parts of the green leaves. Starting at the green end, split each leek in half, with the knife stopping about an inch short of the root end. Spread leaves and white root end apart and wash thoroughly under cold running water.**

NORWEGIAN PEA SOUP WITH PORK

Rib-sticking enough to be the main dish. Good with buttery slices of toasted cracked-wheat or rye bread.
Makes 6 servings.

    1 package (1 pound) green or yellow
        split peas
    2 quarts boiling water
    ¼ pound lean salt pork, in one piece
    1 large carrot, pared and diced
    1 large stalk celery, diced (include tops)
    5 green onions, trimmed and sliced
        (include tops)

2 teaspoons salt (amount will vary
    according to saltiness of pork)
¼ teaspoon pepper

1. Wash and sort peas; place in a large heavy kettle; add boiling water. Bring to boiling; lower heat; cover. Simmer for 1½ hours.

2. Add salt pork, carrot, celery, green onions, the 2 teaspoons salt and the pepper; re-cover; simmer 30 minutes. Uncover; turn heat to lowest point; simmer very slowly 1 to 1½ hours longer, stirring occasionally, until quite thick (about the consistency of gravy). Taste for salt; add an additional ½ teaspoon, if needed. Ladle into a tureen or soup bowls; serve hot.

FRENCH ONION SOUP

Makes 6 servings.

4 large onions, sliced (1½ pounds)
¼ cup (½ stick) butter or margarine
½ teaspoon sugar
½ teaspoon salt
¼ teaspoon pepper
4 cans (13¾ ounces each) beef broth
6 slices French bread, toasted
½ cup grated Parmesan cheese
¼ cup shredded Swiss or Gruyère
    cheese

1. Sauté onions in butter in a covered Dutch oven over very low heat, stirring occasionally, until tender and transparent. Uncover; add sugar, salt and pepper. Cook, stirring, 10 minutes longer, or until onions are a rich golden brown.

2. Add beef broth; bring to boiling; cover; simmer 20 minutes. Taste; add additional salt, if needed.

3. Ladle soup into 6 ovenproof soup bowls or an 8-cup baking dish. Top with bread slices; sprinkle slices with both cheeses.

4. Heat in a hot oven (425°) for 10 minutes, then place under preheated broiler until top is bubbly and lightly browned.

MUSHROOM SOUP

A sherry-spiked, egg-thickened broth holds tissue-thin mushroom slices.

Makes 6 servings.

½ pound mushrooms
2 tablespoons butter or margarine
1 tablespoon lemon juice
1 tablespoon flour
½ teaspoon salt
4 cups water
2 envelopes or teaspoons instant
    chicken broth
2 egg yolks
1 tablespoon dry sherry

1. Wipe mushrooms, trim ends off stems, then cut through caps and stems into tissue-thin slices.

2. Sauté mushrooms, stirring often, in butter in a medium-size saucepan for 2 minutes. Sprinkle with lemon juice; toss lightly to mix.

3. Blend in flour and salt; stir in water and instant chicken broth. Cook, stirring constantly, until mixture thickens and bubbles, 3 minutes.

4. Beat egg yolks well with sherry in a small bowl; blend in about ½ cup of the hot mushroom mixture, then stir back into remaining mixture in saucepan. Heat, stirring constantly, 1 minute longer.

5. Ladle into a tureen or soup bowls. Serve with wheat crackers, if you wish.

QUICK BEEF-VEGETABLE SOUP

A half-hour soup that has all the heartiness of the long-cooking ones.

Makes 6 servings.

½ pound ground chuck
1 large onion, chopped (1 cup)
2 cans condensed beef broth
½ cup chopped celery
1 medium-size potato, pared and cubed (1 cup)
1 can (1 pound) tomatoes
½ cup water
1½ teaspoons salt
⅛ teaspoon pepper
½ teaspoon leaf thyme, crumbled
1 package (10 ounces) frozen peas and carrots
1 can (8 ounces) whole-kernel corn, undrained
2 tablespoons chopped parsley

1. Cook chuck in a large heavy saucepan, breaking up with a spoon, until meat loses its pink color. Add onion; sauté until soft. Add beef broth, celery, potato, tomatoes, water, salt, pepper and thyme. Cook until vegetables are tender, about 10 minutes.
2. Stir in peas and carrots and corn. Heat 5 minutes longer. Ladle into a tureen or soup bowls; sprinkle with parsley. Serve with grated Parmesan cheese, if you wish.

MINESTRONE

Eat some, freeze some in family-size servings. Serve with crusty Italian bread.

Makes about 12 servings.

4 cans (13¾ ounces each) beef broth (7 cups)
2 cans (10½ ounces each) cannelini beans
1 large potato, pared and diced (about 1½ cups)
2 medium-size carrots, pared and sliced (1 cup)
2 stalks celery, sliced (1½ cups)

1 cup shredded green cabbage (¼ medium-size head)
1 medium-size onion, chopped (½ cup)
2 cloves garlic, minced
½ cup chopped sweet green pepper
1 tablespoon vegetable oil
3 small zucchini, cubed (1½ cups)
1 cup green beans, sliced into 2-inch lengths
½ pound spinach, chopped
2 ripe tomatoes, chopped
OR: 1 can (8 ounces) tomato sauce
½ cup small shell macaroni
½ teaspoon leaf oregano, rosemary or basil, crumbled
1 teaspoon salt
½ teaspoon pepper
Grated Parmesan cheese

1. Bring beef broth to boiling in a large kettle or Dutch oven. Add cannelini beans, potato, carrots, celery and cabbage. Lower heat; simmer 15 minutes.
2. Sauté onion, garlic and green pepper in the oil in a small skillet until tender, about 3 minutes; add to kettle. Continue cooking for 15 minutes; add zucchini, green beans, spinach, tomatoes and macaroni. Turn up heat slightly and cook 20 minutes longer. Add herb of your choice, salt and pepper. Ladle into a tureen or soup bowls. Sprinkle top with Parmesan cheese.

To freeze that extra soup: Pour soup into meal-size freezer containers to within ½ inch of top. Cover; seal, label, date and freeze. Keep at 0° for up to 2 months.

SICILIAN SAUSAGE SOUP

Sausage adds a fine, robust flavor to this easy 30-minute soup.

Makes 8 servings.

½ pound pork sausage or sweet Italian sausage
1 large onion, chopped (1 cup)

Sicilian Sausage Soup

1 can (2 pounds, 3 ounces) Italian-style tomatoes

2 cans (13¾ ounces each) chicken broth

1 teaspoon leaf basil, crumbled

½ cup orzo (rice-shaped macaroni)

¼ teaspoon salt

⅛ teaspoon pepper

1. Cook sausage in a large saucepan, breaking up meat with wooden spoon, until meat loses its pink color. (If using Italian sausage, remove casings before cooking.) Add onion; saute until tender, about 3 minutes.

2. Add tomatoes, broth and basil; bring to boiling; stir in orzo, salt and pepper. Lower heat; cover; simmer until orzo is tender, about 10 minutes. Taste and add additional salt and pepper if needed. Ladle into a tureen or soup bowls. Serve with bread sticks or sesame crackers.

BASIC CHICKEN BROTH

It is well worthwhile to make homemade chicken broth. This recipe gives you enough broth and meat to make 2 soups and even extra meat for a salad or casserole, if you wish.

Makes 12 cups.

    2 broiler-fryers, 3 to 3½ pounds each
      Chicken giblets
    2 medium-size carrots, scraped
    1 large parsnip, scraped
    1 large onion, chopped (1 cup)
    2 stalks celery
    2 celery tops
    3 sprigs parsley
    1 leek, well washed
      Water
    2 tablespoons salt
   12 peppercorns

1. Combine chicken, giblets, carrots, parsnip, onion and celery in a large kettle; tie celery tops, parsley and leek with a string; add to kettle. Add enough cold water to cover chicken and vegetables.
2. Heat slowly to boiling; skim; add salt and peppercorns; lower heat. Simmer very slowly 1 to 1½ hours, or until meat falls off the bones. Remove meat and vegetables from broth; discard the bundle of greens.
3. Strain broth through cheesecloth into a large bowl. (There should be 12 cups.)
4. When cool enough to handle, remove and discard skin and bones from chicken; cut meat into bite-size pieces. Use in salads, casseroles, soup or dumplings

> **To store in refrigerator: Pour into covered containers, leaving fat layer until ready to use. Store for up to 4 days.**
> **To store in freezer: Pour into freezer containers in small portions, 1 or 2 cups, in boilable freezer bags or freezer containers, leaving ½ inch at top for expansion in freezing. Freeze at 0° for up to 4 months.**

CHICKEN SOUP WITH DUMPLINGS

A creamy-thick soup with tender little chicken balls and vegetables.

Makes 6 servings.

Chicken Dumplings:
    1 cup diced cooked chicken (from Basic Chicken Broth)
    1 cooked chicken liver
    1 egg
    ⅓ cup flour
    ¼ cup milk
    1 teaspoon salt
      Dash pepper
      Dash nutmeg
    1 tablespoon minced parsley
    1 cup water
    6 cups Basic Chicken Broth
      or 4 cans (13¾ ounces each) chicken broth

Soup:
    ¼ cup chopped green onions
    ¼ cup chicken fat, butter or margarine
    ¼ cup flour
    1 package (10 ounces) frozen mixed vegetables
    ½ teaspoon salt
    1½ cups diced cooked chicken (from Basic Chicken Broth)

1. Combine chicken, liver, egg, flour, milk, salt, pepper and nutmeg in blender; blend at high speed until smooth. Turn into a small bowl; stir in parsley; cover.
2. Bring water and 1 cup of the chicken broth to boiling in large saucepan. Shape chicken mixture, one-half at a time, into ¾-inch balls with a teaspoon. Drop one by one into boiling broth. Simmer gently, uncovered, 8 to 10 minutes; remove with a slotted spoon; keep warm. Repeat with second half.
3. Sauté onions in chicken fat, or butter or margarine in kettle or Dutch oven, until soft but not brown, 3 to 4 minutes; stir in flour; gradually add remaining chicken broth; stirring constantly; bring to boiling; add vegetables and salt; cover. Cook 10

minutes, or until vegetables are tender.
4. Add chicken dumplings, cooking broth and chicken; heat 5 minutes. Ladle into soup bowls; serve with crusty bread.

CLASSIC OYSTER STEW

The Yankee way—so easy to make!
Makes 4 servings.

    2 cups milk
    2 cups light cream or half and half
    ½ teaspoon salt
    ¼ teaspoon paprika
    1 pint (about 24) shucked oysters and juice
        OR: 2 cans (8 ounces each) oysters, undrained
    4 tablespoons (½ stick) butter or margarine

1. Heat milk with cream in a medium-size saucepan over low heat until bubbles appear around edge (do not boil); stir in salt and paprika.
2. Heat oysters and juice in butter in a medium-size saucepan until oyster edges begin to curl; stir in scalded milk mixture.
3. Ladle into soup bowls or mugs. Good with oyster crackers or saltines.

CIOPPINO

A robust colorful soup-stew from the California coast. Always a combination of fish and shellfish, it varies depending on the contents of the day's catch.
Makes 8 servings.

    1 large onion, chopped (1 cup)
    1 medium-size sweet green pepper, halved, seeded and chopped
    ½ cup sliced celery
    1 carrot, pared and shredded
    3 cloves garlic, minced
    3 tablespoons olive oil
    2 cans (1 pound each) tomatoes
    1 can (8 ounces) tomato sauce
    1 teaspoon leaf basil, crumbled
    1 bay leaf
    1 teaspoon salt
    ¼ teaspoon pepper
    1 pound fresh or frozen halibut or turbot
    1 dozen mussels in shell, if available
        OR: 1 dozen fresh littleneck or cherrystone clams, rinsed
    1½ cups dry white wine
    1 package (8 ounces) frozen, shelled, and deveined shrimp
    ½ pound fresh or frozen scallops
    2 tablespoons chopped parsley

1. Sauté onion, green pepper, celery, carrot and garlic in olive oil in a kettle or Dutch over until tender, about 3 minutes.
2. Stir in tomatoes, tomato sauce, basil, bay leaf, salt and pepper; heat to boiling; lower heat; cover; simmer 2 hours, stirring occasionally. Discard bay leaf.
3. While sauce simmers, remove skin from halibut or turbot; cut into serving-size pieces. Using a stiff brush, thoroughly scrub mussels, scraping off their "beards" under running water to remove any residue of mud and sand.
4. Stir wine into sauce in kettle. Add the fish, shrimp and scallops. Simmer, covered, 10 minutes longer.
5. Place mussels or clams in a layer on top of fish in kettle; cover; steam 5 minutes, or until the shells are fully opened and fish just flakes when touched with a fork. (Discard any unopened mussels or clams.)
6. Ladle into soup plates or bowls. Sprinkle with parsley. Serve with sourdough bread, or crusty French or Italian bread.

> **When substituting frozen fish for fresh, you will have better results if you cook it a shorter time. The freezing process tends to soften the fish somewhat, thus it will cook quicker.**

TUREEN SALMON SOUP

A nourishing soup for supper.
Makes 8 servings.

 3 medium-size potatoes, pared and
    diced (1½ to 2 cups)
 1 large onion, chopped (1 cup)
 1 cup thinly sliced celery
 4 tablespoons (½ stick) butter
    or margarine
 ⅓ cup flour
 6 cups milk
 1 bag (about 2 pounds) frozen peas and
    carrots
 2 cans (1 pound each) salmon
 1 teaspoon dillweed
 1½ teaspoons salt
 ¼ teaspoon pepper

1. Cook potatoes, covered, in boiling water to cover in a medium-size saucepan just until tender, about 15 minutes.

2. Sauté onion and celery in butter in a kettle until tender, about 3 minutes. Blend in flour; cook, stirring constantly, until bubbly. Stir in milk; continue cooking and stirring until mixture thickens and bubbles, 1 minute.

3. Stir in peas and carrots; heat slowly to boiling; cover; lower heat. Simmer until vegetables are tender, about 12 minutes.

4. Drain salmon; remove skin and bones; break into large chunks. Stir into vegetable mixture with potatoes and their liquid, dillweed, salt and pepper. Heat slowly, stirring occasionally, until hot.

5. Ladle into a tureen or soup bowls; sprinkle with more dillweed. Good with sesame crackers or breadsticks.

Tureen Salmon Soup

CREAM OF TOMATO AND ORANGE SOUP

Hot or chilled, this soup is a surprisingly pleasing combination of flavors.
Makes 6 servings.

 1 medium-size onion, chopped (½ cup)
 2 tablespoons butter or margarine
 2 tablespoons flour
 1 can condensed chicken broth
 1 can (1 pound, 1 ounce) Italian-style
    tomatoes
 1½ cups water
 1 teaspoon salt
 1 teaspoon sugar
 1 cup orange juice
 ⅛ teaspoon ground cloves
 ½ cup dairy sour cream
    Strips of orange rind

1. Sauté onion in butter in a large saucepan until tender, about 5 minutes. Stir in flour; gradually add chicken broth, stirring constantly. Stir in tomatoes, salt and sugar.

2. Bring to boiling, stirring often; lower heat; cover. Simmer 15 minutes. Press through a sieve or food mill. Return to saucepan; add orange juice and cloves. Bring just to boiling; remove from heat. Add ½ cup hot soup to sour cream in a small bowl, then stir back into saucepan. Serve hot a in tureen or soup bowls with additional sour cream.

FOR CHILLED SOUP: Cool soup, then chill several hours. Serve in chilled glasses or soup bowls garnished with strips of orange rind. Serve with additional sour cream.

VICHYSSOISE

A great hot-weather soup.

Makes 6 servings.

  3 leeks (white part only), well washed and thinly sliced
  1 large onion, thinly sliced
  2 tablespoons butter or margarine
  2 cans (13¾ ounces each) chicken broth (3 cups)
  2 medium-size potatoes, pared and diced
  1 cup milk, scalded
  ½ cup heavy cream
    Chopped chives

1. Sauté leeks and onion slowly in butter in a large saucepan 10 minutes, stirring occasionally. Vegetables should be tender but not brown.
2. Stir in chicken broth and potatoes; cook 15 minutes longer, or until potatoes are tender. Add milk; bring mixture to boiling; remove from heat.
3. Taste; add salt and pepper, if needed. Puree soup through a food mill or in several additions, in container of electric blender. Pour into a bowl.
4. Cool pureed soup, then chill several hours. Stir cream into chilled soup. Serve in chilled cups with a sprinkling of chopped chives.

> **To scald milk: Heat over low heat until tiny bubbles appear around edge and the surface films.**

Gazpacho

GAZPACHO

Makes 6 servings.

  2 cloves garlic
  2 pounds medium-size ripe tomatoes (about 6), peeled and quartered
  1 medium-size cucumber, pared and cut into chunks
  1 large sweet green pepper, seeded and chopped
  2 slices white bread, trimmed and crumbled (1 cup)
  ¼ cup red wine vinegar
  2 cups tomato juice
  1 cup water
  ¼ cup olive or vegetable oil
  ½ teaspoon salt
  ¼ teaspoon black pepper
    Cucumber slices
  ½ cup chopped green onions
  ½ cup packaged garlic-flavored croutons
  ½ cup chopped sweet green pepper

1. Combine garlic, tomatoes, cucumber, green pepper, bread and vinegar in container of electric blender; whirl until smooth.
2. Press mixture through sieve, discarding solids. Add tomato juice, water, oil, salt and pepper to the tomato mixture; chill well.
3. Serve in chilled bowls; garnish with cucumber slices, green onions, croutons and green pepper, if you wish.

CHILLED SENEGALESE SOUP

Makes 8 servings.

  4 tablespoons (½ stick) butter or
        margarine
  1 large onion, chopped (1 cup)
  1 medium-sized tart apple, pared,
        quartered, cored and chopped
  2 teaspoons curry powder
  1 whole chicken breast, split
        (12 ounces)
  ¼ cup flour
  1 teaspoon salt
  1 bay leaf
  4 cups water
  1 cup light cream or half and half

1. Melt 2 tablespoons of the butter in a large heavy saucepan. Sauté onion and chopped apple until soft; stir in curry powder; cook for 1 minute; remove mixture; reserve. Add remaining butter to saucepan; sauté chicken breasts 5 minutes on each side; stir in flour; cook until bubbly. Add salt, bay leaf and water.
2. Heat to boiling; lower heat; cover; simmer 30 minutes or until chicken is tender. Remove saucepan from heat; cool.
3. Remove chicken and bay leaf from soup. Skin and bone chicken; chop.
4. Pour the soup part at a time into container of electric blender; add part of the chicken; cover. Whirl until smooth. (OR: Puree through sieve or food mill.) Repeat with remaining soup and chicken.
5. Pour into a large bowl. Stir in cream. Cover; chill at least 4 hours.
6. Pour into a chilled tureen; garnish with slivers of red apple and mint leaves, if you wish. Serve icy cold.

> When making a flour-based sauce or soup, the flavor is always improved, and the consistency is smoother, if the fat-flour mixture is cooked a few minutes before the liquid is added.

> Spice cookery: Spices like curry powder and chili powder are a combination of several spices. To bring out their full flavor, they should be cooked for a minute or two in the fat used in the recipe, usually at the beginning of the sauce recipe. If the recipe has a range of the amount of spice, it is best to use the minimum amount until you taste and decide.

CHILLED SPINACH SOUP

A pale green, creamy soup with a hint of lemon.

Makes 8 servings.

  2 packages (10 ounces each) spinach
  1 medium-size onion, chopped (½ cup)
  2 tablespoons butter or margarine
  2 cans (13¾ ounces each) chicken broth
  1 teaspoon salt
  ⅛ teaspoon pepper
  ⅛ teaspoon ground mace
  1 teaspoon grated lemon rind
  1 cup light cream or half and half

1. Trim spinach; wash leaves well; shake water off.
2. Sauté onion in butter in a large saucepan until tender. Add spinach; cover. (No need to add any water.) Cook over medium heat 10 minutes, or just until leaves are wilted; do not overcook.
3. Add chicken broth, salt, pepper and mace; simmer 5 minutes; cool slightly.
4. Pour soup, part at a time, into container of electric blender; cover. Whirl until smooth. (OR: Puree soup through a sieve or food mill.)
5. Pour into a large bowl. Stir in lemon rind and cream. Cover; chill several hours or overnight.
6. Ladle into a chilled tureen. Garnish with sieved hard-cooked egg, if you wish. Serve icy cold.

Chilled Spinach Soup, Chilled Senegalese Soup

BAKED TUNA BOAT

Bits of cheese melt while the celery stays crisp in this good-with-soup sandwich.
Bake at 400° for 20 minutes.
Makes 4 servings.

    1 can (7 ounces) tuna, drained
    ½ cup diced celery
    ¼ cup chopped sweet pickles
    2 tablespoons chopped green onions
    ½ cup cubed Muenster cheese (2 ounces)
    ¼ cup mayonnaise
    3 drops liquid red-pepper seasoning
    ½ teaspoon salt
    1 teaspoon lemon juice
    1 loaf unsliced French or Italian bread (15 to 18 inches long)
    2 tablespoons butter or margarine, melted

1. Combine tuna, celery, pickles, onions and cheese in a medium-size bowl.
2. Blend mayonnaise, red-pepper seasoning, salt and lemon juice in a cup. Pour over tuna mixture; toss lightly.
3. Cut thin slice from top of the bread; hollow out, leaving a ½-inch shell. (Use insides for crumbs in other recipes.) Spoon filling into bread. Replace top; brush all over with butter. Wrap in foil; place on a cookie sheet.
4. Bake in a hot oven (400°) for 20 minutes.

WEST COAST HERO

Makes 6 servings.

    2 packages (4 ounces each) alfalfa sprouts
    1 cup shredded carrots
    1 cup mayonnaise
    4 teaspoons lemon juice
    1½ teaspoons salt
       Dash pepper
    1 large round loaf sourdough bread, about 9 inches in diameter
    1 large ripe avocado

    ¼ pound thinly sliced Genoa salami
    1 package (8 ounces) sliced provolone cheese

1. Mix sprouts, carrots, mayonnaise, 2 teaspoons of the lemon juice, salt and pepper in a large bowl. Cut off top half of bread; scoop out center, leaving a shell about 1 inch thick.
2. Halve, pit, peel and slice avocado; sprinkle with the remaining 2 teaspoons lemon juice.
3. Place half the sprouts mixture on bottom of bread. Top with half of avocado slices; cover with a layer of salami and cheese, then remaining avocado slices and sprouts mixture. Replace top of bread. Cut into wedges to serve.

To freshen bread or rolls: Put in a paper grocery bag; close bag securely; sprinkle with water. Heat in a slow oven (325°) for 10 minutes.

MEATBALL HERO SANDWICHES

Makes 9 servings.

    9 individual hero rolls
    1½ pounds ground round
    1 egg, slightly beaten
    1 tablespoon instant minced onion
    1½ teaspoons salt
    ¼ teaspoon pepper
    ¼ cup milk
    2 tablespoons vegetable oil
    1 sweet green pepper, halved, seeded and sliced
    1 sweet red pepper, halved, seeded and sliced
    1 medium-size onion, sliced
    1 tablespoon flour
    ¾ cup chili sauce
    ½ cup water
    1½ teaspoons light brown sugar
    ½ teaspoon dry mustard

Meatball Hero Sandwich

1. Cut a thin slice from the top of each roll; scoop out. Crumble enough insides to make 1¼ cups; reserve. Cover rolls to keep from drying.

2. Combine beef, egg, onion, salt, pepper, milk and the reserved crumbs in a medium-size bowl; mix well; shape into 2-inch balls (about 27).

3. Brown meatballs, part at a time, in 1 tablespoon of the oil in a large skillet; remove to a large bowl.

4. Add remaining oil; saute peppers and onion until tender. Add to meatballs.

5. Stir flour into fat remaining in skillet; heat just until bubbly. Stir in chili sauce and water. Cook, stirring constantly, until sauce thickens and bubbles. Stir in brown sugar and mustard.

6. Add meatball-pepper mixture; cover; simmer 20 minutes to heat through. Spoon meatballs and sauce into rolls.

> To shape meatballs fast, use an ice-cream scoop, leveling off mixture on top. Look for the number on the bar in the scoop, which indicates the number of portions from a quart of mixture.

QUICK AND CRUNCHY PIZZA

Start with a loaf of crisp bread to make a fast sandwich.

Bake at 350° for 15 minutes.
Makes 4 servings.

 1 medium-size onion, chopped (½ cup)
 2 tablespoons vegetable oil
 1 pound ground round
 1 teaspoon salt
 1 jar (15½ ounces) thick Italian-style cooking sauce
 ½ teaspoon leaf oregano, crumbled
 1 loaf Italian or French bread (about 18 inches long)
 1 cup shredded mozzarella cheese (4 ounces)

1. Sauté onion in oil in a large skillet until tender. Stir in beef and salt; cook, stirring constantly, until meat loses its pink color. Stir in sauce and oregano; cook 1 minute.

2. Cut loaf in half; split each half horizontally to make 4 portions. Spread cut surfaces with the tomato-meat sauce. Sprinkle with cheese. Place on cookie sheet.

3. Bake in a moderate oven (350°) for 15 minutes or until cheese is melted.

Provençale Pan Bagna

PROVENÇALE PAN BAGNA

This appealing French sandwich is ideal for a picnic in a park or at the beach. Also called "pan bagnat" or "pain baigné," the name means "bathed bread" as the bread is bathed in olive oil for flavor.

Makes 4 servings.

  4 hard-crusted French rolls or hero rolls
½ cup olive oil
  2 tablespoons red wine vinegar
  2 cloves garlic, minced
¼ teaspoon leaf basil, crumbled
  2 medium-size ripe tomatoes, halved
     and thinly sliced
  1 small sweet green pepper, halved,
     seeded and cut into thin strips
  1 small red onion, sliced and separated
     into rings
    Salt
    Pepper
  4 hard-cooked eggs, sliced
  1 can (2 ounces) flat anchovy fillets,
     drained (12)
10 pitted black olives, halved

1. Cut rolls in half horizontally. Combine oil, vinegar, garlic and basil in a 1-cup mea-sure; stir until blended. Drizzle 1 table-spoon mixture on each cut side of rolls.
2. Arrange tomato slices on bottom halves of rolls, overlapping to fit; top with green pepper strips and onion rings. Sprinkle with salt and pepper. Arrange egg slices over onion rings; top with anchovy fillets and olives. Sprinkle with more salt and pepper; drizzle with any leftover dressing.
3. Carefully place tops of rolls over filled bottoms; press down gently. The flavor of these sandwiches improves on standing a short while. For picnics, wrap in foil or plastic and refrigerate until ready to serve.

THE NEW ORLEANS PEACEMAKER

This legendary sandwich, known also as *La Mediatrice*, was a peace offering from er-rant husbands to their irate wives.

Bake at 350° for 15 minutes.
Makes 4 servings.

¼ cup flour
⅛ teaspoon cayenne
  1 egg, beaten

1 tablespoon milk
¼ teaspoon salt
1 can (8 ounces) whole oysters, drained
½ cup packaged bread crumbs
1 loaf unsliced French bread (15 to 18 inches long)
¼ cup (½ stick) butter or margarine, melted
Vegetable oil
1 cup shredded iceberg lettuce
1 medium-size ripe tomato, thinly sliced
Chili sauce
Lemon wedges

1. Combine flour and cayenne on wax paper. Beat egg with milk and salt in a shallow dish until foamy. Dredge oysters in flour mixture, shaking off excess. Dip in egg mixture, then coat with bread crumbs. Refrigerate about half an hour to set the coating on the oysters.

2. Cut a thin slice from top of loaf; hollow out, leaving a ½-inch shell. (Use insides for crumbs in other recipes.) Brush loaf and top slice inside and out with melted butter. Place on a cookie sheet.

3. Toast in moderate oven (350°) for 15 minutes until golden.

4. Meanwhile, pour oil into a medium-size saucepan to a 1½-inch depth; heat to 375° on a deep-fat frying thermometer. Fry oysters, a few at a time, 2 to 3 minutes or until golden. Drain on paper toweling.

5. Fill hot toasted loaf with a layer of shredded lettuce, then the tomato slices and finally the hot oysters. Cover with loaf top. Cut loaf crosswise to serve. Serve with chili sauce and lemon wedges.

Leftover bread crumbs? Put them in a plastic bag and store in the freezer. Use within 2 months for a breading, sautéed in butter as a casserole topping, in stuffings, or in a bread pudding.

When measuring shredded cheese, let it fall lightly into the measuring cup—do not pack firmly. You can judge the amount of cheese needed to make the required amount of shredded cheese if you remember, 1 pound shredded cheese equals 4 cups.

HAM AND CHEESE HERO SANDWICH

Makes 16 servings.

1 loaf unsliced French or Italian bread (about 18 inches long)
¼ cup mayonnaise or salad dressing
⅓ cup chopped parsley
1 package (8 ounces) cream cheese, softened
¾ cup finely chopped celery
½ cup shredded Cheddar cheese (2 ounces)
2 tablespoons finely chopped onion
¼ teaspoon salt
2 packages (4 ounces each) sliced boiled ham (8 slices)
1 large dill pickle

1. Split bread; hollow out each half with a fork, leaving a ½-inch-thick shell. (Use insides for crumbs in other recipes.)

2. Spread mayonnaise or salad dressing over hollows in loaf; sprinkle parsley over mayonnaise.

3. Blend cream cheese, celery, Cheddar cheese, onion and salt in a medium-size bowl; spoon into bread halves, packing down well with back of spoon and leaving a small hollow down center.

4. Quarter pickle lengthwise; roll each quarter inside a double-thick slice of ham. Place rolls, end to end, in center of bottom half of loaf; cover with remaining half of bread. Wrap loaf tightly in plastic wrap; chill several hours.

5. To serve, cut into 16 slices. Garnish with parsley sprigs, if you wish.

TOMATO-AVOCADO SANDWICHES

They are simple to make and delicious.
Makes 6 servings.

       4 medium-size ripe tomatoes
      ¼ cup vegetable oil
       2 tablespoons red wine vinegar
      ½ teaspoon salt
      ¼ teaspoon pepper
      ¼ teaspoon leaf tarragon, crumbled
       1 small ripe avocado
       2 tablespooon lemon juice
       6 pita breads
       1 container (8 ounces) whipped
           cream cheese
       1 red onion, sliced

1. Core tomatoes; cut into thin slices; place
in a shallow dish. Combine oil, vinegar,
salt, pepper and tarragon; pour over tomatoes. Cover. Chill for 1 hour.
2. Peel, pit and cut avocado into 12 slices
in a shallow dish. Toss with lemon juice.
3. To assemble: Heat pita breads on a
cookie sheet in a very slow oven (250°) for
10 minutes; cut each in half horizontally to
make 2 pockets. Spread cream cheese generously inside each pocket. Place tomato
slices, avocado and red onion in each half;
spoon on additional dressing.

**Bright avocados: To prevent avocado
slices or pulp from turning brown, toss
or sprinkle with a tablespoon or two of
lemon juice.**

JUMBO BACON AND EGG SANDWICHES

With a cup of soup, it's a meal in a roll.
Toast at 375° for 10 minutes.
Makes 4 servings.

       4 poppy-seed rolls
       8 slices bacon
      ½ cup chopped green onions

**For the tenderest scrambled eggs, watch
carefully for the perfect moment—the
eggs will be quite shiny and will have
just a bit of the uncooked portion left,
which will set quickly when you take the
skillet off the heat.**

---

       6 eggs
      ⅓ cup milk
      ½ teaspoon salt
       3 drops liquid red-pepper seasoning

1. Cut a thin slice from the top of each roll.
Scoop out crumbs, leaving about a ½-inch
shell. (Use insides for crumbs in other recipes.) Put rolls on a cookie sheet and toast
in a moderate oven (375°) for 10 minutes,
or until crisp.
2. Cook bacon in a large skillet until crisp.
Drain on paper toweling, then crumble.
Sauté onions in bacon fat remaining in skillet until tender, about 3 minutes.
3. Beat eggs in a medium-size bowl until
frothy. Stir in milk, salt and red-pepper seasoning until well blended.
4. Pour mixture over onions in skillet.
Cook, stirring constantly, over low heat until eggs are softly set. Spoon mixture into
the hot toasted rolls. Sprinkle with crumbled bacon and cover with roll tops.

CROQUE MONSIEUR

This classic French sandwich may be
spread with butter and grilled, or dipped in
butter and fried.
Makes 4 servings.

       8 slices firm white bread, one to
           two days old
       6 tablespoons butter or margarine,
           softened
      12 thin slices cooked ham
       4 thin slices Swiss, Gruyère or
           Muenster cheese
       1 tablespoon flour
      ½ teaspoon salt
      ⅛ teaspoon pepper

Dash paprika or cayenne
1 cup light cream or milk
½ cup shredded Swiss cheese (2 ounces)
3 eggs
3 tablespoons milk

1. Trim crusts from bread. Spread one side of 4 of the slices with 2 tablespoons of the butter. Top with 2 slices ham, 1 slice cheese and 1 slice ham. Cover with remaining bread slices.

2. Melt 1 tablespoon of the butter in a medium-size saucepan; blend in flour, salt, pepper and paprika. Slowly stir in cream. Cook, stirring constantly, until thickened and bubbly. Add the shredded cheese and cook until melted; keep warm.

3. Beat eggs and milk in a small bowl just until blended. Pour mixture into a pie plate. Dip sandwiches on both sides.

4. Melt the remaining 3 tablespoons butter in a large skillet. Sauté sandwiches, turning once, until golden brown. Add more butter, if needed. Serve with cheese sauce spooned over. Or, brown the sauced sandwiches under the broiler.

Bacon-Spinach Junior Club Sandwiches

BACON-SPINACH JUNIOR CLUB SANDWICHES

The flavor is reminiscent of the popular sweet-sour spinach salad with egg and bacon. What makes it a "junior club" are two slices of bread instead of the usual three.

Makes 4 servings.

12 slices bacon
4 eggs
1 medium-size onion, finely chopped (½ cup)
½ cup mayonnaise
2 tablespoons red wine vinegar
1 tablespoon sugar
½ teaspoon salt
Dash pepper
8 slices firm white bread, toasted
¼ pound spinach, washed

1. Cook bacon in a large skillet until crisp; drain on paper toweling. Remove all but about ¼ cup fat from pan. Break eggs, one at a time, into hot fat; fry until firm, breaking yolks with a pancake turner and turning them over. Transfer to a warm platter. Remove and discard all but 1 tablespoon of the fat from pan.

2. Sauté onion until tender. Remove from heat. Stir in mayonnaise, vinegar, sugar, salt and pepper.

3. Spread mayonnaise mixture on each slice of toast. Cover four slices with a layer of spinach leaves, 3 slices bacon, a fried egg and top with more spinach leaves. Cover with remaining slices of toast, mayonnaise-side down. With serrated knife, cut sandwiches into 4 triangles.

CREAM CHEESE, DATE AND NUT SANDWICHES

Makes 6 servings.

2 packages (8 ounces each) cream cheese
¼ cup honey
1 cup chopped pitted dates
1 cup chopped walnuts
12 slices raisin bread

Beat cream cheese in a medium-size bowl with electic mixer until softened. Beat in honey until blended. Stir in dates and walnuts. Spread mixture evenly on 6 of the slices of bread; top with remaining slices. Cut each sandwich into 4 triangles to serve.

GRILLED TURKEY, CHEESE AND TOMATO SANDWICHES

Hearty knife-and-fork sandwiches for a satisfying lunch.

Makes 4 servings.

- 8 slices white, whole-wheat or rye bread
  Butter or margarine, softened
- 4 slices cooked turkey
- 2 slices Swiss cheese
- 8 thin ripe tomato slices (medium-size)
  Salt and pepper
- 2 eggs
- ½ cup milk
- ¼ teaspoon salt
  Dash cayenne
- 2 tablespoons butter or margarine

1. Spread bread slices on one side with butter. Arrange 1 slice turkey, ½ slice cheese and 2 tomato slices on 4 of the buttered sides. Sprinkle with salt and pepper. Top with remaining 4 slices bread, buttered sides in.
2. Beat eggs with milk, salt and cayenne in a shallow dish. Melt the 2 tablespoons butter in a large skillet or griddle. Dip sandwiches in egg mixture to coat both sides, using flat spatula to lift from mixture.
3. Brown sandwiches in butter, turning to brown both sides and melt the cheese.

PEPPER AND STEAK SANDWICHES

Makes 4 servings.

- 4 round hard poppy-seed rolls
- ¼ cup (½ stick) butter or margarine, melted
- ½ teaspoon leaf basil, crumbled
- ½ teaspoon leaf oregano, crumbled
- 1 medium-size onion
- 1 small sweet green pepper, halved, seeded, cut into julienne strips
- 1 small sweet red pepper, halved, seeded, cut into julienne strips
- ¼ cup vegetable oil
- 2 tablespoons butter or margarine
- 4 minute or cubed steaks (about 1¼ pounds), thawed if frozen
- 1 tablespoon red wine vinegar
  Salt
  Pepper

1. Cut rolls in half. Combine melted butter with basil and oregano. Brush on each cut half of roll. Place on cookie sheet.
2. Heat in a preheated moderate oven (350°) 12 minutes.
3. Sauté onion and green and red pepper in the vegetable oil until tender, about 3 minutes. Remove with slotted spoon to platter. Keep warm.
4. Add the 2 tablespoons butter to skillet. Sauté steaks on both sides to desired doneness (about 3 minutes for rare). Remove to platter; keep warm.
5. Add vinegar to pan drippings in skillet. Scrape up brown bits. Cook just until bubbly, but not evaporated. Remove from heat immediately.
6. To assemble: Place a steak on bottom half of roll; top with onion-pepper mixture; drizzle some pan juices over. Salt and pepper sandwich. Cover with top half of roll. Nice with potato sticks.

THE REUBEN

There are a number of versions of this popular restaurant sandwich, but basically it is made with corned beef, Swiss cheese and sauerkraut.

Makes 6 servings.

- 12 slices pumpernickel or rye bread
- ½ cup bottled Russian or Thousand Island dressing
- ½ pound thinly sliced corned beef
- 12 thin slices Swiss cheese
- 1 cup rinsed and drained sauerkraut
- 2 tablespoons Dijon-style mustard
  Softened butter or margarine

1. Spread 6 of the bread slices with Russian dressing. Divide corned beef evenly

The Reuben

over the slices. Top each with 2 slices of cheese and about 2 tablespoons sauerkraut.

2. Spread remaining bread slices with mustard, and press, mustard-side down, over sandwiches.

3. Spread outside surfaces with butter. Broil or grill slowly until cheese melts and bread browns. Serve with dill pickles and potato chips, if you wish.

DOUBLE-QUICK FISH SANDWICHES

Bake at 375° for 20 minutes.
Makes 8 servings.

  4 English muffins or Kaiser rolls
  ¼ cup (½ stick) butter or margarine
  2 packages (8 ounces each) frozen, breaded, fried fish fillets
  ¼ cup mayonnaise
  2 tablespoons chili sauce
  2 tablespoons pickle relish
  1 pound deli coleslaw
  1 large ripe tomato, cored and cut into 8 slices
    Lemon wedges

1. Split muffins; spread each half generously with the butter. Place buttered-side up on a large cookie sheet. Arrange fish fillets on same cookie sheet.

2. Bake in moderate oven (375°) 20 minutes or until muffins are lightly toasted and fish fillets are hot.

3. Make sauce: Combine mayonnaise, chili sauce and pickle relish in a small bowl; mix well.

4. To assemble: Place about ⅓ cup coleslaw on each toasted English muffin half; top with fish fillet, then tomato slice. Spoon sauce on top of each sandwich. Serve with lemon wedges; if you wish.

GRILLED CHEESE SANDWICHES

Makes 4 servings.

  2 tablespoons prepared mustard
  2 tablespoons mayonnaise
  8 slices whole-wheat, rye or white bread
  1 cup shredded Cheddar, Swiss or Muenster cheese (4 ounces)
  ½ cup (1 stick) butter, softened

1. Combine mustard and mayonnaise in a small cup; mix well; spread evenly on all 8 slices of bread

2. Divide the shredded cheese evenly among 4 slices of bread; top with remaining slices, mustard-mayonnaise side down. Spread outsides of bread with the butter.

3. Brown sandwiches on both sides on a griddle or in a large skillet until cheese melts.

Shred cheese right out of the refrigerator when it is nice and cold. When it softens, it is harder to shred. Rub the last few pieces of cheese through the shredder with the heel of your hand to save your fingers and knuckles.

From bottom left, clockwise: Hot Cross Buns (page 56); Orange-Honey Bubble Loaf (page 56); Lemon-Cheese Babka (page 58); Swedish Tea Ring (page 57)

Breads: Yeast and Quick

The aroma of bread baking is a warm welcome to the humblest of homes.
A slice of warm bread is a treat for young and old any time of the day.

GRANDMOTHER'S WHITE BREAD

Bake at 400° for 40 minutes.
Makes 2 loaves.

   1 envelope active dry yeast
 ½ cup very warm water
   3 tablespoons sugar
   2 cups milk
   2 tablespoons butter or margarine
   3 teaspoons salt
   7 to 8 cups all-purpose flour

1. Sprinkle yeast into very warm water in a 1-cup measure; stir in ½ teaspoon of the sugar. ("Very warm water" should feel comfortably warm when dropped on wrist.) Stir to dissolve yeast. Let stand until bubbly, about 10 minutes.
2. Combine remaining sugar, milk, butter and salt in a small saucepan; heat just until butter melts. Pour into a large bowl; cool to lukewarm. Stir in yeast mixture.
3. Stir in 3 cups of the flour; beat until smooth. Gradually stir in enough additional flour to make a soft dough.
4. Turn out onto a lightly floured surface; knead until smooth and elastic, about 10 minutes, using only as much flour as need-

> When a dough has been kneaded to develop elasticity, it is inclined to fight the rolling pin when you want to roll it out. Just let it relax for 10 to 15 minutes, and it will be soft and stretchy again.

> For a soft crust on a freshly baked white or whole-wheat bread, brush the warm crust with softened butter.
>
> To be sure your envelope of yeast is alive and well, you will notice that most of our yeast recipes call for mixing the yeast with a bit of sugar while it is dissolving in the very warm water. An envelope of yeast will bubble nicely within 10 minutes. If not, start with another envelope, and you will not have wasted any of the other ingredients—or your time.

ed to keep dough from sticking.
5. Press into a buttered large bowl; turn to bring buttered side up. Cover with a damp towel. Let rise in a warm place, away from drafts, 1 hour, or until doubled in volume.
6. Punch dough down; turn out onto a lightly floured surface; knead a few times; invert bowl over dough; let rest 10 minutes.
7. Divide dough in half and knead each half a few times. Shape into 2 loaves. Place in two buttered 9x5x3-inch loaf pans; cover.
8. Let rise again in a warm place, away from drafts, 1 hour, or until doubled in volume.
9. Bake in a preheated hot oven (400°) for 40 minutes, or until loaves are golden brown and sound hollow when tapped. If loaves are browning too quickly, cover tops loosely with foil. Remove from pans to wire racks to cool completely.

GEORGIAN CHEESE BREAD

Bake at 375° for 35 minutes.
Makes 1 loaf.

    1 loaf (1 pound) frozen plain bread
        dough, thawed overnight
        in refrigerator
    1 pound Muenster cheese
    2 eggs
    ½ teaspoon salt
    ½ cup dairy sour cream
    1 tablespoon butter or margarine

1. Allow dough to stand at room temperature on a lightly floured surface for 1 hour. Roll dough into a 9-inch circle. Continue to roll and pat dough to make a larger circle, 18 to 20 inches in diameter. Let rest while making filling.
2. Shred cheese into a large bowl. Beat eggs in a small bowl; measure out two tablespoons; reserve; stir remaining beaten egg, the salt and sour cream into cheese in bowl, mixing well.
3. Butter a 9-inch pie plate generously. Place dough loosely in plate, draping excess over side. Spoon in filling, flattening the top. Gather dough loosely to center of filling, turning pan as you go, pleating the folds. Twist ends into a topknot in center. Let rest 30 minutes. Brush top of dough with reserved beaten egg.
4. Bake in a preheated moderate oven (375°) for 35 minutes. If crust is browning too quickly, lower temperature to 350°. Let cool slightly before cutting into wedges.

OLD-FASHIONED RYE BREAD

Bake at 400° for 35 minutes.
Makes 2 loaves.

    2 envelopes active dry yeast
    2½ cups very warm water
    ¼ cup molasses
    4 teaspoons salt
    2 tablespoons vegetable shortening
    2½ cups rye flour

From bottom left, clockwise: Grandmother's White Bread (page 51); Old-Fashioned Rye Bread; Double-Wheat Whole-Wheat Bread

    1 tablespoon caraway seeds
    5½ to 6 cups all-purpose flour
        Cornmeal
    1 egg white
    1 tablespoon water

1. Sprinkle yeast into ½ cup of the very warm water in a 1-cup measure; stir in 1 teaspoon of the molasses. ("Very warm water" should feel comfortably warm when dropped on wrist.) Stir to dissolve yeast. Let stand until bubbly, about 10 minutes.
2. Combine the remaining water and molasses with salt and shortening in a large bowl, stirring to melt shortening. Stir in yeast mixture, rye flour and caraway seeds; add enough of the all-purpose flour to make a soft dough.
3. Turn out onto a lightly floured surface. Knead until smooth and elastic, about 10 minutes, using only as much additional flour as needed to keep dough from sticking.

4. Press into a buttered large bowl; turn dough to bring buttered side up. Cover with a damp towel. Let rise in a warm place, away from drafts, 1 hour, or until doubled in volume.

5. Butter a large cookie sheet. Sprinkle lightly with cornmeal.

6. Punch dough down; turn out onto a lightly floured surface; knead a few times; invert bowl over dough; let rest 10 minutes. Divide dough in half and knead each half a few times. Shape into 2 loaves. Place 4 inches apart on cookie sheet; cover.

7. Let rise again in a warm place, away from drafts, 45 minutes, or until doubled in volume. Beat egg white with water in a small bowl until frothy. Brush over loaves.

8. Bake in a preheated hot oven (400°) for 35 minutes, or until loaves are browned and sound hollow when tapped. Remove from cookie sheet to a wire rack; cool.

> When measuring molasses, corn or other syrups, lightly butter the measuring cup first. Syrup will pour out nicely—with no waste.

DOUBLE-WHEAT WHOLE-WHEAT BREAD

Bake at 400° for 40 minutes.
Makes 2 loaves.

```
2   envelopes active dry yeast
1   cup very warm water
⅓   cup honey
2   cups milk
¼   cup (½ stick) butter or margarine
4½  teaspoons salt
5   cups whole-wheat flour
¼   cup wheat germ
3   cups all-purpose flour
```

1. Sprinkle yeast into very warm water in a 1-cup measure; stir in 1 teaspoon of the honey. ("Very warm water" should feel comfortably warm when dropped on the wrist.) Stir to dissolve yeast. Let stand until bubbly, about 10 minutes.

2. Combine the remaining honey with milk, butter and salt in a small saucepan; heat until butter melts. Pour into a large bowl; cool to lukewarm. Stir in yeast.

3. Stir in whole-wheat flour and wheat germ until smooth; add enough of the all-purpose flour to make a soft dough.

4. Turn out onto a lightly floured surface. Knead until smooth and elastic, about 10 minutes, using only as much additional flour as needed to keep dough from sticking.

5. Press dough into a buttered large bowl; turn to bring buttered side up. Cover with a damp towel. Let rise in a warm place, away from drafts, 1 hour, or until doubled in volume.

6. Punch dough down; turn out onto a lightly floured surface; knead a few times; invert bowl over dough; let rest about 10 minutes.

7. Divide dough in half; knead each half a few times; shape into 2 loaves. Place in two buttered 9x5x3-inch loaf pans.

8. Cover; let rise in a warm place, away from drafts, 45 minutes, or until doubled in volume.

9. Bake in a preheated hot oven (400°) for 40 minutes, or until loaves are browned and sound hollow when tapped. Remove from pans to wire racks to cool completely.

> If you bake with whole-wheat and rye flours only occasionally, keep them fresh and sweet by sealing in freezer weight plastic bags and storing in the freezer until you are ready to use them.
>
> Whole-wheat flour, unlike all-purpose flour, is not sifted, since it contains particles of the bran and germ of the wheat, which would not go through the sieve. Just spoon it lightly into the cup.

ANADAMA CHEESE BREAD

Bake at 375° for 35 minutes.
Makes 2 loaves.

1½ cups water
½ cup yellow cornmeal
2 teaspoons salt
¼ cup vegetable shortening
½ cup light molasses
2 envelopes active dry yeast
Pinch sugar
½ cup very warm water
6 cups all-purpose flour
8 ounces process American cheese,
shredded (2 cups)
Butter or margarine, melted
Cornmeal (for topping)

1. Combine the 1½ cups water, cornmeal, salt, shortening and molasses in a medium-size saucepan. Heat, stirring constantly, until thick and bubbly. Pour into a large bowl; cool to lukewarm.
2. Sprinkle yeast and sugar into the ½ cup very warm water in a 1-cup measure. ("Very warm water" should feel comfortably warm when dropped on wrist.) Stir to dissolve yeast. Let stand until bubbly, about 10 minutes. Stir into cornmeal mixture.
3. Beat in 2 cups of the flour until smooth; stir in cheese, then about 3 more cups of the flour, one cup at a time, until mixture forms a soft dough.
4. Turn dough out onto a lightly floured surface. Knead until smooth and elastic, about 8 minutes, using only as much additional flour as needed to keep dough from sticking.
5. Press into a buttered large bowl; turn to bring buttered side up; cover with a damp towel. Cover; let rise in a warm place, away from drafts, 45 minutes, or until doubled in volume.
6. Punch dough down; knead a few times. Divide in half, then divide one half into 14 even-size pieces, rolling each between palms of floured hands to make a smooth ball. Place a row of 5 balls along each long side of a buttered 9x5x3-inch loaf pan;

place a row of 4 balls down the center. Repeat with the remaining half of dough in a second loaf pan.
7. Brush tops of loaves with melted butter and sprinkle lightly with cornmeal. Let rise in a warm place, away from drafts, 30 minutes, or until doubled in volume.
8. Bake in a preheated moderate oven (375°) for 35 minutes, or until loaves are browned and sound hollow when tapped. Remove from pans to wire racks; cool completely. Loaves will break into separate rolls for serving.

A new, clean, 1-inch paint brush makes a gentle tool for brushing the risen dough with egg wash or butter before baking. Wash with soap and water after using.

ALMOND PRETZEL TWIST

Bake at 350° for 30 minutes.
Makes 1 large coffee cake.

1 envelope active dry yeast
⅓ cup sugar
¼ cup very warm water
¼ cup milk
3 tablespoons butter or margarine
⅓ cup dairy sour cream
2½ cups all-purpose flour
½ teaspoon salt
1 teaspoon grated lemon rind
3 egg yolks
⅓ cup toasted chopped almonds
1 teaspoon water

1. Sprinkle yeast and 1 teaspoon of the sugar over very warm water in a 1-cup measure. ("Very warm water" should feel comfortably warm when dropped on wrist.) Stir to dissolve yeast. Let stand until bubbly, about 10 minutes.
2. Heat milk and butter in a small saucepan just until butter is melted. Pour into a large bowl; cool slightly; stir in sour cream.
3. Stir in the yeast mixture. Add 1½ cups of

the flour, remaining sugar, salt, lemon rind and two of the egg yolks. Beat on medium speed with electric mixer 3 minutes, or until smooth.

4. Stir in the remaining 1 cup flour and ¼ cup of the almonds. Turn out onto a lightly floured surface. Knead until smooth and elastic, about 10 minutes.

5. Press dough into a buttered large bowl, turning to bring buttered side up. Cover, let rise in a warm place, away from drafts, 1 hour, or until doubled in volume.

6. Punch dough down and let rest 10 minutes. Form into a long rope, about 36 inches long, on wax paper. (Squeeze dough from the middle out toward each end.)

7. Form into a pretzel shape; place on a buttered cookie sheet. Cover, let rise again about 30 minutes, until doubled in volume.

8. Stir the remaining egg yolk with water in a small cup; brush over dough. Sprinkle with the remaining almonds.

9. Bake in a preheated moderate oven (350°) for 30 minutes. Remove to wire rack to cool.

JELLY DOUGHNUTS
(Bismarcks)

Makes about 2 dozen doughnuts.

    1¼ cups milk
    ⅓ cup butter or margarine
    5 cups all-purpose flour
    2 envelopes active dry yeast
    ½ cup sugar
    1 teaspoon salt
    1 teaspoon ground nutmeg
    2 eggs
      Vegetable oil for frying
    1 cup raspberry or red currant jelly
      10X (confectioners') sugar

1. Heat milk and butter in a small saucepan over low heat until very warm. ("Very warm" should feel comfortably warm when dropped on wrist.) Butter does not have to melt completely.

2. Combine 2 cups of the flour, yeast, sugar, salt and nutmeg in a large bowl. With electric mixer at low speed, beat in warm milk mixture until smooth.

3. Beat on medium speed 2 minutes, occasionally scraping side of bowl. Beat in ½ cup more flour and eggs.

4. Stir in about 1½ cups more flour with a spoon to make a soft dough. Turn out onto a lightly floured surface; knead until smooth and elastic, about 8 minutes, using only as much additional flour as needed to keep dough from sticking.

5. Press dough into a buttered large bowl, turn to bring buttered side up. Cover bowl with a damp towel; let rise in a warm place, away from drafts, 1 to 1½ hours, or until doubled in volume.

6. Punch dough down; knead 8 minutes to remove any large bubbles; invert bowl over dough; let rest 15 minutes.

7. Roll out dough on a lightly floured surface to ¼ inch thick; cut with a floured 3- to 3⅓-inch biscuit or cookie cutter. Lift off trimmings. Press trimmings together; re-roll and cut. Transfer doughnuts to cookie sheets; cover tops. Let rise in a warm place, away from drafts 45 minutes, or until doubled in volume.

8. Fill a large saucepan or Dutch oven ½ full with vegetable oil. Heat to 370° on a deep-fat frying thermometer.

9. Transfer doughnuts to the hot oil with a flexible spatula or pancake turner, frying 2 or 3 at a time. Fry, turning once, 3 minutes; or until golden. Drain on paper toweling.

10. Cut a slit in the side of each doughnut. Fit a pastry bag with a small plain tube. Spoon jelly into bag; fill doughnuts. Dust filled doughnuts with 10X sugar.

> **All-purpose flour need not be sifted for yeast breads. Part of the flour is beaten in, and the remainder added just until the dough reaches that "feel right" stage.**

ORANGE-HONEY BUBBLE LOAF

Bake at 350° for 30 minutes.
Makes 20 rolls.

> 1 package (13 ounces) hot-roll mix
> ¾ cup very warm water
>   Pinch sugar
> 2 eggs
> ¼ teaspoon ground mace
> 1 tablespoon grated orange rind
> ¼ cup golden raisins
> ⅓ cup orange juice
> 2 tablespoons butter or margarine
> ¼ cup honey
>   Pecan halves
> ¾ cup chopped pecans

1. Sprinkle yeast from roll mix over very warm water in a large bowl; add a pinch of sugar. ("Very warm water" should feel comfortably warm when dropped on wrist.) Stir to dissolve yeast. Let stand until bubbly, about 10 minutes.

2. Beat in eggs, mace, orange rind and raisins; blend thoroughly. Stir in flour from roll mix. Press into a buttered medium-size bowl; turn to bring buttered side up. Let rise in a warm place, away from drafts, about 45 minutes, or until doubled in volume. (Dough will be soft.)

3. While dough is rising, heat orange juice, butter and honey in a small saucepan until butter is melted. Reserve.

4. Butter a 9-inch ring mold or angel cake tube pan; place 2 tablespoons of the orange juice syrup in the bottom of the mold. Arrange pecan halves top-side down in the syrup.

5. Punch dough down; turn out onto a well-floured surface. Knead dough, adding more flour if necessary until the dough is no longer sticky. Shape into 20 balls.

6. Dip each ball into syrup to coat completely; roll in chopped pecans. Arrange in two layers in the prepared pan; cover; let rise in a warm place, away from drafts, about 45 minutes, or until doubled in volume.

7. Bake in a preheated moderate oven (350°) for 30 minutes or until loaf is browned and sounds hollow when tapped. (Cover with foil if top is browning too quickly.) Loosen around the edges with a spatula; invert onto a serving plate; remove mold. Spoon remaining syrup over hot rolls. Cool completely, then break apart with two forks to serve.

HOT CROSS BUNS

Bake at 350° for 30 minutes.
Makes 32 buns.

> 2 envelopes active dry yeast
> ½ cup sugar
> ½ cup very warm water
> ½ cup (1 stick) butter or margarine
> ⅔ cup (1 small can) evaporated milk
> 1 teaspoon salt
> 2 eggs
> ½ cup dried currants or raisins
> 1 container (4 ounces) candied citron, chopped (½ cup)
> 4 to 4½ cups all-purpose flour
> ¼ teaspoon ground cinnamon
> ¼ teaspoon ground nutmeg
>   Sugar Icing (*recipe on page 57*)

1. Sprinkle yeast and 1 teaspoon of the sugar over very warm water in a 1-cup measure. ("Very warm water" should feel comfortably warm when dropped on wrist.) Stir to dissolve yeast. Let stand until bubbly, about 10 minutes.

2. Heat butter, remaining sugar, evaporated milk and the salt in a small saucepan just until butter is melted. Cool to lukewarm.

3. Beat eggs in a large bowl; measure out and reserve 2 tablespoons. Stir cooled milk mixture into the remaining eggs; add yeast mixture, currants, citron, 2 cups of the flour, cinnamon and nutmeg. Beat well until smooth. Stir in 2 cups more flour to make a soft dough.

4. Turn out onto a lightly floured surface; knead until smooth and elastic, about 8 minutes. Press into a buttered large bowl; turn to bring buttered side up. Cover with a damp towel; let rise in a warm place, away from drafts, about 2 hours, or until doubled in volume.

5. Punch dough down; turn out onto a lightly floured surface. Divide in half. Let rest 5 minutes; cover.

6. Grease two 8x8x2-inch pans. Divide each piece of dough into 16 pieces; shape each into a smooth round. Arrange, almost touching, in prepared pans.

7. Cover; let rise in a warm place, away from drafts, about 45 minutes, or until doubled in volume. Brush tops with reserved egg.

8. Bake in a preheated moderate oven (350°) for 30 minutes, or until buns are brown and sound hollow when tapped. Remove from pans; cool on wire racks.

9. When cool, drizzle the Sugar Icing from tip of a teaspoon onto top of buns to make crosses.

SWEDISH TEA RING

Bake at 375° for 25 minutes.
Makes 2 tea rings.

    1 envelope active dry yeast
    ⅓ cup sugar
    ¼ cup very warm water
    ⅓ cup milk
    ¼ cup (½ stick) butter or margarine
    1 teaspoon salt
    2 eggs, beaten
    3 cups all-purpose flour
    ½ teaspoon ground cardamom
    4 tablespoons (½ stick) butter or
        margarine, softened
Filling:
    ½ cup firmly packed brown sugar
    1 teaspoon ground cinnamon
    ⅓ cup raisins
    ⅓ cup chopped walnuts
        Sugar Icing (*recipe follows*)

1. Sprinkle yeast and ½ teaspoon of the sugar over the very warm water in a 1-cup measure. ("Very warm water" should feel comfortably warm when dropped on wrist.) Stir to dissolve yeast. Let stand until bubbly, about 10 minutes.

2. Heat milk, the ¼ cup butter, the remaining sugar and salt in a small saucepan just until butter is melted. Pour into a large bowl; cool to lukewarm.

3. Add eggs and yeast to cooled milk mixture; beat until blended. Add 1½ cups of the flour and the cardamom; beat 2 minutes. Stir in just enough additional flour to make a soft dough.

4. Turn out onto a lightly floured surface. Knead until smooth and elastic, about 8 minutes. Press dough into a buttered medium-size bowl, turning to bring buttered side up. Cover with a damp towel; let rise in a warm place, away from drafts, 1½ hours, or until doubled in volume. Punch dough down; let rest 5 minutes.

5. Divide dough in half; roll to make two 12x9-inch rectangles. Spread rectangles with 2 tablespoons of the softened butter.

6. Make filling: Combine brown sugar, cinnamon, raisins and walnuts in a small bowl; sprinkle half the mixture over each dough rectangle. Roll up each rectangle tightly, jelly-roll fashion, from one long side, pinching along seam to seal well.

7. Place each roll seam-side down on a greased cookie sheet and shape into a ring; pinch ends well to seal.

8. Make cuts ⅔ of the way from the outside edge through the dough and 1 inch apart with scissors or a sharp knife. Turn each section, cut side up. Cover; let rise in a warm place, away from drafts, about 45 minutes, or until doubled in volume.

9. Bake in a preheated moderate oven (375°) for 25 minutes, or until rings are golden brown and sound hollow when tapped. Cover with foil if tops are browning too quickly. Remove to wire rack. Cool. Drizzle with Sugar Icing.

SUGAR ICING: Blend 1 cup *unsifted* 10X (confectioners') sugar with 2 tablespoons milk in a small bowl until smooth. Makes ½ cup.

LEMON-CHEESE BABKA

Tender yeast dough holds a lemony-cheese filling.

Bake at 350° for 40 minutes.
Makes 2 eight-inch cakes.

     1 envelope active dry yeast
    ¼ cup sugar
    ¼ cup very warm water
  3½ to 4 cups all-purpose flour
    ¾ teaspoon salt
     2 teaspoons grated lemon rind
     2 eggs plus 2 egg yolks
    ⅓ cup warm milk
     6 tablespoons (¾ stick) butter or
         margarine, softened
    ½ cup raisins
       10X (confectioners') sugar

Cheese Filling:
     1 package (8 ounces) cream cheese
    ½ cup cottage cheese
     1 egg yolk
    ¼ cup sugar
     1 teaspoon grated lemon rind

Crumb Topping:
     3 tablespoons flour
    ⅓ cup chopped nuts
     3 tablespoons butter or margarine,
         softened
     3 tablespoons sugar
    ¼ teaspoon ground cinnamon

1. Sprinkle yeast and ½ teaspoon of the sugar over very warm water in a 1-cup measure. ("Very warm water" should feel comfortably warm when dropped on wrist.) Stir to dissolve yeast. Let stand until bubbly, about 10 minutes.

2. Combine 2 cups of the flour, salt, lemon rind and the remaining sugar in a large bowl; make a well in the middle. Beat eggs and egg yolks in a small bowl just to mix. Pour eggs, yeast mixture and warm milk into well. Stir liquids into flour until smooth. Beat well.

3. Add softened butter gradually, beating well. Stir in 1 more cup of the flour. Beat until dough leaves the side of the bowl.

4. Knead on a lightly floured surface; until

smooth and elastic, about 8 minutes.

5. Press dough into a buttered large bowl; turn to bring buttered side up; cover. Let rise in a warm place, away from drafts, 1½ to 2 hours, or until doubled in volume.

6. While the dough is rising, make Cheese Filling: Beat cream cheese and cottage cheese in a small bowl with an electric mixer until smooth; beat in egg yolk and sugar. Stir in lemon rind.

7. Make Crumb Topping: Combine nuts, flour, butter, sugar and cinnamon in a small bowl. Grease two 8x1½-inch pans.

8. When dough has doubled, punch down; knead in raisins; divide dough into four equal parts; press two parts into the bottoms and about ½ inch up the sides of each of the prepared pans; spread each with about 1 cup of the cheese filling.

9. Shape remaining dough into two 8-inch circles; place on top of cheese filling. Press the handle of a spoon into dough around edges to seal.

10. Sprinkle half the crumb topping over each. Let rise in a warm place until dough reaches the top of the pans, about 1 hour.

11. Bake in a preheated moderate oven (350°) for 40 minutes; or until the cakes sound hollow when tapped. Cool on a wire rack. (Place foil loosely over the crumb topping; invert onto rack, then turn right side up.) Let cool at least 30 minutes before serving. Sprinkle with 10X sugar.

BAKING POWDER BISCUITS

Flaky, light biscuits to serve with Sunday dinner. Or, try one of our biscuit variations for a tea-time snack.

Bake at 450° for 12 minutes.
Makes 12 biscuits.

     2 cups *sifted* all-purpose flour
     3 teaspoons baking powder
    ½ teaspoon salt
    ¼ cup vegetable shortening
    ¾ cup milk

1. Sift flour, baking powder and salt into a

Cranberry-Pecan Muffins (page 61); Popovers

large bowl. Preheat oven to hot (450°).

2. Cut in shortening with a pastry blender until mixture is crumbly.

3. Add milk; stir lightly with a fork until a soft dough forms.

4. Turn out onto a lightly floured surface. Knead lightly, about 20 times.

5. Roll or pat dough to a ½-inch thickness. Cut into 2-inch rounds with a floured biscuit cutter, working neatly from rim to middle so there will be few scraps to reroll. Place biscuits on an ungreased cookie sheet 1 inch apart.

6. Bake in a preheated hot oven (450°) for 12 minutes, or until golden brown.

CHEESE BISCUITS: Add 1 cup shredded process American cheese to dry ingredients after cutting in shortening.

EASY DROP BISCUITS: Increase milk to 1 cup Drop dough by spoonfuls, 1 inch apart, on ungreased cookie sheets, or fill 12 greased muffin-pan cups ⅔ full.

> **For biscuits with soft sides, place them in baking pan with sides barely touching.**

POPOVERS

Bake at 425° for 40 minutes.
Makes 8 popovers.

    2 eggs
    1 cup milk
    1 tablespoon butter or margarine,
        melted
    1 cup *sifted* all-purpose flour
    ½ teaspoon salt

1. Generously butter eight 5-ounce custard cups; place on a jelly-roll pan. (If you have cast-iron popover pans, heat in oven, then brush cups with melted butter before pouring in batter.) Preheat oven to hot (425°).

2. Beat eggs in a large bowl; add milk and butter. Beat until blended. Add flour and salt; beat until batter is quite smooth. Ladle into prepared cups, filling each half full.

3. Bake in a preheated hot oven (425°) for 35 minutes. Cut a slit in the side of each popover to allow steam to escape. Bake 5 minutes longer, or until popovers are deep brown and very crisp. Serve at once.

APPLE STREUSEL MUFFINS

Mouth-watering muffins chock-full of apple and sprinkled with walnuts for a perfect topping.

Bake at 425° for 20 minutes.
Makes 12 muffins.

- 2 cups *sifted* all-purpose flour
- ½ cup sugar
- 3 teaspoons baking powder
- 1 teaspoon salt
- ½ cup (1 stick) butter or margarine
- 1 medium-size tart apple, pared, quartered, cored and diced (1 cup)
- 2 teaspoons grated lemon rind
- 1 egg
- ⅔ cup milk
- ¼ cup finely chopped walnuts
- 2 tablespoons sugar

1. Sift flour, the ½ cup sugar, baking powder and salt into a large bowl. Cut in butter with a pastry blender until mixture is crumbly. Measure out ½ cup for topping; reserve. Stir apple and 1 teaspoon of the lemon rind into remainder. Preheat oven to hot (425°).

2. Beat egg in a small bowl; stir in milk. Add all at once to apple mixture; stir lightly just until moist. (Batter will be lumpy.) Spoon into 12 greased medium-size muffin-pan cups, filling each ⅔ full.

3. Blend reserved crumb mixture with the remaining lemon rind, walnuts and the 2 tablespoons sugar; sprinkle over batter in each cup.

4. Bake in a preheated hot oven (425°) for 20 minutes, or until golden. Remove from cups to wire rack. Serve warm with butter and jelly.

Not enough muffin pans? Look for the aluminum foil muffin or cupcake pan liners. You can put these right on a cookie sheet and bake without a muffin pan.

Fill muffin pans easily—just use an ice cream scoop. It's neat and quick!

Blueberry Muffins

CORN MUFFINS

Bake at 400° for 20 minutes.
Makes 12 muffins.

- 1 cup *sifted* all-purpose flour
- 3 tablespoons sugar
- 1½ teaspoons baking powder
- ½ teaspoon baking soda
- ½ teaspoon salt
- 1 cup yellow or white cornmeal
- 1 egg, well beaten
- ⅔ cup buttermilk
- ¼ cup vegetable shortening, melted and cooled

1. Sift flour, sugar, baking powder, baking soda and salt into a large bowl; stir in cornmeal. Preheat oven to hot (400°).

2. Mix egg, buttermilk and shortening in a 2-cup measure; add all at once to flour mixture; stir lightly with fork until liquid is just absorbed. (Batter will be lumpy.)

3. Spoon into greased medium-size muffin-pan cups, filling each ⅔ full.

4. Bake in a preheated hot oven (400°) for 20 minutes, or until golden. Remove from pan to wire rack. Serve warm.

BRAN MUFFINS

Bake at 400° for 20 minutes.
Makes 12 muffins.

2¼ cups whole bran
1 cup buttermilk
⅓ cup molasses
¼ cup firmly packed brown sugar
1 cup *sifted* all-purpose flour
1 teaspoon baking powder
1 teaspoon baking soda
1 teaspoon salt
1 egg, slightly beaten
¼ cup vegetable shortening, melted
     and cooled

1. Mix bran, buttermilk, molasses and brown sugar in a small bowl; let stand until liquid is absorbed. Preheat oven to hot (400°).
2. Sift flour, baking powder, baking soda and salt into a large bowl.
3. Stir egg and shortening into bran mixture. Add all at once to flour mixture; stir lightly with a fork just until evenly moist. Spoon batter into greased medium-size muffin-pan cups, filling each ⅔ full.
4. Bake in a preheated hot oven (400°) for 20 minutes. Remove from pans to wire racks. Serve warm.

CRANBERRY-PECAN MUFFINS

Bake at 400° for 20 minutes.
Makes 2½ dozen.

1½ cups coarsely chopped cranberries
¼ cup sugar
3 cups *sifted* all-purpose flour
4½ teaspoons baking powder
½ teaspoon salt
1 cup sugar
½ cup vegetable shortening
1 cup chopped pecans
2 tablespoons grated lemon rind
2 eggs
1 cup milk

1. Combine cranberries and the ¼ cup sugar in a small bowl; let stand while preparing batter. Preheat oven to hot (400°).
2. Sift flour, baking powder, salt and sugar into a large bowl. Cut in shortening with a pastry blender until mixture is crumbly. Stir in pecans and lemon rind.
3. Beat eggs in small bowl until foamy; beat in milk. Add liquid all at once to flour mixture, stirring just until moist. Fold in cranberry mixture. Spoon into greased medium-size muffin-pan cups, filling each ⅔ full.
4. Bake in a preheated hot oven (400°) for 20 minutes. Remove from pans at once; cool on wire racks. Serve warm with butter and honey, if you wish.

BLUEBERRY MUFFINS

Bake at 425° for 20 minutes.
Makes 12 muffins.

2 cups *sifted* all-purpose flour
⅓ cup sugar
3 teaspoons baking powder
1 teaspoon salt
1 egg, well beaten
1 cup milk
¼ cup (½ stick) butter
     or margarine, melted and cooled
1 package (10 ounces) frozen
     quick-thaw blueberries, thawed
     and drained
1 tablespoon sugar
1 teaspoon grated lemon rind

1. Sift flour, the ⅓ cup sugar, baking powder and salt into a large bowl. Mix egg, milk and butter in a small bowl; add all at once to flour mixture; stir lightly with a fork just until liquid is absorbed. Fold in blueberries. Preheat oven to hot (425°).
2. Spoon into greased medium-size muffin-pan cups, filling each ⅔ full. Sprinkle with a mixture of the 1 tablespoon sugar and lemon rind.
3. Bake in a preheated hot oven (425°) for 20 minutes; remove from pans to wire rack. Serve warm.

BUTTERMILK GRIDDLE CAKES

These breakfast treats will disappear fast.
Makes 6 servings.

2 cups *sifted* all-purpose flour
1 tablespoon sugar
1 teaspoon baking soda
1 teaspoon salt
2 eggs
2 cups buttermilk
2 tablespoons vegetable oil

1. Sift flour, sugar, baking soda and salt onto wax paper.
2. Beat eggs in a medium-size bowl until foamy; stir in buttermilk.
3. Add sifted dry ingredients to the buttermilk mixture and beat until smooth; stir in vegetable oil.
4. Pour batter onto medium-hot lightly greased griddle to form 5-inch circles. Cook until edges begin to brown and bubbles appear on top. Turn; cook until other side is golden.
5. Stack griddle cakes; keep warm in a slow oven, until all batter is used.

SWEDISH PANCAKES

Traditionally, Swedish pancakes are cooked in special iron pancake pans (platte panna), but a heavy cast-iron skillet or griddle can be used.

Makes about 50 pancakes.

3 eggs
1 cup light cream or half and half
1 cup *sifted* all-purpose flour
1 tablespoon sugar
Pinch salt
1 cup milk
¼ cup (½ stick) butter or margarine, melted and cooled
Lingonberry or other tart jam

1. Beat eggs and cream in a medium-size bowl with a rotary beater. Add flour, sugar and salt and beat until batter is smooth. Stir in milk and butter.
2. Heat a heavy griddle or skillet; brush lightly with butter. (You will not need to grease it again because pancakes have so much butter in them.) The pan should be almost smoking—so hot that as soon as the batter touches it bubbles begin to form.
3. Drop batter by tablespoonsful onto the griddle to form 3-inch circles. When edges begin to brown, turn pancakes over and cook other side until golden. Stir batter occasionally while making pancakes.
4. Stack pancakes on top of one another and keep warm. Repeat until all batter is used. Serve with jam. If not serving at once, keep hot in a slow oven (325°).

> **Make sure your griddle or skillet is nicely heated for your griddle cakes by flicking on a few drops of water with your hand. When the drops sputter and dance, the griddle is ready.**

FRENCH CRULLERS

Makes about 1 dozen crullers.

1 cup water
¼ cup (½ stick) butter or margarine
¼ cup sugar
½ teaspoon salt
1 cup *sifted* all-purpose flour
3 eggs
Vegetable oil for frying
Honey Glaze (*recipe follows*)

1. Combine water, butter, sugar and salt in a large saucepan; bring to boiling.
2. Add flour all at once. Stir vigorously just until mixture leaves the side of pan. Remove from heat. Add eggs, one at a time, beating well after each addition. Refrigerate mixture for 15 minutes.
3. Cut 12 three-inch squares of foil; oil each. Fit a pastry bag with a ½-inch star tip; fill with dough. Press a 3-inch ring of dough

onto each square.

4. Fill a large saucepan or Dutch oven ½ full with vegetable oil. Heat to 370° on a deep-fat frying thermometer. Hold ring of dough close to the surface of the oil; carefully slip from foil into oil. OR: Drop dough and foil into hot oil. Crullers will slip off foil as they cook; remove foil with tongs. Fry 3 at a time, turning once, about 3 to 5 minutes or until golden and puffed. Drain on paper toweling; cool.

5. Dip top half of crullers into Honey Glaze, letting excess drip back into bowl. Place, glazed side up, on a wire rack set over wax paper; let stand until glaze is dry.

HONEY GLAZE: Combine ½ cup honey and 1 cup 10X (confectioners') sugar in a small saucepan. Heat over low heat just to boiling; use while still warm. (Makes ⅔ cup.)

OLD-FASHIONED CAKE DOUGHNUTS
Makes about 16 doughnuts.

     3¾ cups *sifted* all-purpose flour
      4 teaspoons baking powder
      ½ teaspoon ground mace
      ¼ teaspoon salt
      1 cup granulated sugar
      2 eggs
      3 tablespoons shortening
      ¾ cup milk

Old-Fashioned Cake Doughnuts

Chocolate-Nut Doughnuts (page 64)

      1 teaspoon vanilla
        Vegetable oil for frying
        10X (confectioners') sugar

1. Sift flour, baking powder, mace and salt onto wax paper.
2. Beat sugar, eggs and shortening at medium speed in a large bowl with electric mixer until fluffy; blend in milk and vanilla.
3. Remove bowl from mixer and stir in flour mixture until well-blended.
4. Wrap dough in plastic wrap or wax paper; chill at least 2 hours.
5. Place dough on a lightly floured surface; roll to a ½-inch thickness. Cut out with a lightly floured doughnut cutter.
6. Fill a large heavy saucepan or electric skillet 2/3 full with vegetable oil. Heat to 370° on a deep-fat frying thermometer.
7. Drop doughnuts, 2 or 3 at a time, into hot oil. Fry, turning once, 3 minutes, or until golden. Drain on paper toweling; cool. Sprinkle with 10X sugar or shake in a plastic bag with 1 cup granulated sugar mixed with 1 teaspoon ground cinnamon.

For the tenderest doughnuts, dough should be well chilled. To speed chilling: Press dough onto plastic wrap to a 1-inch thickness. Wrap and place in freezer. Chilled dough can then be rolled with less handling.

CHOCOLATE-NUT DOUGHNUTS

Chocolate all the way, fudgy and dark, and topped with chocolate and pistachios.

Makes 16 doughnuts.

    2 squares unsweetened chocolate
    2 tablespoons vegetable shortening
 3¾ cups *sifted* all-purpose flour
    4 teaspoons baking powder
  ½ teaspoon salt
    2 eggs
    1 cup sugar
  ¾ cup milk
    1 teaspoon vanilla
      Vegetable oil for frying
    1 tub chocolate ready-to-spread frosting
  ½ cup chopped pistachio nuts

1. Melt chocolate and shortening in top of a double boiler over simmering water; cool. Reserve.

2. Sift flour, baking powder and salt onto wax paper.

3. Beat eggs and sugar in large bowl of electric mixer at medium speed until fluffy. Beat in milk, vanilla and cooled chocolate mixture. Remove bowl from mixer.

4. Stir in flour mixture until well-blended. Wrap in plastic wrap; chill at least 2 hours.

5. Roll out dough to ½-inch thickness on a lightly floured surface. Cut with floured doughnut cutter; reroll and cut scraps.

6. Fill a large heavy saucepan or electric skillet ⅔ full with vegetable oil. Heat to 370° on a deep-fat frying thermometer. Drop doughnuts, about 3 at a time, into oil; fry, turning once, 3 to 5 minutes, or until firm. Drain on paper toweling; cool.

7. Frost tops of doughnuts with frosting; sprinkle with nuts.

> **To transfer doughnuts to the hot oil and still keep the nice round shape, scoop them up with a flexible-bladed metal pancake turner. Leave doughnut on the turner in the hot oil until it floats off.**

> **Instead of rerolling the doughnut centers and cutting them out again, you may wish to fry these tasty morsels as special treats for the family. Dip them in a variety of easy coatings—sugar and cinnamon, thinned canned frosting, then in multi-colored sprinkles, chopped toasted peanuts or even chocolate "jimmies." They make great lunchbox treats, too!**

STEAMED BOSTON BROWN BREAD

Traditionally served with Boston Baked Beans, but also delicious with cream cheese or butter.

Steam for 2½ hours.

Makes 2 loaves.

    1 cup *sifted* all-purpose flour
    1 cup whole-wheat flour
    1 cup yellow cornmeal
    2 teaspoons baking soda
    1 teaspoon salt
    1 cup raisins
    2 cups buttermilk
  ¾ cup molasses

1. Grease two 1-pound coffee cans; dust with flour. Combine flour, whole-wheat flour, cornmeal, baking soda, salt and raisins in a large bowl.

2. Blend buttermilk and molasses in a 4-cup measure; pour into flour mixture. Stir until all dry ingredients are moistened. Pour batter into prepared cans, dividing equally. Cover with buttered wax paper and aluminum foil. Tie securely with string.

3. Put cans on a rack in a large kettle or steamer. Add boiling water to come half-way up the side of cans. Cover kettle and steam 2½ hours, or until a cake tester inserted in center of bread comes out clean. Remove from kettle and let stand 15 minutes. Uncover cans and turn out bread. Serve warm with butter or cream cheese.

Bottom: Date-Nut Bread (page 66); middle: Lemon Walnut
Tea Bread (page 67); top: Irish Soda Bread (page 66)

ZUCCHINI BREAD

Bake at 350° for 40 minutes.
Makes 16 servings.

    2 cups *sifted* all-purpose flour
    2 teaspoons baking soda
    1 teaspoon salt
    ¼ teaspoon baking powder
    3 teaspoons ground cinnamon
    3 eggs
    1 cup vegetable oil
 1½ cups sugar
    2 medium-size zucchini, grated
        (2 cups)
    2 teaspoons vanilla
    1 cup raisins
    1 cup chopped walnuts

1. Sift flour, baking soda, salt, baking powder and cinnamon onto wax paper. Preheat oven to moderate (350°).
2. Combine eggs, oil, sugar, zucchini and vanilla in a large bowl; beat until well-mixed. Stir in flour mixture until smooth.
3. Stir in raisins and nuts. Pour mixture into a greased 13x9x2-inch pan.
4. Bake in preheated moderate oven (350°) for 40 minutes, or until a wooden pick inserted in center comes out clean. Cool 15 minutes in pan on wire rack; turn out; cool completely.

IRISH SODA BREAD

Bake at 400° for 40 minutes.
Makes 1 round loaf.

    4 cups *sifted* all-purpose flour
    1 tablespoon sugar
 1½ teaspoons salt
    1 teaspoon baking soda
    1 cup dried currants
 1½ cups buttermilk
    1 egg beaten with 1 tablespoon water

1. Sift flour, sugar, salt and baking soda into a large bowl; stir in currants. Preheat oven to hot (400°).
2. Stir in buttermilk; mix just until flour is moistened. Knead dough in the bowl with lightly floured hands 10 times.
3. Turn dough out onto lightly floured cookie sheet and shape into an 8-inch round. Cut a cross in the top with a floured knife. Brush egg and water over bread.
4. Bake in preheated hot oven (400°) for 40 minutes, or until loaf is golden and sounds hollow when tapped. Cool completely on wire rack before slicing.

DATE-NUT BREAD

Bake at 350 for 1 hour and 10 minutes.
Makes 1 loaf.

    1 package (8 ounces) pitted dates
 1¼ cups boiling water
 1½ cups firmly packed brown sugar
    6 tablespoons (¾ stick) butter or
        margarine, softened
    1 egg, beaten
 2¼ cups *sifted* all-purpose flour
 1½ teaspoons baking soda
 1½ teaspoons salt
    1 cup chopped walnuts

1. Preheat oven to moderate (350°). Cut dates in small pieces into a medium-size bowl; pour boiling water over; cool.
2. Stir in sugar and butter until butter is melted; cool. Stir in beaten egg. Grease a 9x5x3-inch loaf pan.
3. Sift flour, soda and salt onto wax paper; stir into date mixture just until blended. Stir in nuts. Pour into prepared pan.
4. Bake in a preheated moderate oven (350°) for 1 hour and 10 minutes, or until a wooden pick inserted in center comes out clean. Cool in pan on wire rack 5 minutes; turn out; cool completely.

BANANA-PECAN BREAD

Bake at 325° for 1 hour and 20 minutes.
Makes 1 loaf.

 2⅔ cups *sifted* all-purpose flour
    3 teaspoons baking powder
    1 teaspoon salt

¼ teaspoon baking soda

½ cup (1 stick) butter or margarine, softened

1 cup sugar

3 eggs

2 medium-size ripe bananas, peeled and mashed (about 1 cup)

¾ cup finely chopped pecans

2 teaspoons grated orange rind

1. Grease a 9x5x3-inch loaf pan; line the bottom with wax paper; grease the paper. Preheat oven to slow (325°).

2. Sift flour, baking powder, salt and baking soda onto wax paper.

3. Beat butter, sugar and eggs in a large bowl with electric mixer until fluffy.

4. Stir in flour mixture alternately with mashed bananas; fold in pecans and orange rind. Pour into prepared pan.

5. Bake in preheated slow oven (325°) for 1 hour and 20 minutes, or until a wooden pick inserted in the center comes out clean. Cool in pan on a wire rack 10 minutes. Turn out; peel off wax paper; cool.

LEMON WALNUT TEA BREAD

Bake at 350° for 1 hour.
Makes 1 loaf.

2⅔ cups *sifted* all-purpose flour

2¼ teaspoons baking powder

½ teaspoon salt

¾ cup (1½ sticks) butter or margarine, softened

1⅓ cups sugar

3 eggs

3 teaspoons grated lemon rind

¼ cup lemon juice

⅓ cup milk

1 cup chopped walnuts

1. Sift flour, baking powder and salt onto wax paper. Grease and flour a 9x5x3-inch pan. Preheat oven to moderate (350°).

2. Beat butter and sugar in a large bowl with electric mixer until well-blended. Beat

in eggs and lemon rind until fluffy.

3. Add dry ingredients alternately to butter mixture, alternating with lemon juice and milk, and beating well after each addition. Stir in nuts. Turn into prepared pan.

4. Bake in preheated moderate oven (300°) for 1 hour, or until a wooden pick inserted in center comes out clean. Cool in pan 10 minutes; turn out; cool completely.

QUICK APPLE CAKE

Bake at 350° for 45 minutes.
Makes 6 servings.

2 cups *sifted* all-purpose flour

2 teaspoons baking powder

½ teaspoon salt

¼ teaspoon pumpkin-pie spice

1 cup firmly packed light brown sugar

8 tablespoons (1 stick) butter or margarine

¼ cup dried currants

2 eggs

⅔ cup (1 small can) evaporated milk

1 large tart apple, pared, cored and thinly sliced

2 tablespoons sugar

1. Sift flour, baking powder, salt and spice into a large bowl; stir in brown sugar. Preheat oven to moderate (350°).

2. Cut 6 tablespoons of the butter into flour mixture with a pastry blender until crumbly. Measure out ½ cup; reserve for topping; stir currants into the remainder.

3. Beat eggs slightly in a small bowl; stir in evaporated milk. Stir egg mixture into flour mixture until well blended. Spoon into a greased 9-inch pie plate.

4. Arrange apple slices, overlapping, in 2 circles on top. Sprinkle with the ½ cup crumb mixture; dot with the remaining butter; sprinkle with sugar.

5. Bake in a preheated moderate oven (350°) for 45 minutes, or until center springs back when lightly pressed with fingertip. Cool 10 minutes on a wire rack; cut in wedges. Serve warm.

Zucchini and Corn Soufflé

Eggs and Cheese

Two of the most versatile ingredients that need low-heat cooking for best results. Dishes made from either—or a combination—are great for any meal, any season.

ZUCCHINI AND CORN SOUFFLE

Bake at 350° for 55 minutes.
Makes 6 servings.

      2 shucked ears of corn
      2 to 3 medium-size zucchini, washed
      1 teaspoon salt
      6 tablespoons (¾ stick) butter or
          margarine
    ¼ cup chopped green onions
      6 tablespoons flour
    1¼ teaspoons salt
    ¼ teaspoon pepper
    1¼ cups milk
      6 eggs, separated
    ½ cup shredded Swiss cheese (2 ounces)

1. Preheat oven to moderate (350°). Butter an 8-cup soufflé or other straight-sided baking dish.

2. Drop corn into boiling water; simmer 5 minutes. Drain. Cut corn from cob into a small bowl (about 1 cup).

3. Grate zucchini on coarse side of grater to make about 3 cups. Sprinkle with 1 teaspoon of the salt. Let stand 5 minutes. Drain in a sieve, pressing out as much liquid as possible. Sauté in 1 tablespoon of the butter in a large skillet, stirring constantly, 5 minutes; stir in onions.

4. Heat remaining butter in a medium-size saucepan; blend in flour, the remaining salt and pepper; cook and stir until bubbly, 1 minute.

5. Stir in milk. Cook and stir until mixture thickens and bubbles, 3 minutes.

6. Beat egg yolks with a wire whisk in a large bowl until foamy; gradually beat in hot mixture; stir in cheese, corn and zucchini.

7. Beat egg whites in a medium-size bowl until they form soft peaks; stir ⅓ of egg whites into yolk mixture; then carefully fold in the remaining egg whites until no streaks of white remain. Pour into prepared dish.

8. Bake in a preheated moderate oven (350°) for 55 minutes or until puffy and golden brown on top.

A gentle down, over and up procedure is the correct folding technique to incorporate those fluffy egg whites, and since they are responsible for the lightness of the finished product, all steps should be followed to ensure that no air is lost.

Hard-cooked or raw egg? Spin it on countertop; if hard-cooked, it will spin easily.
Leftover whites? Refrigerate in a covered jar for up to 1 week. Use to make a fruit whip or a meringue for a pie, or for those extra whites in a chiffon cake.
Leftover yolks? Refrigerate in a covered jar with water to cover for up to 4 days. Add to scrambled eggs; enrich a butter frosting. If hard-cooked, sieve over potato salad or coleslaw.

TOP-HAT CHEESE SOUFFLÉ

Bake at 350° for 45 minutes.
Makes 4 servings.

- ¼ cup (½ stick) butter or margarine
- ¼ cup flour
- ½ teaspoon salt
- ½ teaspoon dry mustard
- ⅛ teaspoon pepper
  Pinch cayenne
- 1 cup milk
- 1 cup shredded Cheddar cheese (4 ounces)
- 4 eggs, separated
- ¼ teaspoon cream of tartar

1. Preheat oven to moderate (350°). Butter a 6-cup soufflé dish.

2. Melt butter in a medium-size saucepan; blend in flour, salt, mustard, pepper and cayenne; cook, stirring constantly, 1 minute, until well-blended.

3. Stir in milk until smooth; continue cooking and stirring until sauce thickens and bubbles, 1 minute. Remove from heat; add cheese, stirring until melted. Transfer to a large bowl; let cool.

4. Beat egg yolks in a small bowl until thick. Fold into cheese mixture.

5. Beat egg whites with cream of tartar in a large bowl until soft peaks form. Stir about ¼ of egg whites into sauce; fold in remaining egg whites. Pour into prepared dish.

6. For top-hat effect, run the tip of a teaspoon in a groove around soufflé mixture about 1¼ inches from edge.

7. Bake in a preheated moderate oven (350°) for 45 minutes, or until puffed and golden brown. Serve at once.

When egg whites are to be folded into another mixture, they are beaten to *soft* peaks only, as this softer consistency will allow them to be folded into a stiffer mixture without deflating and releasing the air that has been carefully beaten in.

SPINACH-RICOTTA TART

Bright green spinach is combined with a creamy cheese custard and baked in a flaky pastry crust.
Bake at 350° degrees for 50 minutes.
Makes 6 servings.

- ½ package piecrust mix
- 2 packages (10 ounces each) frozen chopped spinach
- 1 small onion, minced (¼ cup)
- 3 tablespoons butter or margarine
- ½ teaspoon salt
- ¼ teaspoon ground nutmeg
  Dash pepper
- 1 container (15 ounces) ricotta cheese
- 1 cup light cream or half and half
- ½ cup grated Parmesan cheese
- 3 eggs, slightly beaten

1. Prepare piecrust mix, following label directions for a one-crust pie. Line a 9-inch pie plate with pastry; flute the edge, making a high rim to hold all the filling. Prick the bottom and sides with a fork to keep the pastry flat while baking. Fit a piece of wax paper in the bottom; add a layer of rice to weigh down.

2. Bake in a hot oven (400°) for 5 minutes; remove paper and rice and let pastry brown, about 6 to 8 minutes longer. Remove from oven to a wire rack.

3. Cook spinach, following label directions. Drain in a large strainer; squeeze out the liquid by pressing spinach against the sides of the strainer with a wooden spoon; or squeeze with hands; reserve.

4. Sauté onion in butter until tender, about 3 minutes. Stir in spinach, salt, nutmeg and pepper.

5. Combine ricotta cheese, cream, Parmesan cheese and eggs in a large bowl; mix thoroughly. Stir in spinach mixture. Pour into baked pastry shell.

6. Bake in a moderate oven (350°) for 50 minutes, or until custard is set and top is lightly browned. Garnish with parsley and cherry tomatoes, if you wish.

> Custard mixtures curdle easily if over-baked. To test for doneness in addition to the time given in the recipe, grasp edge of dish with a pot holder. Shake gently, and watch the center of the custard. If it ripples softly, it is baked enough. If you wait for the center to be as firm as the outside edge, your custard will be overbaked and curdled.

QUICHE LORRAINE

The classic Quiche Lorraine is made with eggs, bacon and cream. This popular variation adds the flavor of onion.

Bake at 425° for 15 minutes, then at 350° for 15 minutes.

Makes 6 servings.

- ½ package piecrust mix
- 6 slices bacon
- 1 medium-size onion, chopped (½ cup)
- 2 cups shredded Swiss cheese (8 ounces)
- 4 eggs
- 2 cups cream or milk
- 1 teaspoon salt
- ¼ teaspoon ground nutmeg
- ⅛ teaspoon pepper

1. Preheat oven to hot (425°). Prepare piecrust mix, following label directions for a single crust. Roll out to a 13-inch round on a lightly floured surface; fit into a 9-inch fluted quiche dish; trim pastry level with rim. Prick pastry all over with fork.
2. Bake pastry shell in a preheated hot oven (425°) for 5 minutes; remove to rack; cool slightly. Increase oven temperature to very hot (450°).
3. Cook bacon in a small skillet until crisp; drain on paper toweling; crumble; reserve. Drain off all but 1 tablespoon fat.
4. Sauté onion in bacon fat in skillet until tender, about 3 minutes. Sprinkle cheese in layer in pastry shell; add bacon and onion.
5. Beat eggs lightly in a medium-size bowl; beat in cream, salt, nutmeg and pepper; pour into shell.

6. Bake in preheated hot oven (425°) 15 minutes. Lower oven temperature to moderate (350°); bake for 15 minutes, or until center is almost set but soft. (Do not overbake; custard will set as it cools.) Let stand 15 minutes. Cut into wedges to serve.

SMOKED SALMON QUICHE

Bake at 450° for 15 minutes, then at 350° for 15 minutes.

Makes 8 servings.

- 1 package piecrust mix
- ½ pound smoked salmon, chopped
- 1 cup shredded Swiss cheese (4 ounces)
- 4 eggs
- 1 cup milk
- ½ cup cream
- ¼ cup grated Parmesan cheese
- 1 tablespoon finely chopped fresh dill
  OR: 1 teaspoon dillweed
- ½ teaspoon salt
- ¼ teaspoon pepper

1. Preheat oven to very hot (450°). Prepare piecrust mix, following label directions. Roll out to a 14-inch round on a lightly floured surface; fit into a 10-inch (6-cup) fluted quiche dish (or use a 10-inch pie plate). Trim pastry even with rim of quiche dish, or for pie plate, trim pastry overhang to ½ inch; turn under. Pinch to make a stand-up edge; flute. Prick shell well over entire surface with a fork.
2. Bake in a preheated very hot oven (450°) for 8 minutes; remove to wire rack; cool.
3. Spread salmon evenly over bottom of pastry shell; top with Swiss cheese.
4. Beat eggs lightly in a medium-size bowl. Add milk, heavy cream, Parmesan cheese, dill, salt and pepper; blend well. Pour into pastry shell.
5. Bake in a preheated very hot oven (450°) 15 minutes; lower oven temperature to moderate (350°) and bake 15 minutes or until center is almost firm but still soft. Let stand 15 minutes before serving.

ZUCCHINI AND ITALIAN SAUSAGE QUICHE

Bake at 450° for 15 minutes, and then at 350° for 15 minutes.

Makes 8 servings.

1 package piecrust mix
1 pound zucchini, shredded (2 cups)
4 tablespoons (½ stick) butter or margarine
5 sweet Italian sausages (½ pound)
1 cup shredded Swiss cheese (4 ounces)
4 eggs
1 cup milk
½ cup heavy cream
¼ cup grated Parmesan cheese
½ teaspoon salt
¼ teaspoon white pepper

1. Preheat oven to very hot (450°). Prepare piecrust mix, following label directions. Roll out to a 14-inch round on a lightly floured surface; fit into a 10-inch (6-cup) quiche dish; trim pastry level with rim .
2. Bake in a preheated very hot oven (450°) for 8 minutes; remove to wire rack; cool slightly.
3. Sauté zucchini in 2 tablespoons of the butter in a large skillet for 5 minutes or until tender. Remove to bowl.
4. Remove casing from 4 sausages; cut remaining sausage into ½-inch rounds. Cook sausage in remaining 2 tablespoons butter in same skillet until no pink remains. Drain on paper toweling.
5. Spread cooked zucchini evenly onto bottom of pastry shell; sprinkle crumbled sausage and Swiss cheese over zucchini.
6. Beat eggs lightly in a large bowl. Add milk, heavy cream, cheese, salt and pepper; blend well. Pour into pastry shell. Arrange sausage rounds around edge of quiche, pressing in slightly.
7. Bake in a preheated very hot oven (450°) for 15 minutes; lower oven temperature to moderate (350°) and bake for 15 minutes or until center is almost firm but still soft. Let stand 15 minutes before serving.

ITALIAN CHEESE AND VEGETABLE PIE

Bake at 375° for 50 minutes.
Makes 6 servings.

3 tablespoons vegetable or olive oil
2 medium-size zucchini, thinly sliced (2 cups)
2 medium-size onions, thinly sliced (1 cup)
2½ teaspoons salt
1 clove garlic, minced
3 tablespoons chopped parsley
1 can (1 pound) tomatoes
1 can (8 ounces) tomato sauce
½ teaspoon leaf oregano, crumbled
Dash pepper
1 container (15 ounces) ricotta cheese
4 eggs
1½ cups milk
1 package (8 ounces) refrigerated crescent rolls
4 ounces mozzarella cheese, sliced
Parsley, black olives, rolled anchovies with capers (*optional*)

1. Heat 2 tablespoons of the oil in a large skillet; add zucchini and onion. Sauté, stirring often, until tender, about 10 minutes. Stir in 1 teaspoon of the salt; remove mixture from skillet to a bowl.
2. Sauté garlic and parsley in oil remaining in skillet, stirring constantly, 1 minute; stir in tomatoes, tomato sauce, oregano, ½ teaspoon of the salt and the pepper. Cook, stirring occasionally and mashing the tomatoes with a spoon, 15 minutes, or until mixture is reduced to about 2 cups.
3. Beat ricotta cheese, eggs and the remaining 1 teaspoon salt in a large bowl; gradually beat in milk.
4. Line a fluted 10-inch quiche dish or 10-inch pie plate with unrolled and separated crescent rolls, overlapping slightly and pressing edges of dough triangles together to form a shell.
5. Spread vegetables in bottom of shell; spoon about ¼ cup tomato sauce over. Place dish on oven shelf, then pour in

cheese mixture.

6. Bake in moderate oven (375°) for 40 minutes, or just until set in center. Arrange mozzarella slices on top of pie; spoon some of the tomato sauce in between slices. Bake 8 minutes longer, or until cheese is melted. Garnish with parsley, black olives and rolled anchovies with capers, if you wish. Serve in wedges with remaining tomato sauce.

TOMATO-CHEESE TART

Bake at 425° for 10 minutes then at 325° for 20 minutes.
Makes 4 servings.

½ package piecrust mix
1 cup shredded Cheddar cheese (4 ounces)
2 packages (6 ounces each) shredded process gruyère cheese
3 ripe medium-size tomatoes
1 teaspoon salt
⅛ teaspoon pepper
1 teaspoon leaf basil, crumbled
1 teaspoon leaf oregano, crumbled
½ cup chopped green onions
2 tablespoons butter or margarine
2 tablespoons soft bread crumbs

1. Prepare piecrust mix, following label directions, adding ½ cup of the Cheddar cheese. Roll out to a 13-inch round on lightly floured surface, fit into a 9-inch pie plate. Trim overhang to 1 inch; turn under; flute to make stand-up edge. Prick with fork.
2. Bake in a preheated hot oven (425°) for 10 minutes, or until golden; cool.
3. Spoon the remaining Cheddar cheese and gruyère into piecrust. Slice the tomatoes into thin wedges. Arrange, slightly overlapping, in a circular pattern over the cheese. Sprinkle with salt, pepper, basil and oregano.
4. Sauté green onions in butter or mar-

garine in a small skillet until tender. Spoon in the center of pie; sprinkle with bread crumbs.
5. Bake in a moderate oven (325°) 20 minutes, or until tomatoes are tender.

ASPARAGUS PIE

Bake at 350° for 30 minutes.
Makes 6 servings.

½ pound fresh asparagus
OR: 1 package (8 ounces) frozen asparagus spears, cooked and drained
2 eggs
1 cup creamed cottage cheese
¼ cup (½ stick) butter or margarine, melted and cooled
¼ cup flour
½ teaspoon baking powder
¼ teaspoon salt
1 cup dairy sour cream
1 medium-size ripe tomato, peeled and thinly sliced
¼ cup grated Parmesan cheese

1. Cut cooked asparagus into 1-inch pieces. Arrange on bottom of well-greased 9-inch pie plate.
2. Beat eggs in a medium-size bowl until frothy. Add cottage cheese and butter; beat until almost smooth. Stir in flour, baking powder and salt. Blend in sour cream.
3. Pour filling into asparagus-lined pie plate. Arrange tomato slices on top. Sprinkle with cheese.
4. Bake in a moderate oven (350°) for 30 minutes, or until firm in center. Let stand in pan 10 minutes. Cut into wedges; serve warm. Good with sliced or boiled ham.

> **All custard-like mixtures and most casseroles benefit from being allowed to stand for 10-15 minutes after they are removed from the oven before serving. Standing time allows steam to settle for easier serving.**

> When separating eggs, don't panic if you should get a bit of egg yolk in the whites. Just lift out the yolk with one of the eggshell halves, or twist a paper towel to a point, and scoop out the yolk.

ALPINE ONION TARTS

Tiny pies with Swiss cheese inside and out—even to the peaks on top.

Bake tarts at 325° for 25 minutes.

Makes 6 servings.

- 1 package piecrust mix
- 1 medium-size onion, chopped (½ cup)
- 2 tablespoons butter or margarine
- 4 eggs, separated
- 1½ cups dairy sour cream
- ¼ teaspoon salt
- ⅛ teaspoon pepper
- 2 tablespoons grated Parmesan cheese
- 8 ounces Swiss cheese, cut in ½-inch cubes
- 1 tablespoon chopped parsley

1. Preheat oven to very hot (450°). Prepare piecrust mix, following label directions. Roll out, half at a time, on a lightly floured surface to a ⅛-inch thickness. Cut 3 six-inch rounds from each half. (A saucer makes a good pattern.) Fit each round into a 4-inch tart-shell pan, pressing pastry firmly against bottom and side. Trim overhang to ½ inch; turn edge under, flush with rim; pinch to make a stand-up edge; flute. Prick shells all over with a fork.

2. Bake in preheated very hot oven (450°) 5 minutes; remove from oven. Lower temperature to slow (325°).

3. Sauté onion in butter or margarine in a small skillet until tender; spoon into partially baked shells, dividing evenly.

4. Beat egg yolks slightly in a medium-size bowl; stir in sour cream, salt, pepper and Parmesan cheese. Reserve ¼ cup of the Swiss cheese cubes; fold remainder into egg-yolk mixture; spoon into shells.

5. Bake in slow oven (325°) 15 minutes.

6. While tarts bake, beat egg whites in a medium-size bowl until they form soft peaks. Remove tarts from oven; spoon beaten egg whites over each, swirling with back of spoon; top with reserved cheese cubes, dividing evenly.

7. Bake in slow oven (325°) 10 minutes, or until cheese is melted. Sprinkle with parsley.

VARIATION: You can vary the type of cheese that is used in the topping, if you wish, substitute Muenster, provolone or a process Swiss.

EGG FOO YUNG

Chinese-style omelets full of crunchy vegetables and pieces of chicken.

Makes 4 servings.

- Egg Foo Yung Sauce (recipe follows)
- 6 eggs
- 1 cup fresh or drained and rinsed canned bean sprouts
- 1 small onion, minced (¼ cup)
- 3 to 4 mushrooms, chopped
  - OR: 1 can (3 ounces) sliced mushrooms
- ½ to 1 cup cooked chicken, chopped
- 2 teaspoons soy sauce
- 1 teaspoon salt
- Vegetable oil

1. Prepare Egg Foo Yung Sauce; cover and keep warm.

2. Beat eggs in a large bowl until foamy. Stir in bean sprouts, onion, mushrooms, chicken, soy sauce and salt.

3. Heat a small skillet (6 to 7 inches); add 1 tablespoon oil. Pour ¼ of the egg mixture (about ½ cup) into skillet; cook 1 to 2 minutes, or until crisp and golden on one side; turn with a wide pancake turner; cook 1 minute longer. Fold in half and arrange on a heated serving platter. Keep warm while using remaining egg mixture to make 3 more omelets. Reheat Egg Foo Yung Sauce. Serve over omelets.

EGG FOO YUNG SAUCE: Mix 1 tablespoon corn starch and 1 tablespoon soy sauce in a small saucepan; gradually stir in 1 cup chicken broth. Cook, stirring constantly, until sauce thickens and bubbles, 1 minute. Makes 1 cup.

FARMER'S BREAKFAST

Makes 4 servings.

6 slices bacon
1 small sweet green pepper, halved, seeded and diced
1 small onion, minced (¼ cup)
3 large potatoes, cooked, peeled and thickly sliced
⅛ teaspoon pepper
  Salt
¼ teaspoon leaf thyme, crumbled
½ cup shredded Cheddar or Swiss cheese (2 ounces)
6 eggs

1. Cook bacon in a large skillet until crisp. Remove from heat; drain on paper toweling; crumble. Pour off all but 3 tablespoons of the bacon fat. Add green pepper, onion and potatoes to skillet. Cook over medium heat, stirring frequently, until potatoes are golden, about 5 minutes.
2. Lower heat; add pepper; taste; add salt if needed. Sprinkle potato mixture with thyme and top with cheese. Break eggs into a small bowl; pour over potatoes.
3. Cook, stirring constantly, until the eggs coat the potatoes and have set.

About cheese: In *shredding* cheese, in general, the semi-hard cheeses, such as Cheddar, Swiss, Edam, Gouda and Muenster; and some soft cheeses, mozzarella, for example, are *shredded* on the small to medium-size openings of the shredder-grater. The hard cheeses, such as Parmesan and Romano, are *grated* on the small sharp projections of the shredder-grater. The soft cheeses would clog the openings if you used the grater side of the utensil.

How to peel a tomato: Dip ripe tomatoes into boiling water for 15 seconds, then plunge into cold water. Core, then the loose skin will slip off easily. Home-grown tomatoes, being vine-ripened, only need a 5-second dip into boiling water. If tomatoes are to be used uncooked, in a salad, for instance, chill them an hour or so before using.

ITALIAN FRITTATA

Here's an easy-cheesy omelet that doesn't need turning.

Makes 4 servings.

½ cup chopped sweet green pepper
1 medium-size onion, chopped (½ cup)
4 tablespoons (½ stick) butter or margarine
1 large ripe tomato, peeled and chopped
½ teaspoon salt
¼ teaspoon leaf oregano, crumbled
8 eggs
½ teaspoon salt
⅛ teaspoon pepper
½ cup shredded provolone cheese (2 ounces)

1. Sauté green pepper and onion in 2 tablespoons of the butter in a small skillet until soft, about 5 minutes; add tomato, ½ teaspoon of the salt and the oregano. Cook slowly, 10 minutes, stirring occasionally, until all liquid is absorbed; reserve.
2. Beat eggs with the remaining ½ teaspoon salt and pepper in a medium-size bowl until foamy-light.
3. Heat a 10-inch skillet until hot. Swirl the remaining 2 tablespoons butter over bottom and side of skillet with a fork.
4. Pour in egg mixture. Cook, stirring with flat of fork and shaking pan back and forth, until omelet is firm on bottom and almost set on top. Spread tomato mixture evenly over top. Sprinkle with cheese; cover skillet for about 2 minutes, or until cheese starts to melt. Cut into wedges to serve.

PUFFY OMELET

Bake at 350° for 10 minutes.
Makes 2 servings.

4 eggs, separated
¼ cup milk or heavy cream
¼ teaspoon salt
⅛ teaspoon pepper
2 tablespoons butter or margarine

1. Beat egg whites in a large bowl with electric mixer until soft peaks form.
2. Beat egg yolks slightly in a medium-size bowl with the same mixer. Add milk, salt and pepper. Beat until thick and light. Fold egg yolk mixture into egg whites until no streaks of white remain.
3. Preheat oven to moderate (350°).
4. Heat a heavy 10-inch skillet with an ovenproof handle over moderate heat. Swirl butter over bottom and side of skillet, but do not let it brown.
5. Pour in egg mixture. Cook over low heat about 3 minutes, or until mixture is set on the bottom and is lightly browned.
6. Bake in preheated moderate oven (350°) for 10 minutes, or until puffy and golden brown on top.
7. Remove omelet from oven. Loosen around edge. Cut a gash down the center; add filling, if using; fold over; turn out onto a heated serving platter. Garnish with parsley, if you wish.

Variations:

CHILI-CHEESE OMELET: Before making omelet, prepare Cheese Sauce. Melt 2 tablespoons butter in a small saucepan. Stir in 2 tablespoons flour and ¼ teaspoon salt; cook 1 minute. Stir in 1 cup milk; cook, stirring constantly, until sauce thickens and bubbles. Stir in 1 cup shredded Swiss cheese; remove from heat; cover; keep warm. Before folding omelet, sprinkle surface with 1 tablespoon chopped canned green chilies; fold; spoon sauce over.

SPANISH OMELET: Sauté ½ cup chopped onion and ½ cup chopped sweet green pepper in 2 tablespoons butter in a small saucepan until tender, about 3 minutes. Stir in ½ teaspoon crumbled leaf marjoram and 3 medium-size peeled and chopped ripe tomatoes. Cook 5 minutes. Spoon filling into omelet before folding. Fold; top with ½ cup dairy sour cream and 1 tablespoon snipped chives.

When making a puffy omelet that finishes cooking in the oven, and you are not sure if your favorite skillet has an ovenproof-handle, wrap the handle in several layers of aluminum foil to protect it.

A puffy omelet, like a soufflé, depends on the air beaten into the eggs whites for its lightness. It is different from a French omelet, in that it is not stirred or turned, and is finished in the oven. It is helpful to crease the finished omelet through the center to give it enough flexibility to fold over, filled or unfilled.

FRENCH OMELET

Fast and fabulous! You can make this in 5 minutes from start to finish.
Makes 2 servings.

3 eggs
1 tablespoon water
⅛ teaspoon salt
Dash pepper
2 tablespoons butter or margarine

1. Beat eggs with water, salt and pepper in a small bowl, just to blend yolks and whites.
2. Heat a heavy 10-inch skillet. Add butter; swirl pan to coat bottom and side with butter. When butter foams and then subsides, pan is ready. Do not allow butter to brown.
3. Pour egg mixture into skillet. Cook, stirring with flat side of fork, and shaking pan back and forth, until omelet is set on bottom, but still slightly soft on top. (Omelet may be filled at this step.)
4. Working with side of omelet opposite handle, quickly fold ⅓ of the omelet over

Puffy Omelet

the center third. Holding the skillet near a warm plate, tip the omelet out of the pan, flipping the remaining ⅓ over the center, so you have a neatly folded oval.

Good Fillings for a French Omelet
FINES HERBES: Add a teaspoon snipped chives, 1 tablespoon chopped parsley and ¼ teaspoon crumbled leaf tarragon to the eggs before cooking.
CHEESE: Sprinkle ½ cup shredded Cheddar, Swiss or Muenster cheese over omelet before folding.
TOMATO AND CHEESE: Fill with creamed cot-

tage cheese; top with heated pizza sauce.
JELLY: Spread with strawberry preserves or orange marmalade; fold; sprinkle lightly with 10X sugar.

> An everyday heavy aluminum skillet can be seasoned quickly to make perfect omelets. Just shine it to glistening brightness with a soapy steel wool pad, then heat a ¼-inch depth of oil over low heat for 10 minutes. Pour off oil, wipe out skillet, and you are ready to cook.

EGGS BENEDICT

The classic brunch and lunch dish.

Makes 6 servings.

½ cup (1 stick) butter or margarine
2 egg yolks
1 teaspoon lemon juice
⅓ cup boiling water
   Dash salt
   Dash cayenne
12 thin slices cooked ham or
   Canadian bacon
3 medium-size ripe tomatoes, halved
6 eggs, poached
6 English muffins, toasted and
   buttered

1. Make Hollandaise Sauce: Divide butter into thirds. Beat egg yolks with lemon juice in the top of a double boiler, then add one-third of the butter. Place over simmering, not boiling, water; cook, beating constantly, until butter melts and sauce starts to thicken; add remaining butter, half at a time, same way. Beat in boiling water slowly; continue cooking and stirring, still over simmering water, 3 minutes, or until mixture thickens; remove from water. Stir in salt and cayenne; cover sauce and keep warm in double boiler.
2. Place ham slices and tomato halves on rack of the broiler pan. Broil, 4 to 5 inches from heat, 5 minutes, or until ham is crisp and tomatoes are heated through.
3. Place 2 English-muffin halves on each of 6 heated serving plates; top with 2 slices of ham and a poached egg. Spoon sauce over eggs. Place a broiled tomato half at side; garnish with watercress, if you wish.

For tender poached eggs: Pour enough water into a large skillet to make a 2-inch depth; salt lightly; bring just to boiling. Break eggs, one at a time into a cup, and slip into water. Simmer, basting often with water in skillet, about 3 minutes, or just until egg is set. Lift out with slotted spoon; drain on paper toweling.

CHILIES RELLENOS

Makes 6 servings.

6 canned whole mild green chilies
   (about two 4-ounce cans)
6 strips (½x½x3-inch) Monterey
   Jack or Longhorn cheese
   Flour
3 eggs, separated
3 tablespoons flour
1 tablespoon water
¼ teaspoon salt
   Vegetable oil for frying
   Seasoned Tomato Sauce
   (*recipe follows*)

1. Rinse chilies; seed and pat dry with paper toweling. Insert cheese strip inside each chile. Roll each in flour to coat all over.
2. Beat egg whites in a small bowl with electric mixer until soft peaks form. Beat yolks with same mixer in a medium-size bowl until fluffy and pale yellow, about 5 minutes. Beat in the 3 tablespoons flour, water and salt into the yolks. Gently fold in beaten egg whites.
3. Heat ½ to 1 inch oil in a small skillet to 370°. Place a lengthwise mound of egg batter about, ½ inch thick and 2 inches wide, on a small saucer. Place chile in center and enclose with more batter on top.
4. Slide batter-coated chile into hot oil; fry 3 or 4 minutes, or until golden brown, turning with two slotted spoons or spatulas. Drain on paper toweling. Keep hot in slow oven until all are cooked. Serve hot with Seasoned Tomato Sauce.

SEASONED TOMATO SAUCE
Makes about 2 cups.

Heat 1 tablespoon vegetable shortening or lard in a small saucepan. Sauté ¼ cup finely chopped green onions and 1 minced clove garlic, 1 minute. Stir in one 15-ounce can tomato sauce, ½ teaspoon salt and ½ teaspoon crumbled leaf oregano. Heat until bubbly-hot.

Ranch-Style Eggs

RANCH-STYLE EGGS

They call them Huevos Rancheros in the Southwest and in Mexico.

Makes 6 servings.

1 large onion, chopped (1 cup)
1 medium-size sweet green pepper, halved, seeded and chopped (1 cup)
1 clove garlic, minced
4 tablespoons vegetable oil
3 medium-size ripe tomatoes, peeled, seeded and diced (3 cups)
  OR: 1 can (28 ounces) tomatoes
1 can (4 ounces) chopped green chilies
¾ teaspoon liquid red-pepper seasoning
1 teaspoon salt
6 canned, frozen or refrigerated tortillas
2 cups shredded Romaine lettuce
½ cup shredded Cheddar cheese (2 ounces)
6 eggs, fried

1. Sauté onion, green pepper and garlic in 2 tablespoons of the oil in a medium-size saucepan until tender, about 3 minutes. Stir in tomatoes, chilies, red-pepper seasoning and salt. Cook sauce, uncovered, stirring occasionally, 10 minutes.

2. Heat remaining 2 tablespoons oil in a large skillet. Fry tortillas, one at a time, just until limp. Drain on paper toweling; keep warm. Chop or shred lettuce and cheese; serve.

3. Line a large serving platter with the lettuce. Arrange tortillas on lettuce. Slip a fried egg onto each tortilla; spoon sauce around eggs. Sprinkle with cheese. Serve with pinto beans, if you wish.

> **Sunny side up, or you may like your eggs over lightly: Here's the way to fry them.** Heat oil, shortening, butter or margarine, or a combination, in a large skillet until sizzling hot but not smoking. Crack eggs, one at a time into a cup, then slip each into hot oil. Cook until whites are just set. Eggs can be turned over to cook the other side, or oil can be spooned over yolks to set tops, or sprinkle in a teaspoon of water; cover skillet. The steam formed will film the yolks.

SCOTCH EGGS

This traditional British picnic favorite is simple to prepare. Make sure that eggs are well chilled—sausage will cling to them more easily.

Makes 6 servings.

6 hard-cooked eggs, well chilled
1 pound sausage meat
2 tablespoons minced parsley
½ teaspoon ground sage
¼ teaspoon pepper
¼ cup flour
2 eggs, beaten

½ to ¾ cup packaged bread crumbs
Vegetable oil for frying

1. Peel hard-cooked eggs.
2. Combine sausage, parsley, sage and pepper in a large bowl; mix well. Divide meat mixture into 6 equal portions.
3. Press meat mixture evenly around eggs with hands, keeping the oval shape. Sprinkle eggs with flour, coating lightly all over. Dip into beaten egg and then roll in bread crumbs to coat well.
4. Pour oil into a deep fryer or large heavy saucepan to fill ½ full. Heat to 350° on deep-fat frying thermometer. Cook one egg at a time for about 4 to 5 minutes, or until meat is well browned. Drain on paper toweling; cool; refrigerate.

> **A sure-fire way to hard-cook eggs:** Put eggs in a saucepan of cold water. Bring to boiling; lower heat; simmer or remove from heat for 14 minutes. Drain; run under cold running water until eggs are cold. If using at once, crack shell on counter top for easy peeling.
>
> **For the most satisfactory hard-cooked eggs, it is better to use eggs that are not spanking fresh, since the shells of fresh eggs cling so tightly to the egg as to make peeling more difficult. Older eggs tend to develop a little air space at one end and are much easier to handle.**

Scotch Eggs

STUFFED EGGS MORNAY

Elegant for brunches, lunches, suppers and special occasions.

Bake at 350° for 30 minutes.
Makes 6 servings.

8 tablespoons (1 stick) butter or margarine
½ cup flour
1 teaspoon salt
Pinch cayenne
¼ teaspoon white pepper
3 cups milk, heated

½ cup shredded Swiss cheese (2 ounces)
6 tablespoons grated Parmesan cheese
12 hard-cooked eggs
½ pound mushrooms, minced
2 tablespoons chopped parsley
½ teaspoon leaf tarragon, crumbled
1 cup fresh bread crumbs (2 slices)
2 tablespoons butter or margarine, melted

1. Melt 4 tablespoons of the butter in a large saucepan. Stir in flour, salt, cayenne and white pepper; cook 1 minute. Add milk slowly, stirring until smooth. Cook, stirring constantly, until thickened and bubbly, about 2 minutes.

2. Add Swiss cheese and 4 tablespoons of the Parmesan. Cook, stirring constantly, until cheese is melted; remove from heat; cover to keep skin from forming.

3. Cut eggs in half lengthwise. Empty yolks into bowl; reserve whites.

4. Heat the remaining 4 tablespoons butter in a small skillet. Sauté mushrooms, stirring occasionally, about 5 minutes, or until mixture is almost dry. Stir in parsley and tarragon.

5. Mash egg yolks with ½ cup of the reserved sauce; add the mushrooms. Fill whites with the mushroom mixture.

6. Spread a thin layer of sauce in a 13x9x2-inch baking dish and arrange the stuffed eggs in the sauce, stuffing side up. Spoon the remaining sauce over.

7. Toss bread crumbs and remaining 2 tablespoons Parmesan with the 2 tablespoons melted butter. Sprinkle over eggs.

8. Bake in a moderate oven (350°) for 35 minutes, or until brown and bubbly.

> **When making a flour-based sauce, the flour-butter mixture is always cooked and stirred about 1 minute to cut down on the raw flour taste and to make a smoother sauce.**

Stuffed Eggs Mornay

Swiss Fondue

SWISS FONDUE

One of the world's most sociable foods—
fun for a gathering of good friends.
Makes 6 servings.

       2 cups shredded Swiss cheese
            (8 ounces)
       2 cups shredded Gruyère cheese
            (8 ounces)
       OR: Use 4 cups shredded Swiss cheese
            (1 pound)
       3 tablespoons flour
       1 clove garlic, halved
       2 cups dry white wine
       3 tablespoons Kirsch
         Paprika
       1 loaf Italian bread

1. Toss cheese with flour in a large bowl.
2. Rub cut ends of garlic around bottom
and side of a fondue pot or large heavy
skillet; pour in wine. Heat slowly just until
bubbles start to rise from bottom of pan.
3. Stir in cheese mixture, a small amount
at a time, with a wooden spoon. (Wait until
all of one addition has melted before adding more cheese. Do not let mixture boil at
any time.)
4. Stir in Kirsch. If skillet has been used for
cooking, pour fondue into a heated chafing
dish to keep hot while serving; sprinkle
with paprika.
5. Cut bread into small pieces, leaving
some crust on each; place in a basket. Set
out fondue or regular forks so everyone
can spear a piece of bread on fork, then
swirl in the velvety cheese sauce.

> **To prevent losing the bread as it is
> swirled in the savory cheese mixture,
> press the tines of the fondue fork
> through the soft bread and into crust.**

WELSH RAREBIT

Makes 4 servings.

       1 cup beer
       1 teaspoon dry mustard
       2 teaspoons Worcestershire sauce
         Few drops liquid red-pepper
            seasoning
       4 cups shredded Cheddar cheese
            (1 pound)
       2 eggs
       8 slices toast

1. Combine beer, mustard, Worcestershire
sauce and red-pepper seasoning in the top
of a double boiler; warm over simmering
water.
2. Stir in cheese, part at a time, until melted.
3. Beat the eggs slightly in a small bowl;
slowly stir in about 1 cup of the hot cheese
mixture; return to double boiler. Cook,
stirring for 3 minutes.
4. Halve each slice of toast diagonally;
place 4 triangles on each serving plate and
spoon cheese mixture over top.

TOMATO RAREBIT

Makes 6 servings.

       2 tablespoons butter or margarine
       2 tablespoons flour
       1 teaspoon dry mustard
       2 drops liquid red-pepper seasoning
      ⅔ cup half and half or evaporated milk
      ⅔ cup tomato juice
      ⅛ teaspoon baking soda
    1½ cups shredded Cheddar cheese
            (6 ounces)
       2 eggs, lightly beaten
       6 English muffins, split and toasted

1. Melt butter in a large saucepan. Add
flour, mustard and red-pepper seasoning;
cook 1 minute. Add half and half, stirring
until sauce is thickened and bubbly.
2. Stir tomato juice, baking soda and
cheese into eggs. Add to sauce; stir over
low heat until cheese melts. Serve over
muffins.

CREAMED TARRAGON EGGS ON ASPARAGUS

Bake at 350° for 20 minutes.

Makes 4 servings.

    4 tablespoons (½ stick) butter or
        margarine
    ¾ cup fresh bread crumbs (1½ slices)
    1 small onion, chopped (¼ cup)
    ¼ teaspoon leaf tarragon, crumbled
    ⅓ cup milk
    1 can condensed cream of celery soup
    2 tablespoons lemon juice
    6 hard-cooked eggs
    ½ pound fresh asparagus, cooked

1. Melt butter in a large skillet; remove 1 tablespoon and combine with bread crumbs in a small bowl; reserve.

2. Sauté onion in the remaining butter until tender. Stir in tarragon, milk, soup and lemon juice until well-blended. Chop the eggs coarsely; stir into sauce.

3. Arrange asparagus in a greased baking dish; pour sauce over; sprinkle with reserved bread crumbs.

4. Bake in a moderate oven (350°) for 20 minutes, or until mixture is bubbly and crumbs are browned.

> **The easiest way to make fresh bread crumbs:** Tear a slice or two (no more) of fresh bread into container of electric blender; whirl 15 seconds; remove. Repeat for as many cups of crumbs as you want. 1 slice of bread = ½ cup of crumbs.

CHEESE STRATA

A perfect casserole to prepare ahead, then to bake at dinnertime.

Bake at 325° for 1 hour.

Makes 6 servings.

    8 slices white bread
    2 cups shredded Cheddar cheese
        (8 ounces)
    2 cups milk
    4 eggs

1. Cut each slice of bread into 4 triangles. Arrange half of the bread triangles, points up and overlapping, in a 9x9x2-inch baking dish; sprinkle with half the cheese; top with remaining bread triangles and cheese.

2. Beat milk and eggs in a medium-size bowl until blended. Pour over bread; let stand 15 minutes.

3. Bake, uncovered, in a slow oven (325°) for 1 hour, or until mixture is puffy and a light golden brown.

> It is important to allow the strata to stand for at least 15 minutes before baking to let the bread absorb the custard mixture. This step will result in the creamy-smooth, puffy texture of a true strata.

GNOCCHI PARISIENNE

This is really a form of pasta. It's easy to make—you can even put it together and refrigerate until ready to bake.

Bake at 350° for 20 minutes.

Makes 4 servings.

    1 cup water
    ¼ cup (½ stick) butter or margarine
    ¼ teaspoon salt
    ⅛ teaspoon cayenne
    1 cup plus 2 tablespoons *sifted*
        all-purpose flour
    ¼ cup grated Parmesan cheese
    ½ teaspoon dry mustard
    4 eggs
    1 tablespoon salt
        Mornay Sauce (*recipe follows*)
    2 tablespoons butter or margarine

1. Combine water, butter, the ¼ teaspoon salt and cayenne in a medium-size saucepan. Bring to boiling.

2. Combine flour, Parmesan cheese and mustard in a small bowl. When liquid is boiling rapidly and butter is melted, add flour mixture all at once and, stirring rapidly, lift pan a few inches above the heat and continue to stir for 30 seconds, or until paste comes away from side of pan and forms a rough ball in center.

3. Add eggs, one at a time, beating vigorously after each addition, until paste is smooth and shiny.

4. Fill a large, deep skillet half full with water, add the 1 tablespoon salt and bring to boiling.

5. With two tablespoons dipped into the hot water, mold dough into egg shapes and drop into the water. Lower heat so that water just simmers. Poach a few at a time for about 15 minutes or until firm, turning each over occasionally with a slotted spoon. Drain on a cookie sheet, covered with paper toweling, and refrigerate while making Mornay Sauce.

6. Spread half the Mornay Sauce on the bottom of a 2-quart shallow baking dish. Arrange gnocchi in the dish and spoon remaining sauce over.

7. Bake in a moderate oven (350°) 20 minutes or until sauce is bubbly hot.

8. Dot with the remaining 2 tablespoons butter; place under broiler, with top about 4 inches from heat, just until glazed and brown.

MORNAY SAUCE
Makes 3 cups.

- 2 cups milk
- 1 bay leaf
  Slice of onion
  A few peppercorns
- 6 tablespoons butter or margarine
- 6 tablespoons flour
- ¼ teaspoon salt
  Dash cayenne
- ½ cup heavy cream
- ½ cup grated Parmesan cheese
- ¼ teaspoon dry mustard

1. Heat milk in a small saucepan to steaming hot with bay leaf, onion and peppercorns.

2. Melt butter in a large saucepan. Stir in flour, salt and cayenne. Remove saucepan from heat and strain hot milk into it, a third at a time, stirring constantly, until mixture is smooth and thick.

3. Stir in cream, Parmesan and mustard, return to heat and cook over low heat for 3 minutes, stirring frequently.

POTATO GNOCCHI

Dumplings, Northern Italian style, tender and cheesy.
Bake at 400° for 15 minutes.
Makes 6 servings.

- 2 pounds potatoes, pared
- 2 eggs, beaten
- 1 teaspoon salt
- 3 cups *sifted* all-purpose flour
- 1 can condensed chicken broth
- 8 cups water
- ½ cup (1 stick) butter or margarine, melted
- 1 cup grated Parmesan cheese

1. Cook potatoes in boiling salted water in a large saucepan until tender; drain and shake over very low heat 2 minutes to dry.

2. Mash potatoes in a large bowl until smooth; beat in eggs and salt. Blend in the flour to make a soft dough. Cover the bowl and chill at least 1 hour.

3. Bring chicken broth and water to boiling in a kettle. Drop dough by teaspoonfuls, a few at a time, into boiling liquid; lower heat; simmer for 5 minutes or until slightly puffed. Remove with a slotted spoon to a shallow baking dish.

4. Drizzle with melted butter and sprinkle with the Parmesan cheese.

5. Bake in a hot oven (400°) 15 minutes, or until puffy and golden.

> **Besides potato gnocchi there are gnocchi made with cream puff dough and those made with semolina.**

Cannelloni alla Florentine

Pasta, Rice, Beans and Grains

The popularity of these ingredients has increased tremendously as cooks have discovered their roles in ethnic, economical and nutritious meals.

CANNELLONI ALLA FLORENTINE

A close cousin to the French crepe.
Bake at 350° for 20 minutes.
Makes 6 to 8 servings.

    1 large onion, chopped (1 cup)
    1 carrot, chopped (½ cup)
    1 clove garlic, minced
    2 tablespoons olive or vegetable oil
    1 package (10 ounces) frozen chopped
        spinach, partially thawed
    ¾ pound chicken livers
    ½ pound ground round
    2 eggs
    1 teaspoon salt
    ¼ teaspoon pepper
    1½ teaspoons leaf oregano, crumbled
    ½ teaspoon leaf basil, crumbled
    ½ cup grated Parmesan cheese
    1 jar (15 ounces) marinara sauce
        Cannelloni Wrappers (*recipe follows*)
    3 tablespoon butter or margarine
    3 tablespoons flour
    1 teaspoon salt
    1½ cups milk

1. Sauté onion, carrot and garlic in oil in a large skillet until tender, about 5 minutes. Add spinach and cook, stirring often, until liquid evaporates. Remove to a bowl.
2. Add chicken livers to the same skillet, adding more oil if needed. Sauté until lightly browned, 8 to 10 minutes. Chop finely; add to vegetable mixture.
3. Cook beef in the same skillet until no pink remains, about 5 minutes. Add to veg-

etable mixture; stir in eggs, 1 teaspoon of the salt, pepper, oregano, basil and ¼ cup of the Parmesan cheese.
4. Spread marinara sauce in bottom of a 13x9x2-inch baking dish. Spoon about ¼ cup filling onto each wrapper; roll up. Place in single layer in sauce in dish.
5. Melt butter in small saucepan; stir in flour and the remaining salt. Cook until bubbly. Gradually stir in milk; cook, stirring constantly, until sauce thickens and bubbles, 1 minute. Pour sauce over cannelloni; sprinkle with remaining cheese.
6. Bake in a moderate oven (350°) for 20 minutes, or until heated through.

CANNELLONI WRAPPERS
Makes 12 to 15 wrappers.

    3 eggs
    1 cup *sifted* all-purpose flour
    ½ teaspoon salt
    1¼ cups water
    1 tablespoon vegetable oil

1. Combine eggs, flour, salt, water and oil in a medium-size bowl; beat with a wire whisk until smooth.
2. Heat a small skillet, 6 or 7 inches, over medium heat; brush with a little oil. Pour 2½ to 3 tablespoons batter into skillet to cover bottom in an even layer; cook slowly until top is dry, but bottom is not yet brown. Turn and cook other side 10 seconds; remove to cookie sheet.
3. Repeat with remaining batter; as cannelloni wrappers cook, stack with wax paper between each.

FUSILLI WITH SPINACH-RICOTTA PESTO

A year-round version of the classic summer sauce made with fresh basil.

Makes 4 servings.

    5 cups spinach leaves (about
        ½ pound untrimmed), washed
        and thoroughly drained
    1 pound fusilli, ziti or rigatoni
    2 tablespoons olive or vegetable oil
    1 large clove garlic
    ½ teaspoon salt
    ¼ teaspoon pepper
    1 teaspoon leaf basil, crumbled
    ¼ cup walnuts
    1 cup ricotta cheese
    2 tablespoons grated Parmesan cheese

1. Remove and discard all woody stems from spinach.
2. Start cooking pasta in boiling salted water, following label directions.
3. Place oil, garlic, salt and pepper in container of electric blender. Cover and whirl until garlic is pureed. Add basil and walnuts and whirl again until nuts are finely ground. Add cheeses; whirl until smooth. Start adding spinach leaves, 1 cup at a time, and blending until smooth. Between batches, scrape mixture down side of blender with a rubber spatula.
4. To serve, stir about 3 tablespoons of the hot pasta cooking water into sauce. Drain pasta and place in a heated serving dish. Add sauce and toss thoroughly. Serve with additional Parmesan cheese.

PEPPERONI PASTA

Makes 4 servings.

    1 pound fettucine, green noodles or
        spaghetti
    ¼ cup olive or vegetable oil
    1 large onion, sliced
    2 cloves garlic, minced
    ½ pound pepperoni sausage, sliced thin
    2 medium-size sweet green peppers,

halved, seeded and sliced
    1 can (1 pound) tomatoes
    1 teaspoon leaf oregano, crumbled
    ½ teaspoon salt
        Grated Parmesan cheese

1. Start cooking pasta in boiling salted water, following label directions.
2. Meanwhile, heat oil in a large skillet over moderate heat. Add onion, garlic, pepperoni and peppers and cook 5 minutes, stirring often. Add tomatoes, oregano and salt; cover and cook 5 minutes longer, stirring 2 or 3 times. Uncover during last minute to thicken sauce slightly.
3. Drain pasta and serve with sauce. Sprinkle with grated Parmesan cheese.

To chop or mash garlic easily: Sprinkle peeled clove with the salt used in the recipe. Chop finely, turn the flat of the knife against the chopping board and rub the chopped garlic and salt until they form a paste. Then scoop up the paste with knife. The salt keeps the garlic from sticking to the knife.

PASTA WITH MOZZARELLA AND TOMATO SALAD SAUCE

Hot pasta topped with cold sauce makes a pleasant taste sensation.

Makes 4 servings.

    1 pound mezzani rigati, rigatoni or
        linguine
    1 small clove garlic
    ½ teaspoon salt
    2 tablespoons red wine vinegar
    6 tablespoons olive oil
    ¼ teaspoon pepper
    1 tablespoon leaf basil, crumbled
    4 cups diced ripe tomatoes
    ⅓ cup diced red onion
    ½ cup small pitted black olives

Clockwise from upper left: Pasta with Mozzarella and Tomato Salad Sauce; Pepperoni Pasta, Fusilli with Spinach-Ricotta Pesto; and Spaghetti with Broccoli, Tomatoes and Walnuts

1 package (8 ounces) whole-milk
    mozzarella cheese, finely diced
½ cup grated Parmesan cheese

1. Start cooking pasta in boiling salted water, following label directions.
2. Mash garlic with salt in a medium-size bowl. Stir in vinegar, oil, pepper and basil. Add the tomatoes, onion and olives and toss to mix.
3. Drain pasta and return to hot kettle. Add Mozzarella and Parmesan and toss until cheese begins to melt. Add tomato mixture and toss to blend.
4. Serve from kettle, with additional Parmesan cheese.

SPAGHETTI WITH BROCCOLI, TOMATOES AND WALNUTS

Makes 4 servings.

1 pound thin spaghetti or linguine
4 tablespoons (½ stick) butter or
    margarine
2 tablespoons olive or vegetable oil
1 pint cherry tomatoes, stems removed

1 large clove garlic, minced
½ teaspoon salt
    Pinch crushed red pepper flakes
1 teaspoon leaf basil, crumbled
1 medium-size bunch broccoli, cut
    into 1-inch pieces (about 6 cups)
½ to 1 cup chicken broth
½ cup grated Parmesan cheese
¼ cup chopped parsley
½ cup coarsely chopped walnuts, toasted

1. Start cooking pasta in boiling salted water, following label directions.
2. Heat 2 tablespoons of the butter with the oil in a medium-size skillet. Add tomatoes and cook, stirring often, 5 minutes, until tomatoes are tender but still hold their shape. Stir in garlic, salt, pepper and basil and cook 2 minutes longer. Remove from heat; cover and keep warm.
3. Add broccoli to pasta during last 5 minutes of cooking time. Drain.
4. Melt remaining 2 tablespoons butter in pasta kettle and return pasta and broccoli to kettle. Toss to coat with butter. Add tomatoes, ½ to 1 cup of the broth, cheese and parsley and walnuts; toss to blend.

Fettucine in Tuna Sauce

FETTUCINE IN TUNA SAUCE

Makes 4 servings.

> 1 package (12 ounces) fettucine
> ½ cup mayonnaise
> 1 can (2 ounces) flat anchovies, drained
> 1 clove garlic
> 2 tablespoons lemon juice
> ½ cup heavy cream or milk
> 1 can (7 ounces) tuna
> 2 tablespoons chopped parsley
> 1 tablespoon finely slivered lemon rind
>   Grated Parmesan cheese

1. Cook fettucine in boiling salted water, following label directions; drain.

2. Combine mayonnaise, anchovies, garlic, lemon juice and cream in container of electric blender; whirl until smooth. Break tuna up with a fork in a small bowl. Pour sauce over tuna.

3. Combine hot fettucine and sauce in heated serving bowl; toss to mix well. Sprinkle parsley and lemon rind over. Serve with Parmesan cheese.

LINGUINE WITH LEMON-PARSLEY CLAM SAUCE

The tangy flavor of lemon gives character to this quick clam sauce.

Makes 2 servings.

> 2 cans (7 to 8 ounces each) minced
>   clams
> 1 small onion, chopped (¼ cup)
> 3 cloves garlic, minced
> ⅓ cup olive or vegetable oil
> 2 tablespoons butter or margarine
> 1 teaspoon leaf oregano, crumbled
> ½ teaspoon salt
> ⅛ teaspoon pepper
> 1 package (8 ounces) linguine or thin
>   spaghetti
> 2 tablespoons chopped parsley
> 1 teaspoon grated lemon rind
> 1 to 2 tablespoons lemon juice
>   Grated Parmesan cheese

1. Drain clam juice from clams; reserve.

2. Sauté onion and garlic in oil and butter in a saucepan until tender, but not brown, about 3 minutes.

3. Add reserved clam juice, oregano, salt and pepper; bring to boiling over high heat. Cook until mixture is reduced to 1 cup, about 5 minutes.

4. Meanwhile, cook linguine, following label directions; drain; keep hot in a heated serving bowl.

5. Lower heat under clam juice mixture; add reserved clams, parsley, lemon rind and lemon juice; heat thoroughly. Pour over hot linguine and toss. Serve with grated Parmesan cheese.

> **All fish, including clams, are easily over-cooked, especially when they have already been processed in a can. Add them at the end of the cooking time to just reheat or to cook quickly in minutes.**

Freshly grated Parmesan, Romano, Romano Pecorino, Asiago or Sardo hard cheeses have infinitely more flavor than the packaged grated product. The easiest way to grate cheese is in the food processor, but the most satisfactory way to achieve that desirable feathery lightness is to use the hand-held grater. The blender or the hand-held rotary grater can also be used.

ROMAN SPAGHETTI

Simple and very tasty.

Makes 6 servings.

- ¼ cup (½ stick) butter or margarine
- ½ pound lean bacon, diced
- 1 to 3 teaspoons pepper
- 1 pound spaghetti
- ⅔ cup grated Romano or Parmesan cheese

1. Melt butter in a large saucepan; cook bacon until crisp; drain on paper toweling crumble. Stir in the pepper, depending on taste, blending well.

2. Cook spaghetti, following label directions, until just barely tender. Drain; turn into a heated serving bowl. Toss half the bacon-butter mixture with the pasta. Pass remaining bacon mixture to sprinkle over each serving. Sprinkle generously with Romano or Parmesan cheese.

Roman Spaghetti

PERCIATELLI WITH EGGPLANT AND TOMATOES

Browned and tender eggplant plus perciatelli, a thick tubular spaghetti, make this a very hearty meatless dish.

Makes 4 servings.

- 1 medium-size eggplant (about 1½ pounds)
- ½ cup olive or vegetable oil
- 1 medium-size onion, thinly sliced
- 2 cloves garlic, minced
- 1 can (1 pound) tomatoes
- 1 teaspoon salt
- ¼ teaspoon crushed red pepper flakes
- 1 teaspoon leaf rosemary or basil, crumbled
- ¼ cup chopped parsley
- 1 package (1 pound) perciatelli or spaghetti
   Grated Parmesan cheese

1. Pare eggplant; cut into ½-inch slices, then into cubes.

2. Heat half the oil in a large skillet. Add half the eggplant, stirring and tossing until eggplant is lightly browned, about 2 minutes. Brown remaining eggplant in remaining oil. Return the first half to the skillet.

3. Add onion and garlic to eggplant. Cook, stirring constantly, until onion is tender, about 1 minute. Stir in tomatoes, salt, red pepper flakes and rosemary. Bring to boiling, stirring and breaking up tomatoes with a wooden spoon. Lower heat; simmer 2 minutes or until eggplant is tender and liquid in skillet is reduced slightly. Stir in parsley. Remove skillet from heat.

4. Cook and drain pasta, following label directions; return to kettle. Reheat sauce; add half to pasta; toss. Divide mixture among 4 heated bowls; top with remaining sauce; serve with cheese.

Pasta Primavera

PASTA PRIMAVERA

Makes 6 servings.

  1 bunch broccoli (about 1 pound)
  2 small zucchini
½ pound asparagus
  1 package (1 pound) linguine
  1 large clove garlic, chopped
  1 pint cherry tomatoes, halved
¼ cup olive oil
¼ cup chopped fresh basil
    OR: 1 teaspoon leaf basil, crumbled
½ pound mushrooms, thinly sliced
½ cup frozen green peas
¼ cup chopped parsley
1½ teaspoons salt
¼ teaspoon pepper
¼ teaspoon crushed red pepper flakes
¼ cup (½ stick) butter or margarine
¾ cup heavy cream
⅔ cup grated Parmesan cheese

1. Wash and trim broccoli, zucchini and asparagus. Cut broccoli into bite-size pieces; cut zucchini into thin slices; cut asparagus into 1-inch pieces. Cook in boiling salted water until crisp-tender; drain; put in a large bowl.

2. Cook and drain linguine, following label directions, until just barely tender.

3. Sauté garlic and tomatoes in oil in a large skillet 2 minutes. Stir in basil and mushrooms; cook 3 minutes. Stir in peas, parsley, salt and pepper and red pepper; cook 1 minute more. Add mixture to vegetables in bowl.

4. Melt butter in same skillet; stir in cream and cheese. Cook over medium-heat, stirring constantly, until smooth. Add linguine; toss to coat. Stir in vegetables; heat gently just until hot.

PASTITSIO

This classic Greek dish is easy to prepare for a supper party.
Bake at 350° for 35 minutes.
Makes 8 servings.

Cream Sauce:
  6 tablespoons butter or margarine
¼ cup flour
  3 cups light cream or half and half
  1 cup chicken broth
½ cup grated Parmesan cheese
  1 teaspoon salt
¼ teaspoon pepper

Meat Layer:
- 1 large onion, chopped (1 cup)
- 2 tablespoons butter or margarine
- 2 pounds ground chuck
  OR: 1 pound ground chuck and 1 pound sausage meat
- ½ teaspoon ground cinnamon
- ½ teaspoon ground nutmeg
- ½ teaspoon ground allspice
- 2 teaspoons salt
- ½ teaspoon pepper
- 1 can (6 ounces) tomato paste
- ¼ cup dry white wine

Pasta Layer:
- 1 pound elbow macaroni or ziti
- 3 eggs
- ¾ cup grated Parmesan cheese
- 2 tablespoons butter or margarine, softened

1. Make Cream Sauce: Melt butter in a large saucepan. Stir in flour; cook 1 minute; Lower heat; stir in cream and broth until smooth. Cook, stirring constantly, until sauce is thickened and bubbly. Stir in cheese, salt and pepper and cook until cheese is melted and blended into sauce; cover; keep warm.

2. For Meat Layer: Sauté onion in butter in a large skillet until tender. Add meat, breaking it up with a spoon and cooking until meat loses its pink color. Drain fat from skillet by pouring onion and meat into a strainer until fat has dripped through. Return meat and onion to skillet; stir in cinnamon, nutmeg, allspice, salt, pepper, tomato paste and wine. Bring to boiling; lower heat; simmer, uncovered, 15 minutes or until slightly thickened.

3. For Pasta Layer: Cook and drain pasta, following label directions. Turn into a warm bowl. Beat eggs, ½ cup of the cheese and the butter in a small bowl until blended. Add to the cooked pasta, blending well.

4. To assemble: Spoon half the pasta mixture into a buttered 13x9x2-inch baking dish. Pour 1 cup cream sauce over in an even layer. Spoon all the meat mixture in a layer over the sauce. Pour over another cup of sauce. Top with remaining pasta mixture and mask with remaining sauce. Sprinkle with remaining ¼ cup cheese.

5. Bake, uncovered, in a moderate oven (350°) for 35 minutes, or until bubbling and browned. Cool on wire rack for 15 minutes before cutting into 3-inch squares to serve.

Pastitsio

Baked Ziti

BAKED ZITI

Sausage, ricotta cheese and tomato sauce flavor this dish.

Bake at 400° for 15 minutes.
Makes 6 servings.

 3 sweet Italian sausages
½ pound ricotta cheese
¼ teaspoon ground nutmeg
½ teaspoon salt
¼ to ½ teaspoon pepper
½ teaspoon sugar
 1 tablespoon chopped parsley
 1 pound ziti, broken in 3-inch lengths
 2 cans (8 ounces each) tomato sauce
½ cup grated Parmesan cheese

1. Remove casings from sausages; break up meat and brown in a small skillet. Place in a strainer to drain off fat.
2. Combine ricotta with nutmeg, salt, pepper, sugar and parsley, blending well.
3. Cook ziti, following label directions, until just tender. Drain; turn into heated bowl and keep warm.
4. Spoon half the tomato sauce into a buttered 13x9x2-inch baking dish. Layer on half the ziti. Cover with all the sausage meat. Spoon over an even layer of the ricotta mixture. Cover with remaining ziti, then with remaining tomato sauce. Sprinkle with Parmesan cheese. Bake, uncovered, in a hot oven (400°) about 15 minutes, or until brown and bubbling.

BAKED STUFFED MACARONI SHELLS

Bake at 375° for 35 minutes.
Makes 10 servings.

 1 package (12 ounces) jumbo macaroni shells
 1 pound ricotta cheese
½ cup creamed cottage cheese
½ pound cooked ham, finely chopped
 1 egg
 1 teaspoon leaf oregano, crumbled
 1 tablespoon chopped parsley
½ teaspoon salt
¼ teaspoon pepper
  Savory Tomato Sauce (*recipe follows*)
  Creamy Cheese Sauce (*recipe follows*)
  Grated Parmesan Cheese

1. Cook shells, following label directions.
2. Combine ricotta, cottage cheese, ham, egg, oregano, parsley, salt and pepper in a large bowl. Spoon about 1 tablespoon of the cheese mixture into each shell, or use a pastry bag (without tip).
3. Alternate layers of stuffed shells, Savory Tomato Sauce and Creamy Cheese Sauce in a buttered 12-cup baking dish, ending with Creamy Cheese Sauce. Sprinkle top with additional grated Parmesan cheese.
4. Bake in a moderate oven (375°) for 35 minutes or until bubbly.

SAVORY TOMATO SAUCE: Sauté 1 cup chopped onion, ½ cup chopped carrot and ½ cup chopped celery in 2 tablespoons butter or margarine in a large saucepan until tender, about 5 minutes. Stir in 1 teaspoon crumbled leaf basil, 1 teaspoon salt and a 1 pound, 1 ounce-can Italian-style tomatoes. Simmer, stirring often, 10 minutes. Makes about 2½ cups.

CREAMY CHEESE SAUCE: Melt 2 tablespoons butter or margarine in a medium-size saucepan. Add 2 tablespoons flour; cook and stir 1 minute. Remove from heat; gradually stir in 1½ cups milk. Cook, stirring constantly, until thickened and bubbly. Stir in ½ cup grated Parmesan cheese and ¼ teaspoon salt. Makes about 1⅔ cups.

RIGATONI WITH PROSCIUTTO AND CREAM

Makes 6 servings.

- 1½ pounds rigatoni (large tubes)
- 8 tablespoons (1 stick) butter or margarine
- 1 pound thinly sliced prosciutto or ham, cut in julienne strips
- 4 egg yolks
- 1½ cups heavy cream
- ⅛ teaspoon ground nutmeg
- 1 cup grated Parmesan cheese

1. Cook rigatoni, following label directions, until just barely tender. Drain; turn into a large bowl; add 2 tablespoons of the butter; keep warm.

2. Melt 4 tablespoons of the butter in a kettle or Dutch oven. Sauté prosciutto for 2 minutes. Add rigatoni, stirring to mix well.

3. Beat egg yolks with cream and nutmeg in a medium-size bowl just until blended. Blend mixture gently into rigatoni mixture; blend in remaining 2 tablespoons butter. Simmer 1 minute over low heat just to heat through, but not to solidify the egg yolks. Serve, passing the cheese to sprinkle over.

Rigatoni with Prosciutto and Cream

SIMPLE, BUT GOOD, MARINARA SAUCE

Makes about 3 cups sauce.

- 1 can (2 pounds, 3 ounces) Italian-style tomatoes
- 1 large onion, diced (1 cup)
- 1 large carrot, diced
- 2 small cloves garlic, minced
- ¼ cup olive oil
- ½ teaspoon salt
  Pinch crushed red pepper flakes
- 1 teaspoon leaf basil, crumbled
- ¼ cup chopped parsley

1. Combine tomatoes, onion and carrot in a medium-size saucepan. Bring to boiling, breaking up tomatoes with a spoon; lower heat; simmer sauce 15 minutes. Puree mixture, a small amount at a time, in container of electric blender.

2. Sauté garlic in oil in a large saucepan 1 minute. Stir in pureed tomato mixture, salt, pepper flakes and basil; cook 5 minutes. Stir in parsley just before serving. Makes enough sauce for 1 pound of cooked pasta.

HOMEMADE TOMATO SAUCE

Makes about 5 cups.

- 1 large onion, chopped (1 cup)
- 1 clove garlic, minced
- ¼ cup olive or vegetable oil
- 1 can (2 pounds, 3 ounces) Italian-style tomatoes
- 1 can (6 ounces) tomato paste
- 2 teaspoons leaf basil, crumbled
- 1 teaspoon salt
  Dash sugar
- 1 cup water

1. Sauté onion and garlic in oil in a large saucepan until tender; stir in tomatoes, tomato paste, basil, salt, sugar and water.

2. Heat to boiling; lower heat and simmer, uncovered, stirring frequently, 30 minutes, or until sauce has thickened. Makes enough sauce for 1 pound of cooked pasta.

KASHA-CHEESE SKILLET

So easy to prepare, you'll make it over and over.

Makes 4 servings.

  1 large onion, chopped (1 cup)
  4 tablespoons butter or margarine
  1 egg, slightly beaten
  1 cup whole-grain kasha
  2 cups water
  1 teaspoon salt
  1 cup creamed cottage cheese
  1 cup frozen corn kernels
  1 cup shredded Cheddar cheese
      (4 ounces)
  2 to 3 ripe tomatoes, cut into wedges

1. Sauté onion in butter in a medium-size skillet with heatproof handle, 10 minutes.
2. Stir egg into kasha in a small bowl; add to onion, stirring constantly, until each grain separates. Stir in water and salt; bring to boiling. Lower heat; cover and cook 15 minutes. Remove from heat.
3. Mix in cottage cheese and corn. Sprinkle with Cheddar cheese.
4. Broil 3 to 5 minutes, about 4 inches from heat, until cheese is melted. Garnish with tomato wedges.

KASHA, CHICKEN AND NOODLES

Makes 8 servings.

  1 egg
  1 cup whole-grain kasha
1½ cups boiling water
  ½ teaspoon salt
  1 whole chicken breast (about 12
      ounces), boned, skinned and cut
      into slivers (10 ounces when
      boned)
  1 tablespoon soy sauce
1½ teaspoons cornstarch
  3 tablespoons sesame seeds
  1 package (9 ounces) frozen Italian
      beans
  8 ounces uncooked broad egg noodles
  2 tablespoons peanut oil
  1 bunch green onions, sliced (1 cup)
  2 slices fresh ginger root
  2 tablespoons peanut oil
  2 tablespoons soy sauce
  1 tablespoon cornstarch

1. Beat egg slightly in a medium-size bowl; stir in kasha, mixing until grains are moistened.
2. Heat a large saucepan (preferably nonstick); add kasha. Stir constantly until all grains are separated and dry, about 2 minutes. Carefully add boiling water and salt; cover. Simmer 15 minutes; remove from heat and let stand, covered, 15 minutes, until softened.
3. Combine chicken, 1 tablespoon of the soy sauce and 1½ teaspoons of the cornstarch in a small bowl; mix to coat evenly.
4. Shake sesame seeds constantly in a small skillet over low heat until toasted; remove from heat; cool.
5. Bring water to boiling in a kettle or Dutch oven; add salt, if you wish. Drop in frozen beans; return to boiling; remove beans with slotted spoon to a large bowl; keep warm. Drop noodles into the same water; bring to boiling; cook, following label directions; remove and reserve 1 cup cooking water. Drain noodles, add to beans; add 2 tablespoons oil and gently toss; keep warm.
6. Sauté chicken, green onions and ginger in remaining 2 tablespoons oil in a large skillet. Combine the remaining soy sauce, cornstarch and reserved cooking water; gradually stir into skillet; cook until slightly thickened, stirring constantly.
7. Combine chicken and kasha with noodle mixture and toss lightly. Spoon into serving dish; sprinkle with toasted sesame seeds.

MAIN DISH SALAD OF KASHA, FISH, PEPPERS, OLIVES AND TOMATOES

This is an unusual treatment for the nutritious and full-flavored grain kasha (roasted buckwheat groats). Use whichever canned fish best suits your taste and budget. Spicy tomato juice and breadsticks are a pleasant accompaniment.

Makes 6 servings.

```
   1   egg
 1¼   cups whole-grain kasha
   2   cups boiling water
   2   large cloves garlic, peeled and
         left whole
  ½   teaspoon salt
  ⅓   cup olive oil
  ¼   cup fresh lemon juice
   2   tablespoons red wine, white wine or
         cider vinegar
   1   teaspoon leaf oregano, crumbled
  ¼   teaspoon crushed red pepper flakes
  ¼   teaspoon pepper
  ¾   teaspoon salt
   1   can (16 ounces) mackerel, tuna or
         salmon
   1   large sweet green pepper, halved,
         seeded and diced (1 cup)
   1   large sweet red pepper, halved,
         seeded and diced (1 cup)
   1   medium-size red onion, diced
         (½ cup)
  ½   cup pimiento-stuffed olives or black
         olives, sliced
  ½   cup chopped parsley
   3   cups shredded chicory or escarole
   1   pint cherry tomatoes, halved
```

1. Beat egg slightly in a medium-size bowl; stir in kasha, mixing until grains are moistened.

2. Heat a large saucepan (preferably nonstick) and add kasha. Stir constantly, until all grains are separated and dry, about 2 minutes. Carefully add water, garlic and ½ teaspoon of the salt; cover. Simmer 15 minutes; remove from heat and let stand, covered, 15 minutes.

3. Combine oil, lemon juice, vinegar, oregano, red pepper flakes, pepper and the remaining ¾ teaspoon salt in a screw-top jar with a tight-fitting lid. Shake well to blend.

4. Drain fish; remove skin and bones, if you wish. Break fish into large pieces in a large bowl; pour half of the dressing slowly over fish.

5. Remove garlic cloves from kasha and add kasha to the bowl with fish; mix gently; cool to lukewarm. Add green and red peppers, onion, olives, parsley and remaining dressing; mix gently to coat. Cover with plastic wrap and chill at least 3 hours for flavors to blend and season.

6. Just before serving, line a large shallow salad bowl with shredded lettuce; mound salad in center; border with halved cherry tomatoes.

GOLDEN SPOON BREAD

Spoon bread, more of a pudding than a bread, is usually eaten, well buttered, as a vegetable side dish.

Bake at 400° for 30 minutes.
Makes 6 servings.

```
   2   cups boiling water
   1   cup yellow cornmeal
   1   cup milk
   4   eggs, well beaten
   3   teaspoons baking powder
   1   teaspoon salt
   1   package (8 ounces) process American
         cheese, shredded (2 cups)
       Paprika
```

1. Pour boiling water over cornmeal in a large bowl. Slowly stir in milk, eggs, baking powder, salt and cheese. Pour into a greased 6-cup baking dish; sprinkle lightly with paprika.

2. Bake in a preheated hot oven (400°) for 30 minutes, or until puffy-firm and golden brown.

BARLEY-VEGETABLE SOUP-STEW

A rich, thick, colorful dish, extremely easy to prepare. The final addition of yogurt and sour cream lends both a creaminess and welcome tart edge. Fill out the simple meal with thick pieces of buttered pumpernickel bread and a dessert of baked apples stuffed with walnuts.

Makes 6 servings.

    2 to 3 meaty ham hocks (1½ pounds)
    2½ quarts water
    1 large onion, quartered and thinly
        sliced (1 cup)
    ⅔ cup medium barley
    1 cup finely chopped celery with leaves
    4 medium-size parsnips, pared and cut
        into ½-inch dice (3 cups)
    4 medium-size carrots, cut into ½-inch
        dice (1½ cups)
    1¼ teaspoons dillweed
    1¼ teaspoons salt
    ¼ teaspoon pepper
    ¾ cup plain yogurt
    ¼ cup dairy sour cream
        Chopped parsley

1. Combine ham hocks and water in a kettle; bring slowly to boiling; skim any foam from liquid. Lower heat; simmer, partly covered, 1 hour, or until meat is tender but not falling apart; remove from broth. When cool enough to handle, remove skin and

bones, cut meat into small dice and return to kettle.
2. Add onion, barley, celery, parsnips, carrots, dillweed, salt and pepper; lower heat; cover. Simmer 35 minutes, or until barley and vegetables are barely tender. Soup improves in flavor if allowed to stand several hours or overnight.
3. Warm on low heat, stirring frequently. Combine yogurt and sour cream in a small bowl and sprinkle with parsley. Ladle the soup into large soup bowls; drop a dollop of the yogurt mixture on each, then stir into soup.

BARLEY BAKED WITH SAUSAGE

Bake at 350° for 60 minutes.
Makes 6 servings.

    1 Polish sausage (Kielbasa),
        about 1 pound
    1 tablespoon vegetable oil
    1¼ cups medium barley
    1 large onion, chopped (1 cup)
    1 large sweet green pepper, halved,
        seeded and chopped (1 cup)
    1 clove garlic, minced
    1 bay leaf, crumbled
    1 teaspoon salt
    2 teaspoons paprika
    ½ teaspoon leaf thyme, crumbled
    3 cups tomato juice
    2 to 3 cups water

1. Remove casing from sausage; cut sausage in half lengthwise, then across into 1-inch pieces. Brown sausage in oil in a Dutch oven or flameproof baking dish. Remove pieces with a slotted spoon to a medium-size bowl as they brown. Reserve.
2. Add barley, onion and green pepper to pot; cook over medium heat, stirring frequently, until barley is browned and vegetables are tender, about 10 minutes. Stir in garlic; cook 1 minute. Add bay leaf, salt, paprika and thyme; mix thoroughly. Add sausages, tomato juice and 2 cups water;

> **Make the protein content of grains even more valuable by combining them with eggs, milk, cheese, a small amount of meat or fish, beans, seeds or nuts.**
> **Cut cholesterol by adding grains to your diet and limiting red meats.**
> **The U.S. Recommended Daily Allowance of protein is 45 grams if the quality is equal to or greater than that of milk protein (65 grams if quality of protein is less than that of milk, as in beans, peas and peanut butter).**

bring to boiling; cover.

3. Bake in a preheated moderate oven (350°) for 1 hour, or until barley is tender and most of the liquid has been absorbed. Add water, if needed, so that there is always a little liquid left in the pot.

4. Either cool and refrigerate the casserole (it improves on standing) or serve immediatly. To reheat, place over very low heat and stir often, adding water as necessary to keep a bit of sauce in the dish.

TABBOULEH

Makes 6 servings.

1 cup bulgur (cracked wheat)
3 medium-size ripe tomatoes, chopped (2 cups)
1 bunch green onions, chopped
3 cups chopped parsley
¼ cup chopped mint
½ cup olive oil
4 to 6 tablespoons lemon juice
½ teaspoon salt
¼ teaspoon pepper
   Romaine or leaf lettuce
   Ground cinnamon (*optional*)

1. Wash bulgur; place in a large bowl and cover with hot water; let stand 30 minutes. Drain thoroughly and squeeze dry with hands.

2. Combine with tomatoes, onions, parsley and mint in a large bowl. Beat oil, lemon juice, salt and pepper together in a 1-cup measure; pour over bulgur mixture; stir until well-blended. Serve in lettuce-lined salad bowl. Sprinkle with ground cinnamon, or pass cinnamon for guests to sprinkle on salad, if you wish.

PHILADELPHIA SCRAPPLE

Makes 4 to 8 servings.

½ pound beef liver
½ pound lean boneless pork
¾ teaspoon leaf thyme, crumbled

> Store rice, barley and kasha (whole buckwheat grain) in tightly closed jars to keep dry.
> Keep a range of other grains in your kitchen cabinet. They store well so you can pick up rye, millet, triticale (a wheat-rye hybrid), cracked oats and cracked wheat whenever you happen to find them. Use as you would rice, if the packages don't have suggestions.
> When you cook up a batch of grain, make extra to use during the week in soups, stuffings, stews or casseroles. Tightly covered and refrigerated barley will keep three to four days, brown rice and kasha for five to six days.

¼ teaspoon ground sage
½ teaspoon pepper
1 teaspoon salt
1½ cups (or more) cornmeal
   Flour
   Butter

1. Place liver and pork in a large saucepan with 8 cups water. Bring to boiling; lower heat; simmer 1½ to 2 hours, or until tender, adding water to cover if necessary. Let stand until cool.

2. Reserve broth; chop meats finely or put through a meat grinder. Measure 3 cups broth (beef broth can be added to make the 3 cups, if necessary) and season with thyme, sage, pepper and salt.

3. Add meat to broth and bring to boiling. Add cornmeal very gradually, stirring constantly, until mixture is very thick and bubbly. If mixture does not thicken well, add a little more cornmeal.

4. Pour into a greased 13x9x2-inch baking pan; chill thoroughly. Cut scrapple into serving slices; dredge with flour and brown quickly on both sides in butter in a large heavy skillet.

POLENTA WITH ZUCCHINI

To northern Italy goes the credit for this specialty. The buttery cornmeal squares are topped with grated cheese and baked.
Bake at 350° for 30 minutes.
Makes 6 servings.

1½ cups yellow cornmeal
2 cups milk
1½ cups water
1 teaspoon salt
8 tablespoons (1 stick) butter or margarine
2 eggs, beaten
2 cups grated Parmesan cheese
6 small zucchini, trimmed and sliced diagonally ¼ inch thick

1. Stir cornmeal into milk in a medium-size bowl.
2. Combine water, salt and 3 tablespoons of the butter in a large saucepan; heat to boiling. Stir in cornmeal mixture slowly.
3. Cook over medium heat, stirring often, 15 minutes, or until mixture starts to pull away from side of pan and is very thick.
4. Very slowly stir in beaten eggs and 1½ cups of the Parmesan cheese. Pour into a 9x9x2-inch baking pan; cool; chill several hours or overnight.
5. Turn chilled cornmeal mixture out of pan onto a cutting board; cut into 2¼-inch squares. (Using a wet knife helps to prevent sticking.) Stand squares, overlapping, in a 6-cup shallow baking dish. Melt 3 tablespoons of the remaining butter in a small saucepan and drizzle over cornmeal squares; sprinkle with the remaining ½ cup Parmesan cheese.
6. Bake in a preheated moderate oven (350°) for 30 minutes, or until golden.
7. While cornmeal bakes, cook zucchini, covered, in boiling salted water in a large saucepan 15 minutes, or until crisply tender; drain; return zucchini to saucepan. Add remaining 2 tablespoons butter. Arrange around cornmeal squares in baking dish.

INDIANA BEAN BAKE

Bake at 325° for 2½ hours.
Makes 8 servings.

1 package (1 pound) dried lima, navy or Great Northern beans
6 cups water
2 teaspoons salt
1 pound ground chuck or round
1 egg
¼ cup seasoned packaged bread crumbs
½ teaspoon salt
2 tablespoons vegetable oil
1 large onion, chopped (1 cup)
½ cup light molasses
½ cup chili sauce
¼ cup prepared mustard

1. Pick over beans and rinse under running water. Combine beans and water in a kettle or Dutch oven. Bring to boiling; cover; boil 2 minutes; remove from heat; let stand 1 hour. Return kettle to heat; bring to boiling; lower heat; simmer 1 hour or until beans are tender. Add the 2 teaspoons salt.
2. Combine ground beef, egg, bread crumbs and the remaining ½ teaspoon salt in a medium-size bowl; shape into small balls.
3. Brown meatballs in vegetable oil in a large skillet; remove with a slotted spoon. Sauté onion in fat in pan; stir in molasses, chili sauce and mustard; bring to boiling.
4. Drain beans, reserving liquid. Combine beans, meatballs and onion mixture in a 12-cup baking dish; add enough reserved liquid to just cover the beans; cover dish.
5. Bake in a preheated slow oven (325°) for 2 hours, adding more reserved liquid, if needed, to prevent beans from drying. Remove cover; bake 30 minutes longer, or until beans are very tender.

> **Do not add salt to beans until they are tender. Salt tends to toughen them. Cook beans at a steady, gentle simmer, which will also ensure tenderness.**

Top: Pinto Bean Pot (page 102); center: Indiana Bean Bake; bottom: Basque Garbanzo Casserole (page 102)

BASQUE GARBANZO CASSEROLE

Bake at 325° for 1 hour.
Makes 8 servings.

½ pound pepperoni sausage, sliced thin
2 tablespoons vegetable oil
1 whole chicken breast (about 12 ounces)
1 large leek, washed and chopped
2 cloves garlic, minced
4 medium-size carrots, sliced
2 cups shredded cabbage (¼ head)
2 cans (1 pound, 4 ounces each) chick-peas (garbanzos) or red kidney beans, drained
1 can (1 pound) tomatoes
3 teaspoons salt
1 teaspoon leaf thyme, crumbled
½ teaspoon pepper

1. Sauté pepperoni in oil in a large skillet for 5 minutes; remove with a slotted spoon. Cut chicken breast into 2-inch pieces.
2. Brown chicken pieces in fat remaining in pan; remove with a slotted spoon. Sauté leek and garlic; stir in carrots and cook 3 minutes; stir in cabbage and cook 2 minutes. Add chick-peas, tomatoes, salt, thyme and pepper; stir to blend well.
3. Spoon chick-pea mixture into a 12-cup baking dish; add browned chicken and pepperoni; cover dish.
4. Bake in a preheated slow oven (325°) for 1 hour.

PINTO BEAN POT

No chili, but tomatoes and green pepper are in this flavorful casserole.

Bake at 325° for 3 hours.
Makes 8 servings.

1 package (1 pound) dried pinto, red kidney, Great Northern or lima beans
5 cups water
3 medium-size onions, chopped (1½ cups)

2 teaspoons salt
1 pound hot Italian sausages, skinned and cut into 1-inch pieces
2 large sweet green peppers, halved, seeded and cut into 1-inch pieces
1 can (1 pound) tomatoes
1 teaspoon leaf oregano, crumbled
½ teaspoon cumin seeds, crushed
½ teaspoon pepper

1. Pick over beans and rinse under running water. Combine beans and water in a large kettle. Bring to boiling; boil 2 minutes; remove from heat; let stand 1 hour. Return to heat; bring to boiling; add onions; lower heat and simmer 1 hour, or until beans are firm-tender; add salt.
2. Brown sausage in a large skillet; remove with a slotted spoon. Sauté green pepper in fat remaining in skillet until soft; stir in tomatoes, oregano, cumin and pepper; heat until bubbling.
3. Drain beans, reserving liquid. Combine with browned sausage in a 12-cup baking dish; add enough reserved liquid to just cover the beans; cover baking dish.
4. Bake in a preheated slow oven (325°) for 2½ hours, adding more reserved liquid, if needed, to prevent beans from drying. Remove cover; bake 30 minutes longer, or until beans are very tender.

> **Great Northern, navy or pea beans are good for baked bean dishes, soups and casseroles; black beans are for Latin American and Caribbean dishes, such as soup or beans and rice. Yellow split peas are good for thick soups and purees. Pinto beans are good for soups, casseroles, salads, Mexican and Southwestern dishes. Cranberry beans are good for chili and New England succotash. Chickpeas or garbanzos are good for antipasto, soups, salads, casseroles, hummus and falafel. Red kidney beans are good for salads and chili. Lima beans are good in soup, stews and casseroles.**

TOP-OF-THE-STOVE BEANS WITH ITALIAN SAUSAGE

Makes 8 servings.

½ pound sweet Italian sausage
½ pound hot Italian sausage
1 tablespoon vegetable oil
1¾ cups chopped onion
¾ pound mushrooms, sliced (3 cups)
3 cans (16 ounces each) pork and
    beans in tomato sauce
⅓ cup tomato juice
1 teaspoon leaf oregano, crumbled
1 teaspoon salt
⅛ teaspoon crushed red pepper flakes
1 cup uncooked long-grain rice

1. Cook sausage in vegetable oil in a large skillet until brown and no pink remains, about 20 minutes. Remove with a slotted spoon to a Dutch oven or heavy saucepan.
2. Pour off all but 2 tablespoons of fat from skillet. Sauté onion and mushrooms until tender, about 3 minutes. Add onion mixture to sausage.
3. Add beans, tomato juice, oregano, salt and pepper to sausage. Bring to boiling; lower heat; simmer 15 minutes.
4. While beans cook, cook rice following label directions. Serve beans over rice.

OLD-FASHIONED BAKED BEANS

These are the kind of beans our great-grandmothers baked for hours.
Bake at 300° for 4½ hours.
Makes 8 servings.

2 cups dried navy beans (1 pound)
6 cups water
1 medium-size onion
2 whole cloves
¾ cup dark molasses
¼ cup firmly packed brown sugar
2 teaspoons dry mustard
¼ pound salt pork

1. Pick over beans and rinse under run-ning water. Combine beans and water in a kettle or Dutch oven. Bring to boiling; boil 2 minutes; remove from heat; cover kettle; let stand 1 hour.
2. Return beans to heat; bring to boiling; cover; lower heat; simmer 1½ hours or un-til beans are tender, but before skins burst. Drain; reserving liquid.
3. Stud onion with cloves. Place in bottom of a 10-cup earthenware bean pot. Add beans.
4. Combine molasses, brown sugar, dry mustard and 1 cup hot bean liquid. Pour over beans; mix well.
5. Cut salt pork almost through at ½-inch intervals. Place, cut-side down, in center of beans. Add enough hot bean liquid to just cover beans (about 1 cup); cover.
6. Bake in a preheated slow oven (300°) for 4 hours. Remove cover. Bake 30 min-utes longer for top of beans to brown. Serve with steamed Boston Brown Bread (page 64), if you wish.

ELEGANT LIMA BEANS

Bake at 350° for 30 minutes.
Makes 4 servings.

4 cups cooked dried lima beans
1 can (15 ounces) tomato sauce
1 cup shredded Swiss cheese (4 ounces)
1 cup coarsely chopped walnuts
¼ teaspoon leaf basil, crumbled
1 sweet green pepper, halved, seeded
    and diced
¾ cup water
½ teaspoon salt
¼ teaspoon pepper

1. Combine lima beans and tomato sauce in a large saucepan or Dutch oven. Bring to boiling; remove from heat.
2. Stir in cheese, walnuts, basil, green pep-per, water, salt and pepper. Spoon into an 8-cup baking dish.
3. Bake in a preheated moderate oven (350°) for 30 minutes. Garnish with pars-ley, if you wish.

Curried Lima Beans and Chicken Wings

CURRIED LIMA BEANS AND CHICKEN WINGS

A hearty, mildly seasoned casserole with peas and carrots.

Bake at 350° for 30 minutes.

Makes about 8 servings.

    1 pound dried lima beans
    3 cups water
    8 chicken wings (about 1¼ pounds)
    ¼ cup (½ stick) butter or margarine
    1 large onion, chopped (1 cup)
    3 carrots, sliced (1½ cups)
    2 teaspoons curry powder
    ¼ teaspoon ground cinnamon
    2 tablespoons flour
    2 teaspoons salt
    1 cup milk
    1 package (10 ounces) frozen peas

1. Pick over beans and rinse under running water. Combine beans and water in a large kettle; cover, let soak overnight. Or, to quick-soak, bring to boiling, boil 2 minutes, remove from heat; let stand 1 hour.

2. Bring soaked beans to boiling; lower heat; partially cover and simmer 35 minutes, or until beans are almost tender.

3. Cut each chicken wing at joint to separate the 2 large sections. Melt butter in a large skillet; add wings and cook slowly until brown on all sides. Remove to paper toweling as they brown.

4. Add onion, carrots, curry powder and cinnamon to fat remaining in skillet. Sauté until onion is tender. Stir in flour and salt. Drain beans, reserving liquid. There should be 2 cups liquid; if not, add water to make that amount.

5. Add reserved liquid to flour mixture; cook, stirring constantly, until thickened and boiling. Add milk and peas; bring to boiling. Combine beans, chicken wings and curry sauce in a 3- to 4-quart baking dish; cover.

6. Bake in a moderate oven (350°) for 30 minutes or until beans are tender, stirring once halfway through baking.

GREEK BEAN SALAD

Prepare the bean mixture the day before. The final preparation is quick, less than 10 minutes to the table.

Makes 8 servings.

    1½ cups dried navy beans
     6 cups water
     ⅓ cup chopped green onions
     ½ cup chopped parsley
     1 tablespoon dried mint leaves, crumbled
     ⅓ cup olive oil
     ¼ cup red wine vinegar
     1 teaspoon salt
     ½ teaspoon pepper
     1 tablespoon drained capers
     2 medium-size ripe tomatoes, cut in chunks
     1 medium-size cucumber, sliced
     ¼ pound feta cheese, cut in chunks
     1 can (5¾ ounces) pitted black olives, drained
     1 medium-size head romaine

1. Pick over, sort and wash beans. Drain and combine beans with 6 cups water in a large saucepan. Bring to boiling; boil 2 minutes; remove from heat; cover and allow to stand 1 hour. Return to heat; simmer 1½ hours or until just tender. Drain.

2. While beans are still warm, transfer to a large salad bowl. Add green onions, parsley, mint, olive oil, vinegar, salt and pepper; toss gently. Cover; refrigerate until well chilled, about 3 hours.

3. Just before serving, add capers, tomatoes, cucumber, cheese and black olives; toss gently. Line serving platter with romaine. Spoon salad onto platter.

> **1 pound dried beans is equivalent to 2 cups, which, after soaking and cooking, yields about 8 servings of ¾ cup each. Dry or canned dry peas, beans and lentils are generous sources of iron, thiamine and vegetable protein.**

LENTIL BURGERS

Makes 10 burgers.

    1 cup dried lentils, rinsed
    ½ cup uncooked brown rice
    3 cups water
    2 teaspoons salt
    1 cup whole-wheat bread crumbs
        (2 slices)
    ½ cup wheat germ
    1 medium-size onion, chopped (½ cup)
    ½ teaspoon celery seed
    ½ teaspoon leaf marjoram, crumbled
    ½ teaspoon salt
    ½ teaspoon pepper
      Wheat germ
    3 tablespoons vegetable oil
      Whole-wheat pita bread
      Lettuce
      Tomato slices

1. Combine lentils, rice, water and the 2 teaspoons salt in a medium-size saucepan. Bring to boiling; lower heat; cover and simmer about 45 minutes, or until beans and rice are tender. Remove from heat; let stand 10 minutes, then mash well with any liquid remaining in pan.
2. Stir in bread crumbs, wheat germ, onion, celery seed, marjoram, the remaining ½ teaspoon salt and pepper.
3. Shape into patties (⅓ cup each); sprinkle with wheat germ; turn and coat other side.
4. Heat oil in large skillet; sauté patties until brown on both sides, about 10 minutes. Serve in pita bread with lettuce and tomato slices.

BAKED LENTILS WITH CHEESE

Bake at 375° for 1 hour and 15 minutes.
Makes 8 servings.

    1¾ cups dried lentils, rinsed
    2½ quarts water
    1 bay leaf

    2 large onions, finely chopped (2 cups)
    2 cloves garlic, minced
    2 tablespoons vegetable oil or
        shortening
    2 large carrots, thinly sliced (1 cup)
    ½ cup thinly sliced celery
    ½ cup chopped sweet green pepper
    1 can (1 pound) tomatoes, drained
    1½ teaspoons salt
    ½ teaspoon pepper
    ¼ teaspoon leaf marjoram, crumbled
    ¼ teaspoon ground sage
    ¼ teaspoon leaf thyme, crumbled
    1 package (8 ounces) process
        American cheese

1. Combine lentils, water and bay leaf in a large saucepan; bring to boiling. Lower heat; cover; simmer 30 minutes or until lentils are tender; drain. Put lentils in a 13x9x2-inch baking dish.
2. Sauté onions and garlic in oil in a medium-size skillet until tender, about 3 minutes. Add to lentils with carrots, celery, green pepper, tomatoes, salt, pepper, marjoram, sage and thyme. Stir to mix. Cover with aluminum foil.
3. Bake in a moderate oven (375°) for 1 hour. Uncover. Slice cheese; layer evenly over top. Bake 15 minutes, or until cheese melts and begins to brown. Let stand 15 minutes before serving.

> Lentils and split peas do not need to be soaked and should never be cooked in a pressure cooker or slow cooker, as they foam up and clog the pressure valves. Both are excellent sources of fiber.

NUTTED ZUCCHINI-RICE LOAF WITH CHEDDAR SAUCE

This dish is a real treat, even for meat lovers, who will be surprised to know meat is missing here. You might serve slices of the firm, nutty loaf with sautéed green peppers and onions and baked whole tomatoes. Pears in wine sauce make a lovely ending to the meal.

Bake at 350° for 55 minutes.
Makes 6 servings.

    1 cup uncooked brown rice
1¾ cups water
    ½ teaspoon salt
    1 pound small zucchini, washed and
        trimmed
    ½ teaspoon salt
    3 eggs
    3 green onions, sliced
    1 cup finely chopped walnuts
    ½ teaspoon leaf sage, crumbled
    ½ teaspoon leaf thyme, crumbled
    ¼ teaspoon pepper
    1 tablespoon butter or margarine
    1 tablespoon plus 2 teaspoons
        cornstarch
    2 teaspoons prepared mustard
    ¼ teaspoon salt
1¼ cups milk
    1 cup shredded Cheddar cheese, (4
        ounces)
    ½ cup buttermilk

1. Combine rice, water and ½ teaspoon of the salt in a medium-size saucepan; bring to boiling over high heat; cover. Lower heat; simmer 35 minutes. Remove from heat and let stand, covered, 20 minutes.
2. Meanwhile, coarsely shred zucchini into a large sieve or colander placed over a medium-size bowl; add another ½ teaspoon salt; let stand 30 minutes while rice cooks. With the back of a wooden spoon press liquid from zucchini until dry.
3. Beat eggs in a large bowl; add zucchini, mixing well to separate strands. Add rice, green onions, walnuts, sage, thyme and pepper; mix well to moisten thoroughly. (Use hands, if necessary.)

4. Spoon mixture into a buttered 8½x4½x2⅝-inch glass baking dish. Spread evenly in dish; cover with aluminum foil.
5. Bake in a moderate oven (350°) for 45 minutes. Remove foil and continue baking an additional 10 minutes. Remove from oven to wire rack. Let stand 15 minutes. Run a spatula around edges of pan to loosen loaf; place a serving dish on top and invert loaf onto dish.
6. While loaf rests, make sauce: Melt butter in a medium-size saucepan, stir in cornstarch, mustard and the remaining ¼ teaspoon salt and continue stirring over medium heat until bubbly. Remove from heat. Gradually add milk, stirring with a wire whisk until mixture is smooth. Return to heat. Cook over low heat, stirring constantly, until mixture thickens. Add cheese; continue to cook until cheese melts; stir in buttermilk. Spoon some sauce over loaf; pour remaining in sauceboat to pass at table. Garnish zucchini-nut loaf with whole walnuts, if you wish.

Supermarkets offer a wide variety of rice for you to choose from. Long-grain white rice, which is used most often in these recipes, is polished rice that cooks up fluffy and separates, as compared to short-grain white rice, preferred by many homemakers, which cooks more moist with the grains less separated. 1 cup uncooked = 4 cups cooked. Processed or converted, another favorite, is the same long-grain rice which has been partially steam-cooked before milling. 1 cup uncooked = 4 cups cooked. Precooked white rice, called instant, is fully cooked, and needs only to stand in boiling water for a short time. 1 cup uncooked = 2 cups cooked. Brown rice is unpolished rice that has only had the husks removed. It takes longer to cook than the white rice. 1½ cups uncooked = 4 cups cooked. Wild rice is not a true rice, but the seeds of a water grass grown in some of our northern states. 1 cup uncooked = 4 cups cooked.

ONE-POT SPANISH RICE

Makes 4 servings.

¾ pound ground chuck
1 medium-size onion, chopped (½ cup)
½ cup chopped sweet green pepper
1 can (1 pound) tomatoes
1 can (12 ounces) vegetable juice
 cocktail
1 cup uncooked long-grain rice
1½ teaspoons salt
¼ teaspoon pepper
½ teaspoon Worcestershire sauce

1. Combine beef, onion and green pepper in a large saucepan or Dutch oven; cook over low heat, stirring occasionally, just until meat browns and vegetables are tender, about 5 minutes; drain off fat.
2. Add tomatoes, vegetable juice cocktail, rice, salt, pepper and Worcestershire; bring to boiling; lower heat; cover. Simmer 25 minutes, or until most of the liquid has evaporated and rice is tender.

BROWN RICE, SPINACH AND CHEESE BAKE

Green chili peppers add pep; brown rice adds nutrition. Good with a tossed lettuce and tomato salad and tortilla chips.
Bake at 350° for 30 minutes.
Makes 6 servings.

1 cup uncooked brown rice
2 cups (1 pound) creamed cottage
 cheese, sieved
2 eggs
1 package (10 ounces) frozen chopped
 spinach, thawed
1 can (4 ounces) green chilies,
 seeded and chopped
1 cup cubed Monterey Jack or
 Muenster cheese (about 6 ounces)
1½ teaspoons salt
⅛ teaspoon pepper

1. Cook rice, following label directions.
2. Combine cottage cheese, eggs, spinach,

green chilies, ½ cup of the Monterey Jack cheese, salt and pepper in a large bowl. Stir in cooked rice.
3. Spoon into an 8-cup shallow baking dish. Dot with remaining cheese.
4. Bake in a preheated moderate oven (350°) for 30 minutes, or until bubbly-hot and cheese has melted.

CHINESE PORK FRIED RICE

Makes 6 servings.

2 cups uncooked long-grain rice
1 pound shoulder pork chops
1 medium-size sweet green pepper,
 halved, seeded and chopped
6 green onions, sliced, with some tops
2 tablespoons vegetable oil
½ cup soy sauce
¼ teaspoon garlic powder
¼ teaspoon pepper
6 eggs, lightly beaten
1 tablespoon butter or margarine

1. Cook rice, following label directions.
2. In the meantime, remove all fat and bone from pork; cut pork into thin strips 2 inches long.
3. Sauté green pepper and onions in oil in a wok or large skillet until tender, about 3 minutes. Remove with a slotted spoon to a small bowl.
4. Add pork to wok; stir-fry about 3 minutes. Add soy sauce, garlic powder and pepper. Cover. Simmer 8 minutes. Add vegetables; simmer 2 more minutes.
5. Scramble eggs in butter in a medium-size skillet until softly set.
6. Stir pork-vegetable mixture into rice. Gently stir in eggs. Serve at once.

> **Use up leftover rice in thrifty ways. Add to waffle or pancake batter, use in place of bread in a meat loaf, make a rice pudding, use to stuff eggplant or zucchini or add to soups or stews.**

Risotto with Chicken Livers

RISOTTO WITH CHICKEN LIVERS

A specialty from Milan, to serve as a tasty main dish.

Makes 6 servings.

    4 slices bacon
    1 pound chicken livers, trimmed
        and halved
 ¼ cup flour
    1 teaspoon salt
 ¼ teaspoon pepper
    1 large onion, chopped (1 cup)
    1 cup uncooked long-grain rice
    2 envelopes or teaspoons instant
        chicken broth
    1 teaspoon leaf basil, crumbled
    1 bay leaf
 2½ cups water
    Chopped parsley

1. Cook bacon in a large skillet until crisp. Drain on paper toweling; crumble; reserve.
2. Shake chicken livers in a plastic bag with flour, salt and pepper.
3. Brown livers in bacon fat remaining in skillet. Remove with a slotted spoon to a bowl as they brown; reserve.
4. Sauté onion in the same skillet until tender, about 3 minutes. (If there is no fat remaining in the skillet, add 2 tablespoons vegetable oil.) Stir in rice, chicken broth, basil, bay leaf and water.
5. Heat to boiling; lower heat; stir rice mixture well; cover. Simmer 10 minutes. Spoon browned chicken livers over rice. Return cover and simmer 20 minutes longer, or until liquid is absorbed and rice is tender; remove bay leaf. Sprinkle with reserved bacon and chopped parsley.

109

ITALIAN RICE BALLS (Suppli al Telefono)

The center of melty mozzarella in each rice ball strings when eaten and gives them their name, Suppli al Telefono or Telephone Wires.

Makes 8 servings.

2 cups uncooked long-grain rice
4 eggs, separated
⅓ cup shredded provolone cheese
1 package (8 ounces) mozzarella cheese, cubed
1 cup packaged herb-flavored bread crumbs
1 can (15 ounces) tomato sauce
¼ cup chopped parsley

1. Cook rice, following label directions. Fold in egg yolks and provolone. Shape into 24 balls, using about ¼ cup for each, placing a cube of mozzarella cheese in the center of each ball, making sure the rice completely covers the cheese.
2. Beat egg whites slightly in a pie plate place bread crumbs in a second pie plate. Gently roll rice balls in egg white, then in bread crumbs, to coat evenly. Chill at least 1 hour, or until firm.
3. Pour enough vegetable oil into a large saucepan to make a 3-inch depth; heat to 375° on a deep-fat frying thermometer.
4. Fry rice balls, 2 or 3 at a time, turning once, about 4 minutes, or until golden. Drain on paper toweling; keep warm.
5. While rice balls cook, heat tomato sauce in a medium-size saucepan.
6. Arrange rice balls on a heated serving platter; spoon the tomato sauce over. Sprinkle with parsley.

> **When you cook rice for a recipe, it is handy to have a little extra for another meal. Refrigerate rice, covered. To reheat: Put rice in a colander over, not in, simmering water. Cover with towel; steam rice 10 minutes.**

WHITE BEANS, PROVENÇALE STYLE (Haricots Blancs À La Provençale)

A hearty and delightful casserole of beans cooked in the French country style. The vigorous flavors of tomato, garlic and olive oil are combined with pungent herbs. Excellent with roast lamb.

Makes 8 servings.

1 package (1 pound) dried Great Northern white beans
8 cups water
2 chicken bouillon cubes
½ pound cured lean salt pork
3 medium-size onions, chopped (1½ cups)
1 large ripe tomato, peeled, seeded and chopped
  OR: 1 cup Italian-style canned tomatoes, drained and chopped
1 large clove garlic, quartered
3 tablespoons olive oil
1 bay leaf
1 teaspoon leaf rosemary, crumbled
½ teaspoon leaf thyme, crumbled
¼ teaspoon leaf sage, crumbled
1 teaspoon chopped parsley

1. Pick over beans and rinse under running water. Combine beans with 8 cups water in a large kettle. Bring to boiling; boil 2 minutes; remove from heat; cover; let stand 1 hour. Drain liquid from beans into a 4-cup measure to measure 3 cups; discard remainder; add bouillon cubes.
2. Rinse cured salt pork; pat dry on paper toweling; cut into 1-inch strips. Brown strips until crisp in a kettle or Dutch oven. (Do not drain off fat.) Add beans, 3 cups reserved liquid, onions, tomato, garlic, oil, bay leaf, rosemary, thyme, sage and parsley.
3. Cover; simmer 2 hours and 15 minutes or until beans are tender. Remove bay leaf. Taste; add salt and pepper, if needed.

VENETIAN RICE AND PEAS
(Risi e Bisi)

Call it a thick soup or a thin stew—it is a delicious dish from a lovely city.

Makes 6 servings.

  3 tablespoons chopped onion
  6 tablespoons (¾ stick) butter or
     margarine
  1 package (10 ounces) frozen peas
  ½ teaspoon salt
  3 cans (13¾ ounces each) chicken
     broth
  1 cup uncooked long-grain rice
  3 tablespoons chopped parsley
  ⅔ cup grated Parmesan cheese

1. Sauté onion in butter in a large saucepan or Dutch oven until tender.
2. Add peas and salt and cook for 2 minutes, stirring often.
3. Add broth; bring to boiling. Add rice; stir thoroughly; lower heat; cover. Cook at a steady simmer for 15 minutes or longer, until rice is tender but firm to the bite, not mushy. Stir from time to time while the rice cooks.
4. Remove from heat. Add parsley and Parmesan cheese just before serving.

OVEN RICE

A no-fuss way of preparing a simple dish of rice. Easy, too!

Bake at 350° for 1 hour.
Makes 6 servings.

1½ cups uncooked long-grain rice
  4 dashes liquid red-pepper seasoning
  1 bay leaf
  4 tablespoons (½ stick) butter or
     margarine
  1 can (13¾ ounces) chicken broth
1¼ cups water
    Salt, if needed
    Chopped parsley

1. Put rice, red-pepper seasoning and bay leaf in a 6-cup baking dish with a tight-fitting lid. Add butter to broth and water. Bring to boiling; pour over rice; mix with a fork; cover dish.
2. Bake in a preheated moderate oven (350°) for 1 hour, or until all the liquid is absorbed and rice is tender.
3. Remove from oven. If kept tightly covered, it will remain hot for 30 minutes if necessary. Fluff up with a fork just before serving. Sprinkle with chopped parsley.

RICE PILAF

Serve with chicken as a flavorful alternate to potatoes or pasta.

Makes 6 servings.

  1 large onion, chopped (1 cup)
  1 clove garlic, minced
  ¼ cup (½ stick) butter or margarine
2½ cups chicken broth
  1 cup uncooked long-grain rice
  ½ cup chopped parsley
  ¼ cup raisins or currants, plumped
  ¼ cup pine nuts (pignoli)
  ½ teaspoon salt
  ¼ teaspoon pepper

1. Sauté onion and garlic in butter in a large saucepan until onion is tender but not brown, about 3 minutes.
2. Add chicken broth; bring to boiling; stir in rice with a fork; cover; lower heat; cook, 25 minutes, or until liquid is absorbed and rice is tender.
3. Add parsley, raisins, pine nuts, salt and pepper. Good with any roast or cold meats.

To plump raisins, place them in a small bowl, pour boiling water over and let stand 20 minutes. Drain; pat dry on paper toweling.

From left: Coleslaw Vinaigrette, Wilted Red Cabbage Slaw with Bacon and Peppers

Salads and Vegetables

Consumption of vegetables and fruits are up in line with nutritionist's recommendation to eat more complex carbohydrates and fiber. And they taste good, too!

COLESLAW VINAIGRETTE

Makes 4 servings.

- 1 small Savoy cabbage (1½ pounds)*
- ¼ cup pimiento-stuffed green olives, sliced
- 1 large carrot, shredded
- ⅓ cup olive oil
- 3 tablespoons red wine vinegar
- 1 tablespoon capers, drained and chopped
- ½ teaspoon salt
- ⅛ teaspoon pepper
- ¼ teaspoon crushed red pepper flakes
- 1 cup cherry tomatoes, halved
- ¼ cup chopped parsley

1. Trim outer leaves from cabbage; quarter and core; chop coarsely. (You will need about 6 cups.) Combine cabbage with olives and carrots in a large bowl.
2. Combine oil, vinegar, capers, salt, pepper and red pepper flakes in a screw-top jar. Cover; shake well. Pour dressing over cabbage and toss to coat. Cover; refrigerate several hours to blend flavors.
3. To serve: Top cabbage with cherry tomatoes; sprinkle with parsley. Toss again before serving.

If you wish, for an attractive presentation, gently remove inner core of cabbage to chop, reserving outer shell to fill.

WILTED RED CABBAGE SLAW WITH BACON AND PEPPERS

Makes 6 servings.

- 1 small red cabbage (1¼ pounds)
- 2 medium-size sweet red peppers, halved, seeded and thinly sliced
- 6 slices bacon
- 1 large clove garlic, minced
- ¼ cup red wine vinegar
- 1½ tablespoons brown sugar
- ½ teaspoon salt
- ½ teaspoon pepper

1. Trim outer leaves from cabbage; quarter and core; shred. (You will need about 7 cups.) Combine in a large bowl with red peppers.
2. Cook bacon in a large skillet until crisp. Drain on paper toweling; crumble and reserve. Measure bacon fat. (There should be ¼ cup; add vegetable oil, if needed.)
3. Return bacon fat to skillet. Sauté garlic until soft, but not browned. Add vinegar, sugar, salt and pepper; bring just to boiling. Pour hot dressing over cabbage; add crumbled bacon and toss well until cabbage starts to wilt. Serve immediately.

> **When buying cabbage, choose a head that looks bright and fresh and is solid and heavy for its size. 1 pound cabbage, shredded, yields 4 cups raw or 3 cups cooked.**

ASPARAGUS VINAIGRETTE

Serve as a first course or as a salad.

Makes 6 servings.

2½ pounds asparagus
⅔ cup olive or vegetable oil
⅓ cup white wine vinegar
½ teaspoon Dijon-style mustard
½ teaspoon salt
⅛ teaspoon pepper
1 tablespoon chopped parsley
1 tablespoon chopped green onion
1 tablespoon sweet pickle relish
1 tablespoon chopped pimiento

1. Wash and trim asparagus. Cook until just tender, about 10 minutes; drain. Rinse with cold water to stop cooking; drain on paper toweling. Arrange on a platter; chill.

2. Combine oil, vinegar, mustard, salt, pepper, parsley, onion, relish and pimiento in a screw-top jar. Shake well; chill 2 hours to blend flavors.

3. Spoon dressing over asparagus about ½ hour before serving.

> Olive oil adds a distinctive flavor to this and other cold and hot dishes. However, it is more expensive and not as unsaturated as other cooking oils. Use half olive and half vegetable oil, if you wish.

MACEDONIAN SALAD

Makes about 10 servings.

2 medium-size eggplants
  (1 pound each)
  Salt
2 medium-size ripe tomatoes,
  diced (2 cups)
1 large unpared cucumber,
  diced (2 cups)
1 small sweet green pepper, halved,
  seeded and diced (1 cup)
1 small sweet red pepper, halved,
  seeded and diced (1 cup)

½ cup sliced green onions
½ cup chopped parsley
½ cup safflower oil
¼ cup olive oil
½ cup white wine vinegar
¼ cup dry red wine
2 tablespoons lemon juice
2 cloves garlic, minced
½ teaspoon leaf oregano, crumbled
½ teaspoon leaf basil, crumbled
½ teaspoon leaf thyme, crumbled
½ teaspoon salt
¼ teaspoon pepper
  Salad greens

1. Pare eggplant; cut into ¾-inch-thick slices; salt lightly. Broil until light brown on both sides (about 4 minutes for each side). Cool; cut into bite-size pieces.

2. Combine eggplant, tomatoes, cucumber, green and red pepper, green onions and parsley in a large bowl.

3. Combine oils, vinegar, wine, lemon juice, garlic, oregano, basil, thyme, salt and pepper in a large screw-top jar. Shake thoroughly; pour over vegetables. Toss gently. Cover; refrigerate several hours for flavors to blend. Serve on salad greens. Top with plain yogurt, if you wish.

SPINACH AND MUSHROOM SALAD

Fresh spinach with a tangy dressing.

Makes 4 servings.

4 slices bacon
2 teaspoons sugar
2 tablespoons cider vinegar
2 tablespoons water
½ teaspoon salt
1 pound spinach
¼ pound mushrooms, sliced
2 medium-size carrots, shredded
2 hard-cooked eggs, cut into wedges

1. Cook bacon in a skillet until crisp; remove to paper toweling to drain; crumble and reserve. Measure bacon fat; return 2 tablespoons to skillet. Stir in sugar, vinegar, water and salt. Keep warm.

2. Wash and remove stems from spinach; dry thoroughly and break into pieces in a salad bowl. Pour warm dressing over and toss until coated and wilted.

3. Top with mushrooms, carrots and bacon; toss. Garnish with eggs.

GREEK CHICK-PEA SALAD

A delicious salad which only takes a few minutes to prepare. It can be assembled early in the day, and the cheese and garnish added just before serving.

Makes 8 servings.

  2 teaspoons prepared mustard
1½ teaspoons salt
1¼ cups olive or vegetable oil
  ½ cup lemon juice
  ¼ teaspoon ground pepper
  2 cans (20 ounces each) chick-peas, drained
  1 medium-size red onion, sliced and separated into rings
  ¼ pound feta cheese, crumbled
  2 tablespoons chopped parsley
    Lettuce leaves

1. Combine mustard, salt, oil, lemon juice and pepper in container of electric blender; whirl until smooth. (Or, shake well in a screw-top jar.)

2. Combine chick-peas and onion in a large bowl. Pour dressing over and toss. Refrigerate 1 hour.

3. Just before serving, add cheese and parsley; toss. Spoon over lettuce.

BIBB LETTUCE MIMOSA

Professional chefs agree there's no better salad than one made with crisp fresh greens tossed with just the right balance of piquant dressing.

Makes 8 servings.

  4 heads Bibb lettuce
    OR: 2 heads Boston lettuce

  2 hard-cooked eggs, finely chopped
    Creamy Italian Dressing
    (*recipe follows*)

Remove the outer leaves of lettuce; use to line a salad bowl. Cut the hearts of lettuce into 4 or 6 wedges through core. Wash, if necessary, and dry well on paper toweling. Arrange spoke-fashion in the salad bowl. Sprinkle with the chopped eggs. Ladle some of the dressing over salad; pass remainder at table.

CREAMY ITALIAN DRESSING
Makes about 1½ cups.

  1 egg
  1 tablespoon Dijon-style mustard
  ½ small onion
  ½ teaspoon salt
  ¼ teaspoon pepper
  1 clove garlic
  ⅛ teaspoon sugar
  2 tablespoons lemon juice
  ¼ cup red wine vinegar
  1 cup olive or vegetable oil

1. Combine egg, mustard, onion, salt, pepper, garlic, sugar, lemon juice and vinegar in container of electric blender. Whirl until smooth and thickened.

2. Add oil slowly through center of the blender cover while the blender is running. The dressing will be quite thick. Refrigerate at least 1 hour to blend flavors.

To add variety to salad dressing, make your favorite oil and vinegar dressing by the quart. At meal time measure the amount you'll need and add blue cheese, onion, garlic, or a favorite herb. For creamy dressings, start with mayonnaise and add fresh herbs, chopped hard-cooked eggs or sour cream.

Trim and wash salad greens (except iceberg lettuce); drain and dry in a salad basket salad spinner or between paper towels. Store in plastic bags in the crisper drawer of the refrigerator; they are ready to use and will keep fresh several days. Twist out the core of the head of iceberg lettuce; rinse under running water. Drain very well and store in a covered bowl or plastic bag in the crisper. Small, delicate greens (watercress, mint, etc.) will keep best if stored in small, individual plastic containers with the covers snapped firmly in place.

Unless badly bruised, shred the dark, outer vitamin-rich leaves of salad greens into a salad or slip into sandwiches, where appearance is not important.

LISA'S CUCUMBER SALAD

Small firm cucumbers are the best choice for this salad, as their seeds are not as large, and they are crisper.

Makes 6 servings.

    3 to 4 small firm cucumbers
    1 tablespoon salt
    1 small onion, minced (¼ cup)
    ¼ cup olive oil
    5 tablespoons white wine vinegar
    ¼ teaspoon white pepper

1. Pare cucumbers; slice paper-thin into a medium-size bowl. Sprinkle with salt; cover; refrigerate for at least 1 hour, several hours would be better.
2. Drain cucumbers, pressing out as much liquid as possible (squeeze with hands). Put cucumbers and onion into a small glass salad bowl.
3. Combine oil, vinegar and pepper in a cup; pour over cucumbers. Toss gently to mix. Chill until ready to serve. Sprinkle with chopped parsley, if you wish.

GARDEN GREENS WITH BUTTERMILK DRESSING

The piquant dressing has only 12 calories per serving.

Makes 4 servings.

    ½ cup buttermilk
    ½ clove garlic, minced
    ¼ teaspoon sugar
    ¼ teaspoon dry mustard
    ¼ teaspoon salt
    ⅛ teaspoon pepper
    1 quart salad greens (chicory, romaine, watercress and Boston lettuce)
    1 cucumber, pared and sliced
    4 radishes, sliced
    4 ounces Swiss cheese, cut into julienne strips

1. For the dressing: Combine buttermilk, garlic, sugar, mustard, salt and pepper in a 1-cup measure; stir to mix well.
2. Wash, dry and tear salad greens into pieces. Place in a salad bowl with cucumber, radishes and cheese.
3. Pour dressing over; toss to coat.

OLD-FASHIONED POTATO SALAD

Makes 6 servings.

    Boiled Dressing (*recipe follows*)
    6 medium-size potatoes (about 2 pounds)
    1 medium-size red onion, chopped (½ cup)
    ¼ cup chopped parsley
    1 teaspoon salt
    ⅛ teaspoon pepper
    Lettuce leaves
    4 hard-cooked eggs

1. Prepare Boiled Dressing; cool.
2. Cook potatoes in boiling salted water to cover in a large saucepan until tender, about 20 minutes. Drain, cool, peel and slice into a large bowl.
3. Add onion, parsley, salt, pepper and

Boiled Dressing. Toss just until potatoes are coated with dressing. Chill until serving time. Spoon into a bowl lined with lettuce leaves. Garnish with hard-cooked eggs, either sliced or chopped.

BOILED DRESSING
Makes 1¼ cups.

   2 tablespoons flour
   ¾ teaspoon dry mustard
   ½ teaspoon salt
   2 tablespoons sugar
   ½ cup water
   ¼ cup vinegar
   2 egg yolks, slightly beaten
   1 tablespoon butter or margarine
   ½ cup light cream or milk

1. Combine flour, dry mustard, salt and sugar in the top of a double boiler. Stir in water, vinegar and egg yolks.
2. Cook over hot, not boiling, water, stirring constantly, until thickened. Remove from heat; stir in butter and cream.
3. Chill in screw-top jar or plastic container. If necessary, thin with additional cream or milk. Keep refrigerated.

GERMAN POTATO SALAD
Makes 6 servings.

   6 medium-size potatoes (about 2 pounds)
   6 slices bacon
   1 medium-size onion, chopped (½ cup)
   1 cup chopped celery
   1½ tablespoons flour
   2 tablespoons sugar
   1 teaspoon salt
   ¼ teaspoon pepper
   ¼ cup vinegar
   1 cup water

1. Cook potatoes in boiling salted water to cover in a large saucepan just until tender, about 20 minutes. Drain, peel and slice into a large bowl; cover.
2. Cook bacon in a large skillet until crisp;

drain on paper toweling. Pour off fat into a cup. Measure ¼ cup fat and return to the skillet.
3. Sauté onion and celery in fat until tender. Stir in flour, sugar, salt, pepper, vinegar and water. Cook, stirring constantly, until mixture is thickened. Pour over potatoes; toss lightly to coat. Crumble bacon and sprinkle over top. Serve warm.

TANGY HAM-POTATO SALAD MOLD
Makes 8 servings.

   6 medium-size potatoes (about 2 pounds)
   ½ cup vegetable oil
   3 tablespoons vinegar
   1 tablespoon prepared mustard
   1 teaspoon salt
   ¼ teaspoon pepper
   1 large sweet green pepper
   1 pound cooked ham, diced (3 cups)
   1 cup diced celery
   1 small onion, chopped (¼ cup)
   ⅔ cup dairy sour cream
   3 hard-cooked eggs, chopped
     Lettuce leaves

1. Cook potatoes in boiling salted water to cover in a large saucepan until tender, about 20 minutes. Drain, peel and cut into ½-inch cubes to make 4 cups.
2. Combine oil, vinegar, mustard, salt and pepper in a large bowl. Add hot potatoes; toss lightly. Let stand at room temperature 20 minutes for potatoes to absorb dressing.
3. Cut pepper in half crosswise; seed. Slice half the pepper into rings for garnish; reserve. Cut remaining half into ¼-inch dice.
4. Add diced green pepper, ham, celery, onion, sour cream and eggs to potatoes; mix well. Press into a 4-quart mold or large round bowl. Cover and refrigerate 2 hours or overnight.
5. To serve, unmold onto a round platter lined with lettuce leaves. Garnish with the reserved green pepper rings.

CAESAR SALAD

Makes 6 servings.

    1 clove garlic, crushed
    ¾ cup olive oil
    3 slices firm white bread
    3 tablespoons fresh lemon juice
    6 anchovy fillets, minced
    ½ teaspoon salt
    ½ teaspoon dry mustard
    ⅛ teaspoon coarse black pepper
    ½ teaspoon Worcestershire sauce
    1 egg
    1 large head romaine lettuce
    ½ cup grated Parmesan cheese

1. Steep garlic in oil overnight; remove and discard. Remove crusts from bread; cut bread into small cubes. Sauté bread cubes in ¼ cup of the garlic oil in a large skillet until golden brown. Drain on paper toweling.
2. Combine the remaining oil, lemon juice, anchovies, salt, mustard, pepper and Worcestershire in a large salad bowl.
3. Heat egg in hot water in a small bowl 10 minutes. Tear romaine in bite-size pieces into salad bowl. (About 3 quarts leaves.)
4. Top romaine with half the Parmesan. Break egg over salad. Toss salad, spooning from bottom of bowl, until leaves are coated with dressing. Sprinkle with remaining Parmesan and the sautéed garlic croutons; toss lightly. Serve at once.

TOMATO GARDEN ASPIC

Makes 12 servings.

    3 envelopes unflavored gelatin
    5 cups tomato juice
    3 tablespoons lemon juice
    1 teaspoon Worcestershire sauce
    ½ teaspoon celery salt
    ½ teaspoon garlic salt
    ½ teaspoon salt
    ½ teaspoon pepper
    ⅛ teaspoon liquid red-pepper
         seasoning

    4 medium-size ripe tomatoes, peeled,
         seeded and chopped
         (about 2½ cups)
    1 medium-size cucumber, pared,
         seeded and chopped (about 1 cup)
    ½ cup chopped green onion, with tops
    ½ sweet green pepper, halved, seeded
         and chopped (½ cup)
         Whipped Horseradish Cream
         (*recipe follows*)

1. Sprinkle gelatin over 2 cups of the tomato juice in a medium-size saucepan; let stand 10 minutes to soften. Stir over very low heat until gelatin is dissolved.
2. Combine the remaining tomato juice with lemon juice, Worcestershire, celery salt, garlic salt, salt, pepper and red-pepper seasoning in a large bowl. Stir in gelatin mixture. Chill until as thick as unbeaten egg white, about 1 hour.
3. Stir in tomatoes, cucumber, green onions and green pepper.
4. Rinse a 10 to 12-cup fluted mold with cold water; pour in gelatin mixture. Chill until set, 4 hours or overnight. To unmold, dip in warm water; loosen around edge with tip of knife. Invert a serving plate over mold; turn right-side up; shake gently. Serve with Whipped Horseradish Cream.

WHIPPED HORSERADISH CREAM: Combine 1 cup heavy cream, 1 tablespoon bottled horseradish, ¼ teaspoon Worcestershire sauce and ⅛ teaspoon liquid red-pepper seasoning in a small bowl; beat until soft peaks form. Makes 2 cups.

PERFECTION SALAD

Makes 4 servings.

    2 envelopes unflavored gelatin
    ½ cup sugar
    1 teaspoon salt
    2½ cups water
    ½ cup white vinegar
    2 tablespoons lemon juice
    2 cups finely shredded cabbage
         (¼ medium-size head)

Caesar Salad

1 cup finely chopped celery
½ cup chopped sweet green pepper
2 tablespoons chopped pimiento
Green Goddess Dressing
(*recipe follows*)

1. Combine gelatin, sugar and salt in a medium-size saucepan; stir in 1 cup of the water. Heat slowly, stirring, until gelatin is dissolved.

2. Remove from heat; stir in the remaining 1½ cups water, vinegar and lemon juice. Pour mixture into a large bowl.

3. Chill until mixture is as thick as unbeaten egg white. Stir in cabbage, celery, green pepper and pimiento. Spoon into a 6-cup ring mold. Refrigerate until firm.

4. Unmold onto a serving plate. Serve with Green Goddess Dressing.

GREEN GODDESS DRESSING: Combine 1 cup mayonnaise, 1 can (2 ounces) anchovy fillets, drained, ¼ cup minced parsley and 2 tablespoons tarragon vinegar in container of electric blender; whirl until smooth, scraping down side of blender as necessary. Refrigerate for 1 hour before serving. Makes 1½ cups.

TOMATO JUICE BLENDER DRESSING
Makes 1½ cups.

½ cup tomato juice
2 tablespoons chopped onion
2 tablespoons lemon juice
1 teaspoon Worcestershire sauce
¼ teaspoon salt
¾ cup vegetable oil

Combine tomato juice, onion, lemon juice, Worcestershire, salt and oil in container of electric blender. Whirl until smooth. Chill well before serving.

SUNSET SALAD

Makes 8 servings.

1 can (1 pound, 4 ounces) crushed pineapple in pineapple juice
2 envelopes unflavored gelatin
¼ cup sugar
½ teaspoon salt
½ cup water
1 cup orange juice
¼ cup vinegar
1½ cups shredded carrots (about 3)
Fruit Dressing (*recipe follows*)

1. Drain pineapple, reserving both juice and pineapple.
2. Mix gelatin, sugar and salt in a small saucepan; stir in reserved juice from pineapple and ½ cup water. Heat slowly, stirring constantly, until gelatin is dissolved; stir in orange juice and vinegar; pour into a large bowl. Refrigerate until mixture is as thick as unbeaten egg white, about 1 hour.
3. Stir carrots and reserved pineapple into thickened gelatin mixture. Pour into a 6-cup mold or an 8x8x2-inch pan. Refrigerate about 4 hours, or until set. Serve with Fruit Dressing.

FRUIT DRESSING: Combine 1 cup dairy sour cream, 1 teaspoon grated orange rind and 2 tablespoons honey in a small bowl. Beat until smooth; chill.

THE PERFECT CHEF'S SALAD

Makes 6 servings.

2 whole chicken breasts (about 12 ounces each)
1 medium-size head Boston lettuce
1 medium-size head Romaine lettuce
1 cup sliced celery
6 slices bacon
1 ripe avocado
1 tablespoon lemon juice
2 ripe tomatoes, cut into thin wedges
3 hard-cooked eggs, sliced

4 ounces blue cheese, crumbled
Herb Vinaigrette Dressing
(*recipe follows*)

1. Cook chicken; skin and bone; chill; then cut into thin slices.
2. Break Boston and romaine lettuce into a large bowl; add celery; cover; refrigerate.
3. Cook and crumble bacon.
4. Halve avocado; peel and pit. Cut into cubes; sprinkle with lemon juice.
5. Top greens with tomatoes, avocado, chicken, bacon, eggs and cheese.
6. Pour ⅓ of the Herb Vinaigrette Dressing over the salad just before serving; toss gently to coat. Pass the remaining dressing separately.

HERB VINAIGRETTE DRESSING: Combine ¾ cup vegetable oil, ½ cup tarragon vinegar, ¾ teaspoon salt, ¼ teaspoon seasoned pepper and ½ teaspoon crumbled leaf basil in a screw-top jar; shake well to blend. Refrigerate to mellow flavors. Shake again just before pouring over salad. Makes 1¼ cups.

> **To cook chicken breasts; Combine 2 whole chicken breasts with 1 bay leaf, ½ cup diced celery, 1 teaspoon salt, ¼ teaspoon pepper in a large skillet. Add water or chicken broth to barely cover. Bring to a boiling; lower heat; cover; simmer 30 minutes, or until tender, turning breasts once. Use broth for soup.**

> **To add variety to salad dressing, make your favorite oil and vinegar dressing by the quart. At meal time, measure the amount you'll need and add blue cheese, onion, garlic or a favorite herb. For creamy dressings, start with mayonnaise and add fresh herbs, chopped hard-boiled eggs or sour cream.**

The Perfect Chef's Salad

CALIFORNIA CHICKEN SALAD

Our version of one of California's favorite salads.

Makes 8 servings.

- 1 large head romaine lettuce
- 1 large head chicory
- 2 ripe avocados, peeled, pitted and sliced
- 3 ripe tomatoes, sliced
- 1 small bunch watercress
- 2 whole cooked chicken breasts (about 12 ounces each), boned and sliced
- 8 slices crisp cooked bacon, crumbled
- 2 hard-cooked eggs, sliced
- 2 tablespoons chopped chives
  Roquefort French Dressing (*recipe follows*)

1. Break romaine and chicory into a large shallow salad bowl to line. Arrange avocados and tomatoes around the edge. Mound watercress in the center. Arrange chicken slices on top of watercress. Sprinkle with bacon. Garnish with egg slices; sprinkle with chives.

2. To serve, pour dressing over salad and toss to mix well.

ROQUEFORT FRENCH DRESSING: Combine ⅓ cup tarragon vinegar, 1½ teaspoons salt, ¼ teaspoon pepper, 1 tablespoon minced parsley, 1 tablespoon chopped chives and ⅔ cup vegetable oil in a screw-top jar; shake until ingredients are well blended. Add 1 cup crumbled Roquefort or blue cheese. Refrigerate at least 2 hours to develop flavors. Makes about 1½ cups.

> **Pineapples do not continue to ripen after they have been harvested. The color of ripe fruit can vary from greenish-yellow to orange. The best way to tell if a pineapple is ripe is to thump the side with a flick of the finger. A ripe pineapple will give a dull thud.**

Fresh Fruit and Savory Cheese Salad

FRESH FRUIT AND SAVORY CHEESE SALAD

Makes 4 servings.

- 1 container (1 pound) creamed cottage cheese
- ½ cup chopped pecans
- 1 tablespoon chopped green onions
- 2 medium-size ripe pineapples
- 1 pint strawberries, washed, hulled and halved
- 2 medium-size bananas, sliced
- 1 kiwi fruit, pared and sliced
- 1 cup seedless green grapes, halved

1. Combine cottage cheese, pecans and green onions in a medium-size bowl; mix lightly; cover; chill 30 minutes.

2. Cut pineapples in half lengthwise through the fruit and plume top. Cut meat from the skin from the 4 halves with a sharp paring knife held at an angle. Cut each removed fruit section in half; slice off the core; then cut pineapple crosswise into thin slices. Use half in the salad and the remainder for another meal.

3. Add strawberries, bananas, kiwi and grapes to pineapple chunks; toss gently.

4. Divide fruit mixture evenly among the four pineapple half shells; top with scoops of the cottage cheese mixture. Garnish with additional chopped pecans, green onion and sprigs of mint, if you wish.

SALADE NIÇOISE
Makes 6 servings.

    10 medium-size potatoes
    ¾ cup olive oil
    ¼ cup vinegar
     1 tablespoon chopped parsley
     1 teaspoon chopped chives
    ¼ teaspoon onion salt
     1 package (10 ounces) frozen whole
         green beans, cooked
     1 small head Boston lettuce, separated
         into leaves
     1 can (about 7 ounces) tuna, drained
         and broken into chunks
     2 large ripe tomatoes, cut into wedges
     2 cans (4 ounces each) small sardines,
         drained
     3 hard-cooked eggs, shelled and halved
     1 can (2 ounces) rolled anchovy fillets,
         drained
    ½ cup pitted black olives, halved

1. Cook potatoes in boiling salted water in a large saucepan until tender, about 30 minutes; drain. Cool until easy to handle, then peel and cut in thick slices.
2. Combine olive oil, vinegar, parsley, chives and onion salt in a screw-top jar; shake well to mix. Drizzle ½ cup of the dressing over potatoes and 2 tablespoons of the dressing over green beans; let each stand 30 minutes to season.
3. Line a large shallow serving platter with lettuce. Layer potato slices and tuna on top, then place green beans in center. Arrange 6 tomato wedges over beans.
4. Place remaining tomato wedges, sardines, egg halves topped with anchovies and the olives in a border around edge of platter. Drizzle remaining dressing over all.

> To ripen tomatoes, place them in a shallow box or basket and slip into a brown paper bag. Close the end and leave at room temperature. The gas released by the tomato ripens the fruit naturally. Never store unripened tomatoes in the refrigerator—it makes the pulp soft and cottony.

GREEN GODDESS SALAD
This salad was originally created for George Arliss, star of *The Green Goddess,* a stage play of 1915.
Makes 6 servings.

    ⅓ cup light cream or half and half
     1 cup mayonnaise
     1 can (2 ounces) anchovy fillets
    ⅓ cup chopped green onion
    ⅓ cup chopped parsley
     2 tablespoons chopped chives
     1 package (1 pound) frozen,
         shelled and deveined shrimp
     2 ripe avocados
     2 tablespoons lemon juice
     1 large head romaine lettuce, broken
     1 can (7 ounces) tuna, drained
         Lemon wedges
         Green Goddess Dressing
         (*recipe, page 119*)

1. Make dressing: Place cream, mayonnaise, anchovies, green onion, parsley and chives in the container of an electric blender, cover. Whirl till smooth, scraping down the side of the blender container if necessary. Refrigerate at least 1 hour to blend flavors.
2. Cook shrimp, following label directions; refrigerate until serving time.
3. Halve avocados; peel and pit. Cut into thin slices; dip into lemon juice.
4. Line a large shallow platter with romaine. Arrange shrimp and avocado slices on top. Place tuna in chunks in the center. Garnish with lemon wedges. Pass Green Goddess Dressing separately.

Lima Bean, Carrot and Zucchini Salad with Cheese

LIMA BEAN, CARROT AND ZUCCHINI SALAD WITH CHEESE

Crunchy with walnuts and a creamy yogurt dressing.

Makes about 4 servings.

- ¾ pound small, firm zucchini, washed and trimmed
- ¾ pound carrots, pared (about 5 or 6 medium-size)
- 1 package (10 ounces) frozen baby lima beans
- 1 teaspoon salt
- 2 tablespoons lemon juice
- ¼ teaspoon leaf marjoram, crumbled
- ¼ teaspoon leaf thyme, crumbled
- ¼ teaspoon pepper
- 1 small clove garlic, minced
- 1¼ cups plain yogurt
- 6 ounces feta or Swiss cheese, cubed
- ¾ cup coarsely chopped walnuts

1. Drop zucchini and carrots into a large saucepan of boiling water. Cook 5 minutes, or just until tender. Remove from water; run under cold water; chill.

2. Combine lima beans in a saucepan with ½ teaspoon of the salt and ½ cup water; cook gently, covered, until just tender, about 10 minutes. Drain and chill.

3. Combine lemon juice, the remaining ½ teaspoon salt, marjoram, thyme, pepper and garlic. Stir in yogurt and chill for at least 1 hour.

4. Cut zucchini and carrots into 2x¼-inch strips. Toss lima beans with cubed cheese.

5. Arrange all vegetables on a serving platter; spoon dressing over and sprinkle with walnuts. Toss before serving.

> Greek feta cheese is made from goat's or sheep's milk, or a mixture of the two. It is a soft, white, crumbly cheese with a salty, tangy flavor. Feta cheese should be submerged in brine.

PESTO RICE SALAD WITH SLIVERED HAM AND BROCCOLI

Chicken or tuna would be equally good in this garlic-and-herb salad.

Makes 6 servings.

- 1¼ cups uncooked long-grain rice
- 2 to 3 cups thin strips of cooked ham
- 4 cups cooked broccoli, cut into 1-inch pieces
- 1 medium-size red onion, sliced and separated into rings
- 2 cups halved cherry tomatoes
  Creamy Pesto Dressing *(recipe follows)*

1. Cook rice, following label directions; cool to room temperature.

2. Combine rice, ham, broccoli, onion and

tomatoes in a serving bowl; toss gently.

3. Add Creamy Pesto Dressing and toss gently to coat thoroughly.

CREAMY PESTO DRESSING
Makes about 1½ cups.

    4 cloves garlic
    2 teaspoons leaf basil, crumbled
    2 teaspoons red wine vinegar
    ½ cup walnut pieces
    1 cup mayonnaise
    ¼ cup grated Parmesan cheese
    ¼ cup parsley sprigs
    ½ teaspoon salt
    ¼ teaspoon pepper

1. Combine garlic, basil and vinegar in container of electric blender. Cover; whirl on low speed until garlic is minced. Add walnuts and whirl until finely ground.
2. Add mayonnaise, Parmesan, parsley, salt and pepper; whirl on medium speed, stopping 2 or 3 times to scrape down side of blender with a rubber scraper, until dressing is smooth. Cover; refrigerate until needed. Tightly covered, dressing will keep 2 or 3 days in the refrigerater. After that, flavor may become too intense.

> **Flat-leafed Italian parsley has more flavor than the regular curly variety. It grows easily from seed indoors and out.**

HOW TO COOK GREAT TASTING ASPARAGUS

1. Select asparagus with firm green stalks and tightly closed tips. Ends should not be woody. Allow 6 to 8 spears per serving.
2. To prepare for cooking: Snap off tough ends; wash stalks well under cold running water. Snip off large or sandy scales with a sharp knife; wash again. (*Tip*: For woody stems, remove thin outer skin on lower portion of stem with a potato peeler.)
3. To cook whole: Tie stalks in serving-size

Fresh Asparagus

bundles. Bring lightly salted water to boiling in a large skillet; add asparagus. Bring to a rapid boil; cover and simmer 10 minutes or until the lower parts of stalks are tender. Drain bundles well on paper toweling. OR: Tie stalks in large bundles; stand upright in a deep saucepan. Pour boiling water to a depth of 2 inches; add a dash of salt; cover. Cook (or steam) and drain as above. (*Tip*: A clean coffeepot is perfect for this. Or, steam in the bottom of a double boiler with insert used as cover.)
4. Boiled Sliced Asparagus: Cut stalks into 1½-inch lengths. Drop into boiling salted water. Cook, covered, 3 to 5 minutes or until just tender and bright green. To serve cold, rinse with cold water immediately to stop cooking; drain well on paper toweling.

LEMON BUTTER SAUCE:
For 2 to 2½ pounds asparagus.
Makes 4 to 6 servings.

Combine 2 tablespoons lemon juice and 2 tablespoons butter in a small saucepan; heat until bubbly. Gradually add 6 additional tablespoons butter, stirring all the time. Spoon over hot asparagus.

STIR-FRIED ASPARAGUS MIMOSA

Makes 6 servings.

1 bunch fresh asparagus (about 1½ pounds)
3 tablespoons peanut oil
2 tablespoons lemon juice
½ teaspoon salt
¼ teaspoon pepper
1 hard-cooked egg yolk
Chopped parsley
Lemon wedges

1. Break woody ends from asparagus and discard; wash stalks well under cold running water. If sandy, cut off scales with the tip of a sharp knife, then wash stalks again. Cut off tips; reserve; cut stalks diagonally into slices about ¼ inch thick and 1 inch long.
2. Heat oil in a large skillet or wok. Add sliced stalks; stir-fry 4 to 5 minutes or just until crisply tender; add asparagus tips; stir-fry 2 to 3 minutes longer. Stir in lemon juice, salt and pepper; cook 30 seconds.
3. Spoon asparagus into heated serving dish; sprinkle with chopped or sieved egg yolk and parsley. Serve with lemon wedges.

> **Fresh bean facts:** The best way to cook beans is to allow ½ to 1 cup boiling water and ½ teaspoon salt for each pound of beans. Snap beans, yellow and green, taste best when cooked just crisply-tender, so allow about 13 to 20 minutes cooking time. Lima beans need about 25 to 30 minutes. All beans are delicious with plain melted butter, but a little coarse ground pepper and fresh herbs are splendid additions.

GREEN BEANS, INDIAN-STYLE

Makes 4 servings.

1 pound green beans
2 tablespoons butter or margarine
2 tablespoons vegetable oil
1 teaspoon mustard seeds
1 medium-size onion, chopped (½ cup)
3 small carrots, thinly sliced (¾ cup)
1¼ teaspoons salt
1 teaspoon ground coriander
⅛ teaspoon ground ginger
1 to 2 tablespoons lemon juice

1. Wash beans; trim ends with a sharp knife. Slice diagonally into 1-inch pieces.
2. Heat butter in a large skillet; add mustard seeds and sauté 30 seconds, or until seeds start to "pop." Stir in onion, carrots and beans; cook, stirring, 5 minutes.
3. Stir in salt, coriander and ginger. Lower heat; cover; cook and stir 8 minutes, or until crisply tender. Stir in lemon juice.

> **To quick-cut green beans, bunch together a handful; cut crosswise or diagonally (Chinese way) into inch-long pieces.**

BROCCOLI RING

Bake at 350° for 40 minutes.
Makes 8 servings.

2½ pounds broccoli, cleaned
4 eggs, beaten
1½ teaspoons salt
¼ cup heavy cream
¼ teaspoon pepper
¼ teaspoon ground nutmeg
2 teaspoons butter or margarine, softened

1. Cook broccoli in boiling salted water in a large kettle or Dutch oven until tender, about 15 minutes. Drain and let cool. Chop into small pieces; place, part at a time, in container of electric blender; puree.
2. Combine broccoli puree, eggs, salt, heavy cream, pepper and nutmeg in a large bowl. Butter a 1-quart ring mold with the softened butter. Spoon broccoli mixture into the mold and cover with foil.
3. Place the mold in a larger pan; pour in

boiling water to a 1-inch depth.

4. Bake in a moderate oven (350°) for 30 minutes or until custard is set. Unmold on-to a heated serving platter.

> Save the woody ends of broccoli, aspar-agus and mushroom stems to simmer in soups. One of the easiest ways to cook broccoli is in the bottom of a double boiler with the stalks covered with boil-ing salted water to within 1 inch of the flowers. Invert the double boiler insert over flowers and simmer 8 to 10 minutes, or until stalks are tender. The flowers steam and do not become over-cooked. Fill the broccoli ring with Car-rots in Dill Butter (see page 128).

SCALLOPED CORN AND PEPPERS

Bake at 350° for 30 minutes.
Makes 4 servings.

    1 medium-size onion, chopped (½ cup)
    1 small sweet green pepper, halved, seeded and chopped
    4 tablespoons butter or margarine
    2 cups cooked, unseasoned, fresh or frozen whole-kernel corn, well drained
    2 tablespoons flour
    1 cup milk
    1 egg, beaten until frothy
    ¾ cup soft bread crumbs (1½ slices)
    1 tablespoon melted butter or margarine

1. Sauté onion and green pepper in 2 ta-blespoons of the butter in a large heavy skillet over moderately high heat, 8 to 10 minutes, or until lightly browned; add corn.

2. Melt the 2 remaining tablespoons but-ter in a small saucepan. Blend in the flour. Stir in milk; heat, stirring, until thickened

and smooth. Turn heat to lowest point and let sauce mellow 3 to 4 minutes. Blend a little hot sauce into the beaten egg; stir back into the pan; then remove the pan from heat. Season sauce with salt, pepper and nutmeg; combine sauce with corn mix-ture.

3. Spoon into a well-buttered 1-quart cas-serole; toss bread crumbs with melted but-ter; place on top of corn mixture.

4. Bake, uncovered, in a moderate oven (350°) for about 30 minutes, or until bub-bly.

CORN ON THE COB WITH FLAVORED BUTTERS

1. Remove husks from corn by peeling back and breaking off the end of cob; re-move silk. Allow two medium-size ears per serving.

2. Fill a large kettle with water; cover; bring to boiling. Add corn, half at a time if the kettle is not large enough for all to cook at once. Boil 5 minutes, or just until tender. Remove corn to a napkin- or towel-lined serving platter, using tongs. Serve hot with seasoned butters.

3. Put second servings in boiling water and repeat as above.

DILL BUTTER: Soften ½ cup (1 stick) butter in a small bowl; stir in 1½ teaspoons freshly snipped dill or ½ teaspoon dillweed.

LEMON BUTTER: Soften ½ cup (1 stick) butter in a small bowl; stir in 2 teaspoons lemon juice.

CHIVE BUTTER: Soften ½ cup (1 stick) butter in a small bowl; stir in 2 teaspoons finely snipped chives.

GARLIC BUTTER: Soften ½ cup (1 stick) butter in a small bowl; stir in ¼ teaspoon garlic salt.

> To remove silk from a husked ear of corn, rub down with a damp paper towel.

CARROTS IN DILL BUTTER

The Scandinavian way with carrots.
Makes 4 servings.

    1 pound small carrots, pared and cut
        into 1-inch pieces
    ½ cup water
    2 tablespoons butter or margarine
    1 teaspoon sugar
    ½ teaspoon salt
    ½ teaspoon dillweed

1. Combine carrots, water, butter, sugar, salt and dillweed in a medium-size heavy saucepan; cover.
2. Bring to boiling; simmer 15 minutes, or until carrots are tender and the liquid has almost evaporated.

SAVORY BAKED HERBED EGGPLANT

Bake at 375° for 45 minutes.
Makes 4 servings.

    2 medium-size eggplants
        (1 pound each)
    1 tablespoon salt
    2 tablespoons packaged bread crumbs
    2 tablespoons chopped parsley
    1 teaspoon leaf oregano, crumbled
  1½ teaspoons leaf basil, crumbled
    2 cloves garlic, minced
    6 tablespoons olive or vegetable oil
    ½ teaspoon salt
    ⅛ teaspoon pepper
    2 tablespoons water
    1 medium-size ripe tomato, thinly sliced

1. Cut eggplants in half lengthwise. Cut deep, long slits in the surface of each half. Sprinkle with the 1 tablespoon salt and let drain, cut-side down, on paper toweling for 1 hour.
2. Combine bread crumbs, parsley, oregano, basil and garlic in a small bowl. Add 1 tablespoon of the oil, the ½ teaspoon salt

and pepper; mix thoroughly.
3. Wipe as much moisture as possible from eggplants with paper toweling. Divide bread-crumb mixture among the eggplant halves, pressing deep into the slits. Arrange eggplants in a baking dish that will just hold them.
4. Pour water and 4 tablespoons of the oil into the dish. Arrange tomato slices, slightly overlapping, lengthwise over eggplants. Drizzle with the remaining tablespoon oil.
5. Bake in a moderate oven (375°) for 45 minutes, basting several times with pan juices. Sprinkle with fresh basil, if you wish, and serve at room temperature.

> Eggplant is sprinkled with salt and allowed to stand a while to draw out any bitterness. It is important to remove the beads of liquid that collect on the surface of the eggplant with paper toweling, or the finished dish will be too salty.

MUSHROOMS STUFFED WITH GINGERED PUREE OF CARROTS

A pretty touch for a festive meal.
Bake at 350° for 10 minutes.
Makes 8 servings.

    8 large mushrooms
    ¼ cup (½ stick) butter or margarine
    1 tablespoon lemon juice
    1 pound carrots, pared and sliced
        ¼ inch thick
    2 tablespoons orange marmalade
    ¼ teaspoon ground ginger

1. Remove stems from mushrooms. (Reserve for another use.) Sauté mushroom caps in butter and lemon juice over moderately high heat until just tender, about 3 minutes.
2. Cook carrots in boiling salted water to cover in a large saucepan until tender, about 8 minutes. Drain; stir in marmalade

and ginger; puree in the container of an electric blender. Pipe puree through a pastry bag into mushroom caps; place on a cookie sheet.

3. Bake in a moderate oven (350°) for 10 minutes, or until heated through.

> **Most mushrooms need only be wiped with a damp paper towel to clean them. Do not peel or soak in water. For exceptionally dirty mushrooms, rinse quickly under running water and pat dry.**

BUTTER-BRAISED ONIONS
Makes 10 servings.

3 dozen small white onions
    (2½ pounds)
3 tablespoons butter or margarine
1 teaspoon sugar

1. Cook onions in boiling salted water to cover in a large saucepan, 15 minutes. Drain; peel onions when cool enough to handle.

2. Heat butter in a large saucepan just until it starts to brown. Add onions and sprinkle with sugar. Cook, stirring often, until golden and slightly glazed.

> **To peel onions without tears, pour boiling water over them in a bowl; let stand a few minutes; then plunge into cold water and proceed peeling—under water.**
>
> **To keep small white onions in shape when boiling, cut an X in the root end of the onion, instead of coring the root end. If the root end is cored out, the onion will fall apart when cooked.**

CREAMED ONIONS
Makes 8 servings.

40 small white onions
 6 tablespoons butter or margarine
 6 tablespoons flour
1½ teaspoons salt
¼ teaspoon white pepper
¼ teaspoon ground nutmeg
 3 cups milk
½ cup heavy cream

1. Cook onions, covered, in boiling salted water in a large saucepan until tender, about 15 minutes. Drain, reserving cooking liquid; peel onions when cool enough to handle.

2. Melt butter in a large saucepan. Stir in flour, salt, pepper and nutmeg; cook 2 minutes. Remove pan from the heat; stir in milk and heavy cream until smooth.

3. Bring to boiling; lower heat; simmer about 5 minutes, stirring constantly, until sauce is thick and smooth. Add onions; heat through. (If too thick, the sauce may be thinned with some of the reserved cooking liquid.)

> **Onions come in many shapes, flavors and colors to enhance countless savory dishes. Popular among the dry mild, sweet onions are the Bermudas, with a thick flat shape; red, white or tan skin; 1½-2 inches in diameter; with a sweet, mild juicy flavor. Spanish onions are much bigger: 3 inches and more in diameter; globelike with yellow or tan skin. Both are great for sandwiches and topping burgers. Small white onions have silver skins and are the preferred variety for creamed onions and adding to braised dishes. Dry strong onions include the familiar yellow onion that is chopped and sautéed to be added to every kind of savory mixture from artichoke stuffing to zucchini sauté.**

SNOW PEAS AND CUCUMBER MEDLEY
Makes 4 to 6 servings.

½ pound snow peas
1 cucumber
2 tablespoons peanut oil
1 small onion, finely chopped (¼ cup)
¼ teaspoon crushed red pepper flakes
1 tablespoon vinegar
½ teaspoon sugar
1 teaspoon salt
⅛ teaspoon ground ginger

1. Snip off tips and remove strings from snow peas; if peas are large, cut each in half diagonally.
2. Pare cucumber; cut in half lengthwise; scoop out and discard seeds. Cut crosswise into ¼-inch-thick slices.
3. Heat oil in a large skillet or wok. Add onion; stir-fry 1 minute; stir in crushed red pepper; cook 5 seconds. Add cucumber slices; stir-fry 1 minute. Stir in snow peas; cook, stirring and tossing, 2 minutes, or just until crisply tender. Stir in vinegar, sugar, salt and ginger; serve at once.

STIR-FRIED PEAS PLUS
Tiny white onions, bacon and green pepper add great flavor to the peas.
Makes 4 servings.

2 slices bacon
18 tiny white onions (½ pound), peeled*
2 cups shelled green peas (2 pounds in shell)
1 small sweet green pepper, halved, seeded and cut into strips
1 envelope or teaspoon instant chicken broth
1 teaspoon flour
½ cup water
2 tablespoons chopped parsley
1 tablespoon butter or margarine

1. Cook bacon in a large skillet until crisp; drain on paper toweling; crumble. Add on-ions to fat in the skillet; sauté over medium heat, stirring often, 10 minutes.
2. Add peas to the skillet; stir-fry 5 minutes, or until bright green. Add green pepper.
3. Blend chicken broth, flour and water in a small bowl until smooth. Stir into the skillet; add 1 tablespoon of the parsley. Cover and cook 3 minutes longer. Stir in the remaining parsley and butter until melted. Spoon into a heated serving dish; sprinkle bacon over top.

If tiny white onions are not available use larger ones, halved or quartered (about ½ to ¾ pound.)

GREEN PEAS WITH A FRENCH TOUCH
Makes 4 servings.

6 to 7 Boston lettuce leaves
2 cups shelled green peas (2 pounds in the shell)
¼ cup water
4 tablespoons butter or margarine
1 teaspoon sugar
½ teaspoon salt
⅛ teaspoon pepper
4 pea pods

1. Line a medium-size saucepan with 3 or 4 of the lettuce leaves. Add peas, water, butter, sugar, salt and pepper. Cover peas with another 2 or 3 lettuce leaves; top with pea pods. Cover the saucepan.
2. Cook over medium heat 12 minutes, or until peas are tender.

Home-gardeners rejoice in the superb qualities of the newest member of the pea family, the Sugar Snap. This edible podded pea can be eaten raw or cooked. It can be used up to and including full-podded stage.

Top, clockwise: Green Beans Indian-Style (page 126), Stir-Fried Peas Plus (page 130), Super-Crisp Ratatouille (page 134), Snow peas and Cucumber Medley (page 130), Stir-Fried Asparagus Mimosa (page 126)

QUICK POTATOES AND MUSHROOMS IN SOUR CREAM

A nice complement to broiled meats, poultry or fish.

Makes 4 servings.

3 tablespoons butter or margarine
1 small onion, minced (¼ cup)
½ pound mushrooms, cut into quarters, or eighths, if large
1 pound potatoes (3 medium), cooked, peeled and cut into ¼-inch-thick slices
1 teaspoon salt
Dash pepper
Dash liquid red-pepper seasoning
½ cup dairy sour cream
1 tablespoon minced fresh dill
OR: 1 teaspoon dried dillweed

1. Melt butter in a large skillet. Add onion and mushrooms; sauté until tender. Add potatoes, salt, pepper and red-pepper seasoning. Cook over medium heat, stirring carefully with a pancake turner, about 5 minutes, or until potatoes are heated.
2. Stir in sour cream. Sprinkle with dill; serve immediately.

POTATOES CACCIATORE

Tomato and herbs cooked briefly in this Italian-style dish add a delicious dash of flavor.

Makes 6 servings.

¼ cup olive oil
2 cloves garlic, minced
2 pounds potatoes (6 medium), cooked, peeled and cut into 1-inch chunks
⅔ cup dry white wine
1 large ripe tomato, peeled and coarsely chopped (1 cup)
2 tablespoons chopped fresh basil
OR: 2 teaspoons dried leaf basil, crumbled
2 tablespoons minced parsley

1 teaspoon salt
Dash pepper
Dash liquid red-pepper seasoning

1. Heat oil and garlic in a large skillet until garlic browns; discard garlic. Add potatoes; cook over medium heat, stirring occasionally with a pancake turner, until potatoes are golden brown on all sides.
2. Add wine; continue to cook until it evaporates. Add tomato, basil, parsley, salt, pepper and red-pepper seasoning. Stir gently. Continue to cook until mixture is thoroughly heated and potatoes have absorbed almost all the liquid.

> If potatoes are boiled 5 minutes, then put into a hot oven, they'll bake in about half the time. As soon as baked potatoes are tender, squeeze them gently, then split them down the center.

POTATO GOULASH

Dill-flavored potatoes in a paprika-sour-cream sauce.

Makes 6 servings.

3 tablespoons butter or margarine
1 medium-size onion, thinly sliced
2 pounds potatoes (6 medium), pared and thinly sliced
¾ cup beef broth or water
1½ teaspoons salt
Dash pepper
2 tablespoons paprika
2 teaspoons dill seed
2 bay leaves
2 tablespoons cider vinegar
½ cup dairy sour cream, at room temperature
1 tablespoon snipped fresh dill
OR: 1 teaspoon dried dillweed

1. Melt butter in a large saucepan. Add onion; cook, stirring constantly, until soft and golden. Add potatoes, broth, salt, pepper, paprika, dill seed and bay leaves.

2. Heat to boiling; lower heat; cover; simmer 10 minutes, or until potatoes are tender, stirring carefully with a pancake turner. If necessary, add a little more broth, 1 tablespoon at a time, to prevent scorching. The dish should not be soupy.

3. Remove bay leaves; stir in vinegar and cook 2 minutes more. Remove from heat; gently stir in sour cream. Sprinkle with dill; serve immediately.

SWEET POTATOES GLAZED WITH MAPLE SYRUP

Bake at 350° for 35 minutes.
Makes 10 servings.

    3 pounds sweet potatoes or yams
    ¼ cup (½ stick) butter or margarine
    ½ to ⅔ cup maple syrup or maple-
         flavored syrup
    1 tablespoon shredded orange rind
    ⅓ cup orange juice
    ½ teaspoon salt

1. Scrub potatoes; cook in boiling salted water to cover in a large saucepan, 35 minutes, or until just tender. Drain; cool; peel. If large, slice crosswise into ¼-inch-thick slices; if small, leave whole or cut in half.

2. Arrange potatoes in a shallow baking dish. Heat butter, syrup, orange rind and juice and salt to boiling in a small saucepan. Boil, 2 minutes; pour over potatoes.

3. Bake in a moderate oven (350°) 35 minutes, basting several times, until well glazed and heated through.

> **Sweet potatoes are vines of the morning glory family. The tubers grow underground, just like yams. However, sweet potatoes are smaller and have a mealier, drier, yellow flesh compared with the sweet, moist, yellow to orange flesh of bigger, plumper yams. They can be used interchangeably in most recipes.**

> **Know your potatoes for best results:**
>
> **ROUND WHITE: Waxy, more moisture, less starch; good for boiling, pan frying, pan roasting, salads.**
> **ROUND RED: Same as above.**
> **RUSSET or IDAHO: More starch, less moisture, giving a dry, fluffy, mealiness; good for baking and French Fries.**
> **LONG WHITE: Mostly from California; good for mashed, pan-fried, pan-roasted or boiled.**

CHEESE-STUFFED POTATOES

Bake at 350° for 20 minutes.
Makes 4 servings.

    8 red new potatoes (2 inches
         in diameter)
    ½ teaspoon salt
       Water
    1½ tablespoons butter or margarine
    ⅓ cup shredded Cheddar cheese
    1 egg
    ⅛ teaspoon salt
    ⅛ teaspoon pepper

1. Scrub potatoes and place in a large saucepan. Add the ½ teaspoon salt and water to cover; simmer 15 minutes, or until just tender. Drain well and let stand until cool enough to handle.

2. Cut potatoes in half. Scoop out centers, using a melon-ball scoop or a small spoon, leaving ¼- to ⅜-inch shell. Mash potato centers with butter until smooth; stir in cheese, egg, the ⅛ teaspoon salt and pepper. Spoon or pipe mashed potato filling back into potato shells, mounding high; place on a cookie sheet.

3. Bake in a moderate oven (350°) for 20 minutes, or until lightly browned.

SUPER CRISP RATATOUILLE

Here's our version of the popular French eggplant-based vegetable combination.
Makes 6 servings.

    1 sweet green pepper
    1 cucumber
    ¼ pound mushrooms
    1 small eggplant (½ pound)
    5 tablespoons olive or vegetable oil
    1 large onion, sliced
    1 clove garlic, minced
  1½ teaspoons salt
    ¼ teaspoon pepper
    1 teaspoon leaf basil, crumbled
    1 tablespoon chopped parsley
    ½ pint cherry tomatoes, halved

1. Wash pepper; halve, seed and cut into 1-inch dice. Pare cucumber; halve lengthwise; scoop out and discard seeds. Slice cucumber ¼ to ½ inch thick. Wipe mushrooms with a damp cloth; cut into quarters through the stems. Wash eggplant (do not peel); cut into about ½-inch dice.
2. Heat 2 tablespoons of the oil in a large skillet or wok. Add pepper, cucumber, mushrooms, onion and garlic; stir-fry over high heat 4 to 5 minutes. Remove with a slotted spoon to a heated bowl.
3. Heat the remaining oil in the skillet. Add eggplant; stir and toss 3 to 4 minutes, or just until tender.
4. Return vegetables to the skillet; sprinkle with salt, pepper, basil and parsley. Add tomatoes; stir gently. Cover; simmer 3 minutes, or until heated through.

SPINACH WITH MUSHROOMS

Makes 4 servings.

    1 pound spinach
    6 medium-size mushrooms
    3 tablespoons vegetable oil
    1 small onion, finely chopped (¼ cup)
    1 clove garlic, minced
    1 tablespoon dry sherry or lemon juice
    1 teaspoon salt
    1 teaspoon sugar
      Dash ground nutmeg

1. Remove stems and any blemished leaves from spinach; wash well in several changes of water; drain. Wipe mushrooms with a damp cloth; trim stem ends; cut through stems and caps into thin slices.
2. Heat oil in a large skillet or wok; add onion, garlic and mushrooms; stir-fry 3 minutes over medium-high heat. Add spinach; cook, turning and stirring gently, 2 to 3 minutes, or until spinach is wilted. Stir in sherry, salt, sugar and nutmeg; cook 30 seconds. Serve immediately.

WILTED SPINACH AND LETTUCE

Country-style wilted lettuce has always been a popular vegetable. We've embellished the original with spinach and a touch of mint.
Makes 6 servings.

    ¾ pound spinach
    1 head Boston lettuce
    4 slices bacon
    1 medium-size onion, sliced
    1 tablespoon sugar
    ½ teaspoon salt
    ⅛ teaspoon pepper
    ⅓ cup tarragon vinegar
    1 tablespoon chopped mint
    1 hard-cooked egg, chopped

1. Wash spinach and lettuce; dry on paper toweling; tear larger leaves into bite-size pieces (about 4 cups each).
2. Sauté bacon in a large skillet or Dutch oven until crisp; drain on paper toweling; Crumble. Sauté onion in bacon fat remaining in skillet until tender, about 3 minutes. Add sugar, salt, pepper, vinegar and mint; bring to boiling. Add spinach and lettuce; toss with the hot dressing just until wilted. Turn into a heated serving dish. Sprinkle bacon over the top; sprinkle with chopped hard-cooked egg.

Stuffed Vegetables (page 137)

GINGERED BUTTERNUT SQUASH

For a festive crowd.

Makes 8 servings.

2 butternut squash (about 4 pounds)
4 tablespoons butter or margarine
1 tablespoon maple syrup
2 tablespoons finely chopped
    crystallized ginger
1 teaspoon salt
⅛ teaspoon pepper
¼ teaspoon ground nutmeg
½ cup heavy cream

1. Split squash in half; scoop out seeds and membranes; pare; cut into chunks. Cook in boiling salted water in a kettle 30 minutes, or until tender; drain.

2. Return squash to low heat for a few minutes, shaking occasionally to dry. Add butter, syrup, ginger, salt, pepper and nutmeg. Beat with an electric mixer until smooth. Gradually beat in heavy cream.

3. Spoon into a heated serving dish; keep hot. Garnish with additional chopped crystallized ginger, if you wish.

> **WINTER SQUASH:** Butternut, acorn, hubbard and turban. 1 pound makes 2 servings. Can be baked, boiled or steamed.
> **SUMMER SQUASH:** Yellow crookneck, summer yellow, zucchini, pattypan and spaghetti squash. 1 pound makes 2 to 3 servings. Can be steamed, sautéed, boiled and baked.

ACORN SQUASH WITH BROCCOLI PUREE

A colorful touch for any meal.

Bake at 375° for 55 minutes.

Makes 8 servings.

2 large acorn squash (about 4 pounds)
8 tablespoons (1 stick) butter
    or margarine
1 teaspoon salt
½ teaspoon pepper
1 bunch broccoli (about 1 pound)
    Boiling water

1. Cut each squash into quarters; scoop out seeds. Place each piece hollow-side up on a square of aluminum foil large enough to enclose it. Dot squash with 4 tablespoons of the butter. Sprinkle with half of the salt and half of the pepper. Fold foil tightly around squash. Place on a cookie sheet.

2. Bake in a moderate oven (375°) for 45 minutes, or until squash is tender.

3. Trim broccoli of stem ends and leaves. Wash and separate into stalks and pieces of equal size. Cover with water; add the remaining salt and pepper. Simmer, covered, 15 minutes, or until tender. Drain thoroughly; return to pan. Add the 4 remaining tablespoons butter and shake over very low heat just until butter melts. Turn into the container of an electric blender; puree.

4. Pipe puree through a pastry bag or spoon onto the baked squash. Return to the oven for 10 minutes, or until thoroughly heated.

DEVILED CHERRY TOMATOES

Makes 4 servings.

¼ cup (½ stick) butter or margarine
3 tablespoons lemon juice
1 tablespoon prepared mustard
1 tablespoon light brown sugar
1 pint cherry tomatoes,
    stemmed and halved
2 tablespoons sliced green onions

1. Melt butter in a medium-size skillet. Stir in lemon juice, mustard and brown sugar until mixture is smooth and comes to boiling. Add cherry tomatoes and heat thoroughly.

2. Remove from heat; toss with green onions. Spoon into a heated serving dish.

ZUCCHINI WITH A DIFFERENCE

Makes 4 servings.

    4 medium-size zucchini
    1 teaspoon salt
    4 tablespoons butter or margarine
    ¼ cup thinly sliced green onions
    ½ cup dairy sour cream
    1 tablespoon chopped fresh basil

1. Wash and trim zucchini. Grate on the coarsest side of grater; sprinkle with salt. Let stand 5 minutes. Drain in a sieve, pressing out as much liquid as possible.
2. Heat butter in a skillet. Add green onions; cook and stir 1 minute; add zucchini. Cook and stir until just tender, about 5 minutes. Quickly stir in sour cream and basil; serve immediately.

ZUCCHINI AND WALNUTS

Makes 6 servings.

    3 tablespoons butter or margarine
    ½ cup coarsely chopped walnuts
    1½ pounds zucchini
    ½ teaspoon salt
      Pepper

1. Heat 1 tablespoon of the butter in a large skillet; stir and toss walnuts until lightly browned (about 5-10 minutes). Remove from skillet.
2. Wash and trim ends from zucchini. Slice ½-inch thick. Heat the remaining 2 tablespoons butter in the skillet; sauté zucchini slices until they begin to soften.
3. Combine walnuts and zucchini in a heated serving dish; add salt and pepper; toss and serve.

ZUCCHINI AU GRATIN

Makes 4 servings.

    3 medium-size zucchini, sliced
    1 small onion, sliced
    ⅓ cup water
    ½ teaspoon salt
    1 slice bread, cut into ¼-inch cubes
    3 tablespoons butter or margarine
    ½ cup shredded Cheddar cheese
      (2 ounces)

1. Combine zucchini, onion, water and salt in a large saucepan; bring to boiling; lower heat; simmer until tender, about 10 minutes. Drain; keep warm.
2. Sauté bread cubes in butter in a small skillet until golden brown. Sprinkle bread cubes and cheese over zucchini.

STUFFED VEGETABLES

Bake at 350° for 30 minutes.
Makes 6 servings.

    6 medium-size zucchini, halved
      lengthwise
      OR: 6 medium-size ripe tomatoes
      OR: 1 large eggplant (2½ to 3 pounds),
      scooped out and drained
    ½ pound hot Italian sausage
    1 small onion, chopped (¼ cup)
    1 clove garlic, crushed
    ⅓ cup packaged Italian-flavored bread crumbs
    ¼ cup grated Parmesan cheese
    1 cup shredded mozzarella cheese,
      (4 ounces)

1. Cook zucchini in boiling salted water in a large skillet 10 minutes. Drain, scoop out insides, leaving a ¼-inch shell. Mash insides; drain well. Put shells in a shallow baking dish.
2. Remove casings from sausage; break up meat. Cook sausage in same skillet 5 minutes. Add onion and garlic; sauté until tender, 3 minutes. Stir in mashed zucchini and bread crumbs. Spoon mixture into shells; sprinkle with cheese.
3. Bake in a moderate oven (350°) 30 minutes, or until piping-hot.

Oven Beef Burgundy

Meats: Beef, Pork, Lamb, Veal

Wonderful ways to prepare different cuts
for family meals and entertaining.

OVEN BEEF BURGUNDY
An adaptation of the French classic.
Bake at 350° for 2 hours.
Makes 6 servings.

    2 pounds top round, cut in 1-inch
       cubes
  ¼ cup flour
    1 teaspoon salt
  ¼ teaspoon pepper
    2 to 4 tablespoons butter or margarine
    2 tablespoons brandy
  12 to 18 small white onions, peeled
  ½ pound medium-size mushrooms,
       halved
    1 clove garlic, minced
    2 tablespoons chopped parsley
  ¼ teaspoon leaf thyme, crumbled
    1 can condensed beef broth
    1 cup dry red wine
    1 bay leaf

1. Shake meat with flour, salt and pepper
in a plastic bag to coat well; reserve any
remaining flour mixture.
2. Brown beef, part at a time, in hot butter
in a large skillet or Dutch oven. Lift out beef
as it browns and transfer it to a 2½- to
3-quart baking dish. Heat brandy in a small
saucepan; ignite and pour over beef. Add
onions and mushrooms. Sprinkle with any
reserved flour mixture.
3. Stir garlic, parsley and thyme into fat
remaining in skillet; cook 1 minute. Add
beef broth and wine; heat, stirring to
loosen browned bits, until mixture comes
to boiling. Pour over beef and vegetables;

add bay leaf. Cover.
4. Bake in a moderate oven (350°) for 2
hours, or until meat is tender. Let stand 10
minutes before serving.

Spirits or liqueurs that are to be used for
flaming should be warmed gently before
they are poured over the ingredients or
finished dish. Ignite with a long kitchen
match, and stand back. Wait until the
flames die down before proceeding.

Braising is a moist-heat cooking method
recommended for less tender cuts of
meat. The meat may be dipped in seasoned flour, if desired, then browned
slowly in a small amount of fat in a heavy
kettle or skillet. The fat can be poured off
before adding the liquid, such as water,
tomato juice or chicken or beef broth;
then the meat is covered and cooked
slowly on the top of the stove or in a
moderate oven (350°). Pot roasting is a
popular term applied to braising large
cuts. When enough liquid is added to
cover the meat, it is called stewing.
Whether braising or stewing, the meat is
cooked until it is fork-tender. Over-
cooking produces greater shrinkage and
decreased tenderness and juiciness. It
also results in less meat and, therefore, a
higher cost per serving.

VINTNER'S POT ROAST

An excellent choice for preparing the day before, then reheating and serving with tender vegetables.

Braise at 325° for 3½ hours.
Makes 12 servings.

- 1 boneless rolled rump roast (about 5 pounds)
- 1 teaspoon leaf thyme, crumbled
- 2 cloves garlic, minced
- ½ teaspoon pepper
- 1 bay leaf
- 3 whole cloves
- 3 cups dry red wine
- ⅓ cup brandy
- 3 tablespoons olive or vegetable oil
- 4 tablespoons flour
- 1 teaspoon salt
- 2 tablespoons butter or margarine
- 1 large onion, chopped (1 cup)
- ½ cup chopped carrot
- 1 stalk celery, chopped
- 1 can condensed beef broth

1. Place meat in a large glass or other non-metal bowl; add thyme, garlic, pepper, bay leaf, cloves, wine, brandy and oil. Cover and let stand to marinate 4 hours at room temperature or overnight in the refrigerator, turning meat several times.

2. When ready to cook meat, remove from marinade; pat dry with paper toweling. Rub flour and salt over surface of meat. Melt butter in a heavy kettle or Dutch oven; brown meat on all sides.

3. While meat is browning, heat marinade in a large saucepan; boil rapidly 5 minutes to reduce to 2½ cups.

4. Spoon onion, carrot and celery around meat. Cook vegetables 5 minutes, stirring occasionally. Add boiling marinade and beef broth. Cover.

5. Braise in a slow oven (325°), turning meat several times, 3½ hours, or until meat is tender. Remove meat to a heated platter. Remove strings. Keep hot.

6. Strain cooking liquid into a deep bowl, pressing all juices out of the vegetables; discard vegetables. Skim fat from liquid; return liquid to Dutch oven; boil rapidly to reduce to about 3½ cups.

7. Carve meat into ¼-inch slices. Arrange slices overlapping on a heated serving platter. Serve with the reduced cooking liquid, buttered carrots, whole white onions or any preferred vegetables, if you wish.

ROLLED STUFFED FLANK STEAK

Makes 6 servings.

- 1 medium-size onion, chopped (½ cup)
- ⅓ cup diced sweet red or green pepper
- ⅓ cup chopped celery, including some leaves
- 6 tablespoons butter or margarine
- 1 package (8 ounces) cornbread stuffing mix
- 1 egg, slightly beaten
- 1 to 2 canned jalapeño peppers, rinsed, seeded and chopped
- ½ teaspoon leaf oregano, crumbled
- ½ cup hot water
- 1 large flank steak (2 to 2½ pounds), well trimmed and butterflied
- 1 can (13¾ ounces) beef broth
- 2 tablespoons flour

1. Sauté onion, pepper and celery in 4 tablespoons of the butter in a large saucepan until just tender; remove from heat. Add cornbread stuffing mix, egg, jalapeño pepper, oregano and water; mix well.

2. Spread flank steak flat on a board; pound lightly with a meat mallet or the edge of a plate. Spead stuffing over steak; roll up jelly-roll style, tucking ends in. Secure with skewers or tie with string.

3. Heat the remaining butter in a skillet or Dutch oven. Brown rolled steak slowly and evenly all over. Pour in beef broth; bring to boiling; lower heat; cover.

4. Simmer, turning meat once or twice, for 1 hour, or until tender. Remove meat to a heated serving platter; keep warm while making gravy.

5. Make a smooth paste with the flour and about 3 tablespoons cold water; add to juices in pan; cook, stirring constantly, until gravy thickens and bubbles 3 minutes.

6. Carve meat into slices; spoon gravy over.

BARBECUED STEAK

Makes 8 servings.

  1 top sirloin steak, cut 2 inches thick
     (about 2½ pounds)
    OR: 1 flank steak (about 2 pounds)
 ¾ cup catsup
 ¾ cup chili sauce
1½ tablespoons soy sauce
  3 tablespoons honey
  3 tablespoons Hoisin sauce (*optional*)
  3 tablespoons minced green onions
  3 cloves garlic, minced
 ½ teaspoon salt
 ⅛ teaspoon pepper

1. Put steak in a plastic food bag. (If using flank steak, score top diagonally on both sides.)

2. Combine catsup, chili sauce, soy sauce, honey, Hoisin sauce, green onions, garlic, salt and pepper in a small bowl; mix well.

Pour mixture into bag with steak. Fasten bag securely with wire tape. Place bag in a shallow pan. Let marinate in refrigerator 24 hours, turning occasionally.

3. Lift steak out of marinade; pat with paper toweling. Broil, 4 inches from heat, brushing several times with marinade, about 8 minutes on each side for sirloin, or 5 minutes on each side for flank steak. If grilling outdoors, grill 6 inches from grayed coals, about the same time. Serve with fresh corn on the cob and grilled tomatoes; garnish with whole green onions, if you wish.

Meat tenderizing can be done in several ways; pounding with a mallet or rolling pin, needling by a commercial machine, or sprinkling with a commercial tenderizer, containing naturally-occurring enzymes on a cut of meat, or in a marinade. A marinade containing an acid (such as wine, lemon juice or tomato, for example) adds flavor and has a slight tenderizing effect. The use of tenderizers by the meat industry increases tenderness but does not change the grade of beef. Papain, the enzyme used in most commercial tenderizers, is extracted from papayas.

Barbecued Steak

RIB ROAST OF BEEF

Allow 2 to 2½ servings per pound. Place beef, fat side up, in a shallow roasting pan. If using meat thermometer, insert so bulb is not touching bone or resting in fat. It is not necessary to add water or to baste. Roast in a slow oven (325°) for 23 minutes a pound for rare (140°) on meat thermometer, 27 minutes for medium (160°) or 32 minutes for well done (170°). Meat should be allowed to rest a short time for easier carving. Since it will continue to cook when removed from oven, it should be removed when thermometer registers about 10° below selected temperature. Carve in slices across the grain, using tip of knife to loosen slices as you carve. Serve with Whipped Horseradish Cream and Potato Nests filled with lima beans (*recipes follow*).

WHIPPED HORSERADISH CREAM: Combine 1 cup heavy cream, 1 tablespoon prepared horseradish, ¼ teaspoon Worcestershire sauce and a dash of liquid red-pepper seasoning in a small bowl. Beat until soft peaks form. Refrigerate. Makes about 2 cups.

POTATO NESTS: For each nest, pare and shred 2 medium-size baking potatoes into cold water. Pat dry on paper toweling. Fill a large saucepan ⅔ full with vegetable oil; heat to 400° on a deep-fat frying thermometer. Dip bottom of a wire potato basket in hot oil. Press about 1½ cups shredded potatoes into basket; leaving center open. Dip basket top in oil; press halves together; secure with clip. Lower slowly into oil; fry 4 to 5 minutes, or until golden brown. Remove nest from basket to paper toweling; keep warm. Fill with buttered lima beans. Can be reheated in a moderate oven (375°).

SAUERBRATEN

Plan this old-time favorite days ahead, as it should season in a spicy marinade a few days before cooking.
Braise at 350° for 3 to 3½ hours.
Makes 6 to 8 servings.

    1 boneless rump roast (about 4 pounds)
    4 cups water

			APPROXIMATE	
CUT	**APPROXIMATE WEIGHT**	**OVEN TEMPERATURE**	**ROASTING TIME**	**INTERNAL TEMPERATURE**
Rib roast: Time based	4 lbs.	325°F	1¾ hours	140°F (rare)
on short cut, 6 inches		325°F	2¼ hours	160°F (medium)
from tip of the rib to the		325°F	3 hours	170°F (well done)
chine bone (back bone).				
If cut longer than 6	6 lbs.	325°F	3¼ hours	140°F (rare)
inches, roast will take		325°F	3¾ hours	160°F (medium)
less time per pound.		325°F	4¼ hours	170°F (well done)
Beef rib eye roast	4 to 6 lbs.	350°F	1¼ to 2 hours	140°F (rare)
		350°F	1½ to 2¼ hours	160°F (medium)
		350°F	2¼ to 2½ hours	170°F (well done)
Tenderloin	4 to 6 lbs.	425°F	¼ to 1 hour	140°F (rare)

ROASTING CHART/BEEF

2 cups red wine vinegar
2 tablespoons sugar
1 medium-size onion, finely chopped
    (½ cup)
¾ cup finely chopped celery
¼ teaspoon salt
  Pinch pepper
1 teaspoon mixed pickling spices
2 tablespoons vegetable shortening
24 crushed gingersnaps (1½ cups
    crumbs)

1. Trim all but a thin layer of fat from meat. Place in a large glass or other nonmetal bowl.
2. Add water, vinegar, sugar, onion, celery, salt, pepper and pickling spices to the bowl, stirring to mix. Cover with plastic wrap; refrigerate 4 or 5 days, turning meat each day.
3. Remove meat from marinade; reserve marinade; pat meat dry with paper toweling. Heat shortening in a kettle or Dutch oven. Brown meat on all sides, about 15 minutes. Drain off fat from kettle. Pour marinade over meat.
4. Braise, uncovered, in a moderate oven (350°) for 30 minutes. Cover; braise 2½ to 3 hours longer, or until meat is tender. Remove meat to heated platter; keep warm.
5. Strain marinade; remove fat and return marinade to pan. Stir in gingersnap crumbs. Heat until thickened; strain again. Slice meat and serve with gravy. Nice with potato pancakes and red cabbage.

In comparing prices of different cuts of meat, be sure to calculate the price per serving. You will need to know that:
1 pound of bony meat (spare ribs, short ribs) equals 1 serving;
1 pound small-bone meat (sirloin steak, chuck steak) equals 2 servings;
1 pound boneless meat equals 3 to 4 servings.

Low to moderate temperatures are best for cooking meat, whatever the cooking method. For example, a 325°F temperature for oven roasting, and a simmering (not boiling) temperature when cooking meat in moisture are best. Meat is more uniformly cooked and tender when cooked slowly.

SKILLET SWISS STEAK
Makes 4 servings.

3 stalks celery, sliced (2 cups)
1 large onion, sliced
2 tablespoons vegetable oil
¼ cup flour
1½ teaspoons salt
1 round steak, cut 2-inches thick
    (about 2 pounds)
2 cups hot water
1 envelope or teaspoon instant
    beef broth
1 teaspoon dry mustard
¼ cup chili sauce
¼ teaspoon pepper
3 medium-size potatoes, pared and
    quartered
3 carrots, quartered
2 tablespoons chopped parsley

1. Sauté celery and onion in 1 tablespoon of the oil in a large skillet until tender; remove; reserve.
2. Pound mixture of flour and 1 teaspoon of the salt into both sides of the meat. Brown meat on both sides in remaining 1 tablespoon oil in the skillet.
3. Stir 1 cup of the hot water into broth and mustard in a 2-cup measure. Add to skillet with chili sauce, pepper, reserved celery and onion; cover.
4. Simmer 1 hour and 15 minutes. Stir in remaining 1 cup water to thin gravy. Add potatoes and carrots; sprinkle with the remaining ½ teaspoon salt.
5. Continue cooking, covered, 30 minutes, or until meat is tender.

CHICKEN-FRIED STEAK WITH PAN GRAVY

Sometimes called "country-fried" but always called good eating.

Makes 4 servings.

    1 round steak, cut ½ inch thick (about 1¾ pounds)
    2 eggs
    2 tablespoons water
    ⅓ cup flour
    ⅓ cup cornmeal
    1 teaspoon salt
    ½ teaspoon pepper
    1 cup flour
    4 to 6 tablespoons vegetable oil
       Pan Gravy (recipe follows)

1. Pound steak to ¼-inch thickness, or ask butcher to tenderize; cut into 4 pieces.

2. Beat eggs and water together in a pie plate. Mix the ½ cup flour, cornmeal, salt and pepper on a piece of wax paper. Put the 1 cup flour on another piece of wax paper. Dip steaks in flour, then in egg mixture, then in cornmeal mixture.

3. Brown meat, 2 pieces at a time, in hot oil on both sides in a large heavy skillet. Return all meat to skillet; lower heat; cover. Cook 10 minutes, or until tender. Remove steaks to heated platter. Pour off all but 3 tablespoons of the pan fat.

PAN GRAVY

    3 tablespoons pan fat
    2 tablespoons flour
    ½ teaspoon salt
    ⅛ teaspoon pepper
    1½ cups milk (about)

Blend flour, salt and pepper into fat; stir in milk. Continue cooking and stirring until gravy thickens and bubbles 1 minute. If gravy is too thick, add more milk.

> **Browning meat in oil or melted fat develops flavor, seals in juices and improves the appearance of the finished dish.**

> A primal, or wholesale, cut of beef is a whole section, such as the whole chuck or shoulder, rib, whole loin or whole round. These are divided into smaller sections by cutting out whole muscles, called subprimals. Top round, whole tenderloin and rib eye are examples that can be found in supermarket meat cases. There is usually substantial savings in buying subprimal cuts and cutting them at home into roasts, steaks, stew meat and meat for grinding. Dark surface color on vacuum-packed subprimal cuts is due to elimination of air from the package. When the wrapper is removed and the beef is cut, it will turn bright red.

BEEF STROGANOFF

The celebrated classic of Continental cuisine, rich with sour cream.

Makes 4 servings.

      1 tablespoon flour
      ½ teaspoon salt
      1 sirloin steak, cut ½ inch thick (about 1 pound)
      4 tablespoons butter or margarine
      ½ cup thinly sliced mushrooms (¼ pound)
      1 medium-size onion, chopped (½ cup)
      1 small clove garlic, minced
      3 tablespoons flour
      1 tablespoon tomato paste
    1½ cup condensed beef broth
      1 cup dairy sour cream
      2 tablespoons dry sherry

1. Cut meat into ¼-inch-thick strips.

2. Combine the 1 tablespoon flour and salt in a paper or plastic bag; shake meat in mixture until coated. Heat 2 tablespoons of the butter in a large skillet. Brown meat on both sides. Add mushrooms, onion and garlic; cook about 3 minutes, or until onion is barely tender. Remove meat and mushrooms from the skillet.

3. Add the remaining 2 tablespoons butter to skillet; blend in the 3 tablespoons flour; cook 1 minute. Stir in tomato paste; stir in broth slowly. Cook, stirring constantly, until mixture thickens and bubbles. Return meat and mushrooms to skillet. Stir in sour cream and sherry; heat but do not boil, or sour cream will curdle. Serve with rice or noodles.

NEW ENGLAND BOILED DINNER

Makes 10 servings.

    1 corned beef brisket (about 4 pounds)
    3 large yellow turnips, pared and cut
        into ½-inch slices
    1 pound carrots, halved
    6 medium-size potatoes, pared and
        halved
    1 bunch beets
    2 medium-size heads of cabbage, each
        cut into 6 wedges
    ¼ cup (½ stick) butter, melted
        Chopped parsley, horseradish sauce
        and mustard

1. Simmer corned beef in water to cover in a large kettle for 2 hours. Add the turnips; cook 30 minutes. Add the carrots and potatoes; cook 30 minutes longer, or until meat and vegetables are tender.
2. About 1 hour before meat is tender, cook beets in water to cover in a large saucepan until tender; skin; keep warm.
3. Start cooking cabbage in a large kettle, about 30 minutes before meat is tender.
4. Slice meat; arrange on a large warm platter. Spoon hot vegetables around meat; pour melted butter over vegetables; sprinkle with parsley. Serve with horseradish sauce and mustard.

> **Plan on cooking a larger piece of corned beef brisket than you need for the Boiled New England Dinner. Leftovers make terrific corned beef hash or Reuben Sandwiches (page 48).**

TEXAS CHILI BEEF STEW

Chili adds its own sweet spiciness to this rib-sticking stew with beef and beans.

Makes 8 servings.

    4 pounds beef short ribs
    1 large onion, chopped (1 cup)
    1 sweet green pepper, halved, seeded
        and diced
    2 cloves garlic, minced
    2 tablespoons chili powder
    1 can (1 pound) tomatoes
    1 can (4 ounces) green chilies, drained
        and chopped
    1 envelope or teaspoon instant beef
        broth
    1 cup boiling water
    1 teaspoon salt
    2 tablespoons flour
    ¼ cup water
    2 cans (1 pound each) kidney beans,
        drained
    1 can (1 pound) whole-kernel corn,
        drained

1. Heat a heavy kettle or Dutch oven; rub fat edges of short ribs over bottom until about 2 tablespoons of the fat is melted. Brown short ribs well on all sides; remove. Drain off fat into a cup. Return 1 tablespoon fat to kettle.
2. Sauté onion, green pepper and garlic in fat in kettle. Stir in chili powder; cook, stirring constantly, about 2 minutes. Add tomatoes and green chilies. Dissolve instant beef broth in boiling water; stir into tomato mixture. Return ribs to pan. Bring to boiling; lower heat; cover. Simmer 2 hours, or until meat is very tender and falls away from the bones. Remove any loose bones.
3. Remove meat to a heated serving bowl; keep warm. Carefully remove remaining bones and skim fat from the sauce in the pan. Blend the flour and water in a cup; mix well. Stir into sauce. Cook, stirring constantly, until sauce thickens and bubbles. Add kidney beans and corn; heat about 5 minutes. Spoon over the meat in the serving bowl.

New England Boiled Dinner (page 145)

BEEF SAUSAGE AND EGGS

Try this spicy beef for breakfast and you may not go back to pork sausages.

Makes 4 servings.

    1   pound ground chuck
    1   small onion, grated
    ¼   cup water
    1½ teaspoons salt
    1½ teaspoons leaf marjoram, crumbled
    ½   teaspoon ground allspice
    ¼   teaspoon ground nutmeg
    ⅛   teaspoon cayenne
    8   eggs
    ⅓   cup milk
    ⅛   teaspoon pepper
    2   tablespoons butter or margarine

1. Combine beef, onion, water, 1 teaspoon of the salt, marjoram, allspice, nutmeg and cayenne in a medium-size bowl until well mixed. Shape into a roll about 2½ inches in diameter and 7 inches long. Wrap in wax paper; chill several hours or overnight until firm enough to slice.
2. Cut sausage roll into ½-inch slices with a sharp knife. Cook slices in skillet until

well browned, turning often.
3. While sausage cooks, beat eggs, milk, the remaining ½ teaspoon salt and pepper in a medium-size bowl. Melt butter in a large skillet. Add beaten eggs; cook until eggs are thickened but still moist. Transfer to heated platter; arrange sausages on top.

THE TOREADOR BURGER

The wide-awake taste of a pungent Mexican chili topping deserves a hearty *olé!*

Makes 4 servings.

    1   tablespoon vegetable oil
    1   medium-size onion, chopped (½ cup)
    1   clove garlic, minced
    1   tablespoon chili powder
    1   can (1 pound) tomatoes
    1   can (1 pound) red kidney beans,
          drained
    1½ teaspoons salt
    ¼   teaspoon pepper
    ⅛   teaspoon liquid red-pepper seasoning
    1   pound ground round or chuck
    ⅛   teaspoon pepper

2 tablespoons butter or margarine
Shredded lettuce
4 hamburger rolls, split, toasted and
buttered
1 cup shredded sharp Cheddar cheese (4
ounces

1: Heat oil in a large saucepan; sauté onion and garlic until tender. Add chili powder; stir 1 minute. Add tomatoes, beans, ½ teaspoon of the salt, ⅛ teaspoon of the pepper and red-pepper seasoning. Simmer 30 minutes, or until thick.

2. Season beef with the remaining salt and pepper; shape into 4 equal-size patties, about the size of the rolls.

3. Heat butter in a skillet. Pan-fry hamburgers about 4 minutes on each side, or until done as you like them.

4. Arrange shredded lettuce on bottom halves of rolls; top with burgers. Spoon chili mixture over burgers. Place more shredded lettuce and shredded cheese on top of chili. Garnish with red-onions rings, if you wish. Top each with remaining half of roll.

HAMBURGERS PARMIGIANA

A favorite Italian flavor has come into the popular American ground beef patty.
Makes 4 servings.

1 pound ground round or chuck
1 teaspoon salt
¼ teaspoon pepper
½ teaspoon Italian seasoning
1 egg
¼ cup packaged seasoned bread crumbs
3 tablespoons grated Parmesan cheese
1 tablespoon vegetable oil
1½ cups bottled Italian cooking sauce
Mozzarella cheese slices
Italian bread or rolls

1. Lightly mix beef with salt, pepper and Italian seasoning in a large bowl; shape into 4 equal-size patties.

2. Beat egg in a pie plate until foamy. Combine bread crumbs and Parmesan cheese on a sheet of wax paper.

3. Dip each hamburger into egg, then coat with crumb and cheese mixture.

4. Heat oil in a large skillet. Pan-fry burgers over medium heat 4 minutes on each side, or until done as you like them.

5. Remove hamburgers from the skillet; drain off any fat. Add Italian cooking sauce to skillet; bring to boiling, scraping up brown bits. Add hamburgers to sauce, coating evenly. Top burgers with cheese slices. Lower heat; cover skillet until cheese melts.

6. Place hamburgers on toasted and buttered Italian bread slices or rolls.

HAMBURGERS AU POIVRE

Makes 4 servings.

1 pound ground round or chuck
½ teaspoon salt
1 to 2 teaspoons cracked black pepper
1 tablespoon vegetable oil
2 tablespoons water, dry red wine or
beef broth
4 slices white bread, toasted and
buttered

1. Shape beef into 4 equal-size patties. Sprinkle each with salt; press black pepper into both sides of patties.

2. Heat oil in a large skillet. Pan-fry the hamburgers over medium heat 4 minutes on each side, or until done as you like them. Remove and keep warm. Pour off fat from the skillet; add water, swirling around to deglaze pan.

3. Place each hamburger on a slice of toast; pour deglazing liquid over each of the burgers. Garnish with either chopped parsley or chopped chives, if you wish.

Handle ground meat with a light touch when shaping into patties for tender, juicy burgers.

BEEF PATTIES DIANE

Makes 6 servings.

    2 pounds ground chuck or round
    2 tablespoons butter or margarine
    ⅓ cup chopped parsley
    ¼ cup chopped chives
    ¼ cup brandy
    ¼ cup beef broth
    2 teaspoons Worcestershire sauce
    ½ teaspoon salt

1. Shape chuck into 6 oval patties about ¾-inch thick.

2. Heat butter in a large skillet over medium heat. Add patties; pan-fry until browned on each side and done as you like them. Remove to a heated serving platter; keep warm.

3. Add parsley, chives and brandy to pan juices; simmer 1 minute. Add broth, Worcestershire and salt; cook 1 minute longer. Spoon over patties.

BAVARIAN BURGERS

Onion and sauerkraut add a robust flavor to this hamburger.

Makes 4 servings.

    1 slice rye bread with caraway seeds
    2 tablespoons hot water
    1 pound ground round or chuck
    1 small onion, finely chopped (¼ cup)
    1 teaspoon salt
    ¼ teaspoon pepper
    1 tablespoon vegetable oil
    1 can (8 ounces) sauerkraut
    ⅓ cup dairy sour cream
    ½ teaspoon flour
    ⅛ teaspoon dillweed
    4 hamburger buns, split, toasted and
        buttered

1. Soak bread in water in a large bowl; let stand 10 minutes; mash with a fork.

2. Add ground round, onion, salt and pepper to the bowl; mix lightly. Shape into 4 equal-size patties.

3. Heat oil in a large skillet. Pan-fry hamburgers 4 minutes on each side; or, broil or grill 5 to 6 inches from heat, turning once. Remove and keep warm. Drain off any fat from the skillet into a 1-cup measure; return 1 tablespoon fat to skillet.

4. Turn sauerkraut into a strainer; rinse under running water; drain but do not squeeze dry. Combine in a small bowl with sour cream, flour and dillweed; stir into fat in skillet; cook over low heat stirring constantly, until well blended.

5. Place hamburgers on bottom halves of buns; divide sauerkraut mixture evenly over each burger; cover with tops of buns.

PINWHEEL MEATLOAF

Bake at 350° for 55 minutes.
Makes 8 servings.

    2 pounds ground round or chuck
    2 eggs
    ½ cup packaged bread crumbs
    2 teaspoons salt
    1 package (8 ounces) sliced
        cooked ham
    1 package (8 ounces) sliced
        Swiss cheese
    1 cup torn celery leaves
    ½ cup parsley leaves
    ⅓ cup catsup

1. Combine beef, eggs, bread crumbs and salt in a large bowl. Roll meat mixture between sheets of foil and wax paper to a 16x12-inch rectangle, about ½-inch thick.

2. Remove top sheet of wax paper. Top meatloaf mixture with ham and cheese to within 1 inch of edges. Sprinkle with celery and parsley leaves. Roll up, beginning with short edge, lifting away foil as you roll but leaving roll on foil at the end. Carefully move roll to center of foil, seam-side down. Crimp foil to enclose meatloaf. Place in a shallow baking pan.

3. Bake in a moderate oven (350°) for 45 minutes. Unwrap meatloaf; brush all over with catsup. Bake 10 minutes longer.

Beef Patties Diane

REFRIGERATOR STORAGE TIME CHART	
Fresh Meats—Beef, Lamb, Pork, Veal	**Recommended Storage Time For Maximum Quality**
Roasts	3 to 5 days
Steaks, Chops	3 days
Ribs	3 days
Stew Meats	2 days
Ground Meat	1 to 2 days
Variety Meats	1 to 2 days
(Heart, Tongue, Liver, Kidneys, Brains, Sweetbreads)	
Pork Sausage	2 to 3 days
Processed Meats (after package is opened)	
Hams, Picnics—whole, half or slices	7 days
Bacon	5 to 7 days
Dried Beef	10 to 12 days
Frankfurters	4 to 5 days
Luncheon Meats, sliced	3 days
Bologna Loaves, wafer-thin, sliced and unsliced	4 to 6 days
Dry and Semi-Dry Sausage, unsliced	2 to 3 weeks
Liver Sausage, unsliced	4 to 6 days
Corned Beef	5 to 7 days
Tongue	6 to 7 days

For unopened packages see freshness date (open date) information on package.

To vary meatloaf shapes: Press ground meat into a pie plate. Mark it into wedges and outline each with catsup, if you wish. Cut between marks after baking; lift out each sauce-topped wedge with a spatula. Bake meatloaf in a shallow round, square or oblong baking dish that can go right to the table. Or, shape meat loaf mixture into individual loaves; place in shallow baking dish and bake about half the time.

MARVELOUS MEATLOAF

Bake at 350° for 1¼ hours.
Makes 8 servings.

 2 slices whole-wheat bread
 ½ cup milk
 ½ pounds lean ground pork
 ½ pound sausage meat
 1 egg, slightly beaten
 ½ cup finely diced apple
 ½ cup finely diced celery
 ¼ cup wheat germ
 2 tablespoons chopped parsley
 1 teaspoon salt
 ½ teaspoon pepper
 ¼ teaspoon leaf basil, crumbled
   Pinch leaf thyme
   Pinch ground nutmeg
   Stir-Fried Apples and Celery
   (recipe follows)

1. Crumble bread into milk in a large bowl Add pork, sausage, egg, apple, celery, wheat germ, parsley, salt, pepper, basil, thyme and nutmeg; stir until well blended. Shape into a loaf in shallow baking pan.
2. Bake in a moderate oven (350°) for 1¼ hours. Serve with Stir-Fry Apples and Celery.

STIR-FRIED APPLES AND CELERY
 2 tablespoons butter or margarine
 2 tablespoons vegetable oil
 1 tablespoon lemon juice
 2 cups thinly sliced celery
 2 medium-size apples, quartered, cored and sliced (2 cups)
 ½ teaspoon salt
 ¼ teaspoon pepper

1. Heat butter and oil in a large skillet. Add lemon juice and celery; stir-fry over high heat for 3 minutes, or until celery is almost tender.
2. Add apples; continue cooking and stirring for 5 minutes, or until tender. Sprinkle with salt and pepper.

BEEF LOAF WITH CANADIAN BACON

The beef mixture alternates with the good smoky flavor of Canadian bacon for a pleasant change of pace.
Bake at 350° for 1 hour.
Makes 8 servings.

 2 pounds ground round or chuck
 2 cups soft bread crumbs (4 slices)
 1 teaspoon salt
 ¼ teaspoon leaf savory, crumbled
 ¼ teaspoon ground allspice
 ⅛ teaspoon pepper
 ½ cup thinly sliced green onions
 1 clove garlic, minced
 2 eggs
 1 can condensed beef broth
 8 slices Canadian bacon
   (about ¼ pound)
   Sauce Robert (recipe follows)

1. Line bottom and ends of a 9x5x3-inch loaf pan with heavy-duty foil, leaving some foil extending above pan at either end.
 2. Combine beef, bread crumbs, salt, savory, allspice, pepper, green onions, garlic, eggs and ½ cup of the beef broth in a large bowl. (Reserve remaining broth for sauce.) Mix until well blended.
3. Alternate meat mixture with slices of Canadian bacon along length of pan.
4. Bake in a moderate oven (350°) for 1 hour. Remove pan from oven; loosen loaf

along sides of the pan; lift out with the help of the foil strips. Place on a heated serving platter; keep warm while making sauce.

SAUCE ROBERT: Pour accumulated juice from meatloaf into a 1-cup measure. Melt 2 tablespoons butter in a medium-size saucepan; stir in 3 tablespoons flour. Cook, stirring constantly, over medium heat, until light brown, about 2 minutes. Add water to remaining beef broth to make 1 cup. Gradually stir into flour mixture; cook, stirring constantly, until sauce thickens and bubbles 2 minutes. Add juices from meatloaf, 2 tablespoons sherry and 1½ teaspoons Dijon-style mustard. Simmer 1 minute.

Meat labeled *ground beef* must be pure beef, ground only from skeletal meat (the beef muscle attached to the skeleton) with no variety meats, other meats or ingredients added. Ground beef can contain varying degrees of leanness, from 70 percent to 90 percent or more and must be labeled accordingly. But it cannot contain less than the minimum of 70 percent lean (or maximum of 30 percent fat).

SKILLET BEEF LOAF

This colorful, skillet-baked, upside-down meatloaf has its own zingy sauce.

Bake at 350° for 1 hour.
Makes 8 servings.

1 large Bermuda or Spanish onion
1 clove garlic, minced
2 tablespoons butter or margarine
2 teaspoons paprika
2¼ pounds meatloaf mixture (beef, veal and pork)*
2 cups soft bread crumbs (4 slices)
1 teaspoon salt
½ teaspoon caraway seeds, crushed

¼ teaspoon pepper
2 eggs
½ cup dairy sour cream
1 can condensed chicken broth
1 large carrot, pared and sliced
1 medium-size yellow squash, sliced
    Paprika Sauce (*recipe follows*)

1. Peel onion; cut a slice, ½ inch thick, from center; reserve for Step 3. Chop remaining onion; measure and reserve ½ cup for Paprika Sauce.
2. Heat butter in a 10-inch skillet with a heatproof handle; sauté the remaining onion until tender, about 3 minutes. Stir in paprika; cook, stirring constantly, 1 minute. Cool slightly.
3. Combine meatloaf mixture, bread crumbs, salt, caraway seeds, pepper, eggs, sour cream and ½ cup of the chicken broth in a large bowl. (Reserve remaining broth for Paprika Sauce.) Add cooled onion mixture; mix just until well blended.
4. Arrange onion slice, carrots and yellow squash in a pattern in the bottom of the same skillet; spoon meat mixture over and pack it down firmly.
5. Bake in a moderate oven (350°) for 1 hour. Pour accumulated juices into a 1-cup measure. (There should be about ½ cup.) Invert a serving plate over skillet; turn upside down; lift off skillet. Keep warm while making sauce.

PAPRIKA SAUCE: Sauté reserved ½ cup chopped onion in 2 tablespoons butter in a medium-size saucepan until tender, about 3 minutes. Stir in 1 tablespoon paprika; cook, stirring constantly, 1 minute; stir in 2 tablespoons flour. Gradually add remaining chicken broth and juice from the meatloaf. Cook, stirring constantly, until sauce thickens and bubbles 3 minutes. Remove from heat; slowly stir in ½ cup sour cream. Makes about 1¼ cups.
Variation: Ground round may be substituted for the meatloaf mixture. There will be very little difference in taste, and the baking time will be the same.

STIR-FRIED BEEF AND ZUCCHINI

Makes 4 servings.

⅓ cup water
2 tablespoons cornstarch
2 tablespoons soy sauce
2 teaspoons sugar
1 teaspoon salt
1 tablespoon sesame seeds
3 tablespoons vegetable oil
1 large onion, sliced
2 medium-size zucchini, cut in thin diagonal slices
1 pound ground round
1 can (8 ounces) sliced bamboo shoots, drained

1. Combine water, cornstarch, soy sauce, sugar and salt in a small bowl.
2. Heat sesame seeds in a large skillet, stirring constantly, until golden brown. Remove to paper toweling. Add oil; swirl to coat pan. Add onion and zucchini. Stir-fry until the vegetables are tender-crisp. Remove with slotted spoon to a heated serving platter.
3. Add beef; stir-fry over high heat until well browned. Restir cornstarch mixture; add to beef; cook until thickened. Return vegetables to pan; add bamboo shoots; stir-fry until heated. Spoon onto a heated serving platter; sprinkle with toasted sesame seeds.

SWEDISH MEATBALLS

Makes 6 servings.

4 slices white bread
⅔ cup milk or light cream
2½ pounds meatloaf mixture or ground round
2 eggs
1 medium-size onion, chopped (½ cup)
1 teaspoon ground allspice
½ teaspoon ground nutmeg
2 teaspoons salt
½ teaspoon pepper

4 tablespoons vegetable oil
2 envelopes or teaspoons instant beef broth dissolved in 2 cups boiling water
¼ cup (½ stick) butter or margarine
¼ cup flour
1 cup (8 ounces) dairy sour cream, at room temperature
⅓ cup chopped fresh dill
    OR: 2 tablespoons dillweed
    Hot cooked noodles

1. Soak bread in milk in a large bowl. Mash with a fork. Add meat, eggs, onion, allspice, nutmeg, salt and pepper; mix well. Shape into 2-inch balls. Brown, part at a time, in oil in a large skillet; remove as browned.
2. Pour off fat from skillet. Add broth to skillet, return meatballs. Bring to boiling. Lower heat; cover; simmer 30 minutes.
3. Remove meatballs with a slotted spoon to bowl. Strain cooking liquid; reserve.
4. Heat butter in skillet. Add flour; cook and stir 1 minute. Gradually stir in strained liquid. Cook slowly, stirring constantly, until thickened and bubbly. Add meatballs and heat thoroughly.
5. Stir in sour cream slowly; add dill; heat 5 minutes. (Do not allow to boil or sour cream will curdle.) Serve over noodles. Garnish with fresh dill, if you wish.

OVEN-BAKED MEATBALLS WITH DILL SAUCE

Brown the meatballs the easy way—in the oven!

Bake at 400° for 15 minutes.

Makes 6 servings.

1½ pounds ground chuck or round
1 cup soft bread crumbs (2 slices)
⅓ cup water
¼ cup minced green onions
1 egg
2 teaspoons salt
¼ teaspoon pepper
¼ cup (½ stick) butter or margarine
3 tablespoons flour

2 cups milk
2 tablespoons chopped fresh dill
OR: 2 teaspoons dillweed

1. Combine beef, bread crumbs, water, onions, egg, 1½ teaspoons of the salt and pepper in a large bowl; mix lightly. Shape into 24 meatballs. Place on a jelly-roll pan.
2. Bake in a hot oven (400°) for 15 minutes, or until browned.
3. Meanwhile, heat butter in a medium-size saucepan. Add flour; cook until bubbly. Remove from heat; gradually stir in milk until smooth. Return to heat; cook until thickened, stirring constantly. Stir in dill and the remaining ½ teaspoon salt. Spoon over meatballs. Serve with hot buttered noodles, if you wish.

KOENIGSBERG MEATBALLS

Makes 8 servings.

    4 slices white bread
    ½ cup milk
    2 pounds meatloaf mixture (beef, veal and pork)
    3 eggs
    1 small onion, grated
    2 tablespoons grated lemon rind
    1 teaspoon salt
    ¼ teaspoon pepper
    1 can (2 ounces) anchovy fillets, drained and chopped
    2 envelopes or teaspoons instant beef broth
    4 cups water
    ¼ cup (½ stick) butter or margarine
    ¼ cup flour
    1 teaspoon sugar
    ½ cup dry white wine
    2 tablespoons drained capers
    1 tablespoon lemon juice

1. Soak bread in milk in a large bowl. Mash with a fork. Add meatloaf mixture, eggs, onion, lemon rind, salt, pepper and half the anchovies; mix well. Shape into 32 meatballs.
2. Combine beef broth and water in a large skillet; heat to boiling; lower meatballs into boiling broth with a slotted spoon. Lower heat; simmer, uncovered, 15 minutes or until no longer pink in center. Remove with a slotted spoon to a deep, hot, serving platter; reserve cooking liquid.
3. Make sauce: Heat butter in a medium-size saucepan; stir in flour and sugar; cook until bubbly, stirring constantly. Gradually add wine and 2 cups of the cooking liquid, continuing to stir until mixture thickens and bubbles 1 minute. Stir in capers, lemon juice and the remaining anchovies, stirring until anchovies are blended into the sauce. Spoon over meatballs. Serve with sauerkraut and boiled potatoes, if you wish.

SKILLET HONEY-GLAZED HAM STEAK

An easy dinner for ham lovers.
Makes 6 servings.

    1 3 to 4-pound fully-cooked ham steak, 1½ to 2-inches thick
    1 tablespoon butter or margarine
    ½ cup honey
    1 lemon, sliced
    ¼ teaspoon ground cloves
    ¼ teaspoon ground allspice
    12 small white onions (about 1 pound)
    6 large carrots, sliced (3 cups)

1. Score fat edge of ham steak to prevent it from curling up during cooking. Heat butter in a large skillet; add ham steak and brown on both sides.
2. Add honey, lemon slices, cloves and allspice; cover. Cook over medium heat, basting often with honey glaze, 30 minutes.
3. Meanwhile, parboil onions in boiling salted water, 5 minutes,; drain; peel. Add onions and carrots to skillet; cover. Cook 15 minutes longer, basting ham and vegetables once or twice. Remove cover and cook, stirring often, 5 minutes or until vegetables are richly glazed. Arrange ham and vegetables on a heated serving platter. Garnish with parsley, if you wish.

> Water is an essential part of the manufacturer's curing process for ham. During cooking, some of the added moisture from the cure is lost. Hams that return to their original weight are labeled "ham." However, when ham returns to within 10 percent over the original weight, it is labeled "ham, water added." The added moisture cannot exceed 10 percent of the weight of the fresh uncured ham. The same labeling regulation applies to picnic shoulders.

STUFFED BAKED HAM, MARYLAND-STYLE

Garden greens tucked down into little pockets add a marvelous flavor.

Bake at 325° for 2½ hours.
Makes 8 generous servings plus enough for another meal.

    1 fully cooked ham (about 10 pounds)
    1 package (10 ounces) frozen chopped kale
    1 cup finely chopped fresh spinach
    1 large onion, finely chopped (1 cup)
    ¾ cup finely chopped watercress
    ½ cup finely chopped celery tops
    ½ teaspoon salt
    ¼ teaspoon pepper
    ½ cup honey
    2 tablespoons vinegar
    2 teaspoons dry mustard

1. Trim rind, if any, from ham. Shave ham fat covering to about ¼ inch. Make X-shaped cuts with a small paring knife, 2 inches deep and 1 inch apart, staggering all over the fat side.
2. Cook kale in boiling salted water to cover, following label directions; drain; cool; squeeze out excess water with hands.
3. Combine kale, spinach, onion, watercress, celery tops, salt and pepper in a medium-size bowl.
4. Press greens mixture into ham pockets, packing down well. Place ham, fat-side up, in a large shallow baking pan.

5. Bake in a slow oven (325°) for 2 hours.
6. Stir honey with vinegar and dry mustard; brush part over ham. Continue baking and brushing with remaining honey mixture, 30 minutes, or until top is richly glazed. Remove ham from pan and let stand about 20 minutes for easier carving.
7. Carve ham carefully, holding slices to keep filling intact. Garnish platter with watercress, if you wish.

SCALLOPED POTATOES AND HAM

Stretch your leftover ham with potatoes and cheese in this hearty casserole.
Bake at 350° for 1½ hours.
Makes 6 servings.

    ½ cup (½ stick) butter or margarine
    ½ cup flour
    2 teaspoons salt
    ¼ teaspoon pepper
    3 cups milk
    3 cups cubed cooked ham (about ½ pound)
    1 large onion, chopped (1 cup)
    1 large sweet green pepper, halved, seeded and chopped (1 cup)
    ½ cup shredded sharp or mild Cheddar cheese (2 ounces)
    5 cups sliced, pared potatoes (about 2 pounds)

1. Heat butter in a large saucepan over low heat; blend in flour, salt and pepper. Cook, stirring constantly, 1 minute. Remove from heat; gradually stir in milk. Return to heat; cook until thickened and bubbly.
2. Fold in ham, onion, green pepper and cheese. Pour over potatoes in a large bowl. Stir gently, then pour into a buttered 13x9x2-inch baking dish; cover with foil.
3. Bake in a moderate oven (350°) for 30 minutes. Uncover and continue baking for 1 hour, or until browned and bubbly. Let stand 10 minutes before serving.

Stuffed Baked Ham, Maryland-Style

ROASTING CHART / PORK, CURED AND SMOKED

CUT	APPROXIMATE WEIGHT	OVEN TEMPERATURE	APPROXIMATE ROASTING TIME	INTERNAL TEMPERATURE
Ham, cook before eating, bone-in half	5 to 7 lbs.	325°F	2½ to 3 hours	160°F
Ham, fully cooked bone-in half	5 to 7 lbs.	325°F	1½ to 2¼ hours	140°F
Ham, fully cooked, Boneless, half portion	3 to 4 lbs.	325°F	1¼ to 1¾ hours	140°F
Arm picnic shoulder bone-in	5 to 8 lbs.	325°F	2½ to 4 hours	170°F
Boneless shoulder roll	2 to 3 lbs.	325°F	1½ to 1¾ hours	170°F

HAM LOAF WITH MUSTARD SAUCE

Bake in the cool of the morning, then refrigerate until dinner, or serve it hot if you wish.

Bake at 350° for 1 hour.

Makes 8 servings.

- 1¼ pounds ground cooked ham
- ¾ pound ground lean pork
- 1 cup mayonnaise
- 1 package (8 ounces) herbed poultry stuffing mix
- 1 envelope (2 to a package) onion soup mix
- 2 eggs
- ¼ cup chopped parsley
- 2 tablespoons prepared horseradish
- 1 tablespoon Dijon-style mustard
- 1 teaspoon leaf marjoram, crumbled
- ¼ teaspoon leaf rosemary, crumbled
- ¼ teaspoon ground allspice
- ⅛ teaspoon ground ginger
- 1 cup apple juice or cider
  Mustard Sauce (*recipe follows*)

1. Line bottom and sides of a 9x5x3-inch loaf pan with foil; grease foil.

2. Combine ham, pork, mayonnaise, poultry stuffing mix, soup mix, eggs, parsley, horseradish, mustard, marjoram, rosemary, allspice, ginger and apple juice in a large bowl; mix well. Press firmly into prepared pan, smoothing top.

3. Bake in a moderate oven (350°) for 1 hour or until loaf begins to pull from sides of pan and is firm. Remove loaf to wire rack. Loosen around edges with a spatula; cool to room temperature. Drain off any juices from pan. Invert loaf onto a sheet of heavy-duty foil; remove foil lining; wrap; chill. Slice and serve with Mustard Sauce. Garnish with celery leaves, cherry tomatoes and pickles, if you wish.

Mustard Sauce: Combine 1 cup dairy sour cream, 2 tablespoons Dijon-style mustard, 2 tablespoons mayonnaise, ¼ teaspoon dillweed, pinch leaf marjoram and 3 tablespoons milk in a small bowl. Stir until well blended. Cover; chill until ready to serve. Stir well again, adding a little more milk, if needed. Makes 1½ cups.

BRAISED HAM IN RED WINE SAUCE

If you are looking for something different from the ordinary sweet glazed hams, here's one that is sure to please: a ham that is braised with vegetables and red wine, and served with a sauce made from the braising liquid.

Bake at 325° for about 2 hours.

Makes 10 servings, plus leftovers.

- 3 tablespoons butter or margarine
- 2 stalks celery with tops, chopped (1 cup)
- 2 to 3 carrots, chopped (1 cup)
- 1 large onion, chopped (1 cup)
- 6 sprigs parsley
- 1 bay leaf
- 8 whole cloves
- 3 strips (about 3x1-inches each) orange peel, (no white)
- 3 cups dry red wine
- 1 fully-cooked ham, about 10 pounds, skin and excess fat removed
- 2 tablespoons 10X (confectioners') sugar (*optional*)
- ⅓ cup red currant jelly
- ¼ cup dry red wine
- 2 tablespoons cornstarch
- 1 teaspoon Dijon-style mustard

1. Heat butter in a large skillet; add celery, carrots and onion and sauté, stirring often, until tender and lightly browned, about 5 minutes. Add parsley, bay leaf, cloves, orange peel and the 3 cups wine; bring to boiling, then pour into a covered roaster or Dutch oven large enough to hold ham. Place ham, in roaster, fat side up; cover.

2. Bake in a moderate oven (325°) about 2 hours, or 15 minutes per pound, basting with wine mixture every 20 minutes. (If you don't have a covered roasting pan or Dutch oven, use a baking pan and cover tightly with heavy-duty aluminum foil.)

3. If you wish to glaze ham after braising, place it on a rack in the roasting pan; sprinkle the 10X sugar through a sieve on top and sides of ham.

4. Bake in a very hot oven (450°) for 10 minutes or until sugar is brown. Remove ham from oven and let stand 20 minutes for easier carving. Or, leave in turned-off oven with door ajar.

5. Make sauce: Strain braising liquid into 4-cup measure. Skim off and discard fat. (You should have about 2 cups liquid.) Turn into large saucepan; add red currant jelly. Bring to boiling; boil rapidly 5 minutes, stirring often, until jelly is dissolved. Mix cornstarch with the ¼ cup red wine in a small cup; add to boiling mixture, stirring constantly, until sauce thickens and bubbles 1 minute; stir in mustard. Taste; add salt and additional mustard if needed. To serve: Place ham on a large serving platter. Garnish with parsley. Serve sauce separately. Good with small glazed potatoes and creamed spinach.

ROASTED FRESH HAM (Leg of Pork) WITH CUMBERLAND SAUCE

Wonderful for special occasions.

Roast at 325° for 20 to 24 minutes per pound.

Makes 12 to 16 servings.

    1 fresh ham (leg of pork), 14 to 16
        pounds
    2 teaspoons salt
    ½ teaspoon pepper
    1 large onion, sliced
    6 medium-size baking potatoes, pared
        and quartered lengthwise
        Cumberland Sauce (*recipe follows*)

1. Score skin on pork in a small diamond pattern. Rub skin with salt and pepper.

2. Put meat on a rack in roasting pan. If using a meat thermometer, insert into thickest part of meat so bulb is not touching bone or resting in fat.

3. Roast in a slow oven (325°) for 22 to 24 minutes per pound, or until thermometer registers 170°.

4. One hour before the end of roasting time, pour off all juices from pan; measure and return ¼ cup to pan; reserve all remaining juices for sauce. Remove pork from rack; return pork to pan. Add onion and potatoes; continue roasting, turning potatoes once or twice, until pork and potatoes are done. Meanwhile, make Cumberland Sauce to serve with pork. Serve potatoes with pork and garnish platter with watercress.

CUMBERLAND SAUCE
Makes 1⅔ cups.

    Roast pork pan juices
    2 naval oranges
    ⅓ cup orange juice
    2 tablespoons cornstarch
    1 cup ruby port wine
    ½ cup currant jelly
    5 drops liquid red-pepper seasoning

1. Skim fat from reserved pan juices; discard fat. Measure juices—you will need 1 cup. Add water if necessary.

2. Pare thin orange zest from both oranges; parboil 5 minutes; cut into thin shreds. Squeeze oranges; measure ⅓ cup juice.

3. Stir cornstarch into orange juice in a medium-size saucepan. Stir in port, currant jelly and red-pepper seasoning. Bring to boiling, stirring constantly; cook until bubbly; cook 1 minute longer. Stir in orange rind. Serve with the fresh ham.

157

ROASTING CHART/FRESH PORK				
CUT	APPROXIMATE WEIGHT	OVEN TEMPERATURE	ROASTING TIME	INTERNAL TEMPERATURE
Leg (fresh ham)				
half, bone-in	7 to 8 lbs.	325°F	4 to 4½ hours	170°F
whole, bone-in	14 to 16 lbs.	325°F	5½ to 6 hours	170°F
Loin, center, bone-in	3 to 5 lbs.	325°F	1¾ to 2½ hours	170°F
boneless	3 to 5 lbs.	325°F	2 to 3 hours	170°F

SAGE-STUFFED PORK SHOULDER

Roast at 325° for about 3 hours and 20 minutes.

Makes 8 servings plus leftovers.

1 fresh pork shoulder, boned (about 5 pounds)
1 large onion, chopped (1 cup)
¼ cup (½ stick) butter or margarine
1 teaspoon leaf sage, crumbled
6 slices white bread, cubed (3 cups)
1 teaspoon salt
¼ teaspoon pepper
¼ cup hot water
Savory Pork Gravy (recipe follows)

1. Trim excess fat from pork and score remaining fat.

2. Sauté onion in butter in a large skillet until soft; stir in sage, bread cubes, salt and pepper. Add water; toss until evenly moist.

3. Spoon stuffing lightly into pocket in pork (where the bone was removed); tie into a compact shape with string. Place on rack in roasting pan; sprinkle with additional salt and pepper. If using a meat thermometer, insert into thickest part of meat so bulb is not resting in fat.

4. Roast in a slow oven (325°) 40 minutes per pound, or until the meat thermometer registers 170°. Remove strings from roast; place on a heated serving platter; keep warm while making Savory Pork Gravy.

SAVORY PORK GRAVY: Pour all fat from roasting pan, leaving juices in pan. Return ½ cup of fat to pan; blend in ½ cup flour. Cook, stirring constantly, 1 minute. Stir in 4 cups water. Cook, stirring constantly, until gravy thickens and bubbles, 3 minutes. Stir in ½ teaspoon salt and ¼ teaspoon pepper. Taste; add additional salt and pepper, if you wish. Makes 4½ cups.

HOT AND HEARTY TEXAS SPARERIBS

Pre-baking ribs assures their tenderness when glazed on barbecue or broiler.

Bake at 450° for 30 minutes.

Makes 6 servings.

5 pounds country-style spareribs
1 medium-size onion, finely chopped (½ cup)
1 clove garlic, minced
2 tablespoons butter or margarine
1 bottle (12 ounces) chili sauce
¼ cup lemon juice
¼ cup firmly packed light brown sugar
1 teaspoon prepared horseradish
1 teaspoon salt

1. Cut ribs into serving-size portions. Put in a shallow baking pan in a single layer.

2. Bake in a very hot oven (450°) for 30 minutes, turning once. Drain off fat.

3. While ribs are baking, prepare the sauce: Sauté onion and garlic in butter in a medium-size saucepan until tender, about 3 minutes. Add chili sauce, lemon juice, sugar, horseradish and salt. Bring to boiling; lower heat; simmer sauce 15 minutes, stirring occasionally.

4. Brush spareribs with sauce. Grill over grayed coals or broil 6 to 7 inches from heat, 20 minutes, brushing with sauce and turning several times until ribs are nicely glazed.

TANGY GLAZED LOIN OF PORK

Roast at 325° for 3½ hours.
Makes 12 servings.

    2 tablespoons vegetable oil
    1 large onion, finely chopped (1 cup)
    2 cloves garlic, minced
    1 cup bottled chili sauce
    ½ cup lemon juice
    ⅓ cup molasses
    3 tablespoons Dijon-style mustard
    1 tablespoon Worcestershire sauce
    ¼ cup dark rum
    1 loin of pork (6 to 7 pounds)

1. Heat oil in medium-size saucepan; add onion and garlic. Sauté 5 minutes until onion is tender but not brown.
2. Stir in chili sauce, lemon juice, molasses, mustard and Worcestershire; bring to boiling; lower heat; cover; simmer 20 minutes. Stir in rum.
3. Place meat on a rack in large shallow baking pan. Do not add water or cover.
4. Roast in a slow oven (325°) for 2½ hours. Brush meat with glaze.
5. Continue roasting for 1 hour, or until meat registers 170° on meat thermometer, basting frequently with additional glaze.
6. Garnish with sugared grapes, spiced crabapples, whole canned apricots and chicory, if you wish.

SWEET-AND-SOUR PORK

Makes 4 servings.

    1 can (20 ounces) pineapple chunks in pineapple juice
    4 teaspoons cornstarch
    ¼ cup water
    ½ cup firmly packed brown sugar
    1 teaspoon ground ginger
    ¼ cup soy sauce
    3 tablespoons red wine vinegar
    1 tablespoon dry sherry
    3 tablespoons vegetable oil
    1 pound boneless pork loin, cut into 2x¼-inch strips
    3 cloves garlic, minced
    1 large sweet green pepper, halved, seeded and cut into ¼-inch strips
    2 cups matchstick-cut carrot strips
    4 cups hot cooked rice

1. Drain pineapple; reserve fruit and juice separately.
2. Blend cornstarch and water in a small saucepan. Stir in reserved pineapple juice, brown sugar, ginger, soy sauce, vinegar and sherry. Bring to boiling; lower heat. Simmer, stirring constantly, until thickened and bubbly. Remove from heat; reserve.
3. Heat 2 tablespoons of the oil in a large skillet or a wok. Stir-fry pork for 10 minutes. Add remaining 1 tablespoon oil, garlic, green pepper and carrots; stir-fry 4 minutes longer.
4. Add pineapple and sweet-sour sauce. Simmer 2 minutes. Serve over hot rice.

All meat shrinks during cooking, whether it is cooked at home or in a processing plant. During processing the cured but still uncooked hams are placed in cans by weight. About one ounce of gelatin, depending upon the size of the ham, is added to the can with the ham before it is vacuum sealed. The hams then move through a hot-water cooking chamber. As the ham cooks, some juices cook out of the meat just as they do when meat is cooked at home. The juices remain in the sealed can and are reabsorbed or are set with the gelatin when chilled. Because ham is cooked in the can, only a relatively small amount of shrinkage takes place, approximately 7 to 15 percent. A pork roast in an open pan in the kitchen range will shrink about 20 to 25 percent.

BONELESS ROAST PORK LOIN MARINATED IN WHITE WINE

The cooking of southern France inspires this tender, moist roast pork loin. A 4½ pound loin of pork yields about 3 pounds of solid meat when boned.

Roast at 325° for about 1½ hours.
Makes 6 to 8 servings.

    1 center cut loin of pork (about
          4¼ pounds)
 1½ cups dry white wine
    ½ cup white wine vinegar
    1 large onion, sliced
    2 cloves garlic
  10 peppercorns
    1 teaspoon leaf thyme, crumbled
    1 bay leaf
    1 teaspoon salt
    ¼ teaspoon pepper

1. Bone loin of pork; reserve bones. Tie boned meat at 2-inch intervals with kitchen string to keep compact shape.
2. Combine wine, vinegar, onion, garlic, peppercorns, thyme and bay leaf in a nonmetal baking dish just large enough to hold the pork loin and the bones. Put pork and bones in marinade, meat-side down; refrigerate overnight.
3. The next morning, remove from refrigerator. Turn pork several times during the day until ready to roast.
4. Drain pork and bones; sprinkle with salt and pepper; put in roasting pan. If using a meat thermometer, insert in thickest part of meat so that bulb is not resting in fat. Add ½ cup of the marinade, onion and garlic.
5. Roast in a slow oven (325°), basting occasionally with marinade, allowing 30 minutes per pound, or until the meat thermometer registers 170°.
6. Remove meat from roasting pan to a heated serving platter; pour off all fat, leaving the brown drippings. Add a few tablespoons of the remaining marinade and deglaze the pan, stirring to scrape up brown bits. Slice meat and arrange on platter.

Spoon pan liquid over meat; the sauce will be small in quantity, but full of flavor. Serve bones separately; they are nice to eat with your fingers.

HERB-STUFFED PORK CHOPS

Bake at 350° for 1 hour.
Makes 4 servings.

    ½ pound medium-size mushrooms
    ⅓ cup chopped onion
    ⅓ cup chopped celery
    ½ cup (1 stick) butter or margarine
    1 cup packaged bread crumbs
    ¼ teaspoon ground sage
    ½ cup chopped parsley
    4 double center loin pork chops with
          pockets
    ½ teaspoon salt
    ¼ teaspoon pepper
    ½ cup dried apricots
    1 cup dry white wine

1. Reserve 4 mushrooms for garnish; thinly slice remainder. Sauté sliced mushrooms, onion and celery in ¼ cup of the butter in a large flameproof baking dish or skillet with an ovenproof handle until tender, about 3 minutes. Add bread crumbs, sage and parsley.
2. Sprinkle pork chops inside and out with salt and pepper. Reserve 4 apricots; chop remainder; add to skillet mixture. Stuff pork chop pockets loosely with mixture. Secure openings with wooden picks. Wipe out baking dish.
3. Brown chops on both sides in remaining ¼ cup butter in same ovenproof dish. Pour wine around chops; cover.
4. Bake in a moderate oven (350°) for 1 hour, or until chops are tender. Garnish with reserved mushrooms and apricots, and add a few crisp celery tops for color.

PORK CHOP AND SCALLOPED POTATO CASSEROLE

Bake at 350° for 1 hour and 10 minutes.
Makes 4 servings.

- 4 loin pork chops, about ¾ inch thick
- 2 tablespoons vegetable oil
- 1 large onion, sliced and separated into rings
- 3 tablespoons butter or margarine
- 3 tablespoons flour
- 1 teaspoon salt
- ¼ teaspoon pepper
- 1 cup milk
- 1 cup chicken broth
- 4 medium-size potatoes, pared and thinly sliced (4 cups)
- 1 tablespoon chopped parsley

1. Brown chops in oil in a large skillet, about 3 minutes on each side. Remove. Add onion rings to fat remaining in skillet; sauté until tender, about 3 minutes. Remove from heat; reserve.

2. Heat butter in a medium-size saucepan. Stir in flour, salt and pepper; cook 1 minute. Add milk and broth slowly. Cook, stirring constantly, until sauce thickens and bubbles. Remove from heat.

3. Arrange sliced potatoes in a buttered 11x7x2-inch baking dish. Top with reserved onion rings. Pour sauce evenly over potatoes and onions. Top with chops. Cover baking dish tightly with foil.

4. Bake in a moderate oven (350°) for 1 hour. Uncover; bake 10 minutes longer, or until chops and potatoes are tender. Sprinkle top with chopped parsley.

> **While fresh pork was formerly recommended to be roasted to 185° on the roast meat thermometer, research has determined that any possible disease causing parisites which might be present in the meat are killed at 140°. The recommended temperature is now 170°, for a juicier, less dry product.**

PORK CHOPS VALENCIA

Bake at 350° for 40 minutes.
Makes 4 servings.

- ¼ cup chopped celery
- 2 tablespoons butter or margarine
- ⅔ cup water
- ½ package (6-ounce size) cornbread stuffing mix
- 2 tablespoons chopped parsley
- 1 naval orange, cut into 6 wedges and thinly sliced
- 1 tablespoon vegetable oil
- 8 to 10 thin loin pork chops
- ½ teaspoon salt
- ¼ teaspoon pepper
- ⅓ cup thawed frozen orange juice concentrate
- ⅔ cup water
- ⅓ cup chili sauce
- 1 teaspoon Worcestershire sauce

1. Sauté celery in butter in a large saucepan until tender, about 3 minutes. Add the ⅔ cup water, the half package stuffing mix, ½ the packet of seasoning from the stuffing mix, parsley and about ⅔ of the sliced orange. Toss lightly with a fork; cover; let stand while browning chops.

2. Heat oil in a large skillet; brown pork chops on both sides over high heat, removing them as they brown to a 13x9x2-inch baking dish. When all are browned, sprinkle with salt and pepper; add orange juice concentrate, the remaining ⅔ cup water, chili sauce and Worcestershire to skillet, stirring to loosen any brown bits. Remove from heat; add remaining sliced orange.

3. Arrange chops, overlapping, in baking dish with a spoonful of stuffing between each. Heat sauce to boiling, spoon around chops.

4. Bake, uncovered, in a moderate oven (350°), 40 minutes, or until tender, spooning sauce over meat several times. Garnish with celery leaves, parsley and orange, if you wish.

SOUTH AMERICAN PORK AND CORN PIE

For a Saturday night supper or buffet party. Thrifty, too!

Bake at 450° for 20 minutes.
Makes 6 servings.

    7 tablespoons butter or margarine, melted
    1 medium-size onion, chopped (½ cup)
 1½ cups leftover diced cooked lean pork
    1 tablespoon flour
    2 tablespoons chili powder
    1 can (13¾ ounces) chicken broth
    ¼ teaspoon salt
    1 can (17 ounces) whole-kernel corn
    ½ cup seedless raisins
    ½ cup pitted green or black olives, coarsely chopped
    1 tablespoon lemon juice
 1½ cups milk
    1 cup yellow cornmeal
    ½ cup *sifted* all-purpose flour
    ¼ teaspoon salt
    2 eggs
    3 teaspoons baking powder
    ½ teaspoon baking soda

1. Make filling: Heat 3 tablespoons of the melted butter in a large skillet. Add onion and sauté until limp; add diced pork and brown lightly. Stir in flour and chili powder; add broth and stir until blended. Add salt, corn, raisins and olives. Blend and stir until liquid thickens.

2. Preheat oven to very hot (450°).

3. Make topping: Stir lemon juice into milk; reserve. Mix the cornmeal, flour and the remaining salt in a large bowl. Add milk mixture, eggs, baking powder, soda and remaining melted butter *without mixing* in the order listed.

4. To assemble pie: Reheat pork mixture to steamy hot. Spoon into a shallow 8-cup baking dish. Stir up the topping mixture; pour over pork.

5. Bake in a preheated very hot oven (450°), until topping is firm and lightly browned, about 20 minutes.

SUPER ENCHILADAS

Bake at 350° for 20 minutes and at 425° for 5 minutes.
Makes 8 servings.

    3 tablespoons vegetable oil
    2 to 3 tablespoons chili powder
    1 tablespoon flour
    1 can condensed beef broth
    1 can (1 pound, 12 ounces) whole tomatoes
    2 packages (9 ounces each) refrigerated or frozen (thawed) tortillas
    4 Chorizos (Spanish sausages)
    1 large onion, chopped (1 cup)
    1 can (15¼ ounces) red kidney beans
    3 cups shredded Cheddar cheese (¾ pound)
      Vegetable oil
    2 ripe tomatoes, diced
    1 large ripe avocado, peeled and diced
    1 to 2 canned green chilies, finely diced
    1 tablespoon chopped parsley
      Shredded iceberg lettuce

1. Heat the 3 tablespoons oil in large saucepan. Stir in chili powder and flour; cook 1 minute; remove from heat. Gradually add beef broth, stirring constantly until smooth. Add tomatoes; bring to boiling, crushing tomatoes with back of spoon. Simmer, uncovered, over low heat, stirring often, 20 minutes, or until thickened.

2. Remove and discard casings from sausages; chop meat coarsely. Sauté sausage in large heavy skillet over medium heat until lightly browned; lift out with slotted spoon. Pour off all but 2 tablespoons of the sausage fat from the skillet.

3. Sauté onion in drippings 5 minutes. Drain beans, reserving liquid, and add to skillet. Cook over low heat, mashing beans with back of spoon until almost smooth; add a little of reserved liquid if mixture is too dry. Return sausage to skillet and add 1½ cups of the cheese; mix well.

4. Heat oil to a depth of 1½ inches in a small skillet until hot. Dip tortillas one at a time in hot oil, just until limp, 5 to 10 seconds on each side. (Do not let them become crisp.) Stack fried tortillas between paper towels.

5. Dip tortillas in chili sauce and top each with a rounded tablespoon of filling; roll up. Place seam-side down in a 15x8x2-inch baking dish, or divide into two smaller dishes, 10x6x2 inches, making 2 layers. Pour remaining sauce over; cover with foil.

6. Bake in moderate oven (350°) for 20 minutes, or until heated through. Increase oven temperature to 425°. Remove cover; sprinkle remaining cheese over top. Bake uncovered 5 minutes, or until cheese is melted and bubbly.

7. Mix tomatoes, avocado, green chili and parsley in a small bowl. Sprinkle casserole with a little shredded lettuce and the tomato mixture. Serve remaining lettuce and the tomato mixture separately to spoon over each serving.

Note: A half-pound of breakfast sausages or 2 cups shredded cooked chicken or turkey may be substituted for Chorizos, but the taste will not be quite as spicy. Hot Italian sausage is also an acceptable substitute for the Chorizos.

Super Enchiladas

Choucroute Garni

CHOUCROUTE GARNI

A flavorful, nourishing meal-in-one-pot from Alsace in France.
Makes 6 servings.

    2 cans (1 pound, 11 ounces each)
          sauerkraut, drained
    6 ham hocks, weighing about 3 pounds
    2 cups dry white wine
    1 bay leaf
    6 whole cloves
    1 medium-size onion, peeled
 1½ pounds knockwurst
    1 red apple, pared, cored and sliced
  12 new potatoes (about 1¼ pound)

1. Soak sauerkraut 5 minutes in cold water in a large bowl; drain well.
2. Place ham hocks in a Dutch oven or a large flameproof casserole. Add drained sauerkraut, wine and bay leaf. Press cloves into onion; press onion down into sauerkraut. Heat to boiling; lower heat; cover. Simmer very slowly, 1½ hours, tossing with a fork once or twice, or until ham hocks are almost tender.
3. Score knockwurst with a sharp knife; place on top of sauerkraut; simmer 20 minutes longer. Add apple slices, pushing down into sauerkraut; cook 10 minutes.
4. Scrub potatoes well; cook in boiling salted water to cover in a medium-size saucepan 20 minutes, or until done.
5. Arrange sauerkraut and meat with potatoes on a heated large deep platter. Serve with an assortment of mustards.

HERB-STUFFED ROAST LEG OF LAMB

A succulent, special-occasions lamb roast with a masterfully seasoned herb stuffing.
Roast at 350° for about 65 minutes.
Makes 6 servings.

    1 leg of lamb, (about 7 pounds)
          Herb Stuffing (*recipe follows*)
   ¼ teaspoon salt
   ⅛ teaspoon pepper
    2 tablespoons olive oil
    1 small sweet green pepper, halved,
          seeded and cut into thin strips
   ½ cup finely chopped carrots
    1 medium-size onion, chopped (½ cup)
   ½ cup finely chopped celery
    2 cloves garlic, minced
    2 cans condensed beef broth
   ¼ cup flour
   ½ cup cold water
          Watercress

1. Have your butcher bone and roll the leg of lamb. Remove strings from rolled leg of lamb carefully and unroll meat. Spoon Herb Stuffing onto surface. Retie lamb, following butcher's original ties. Season with salt and pepper.
2. Heat oil in a rectangular heavy roasting pan or a heavy skillet; brown lamb on all sides. (This will take about 15 minutes.) Transfer lamb to oven in the heavy roasting pan or transfer from skillet to regular roasting pan. Insert meat thermometer into thickest part of roast.
3. Roast in a moderate oven (350°) 30 minutes. Stir pepper, carrots, onions, celery and garlic into pan drippngs.
4. Roast 35 minutes longer, or until meat thermometer registers 140° for rare, or 150° for medium. Transfer meat to a heated serving platter and keep warm.
5. Place roasting pan over heat and add beef broth. Heat to boiling; lower heat; simmer 5 minutes. Strain liquid into a medium-size saucepan and discard vegetables. Skim fat from surface of liquid. Heat slowly to boiling.

		ROASTING CHART / LAMB		
CUT	APPROXIMATE WEIGHT	OVEN TEMPERATURE	ROASTING TIME	INTERNAL TEMPERATURE
Leg, bone-in	5 to 9 lbs.	325°F	2¼ to 3¾ hours 2½ to 4 hours	140°F (rare) 170°F (well done)
Leg, boneless	3 to 5 lbs.	325°-350°F	1½ to 2¼ hours	140°F (rare)

6. Combine flour and water in a cup to make a smooth paste.

7. Stir paste slowly into boiling liquid and continue to stir until mixture thickens and bubbles 3 minutes. Keep warm until serving time.

8. Carve part of lamb into slices, removing strings as you carve. Arrange lamb slices on a heated serving platter. Garnish with watercress.

HERB STUFFING

Makes enough to stuff a 7-pound leg of lamb.

- ¼ teaspoon leaf marjoram, crumbled
- 1 small bay leaf, crumbled
- ¼ teaspoon leaf basil, crumbled
- ¼ teaspoon leaf sage, crumbled
- ¼ teaspoon leaf rosemary, crumbled
- 1 teaspoon salt
- ¼ teaspoon pepper
- ½ cup (1 stick) butter or margarine, softened
- 1½ cups soft white bread crumbs (3 slices)
- 1 tablespoon lemon juice

Combine marjoram, bay leaf, basil, sage, rosemary, salt and pepper in container of electric blender. Whirl until finely pulverised. Add to softened butter in a small bowl along with bread crumbs and lemon juice; blend well.

LAMB KEBOBS WITH VEGETABLES

Makes 6 servings.

- ½ cup vegetable oil
- ½ cup lemon juice
- 1 small onion, minced (¼ cup)
- 1 teaspoon leaf oregano, crumbled
- 2 teaspoons leaf marjoram, crumbled
- ¼ cup chopped parsley
- 1 clove garlic, minced
- 2 pounds boneless lamb (leg or shoulder), cut in 1½-inch cubes
- 1 pint cherry tomatoes
- 2 medium-size sweet red peppers, cut into squares
- 2 medium-size sweet green peppers, cut into squares
- 1 pound large mushrooms, stems removed
- 2 summer squash, cut into chunks
- 1 small eggplant, cubed, or 6 baby eggplants

1. Combine oil, lemon juice, onion, oregano, marjoram, parsley and garlic in a large deep bowl. Stir in lamb; cover; let marinate overnight in refrigerator.

2. Thread lamb on 6 metal skewers. Grill or broil, 6 inches from heat, 15 minutes, turning and basting frequently with marinade. Thread vegetables on separate skewers and continue grilling lamb and vegetables, turning and basting, for about 15 minutes longer, or until meat is done as you like it and vegetables are tender.

> When sautéeing an amount of meat cubes, meatballs or slices, you will have a better browning if the meat is sautéed a small amount at a time. Crowding all the meat into the skillet at once steams the meat instead of a quick browning, which seals in the juices.

Spring Lamb Stew

SPRING LAMB STEW

A savory lamb stew from France, abundant with spring vegetables.

Makes 8 servings.

3 pounds lean boneless lamb, cut into
    1½-inch cubes
3 tablespoons olive or vegetable oil
3 tablespoons flour
3 tablespoons finely chopped shallots
    or green onions
1 clove garlic, minced
1 can condensed beef broth
1 can (1 pound) tomatoes

OR: 1 cup peeled and chopped
    ripe tomatoes
1 to 1½ teaspoons salt
½ teaspoon leaf thyme, crumbled
2 tablespoons butter or margarine
12 small white onions, peeled
4 small turnips, pared and quartered
3 to 4 carrots, pared and cut into
    2-inch lengths
12 small new potatoes, pared (1 pound)
1 cup frozen peas
2 tablespoons chopped parsley

1. Heat oil in a large skillet; brown lamb, a few pieces at a time. Remove pieces as they brown to a Dutch oven. Sprinkle flour over meat; cook over moderate heat, stirring and tossing meat with wooden spoon, until evenly coated, about 5 minutes. (This browns flour slightly.)

2. Pour off all but 1 tablespoon fat from skillet; add shallots and garlic; sauté, stirring often, 3 minutes, or until golden brown. Stir in beef broth and tomatoes; bring to boiling, stirring constantly to loosen brown bits in skillet. Add to lamb. Stir in 1 teaspoon of the salt and the thyme. Bring to boiling; lower heat, cover. Simmer 1 hour. Skim off fat, if any.

3. While meat simmers, heat butter in same skillet; add onions, turnips and carrots. Sauté, stirring, 10 minutes, or until vegetables are browned and glazed.

4. Add glazed vegetables and potatoes to lamb, pushing down under liquid; cover; simmer 45 minutes longer, or until lamb and vegetables are tender. Stir in peas and parsley; cover; simmer 5 to 10 minutes longer. Sprinkle with additional parsley and add more salt, if needed.

ALGERIAN COUSCOUS
(Lamb and Chicken Stew)

The semolina grain *couscous* is a staple food in the Middle East. It is used much the same as the rice and pasta of other Mediterranean countries.

Makes 8 servings.

- 2 large onions, chopped (2 cups)
- 2 tablespoons olive oil
- 1 broiler-fryer (about 2½ pounds), cut up
- 1 pound lean lamb, cut into 1½-inch cubes
- 4 cups water
- 4 carrots, pared and cut into 1-inch pieces
- 4 teaspoons salt
- ¼ teaspoon pepper
- ¼ teaspoon ground ginger
- 1 three-inch piece stick cinnamon
- 1 package (1 pound, 1¾ ounces) couscous* (2¾ cups)
- 4 small zucchini, washed and cut into ½-inch slices
- 2 ripe tomatoes, chopped
- 1 can (1 pound, 4 ounces) chick-peas, drained
- 1 cup seedless raisins
- 6 tablespoons (¾ stick) butter or margarine, melted

1. Sauté onions in oil in a large skillet until golden brown, about 5 minutes. Transfer to a kettle or Dutch oven. Brown chicken and lamb in same skillet; transfer to kettle as browned.

2. Add 3 cups of the water to skillet; bring to boiling, scraping off brown bits. Pour over meat. Stir in carrots, 3 teaspoons of the salt, pepper, ginger and cinnamon. Bring to boiling.

3. For couscous, dissolve the remaining 1 teaspoon salt in the remaining cup water; sprinkle about ½ cup over couscous in a large bowl to moisten; place in a large, fine-mesh sieve. Hang sieve on edge of stock pot over stew, not touching stew. Cover tightly with foil to keep steam in. Simmer 40 minutes.

4. Remove sieve; stir zucchini, tomatoes, chick-peas and raisins into stew. Sprinkle remaining salted water over couscous; mix or stir with a fork. Set sieve over stew again to steam. Simmer 30 minutes longer, or until meats and vegetables are tender. Thicken stew with a little flour mixed with water, if you wish. Turn couscous into a large bowl; drizzle melted butter over; toss to mix.

5. To serve, spoon stew into center of a deep platter. Arrange the steamed, buttered couscous around edge.

Or you may substitute brown or white rice or kasha for the couscous and cook, following label directions.

STUFFED BREAST OF VEAL

Vermouth is *the* braising liquid—a natural for cooking veal since it is already flavored with aromatic herbs. For a full, robust flavor, use it straight. For a more delicate flavor, dilute slightly with water or broth.
Makes 10 servings.

    4 long thin carrots
    ½ pound fresh spinach, washed
    ½ pound sausage meat
    ½ cup soft white bread crumbs (1 slice)
    1 egg
    1 boned breast of veal (about 4 pounds)
    2 tablespoons olive or vegetable oil
    1 large onion, sliced
 1⅓ cups dry vermouth
    1 can (16 ounces) stewed tomatoes
    ½ teaspoon salt
    ½ teaspoon leaf basil, crumbled
    ½ cup pitted green olives, drained

1. Parboil carrots in boiling salted water in a medium-size saucepan 10 minutes; drain. Cool. Cook spinach in water clinging to leaves, just until wilted, about 3 minutes. Drain well, then squeeze dry with hands.
2. Combine sausage, bread crumbs and egg in a small bowl; beat with a wooden spoon or fork until smooth.
3. Spread veal flat, skin-side down, on a board. Spread sausage mixture evenly over veal to within 1-inch from edges. Spread spinach over sausage, then arrange carrots evenly spaced crosswise over meat.
4. Roll in jelly-roll fashion, starting at one of the shorter sides. (Carrots go lengthwise through roll.) Fasten edge with skewers. Tie with string at 1½-inch intervals.
5. Brown roll in oil in a Dutch oven or large deep skillet, about 10 minutes. Add onion; sauté 5 minutes. Stir in vermouth, tomatoes, salt and basil. Bring to boiling; lower heat; cover. Simmer, basting and turning meat several times, 2½ hours, or until meat is very tender. Lift roll to a heated serving platter; keep warm.
6. Add olives to sauce; simmer 10 minutes.
7. Remove string and skewers from veal; slice about ½-inch thick. Serve with a packaged rice pilaf or curry, and sprinkle with chopped celery tops and shredded orange rind, if you wish.

VEAL STEW MILANESE

Makes 8 servings.

 2½ pounds boneless shoulder or breast of veal
    2 tablespoons flour
 1½ teaspoons salt
    ¼ teaspoon pepper
    2 tablespoons vegetable oil
    2 tablespoons butter or margarine
    1 cup chopped leek or onion
    ½ cup finely diced celery
    ½ cup finely diced carrot
    ¼ cup chopped parsley
    1 teaspoon leaf basil, crumbled
    ¾ cup dry white wine
    1 can (1 pound) whole tomatoes
    1 package (10 ounces) frozen peas
    2 teaspoons chopped lemon rind (yellow only)
    1 small clove garlic, minced
    2 tablespoons chopped parsley

1. Cut veal into 2-inch cubes. Shake in a mixture of flour, salt and pepper in a plastic bag to coat evenly.
2. Heat oil and butter in a heavy kettle or Dutch oven. Brown veal pieces, half at a time, removing pieces as they brown.
3. Sauté leek, celery and carrot in same kettle until soft, about 5 minutes. Stir in parsley, basil and wine. Bring to boiling; simmer, uncovered, until slightly reduced, 4 minutes. Add tomatoes and veal; cover.
4. Simmer, stirring occasionally, 2 hours, or until meat is tender. Stir in peas; cook, covered, 5 minutes, or just until tender.
5. Combine lemon rind, garlic and remaining 2 tablespoons parsley in a cup. Sprinkle over stew just before serving. Serve with hot cooked rice or buttered noodles, if you wish.

Stuffed Breast of Veal

Bottom left: Chicken Provençale; Chicken Parmesan

Poultry: Chicken, Turkey, Duck

Good buys that invite creativity in fixing
dozens of tasty, good-loking combinations.

CHICKEN PARMESAN
Speedy and delicious.
Makes 4 servings.

2 whole chicken breasts (about 14
   ounces each), split
1 tablespoon flour
½ teaspoon salt
⅛ teaspoon pepper
1 egg
1 tablespoon water
½ cup packaged bread crumbs
2 tablespoons grated Parmesan cheese
1 tablespoon butter or margarine
1 tablespoon vegetable oil
½ cup dry white wine or chicken broth
1 tablespoon drained capers
4 thin lemon slices

1. Skin and bone chicken; flatten slightly
between sheets of wax paper with a rolling
pin or the flat side of a meat mallet. Combine flour, salt and pepper on wax paper;
turn chicken in flour to coat on both sides.
2. Beat egg slightly in a shallow dish; stir in
water. Combine bread crumbs and cheese
on wax paper. Dip chicken in egg mixture,
then in crumbs, repeating until all coating
mixtures are used. Chill at least 30 minutes.
3. Heat butter and oil in a large skillet.
Sauté chicken 3 minutes on each side. Remove to a heated serving platter; keep
warm.
4. Add wine to the skillet, stirring and
scraping up browned bits, about 3 minutes;
stir in capers. Spoon sauce over chicken;
top each piece with a slice of lemon.

CHICKEN PROVENÇALE
Savory chicken breasts with the hearty
country flavor of Southern France's cuisine.
Makes 4 servings.

2 whole chicken breasts (about 14
   ounces each), split
2 tablespoons flour
½ teaspoon salt
⅛ teaspoon pepper
1 tablespoon butter or margarine
1 tablespoon vegetable oil
1 clove garlic, minced
1 small onion, chopped (¼ cup)
1 can (8¼ ounces) tomatoes, drained
   and chopped
½ cup dry white wine or chicken broth
½ cup sliced pitted black olives
2 tablespoons chopped parsley

1. Skin and bone chicken; flatten slightly
between sheets of wax paper with a rolling
pin or the flat side of a meat mallet. Combine flour, salt and pepper on wax paper;
turn chicken in flour to coat on both sides.
2. Heat butter and oil in a large skillet.
Sauté chicken for 3 minutes on one side
only; remove to a plate.
3. Sauté garlic and onion in the skillet until tender, about 3 minutes. Stir in tomatoes
and wine.
4. Return chicken to the skillet, uncooked-side down. Spoon some sauce over chicken. Lower heat and simmer until sauce is
slightly thickened, about 5 minutes. Add
olives; heat 1 more minute. Sprinkle with
parsley.

171

OVEN-BAKED CHICKEN KIEV

This classic of Russian cuisine is a boneless breast of chicken, wrapped around herbed butter. Be careful when you cut it open at the dinner table—the butter will spurt out.

Bake at 425° for 5 minutes, then at 400° for 25 minutes.

Makes 6 servings.

> 7 tablespoons butter or margarine, softened
> 2 tablespoons chopped parsley
> ½ teaspoon leaf tarragon, crumbled
> ¼ teaspoon salt
> ⅛ teaspoon pepper
> 3 whole chicken breasts (about 2½ pounds)
> 1½ cups packaged bread crumbs
> 2 tablespoons flour
> 1 egg

1. Combine 6 tablespoons of the butter, parsley, tarragon, salt and pepper in a small bowl. Spread mixture on wax paper to a 4x3-inch rectangle. Place mixture in freezer to harden.

2. Split chicken breasts; remove skin; carefully cut meat from bones, keeping the meat in whole pieces (6 in all). Place each piece, smooth-side down, between 2 sheets of wax paper. Flatten with a meat mallet to about ¼-inch thickness, being careful not to break the meat.

3. Remove parsley butter from freezer. Cut into 6 equal finger-size pieces.

4. Place a "finger" of parsley butter in the center of each flattened chicken breast. Bring long sides of the chicken over butter; then fold ends over, being sure butter is completely covered by chicken. Fasten securely with wooden picks.

5. Thoroughly combine bread crumbs and the remaining 1 tablespoon butter on wax paper; place flour on another piece of wax paper; beat egg in a small bowl. Roll each chicken roll completely in flour, then egg, then in crumb mixture to coat completely.

Refrigerate 2 hours to set coating.

6. Place chicken rolls in a single layer in a jelly-roll pan.

7. Bake in a very hot oven (425°) for 5 minutes. Lower heat to 400°; bake 25 minutes longer. Good with rice pilaf.

> **When breading chicken pieces before frying, take the time to refrigerate the coated chicken for at least 30 minutes. The extra step will pay a good dividend: the chilling sets the crust and keeps it on the chicken instead of in the skillet.**

CHICKEN BREASTS IN TARRAGON

Makes 4 servings.

> 2 whole chicken breasts (about 12 ounces each), split
> 2 tablespoons butter or margarine
> 2 teaspoons flour
> ½ teaspoon salt
> ½ teaspoon leaf tarragon, crumbled
> OR: 1½ teaspoons chopped fresh tarragon
> 1 teaspoon Dijon-style mustard
> ½ cup dry white wine
> ½ cup half and half

1. Skin and bone chicken breasts; sauté in butter in a large skillet about 3 minutes on each side, or until they feel springy to the touch. (Don't overcook.) Remove to plate; keep warm.

2. Add flour, salt, tarragon and mustard; gradually stir in wine; cook, stirring to scrape up browned bits in pan; add half and half; cook until the mixture thickens slightly. Pour over the chicken breasts.

> **Chicken, how much to buy:** On the bone, allow ¾ to 1 pound per person.

CASSEROLE-BRAISED CHICKEN

Bake at 325° for 1¼ hours.
Makes 4 servings.

    1 whole broiler-fryer (about 3 pounds)
1½ teaspoons salt
 ¼ teaspoon pepper
 16 small white onions
 12 small red new potatoes
    3 tablespoons butter or margarine
    3 tablespoons vegetable oil
 ½ cup boiling water
    1 envelope or teaspoon instant
         chicken broth
    1 teaspoon leaf basil, crumbled
    1 teaspoon salt
    1 tablespoon chopped parsley

1. Sprinkle chicken cavities with ½ teaspoon of the salt and the pepper. Peel onions. Scrub potatoes; pare a band around the center of each.

2. Melt butter with vegetable oil in a large heavy flameproof casserole or Dutch oven. Add chicken; brown on all sides.

3. Combine boiling water and chicken broth in a 1-cup measure, stirring until dissolved; add to casserole with chicken.

4. Place onions and potatoes around chicken; sprinkle with basil and the remaining 1 teaspoon salt; cover.

5. Bake in a slow oven (325°), basting once or twice with the juices, 1¼ hours, or until chicken and vegetables are tender. Sprinkle with parsley.

ROAST CHICKEN, INDIAN STYLE

An intriguing blend of spices, herbs and yogurt gives the chicken its rich golden color and delicious pungent flavor.

Roast at 350° for about 2½ hours or 20 minutes per pound.
Makes 8 servings.

 ⅛ teaspoon powdered saffron
    1 teaspoon hot water
    1 container (8 ounces) plain yogurt
    3 tablespoons lime juice
1½ teaspoons salt
    2 cloves garlic, minced
    1 teaspoon curry powder
 ½ teaspoon ground cumin
 ¼ teaspoon ground cardamom
 ¼ teaspoon ground ginger
    1 roasting chicken (about 6 pounds)
    3 tablespoons vegetable oil
    3 medium-size onions
1¼ cups chicken broth
    2 tablespoons flour
         Hot cooked couscous or rice

1. Soak saffron in hot water in a small bowl; stir in 4 tablespoons of the yogurt, the lime juice, salt, garlic, curry powder, cumin, cardamom and ginger.

2. Rub about 2 tablespoons of the yogurt mixture inside the chicken; rub remainder over skin to coat completely and evenly. Tie legs together. Let marinate at least 1 hour at room temperature, or several hours refrigerated. Place, breast-side up, in shallow roasting pan. Brush with oil.

3. Roast in a moderate oven (350°) for 1 hour; brush with pan juices. Cut each onion into 6 wedges; arrange around chicken. Continue roasting and basting 1 to 1½ hours longer or until drumstick moves easily at joint. Arrange chicken and onions on heated platter with couscous or rice. Keep warm.

4. Add chicken broth to roasting pan; set pan over a burner and heat while stirring to loosen browned bits. Strain pan juices into a 2-cup measure; skim fat; measure 2 tablespoons fat into a small saucepan. Stir in flour; cook and stir over medium heat 1 minute. Stir in skimmed pan juices; continue cooking and stirring until sauce thickens and bubbles 2 minutes. Stir in remaining yogurt. Taste; add more salt and lime juice if needed. (Sauce will look slightly curdled.) Serve with chicken. Garnish platter with parsley, lime wedges and kumquats, and serve with chutney, if you wish.

Herb-Roasted Chicken

ROAST CHICKEN WITH LEMON

Deliciously simple.
Bake at 350° for 35 minutes, then at 400° for 15 minutes.
Makes 4 servings.

- 1 whole broiler-fryer (about 2½ pounds)
- 1 teaspoon salt
- ¼ teaspoon pepper
- 2 small lemons

1. Wash chicken; pat dry inside and out with paper toweling. Sprinkle with salt and pepper, rubbing into all surfaces inside and out.

2. Soften lemons by pressing and rolling back and forth on countertop with hands. Pierce each lemon in at least 20 places with a skewer. Put lemons in chicken cavity.

3. Close cavity with string and skewers. Tie legs together very loosely. Place chicken breast-side down on a rack in a roasting pan.

4. Roast in a moderate oven (350°) in top third of oven for 15 minutes. Turn, being careful not to break skin. (If skin is not broken, chicken will swell like a balloon.) Continue roasting for 20 minutes. Turn oven heat to hot (400°) and roast an additional 10 to 15 minutes. Serve chicken with all the juices.

HERB-ROASTED CHICKEN

Bake at 375° for 2½ hours.
Makes 6 servings.

- 1 roasting chicken (about 5 pounds)
- 1 teaspoon salt
- ¼ teaspoon pepper
  Buttery Bread Stuffing
  (*recipe follows*)
- ½ cup (1 stick) butter or margarine, melted
- 1 tablespoon chopped chives
- 1 tablespoon chopped parsley
- ½ teaspoon leaf rosemary, crumbled
- ½ teaspoon leaf thyme, crumbled
- 1 clove garlic, minced
- 2 tablespoons flour
- 1 can (13¾ ounces) chicken broth
- ½ cup dry white wine

1. Sprinkle chicken cavities with salt and pepper.

2. Stuff neck and body cavities lightly with Buttery Bread Stuffing. Skewer neck skin to back; close body cavity and tie legs to tail. Place chicken on a rack in a roasting pan. Combine melted butter with chives, parsley, rosemary, thyme and garlic. Brush part of mixture over chicken.

3. Roast in a moderate oven (375°), basting every 30 minutes, 2½ hours or until tender. Remove strings or skewers. Transfer to a heated serving platter; keep warm.

4. Make sauce: Pour off excess fat from roasting pan. Stir flour into pan juices; cook, stirring constantly, 1 minute. Blend in chicken broth and wine; cook, stirring constantly, until mixture thickens and bubbles. Serve separately.

5. Serve chicken with pan-browned potatoes and green beans, if you wish.

BUTTERY BREAD STUFFING
Makes 5 cups.

- 4 cups firm white bread cubes
- ½ cup (1 stick) butter or margarine
- 3 medium-size onions, finely chopped (1½ cups)
- 1 cup finely chopped celery with tops

¼ cup chopped parsley
1 teaspoon poultry seasoning
1 teaspoon salt
¼ teaspoon pepper

1. Place bread cubes in a single layer on a jelly-roll pan. Toast in a moderate oven (350°) for 10 minutes.
2. Melt butter in a large skillet; sauté onion and celery until tender, about 5 minutes. Add bread cubes, parsley, poultry seasoning, salt and pepper; toss until moistened.

ROAST CHICKEN WITH WILD RICE AND FRUIT DRESSING

Roast at 350° for 1¾ hours.
Makes 8 servings.

2 tablespoons leaf rosemary, crumbled
2 tablespoons leaf tarragon, crumbled
⅓ cup dry white wine or chicken broth
½ cup (1 stick) butter or margarine, softened
2 whole broiler-fryers (3½ pounds each)
1 teaspoon salt

½ teaspoon pepper
1 fresh pear, cored and chopped
1 package (6 ounces) wild rice mix, cooked following label directions

1. Combine rosemary, tarragon and wine in a small bowl; let stand 1 hour. Strain; reserve herbs and liquid separately. Blend butter into herbs.
2. Sprinkle cavity of each chicken with part of the salt and pepper; add 1 tablespoon of the herb butter. Loosen skin over breast; press in about 2 tablespoons of the herb butter.
3. Sauté chopped pear in 1 tablespoon of the herb butter. Blend with cooked wild rice. Stuff chickens with wild rice; truss.
4. Combine remaining tablespoon of herb butter with 1 tablespoon of the reserved liquid. Brush over birds. Sprinkle with remaining salt and pepper.
5. Roast in a moderate oven (350°), basting frequently with pan juices for 1¾ to 2 hours, or until leg moves easily and juices are no longer pink.
6. Serve with sautéed zucchini, broccoli, yellow squash and carrots, if you wish.

Roast Chicken with Wild Rice and Fruit Dressing

> The popular broiler-fryer chicken, available from 1½ to 3½ pounds, is a most versatile bird. In addition to frying, broiling and simmering, the bird makes an excellent roast. Roasting at 375° instead of 325° keeps the bird tender.

LEMON-BUTTER BROILED CHICKEN

Chicken quarters broiled with lemon and herbs have a wonderful flavor.

Broil 40 minutes.
Makes 4 servings.

- 1 broiler-fryer (3 pounds), quartered
- 1 teaspoon seasoned salt
- ¼ teaspoon pepper
- ¼ cup (½ stick) butter or margarine
- 2 tablespoons lemon juice
- ½ teaspoon leaf tarragon, crumbled
- ½ teaspoon leaf chervil, crumbled
- 2 tablespoons dry vermouth

1. Sprinkle chicken quarters on both sides with salt and pepper.
2. Melt butter in small saucepan; add lemon juice, tarragon, chervil and vermouth; brush part over chicken.
3. Place chicken, skin side down, on rack of broiler.
4. Broil, 6 inches from heat, 20 minutes, basting frequently. Turn; broil 15 to 20 minutes longer, or until nicely browned, brushing with remaining lemon-butter.

CHICKEN FLAUTAS WITH SALSA

Makes 6 servings.

- 1 medium-size onion, chopped (½ cup)
- 1 clove garlic, minced
- 2 tablespoons vegetable shortening or lard
- 1 tablespoon cornstarch
- 1¼ teaspoons salt
- ¼ teaspoon pepper
- ½ cup chicken broth
- 2¼ cups chopped or shredded cooked chicken
- 1 can (4 ounces) chopped green chilies
  Vegetable oil for frying
- 12 canned, refrigerated, or thawed, frozen corn tortillas
  Salsa (*recipe follows*)

1. Sauté onion and garlic in shortening in a large saucepan until tender, about 3 minutes. Stir in cornstarch, salt and pepper; mix well. Stir in broth, chicken and chilies. Cook, stirring constantly, until very thick and bubbly.
2. Heat a ¼-inch depth of oil in a large skillet. Dip tortillas into hot oil for a few seconds to soften; drain on paper toweling. Spoon a heaping tablespoon of filling in center of each tortilla; roll up.
3. Sauté flautas, a few at a time, in hot oil in the skillet, turning often, until crisp, about 2 minutes. Keep flautas warm until all are cooked. Serve with Salsa. Garnish with lettuce, if you wish.

SALSA: Chop 2 medium-size ripe tomatoes, 1 medium-size onion and 1 medium-size halved and seeded green pepper. Combine with ¼ cup chopped parsley, 1 minced clove garlic, ½ teaspoon salt, ⅛ teaspoon pepper and ⅛ teaspoon ground cumin in a small bowl; mix well. Refrigerate 1 hour, or until cold.

> An egg for thickening or enriching a hot sauce or gravy can be handled easily. Just beat the egg with an equal amount of cream before stirring into the hot sauce. Mixing the egg with the cream first, prevents curdling and results in a smooth sauce.

POLLO VERDE

In Mexico there are many versions of "green chicken." This one includes yellow squash and two kinds of green peppers. Makes 6 servings.

    3 tablespoons olive or vegetable oil
    ½ teaspoon salt
    ¼ teaspoon pepper
    1 broiler-fryer (about 3 pounds),
        cut up
    2 large onions, chopped (2 cups)
    3 cloves garlic, minced
    1 can (4 ounces) chopped green
        chilies, drained
    1 can (13¾ ounces) chicken broth
    3 medium-size yellow squash, diced
    2 sweet green peppers, halved, seeded
        and thinly sliced
    1½ cups uncooked long-grain rice

1. Heat oil in a very large skillet or Dutch oven over moderate heat. Sprinkle salt and pepper over chicken; sauté 5 minutes on each side. Remove; reserve.

2. Add onions, garlic and chilies to the skillet and cook until onion is tender, about 3 minutes. Stir in broth and bring to boiling.

3. Return chicken to the skillet; lower heat; cover; simmer 10 minutes.

4. Add squash, green pepper and rice to the skillet, taking care that rice is submerged in liquid. Cover and cook over low heat 20 minutes, or until rice and chicken are tender.

COUNTRY CAPTAIN

A famous Southern curry dish. Makes 8 servings.

    ¼ cup flour
    2 teaspoons salt
    ½ teaspoon pepper
    2 broiler-fryers (about 2½ pounds
        each), cut up
    3 tablespoons vegetable oil
    1 large onion, chopped (1 cup)
    1 large sweet green pepper, halved,
        seeded and chopped
    1 large clove garlic, minced
    3 teaspoons curry powder
    1 can (1 pound) tomatoes
    ½ cup raisins or currants
        Hot cooked rice

1. Combine flour with 1 teaspoon of the salt and ¼ teaspoon of the pepper in a plastic bag. Add chicken pieces, a few at a time, and shake in flour mixture to coat; shake off excess.

2. Brown chicken, a few pieces at a time, in oil in a heavy kettle or Dutch oven. Remove chicken to a heated dish; keep warm.

3. Add onion, green pepper, garlic and curry powder to fat remaining in the kettle; sauté until tender. Add tomatoes (breaking with a spoon), raisins, the remaining salt and pepper and reserved chicken; cover. Simmer 40 minutes, or until chicken is tender. Arrange chicken on a bed of hot cooked rice. Spoon sauce over.

CHICKEN FACTS:

Dieter's choice: Poultry is a good choice for the dieter. Chicken breasts can be pan-fried in a skillet, without fat, by cooking skin side down very slowly, until the meat yields enough of the natural fat present in the chicken to continue cooking. Since most of the fat is in the skin, removing the skin after cooking will make the calorie count even less.

To freeze fresh chicken: Remove store wrapping and cardboard or plastic tray. Rinse chicken in cold water; pat dry. If chicken is cut up, wrap pieces separately, then bundle together in a plastic freezer-weight bag. Label and date. (It is easier to defrost the separated pieces.) Store at 0° for up to 3 months.

Money saver: Save the giblets when buying whole birds and keep them in the freezer. When you have a pound or so, make a hearty spaghetti sauce.

OVEN-FRIED CHICKEN WITH BISCUITS AND CREAM GRAVY

Bake at 425° for 1 hour.
Makes 4 servings.

- ½ cup flour
- 2 teaspoons salt
- 1 teaspoon paprika
- 1 teaspoon leaf thyme, crumbled
- ¼ teaspoon pepper
- 1 broiler-fryer (2½ pounds), cut up
- ¼ cup vegetable shortening or oil
- ¼ cup (½ stick) butter or margarine
  Biscuits (*recipe follows*)
  Cream Gravy (*recipe follows*)

1. Measure flour, salt, paprika, thyme and pepper into a large plastic bag. Add chicken pieces, a few at a time; shake to coat thoroughly. Reserve seasoned flour for gravy.
2. Melt shortening and butter in a 13x9x2-inch baking pan in a hot oven (425°), about 5 minutes. Remove pan from oven and arrange chicken in one layer in butter-oil mixture, turning to coat. Return to oven and bake for 40 minutes, turning once or twice.
3. Prepare biscuits: Push chicken to one side of pan. Drop biscuits into 8 large mounds; return to oven. Bake an additional 20 minutes, or until biscuits are brown.
4. Place chicken and biscuits on a heated platter; keep warm. Prepare the gravy.

BISCUITS: Sift 2 cups *sifted* all-purpose flour with 1 tablespoon baking powder and ½ teaspoon salt. Cut in ¼ cup shortening until mixture has the consistency of cornmeal. Stir in 1 cup milk with a fork.

CREAM GRAVY: Drain off all but 2 tablespoons fat from the baking pan; heat in pan over low heat. Stir in 2 tablespoons of the reserved seasoned flour; cook and stir 1 minute. Gradually stir in 1½ cups milk, light cream or half and half, scraping up browned bits in the pan. Bring to boiling, stirring constantly; lower heat; cook until mixture is thickened and bubbly; stir in 1 teaspoon grated lemon rind; cook 2 minutes longer. Serve with chicken and biscuits to spoon over each serving.

SOUTHERN BARBECUED CHICKEN WITH SAUCE

Try this savory chicken for a cookout.
Makes 4 servings.

- 2 broiler-fryers (about 2½ pounds each), split
- 1 tablespoon vegetable oil
  Salt and pepper
- 2 tablespoons butter or margarine
- 6 tablespoons vinegar
- ¼ cup water
- 1½ cups catsup
- 2 tablespoons Worcestershire sauce
- ¼ teaspoon liquid red-pepper seasoning
- 2 cloves garlic, minced
- 3 tablespoons vegetable oil
- ½ teaspoon salt
- ¼ teaspoon pepper
- ¼ teaspoon crushed red pepper flakes
- ½ bay leaf
- 2 tablespoons sugar
- 1 teaspoon paprika
- 2 tablespoons lemon juice

1. Place chickens skin-side up on a flat surface and flatten with the heel of the hand or a mallet to keep them flat on the grill. Rub with oil and sprinkle with salt and pepper.
2. Make a southern barbecue sauce: Combine butter, vinegar, water, catsup, Worcestershire, red-pepper seasoning, garlic, oil, salt and pepper, crushed red pepper, bay leaf, sugar, paprika and lemon juice in a saucepan. Heat on side of the grill but do not allow to boil.
3. Grill chicken skin-side up 6 inches from the hot coals, about 10 minutes, or until browned. Brush with sauce; turn and brush the bone side with sauce. Continue grilling, brushing often with sauce, until chicken is tender, but not dry, about 30 minutes in all.
4. Remove chicken to a serving platter and give a final brushing with sauce.

Beer Batter Fried Chicken

MARYLAND FRIED CHICKEN WITH CREAM GRAVY AND BISCUITS

Fried chicken served Southern-style is a favorite all around the country.

Makes 4 servings.

    1 broiler-fryer (3 pounds), cut up
    ½ cup flour
    2 teaspoons salt
    ½ teaspoon pepper
    ½ teaspoon leaf marjoram, crumbled
        Vegetable oil
    1 cup half and half
    1 package (4.5 ounces) refrigerated
        buttermilk biscuits

1. Shake chicken in plastic bag with flour, salt, pepper and marjoram until thoroughly coated. Reserve 2 tablespoons of the flour mixture.

2. Pour enough vegetable oil into a large skillet to make a 1-inch depth. Heat to 375° on a deep-fat frying thermometer, or until a cube of bread turns golden in 60 seconds.

3. Sauté chicken, a few pieces at a time, until brown. Remove and drain on paper toweling. Pour off oil from skillet into measuring cup. Return 2 tablespoons to skillet.

4. Return chicken pieces to skillet, skin-side up. Cover; cook over low heat, 30 minutes, or until chicken is tender. Uncover and cook 10 minutes longer to crisp skin. Remove to serving platter; keep warm.

5. Sprinkle the reserved 2 tablespoons flour into fat in skillet; cook 1 minute. Add half and half, stirring and scraping up browned bits. Cook, stirring constantly, until thickened and bubbly. Pour into gravy boat.

6. Bake biscuits following label directions; serve with chicken. Pass gravy to spoon over biscuits and chicken.

BEER BATTER FRIED CHICKEN

This light batter makes a crunchy coating for the chicken.

Makes 8 servings.

    1¾ cups *sifted* all-purpose flour
    1½ teaspoons salt
    ½ teaspoon pepper
    1 can (12 ounces) beer
    2 broiler-fryers (2½ pounds each),
        cut up
        Vegetable oil

1. Combine flour, salt and pepper in a medium-size bowl. Beat in beer with a wire whisk or rotary beater until smooth. Let stand 30 minutes.

2. Pour enough vegetable oil into a large skillet or saucepan to make a 1-inch depth. Heat to 375° on a deep-fat frying thermometer or until a cube of bread turns golden in about 60 seconds.

3. Dip chicken pieces into the beer batter a few at a time, allowing excess to drain back into the bowl.

4. Fry chicken pieces, turning once, for 30 minutes, or until chicken is browned. Garnish with parsley and serve with onion rings, if you wish.

> **Beer batter will fry crisper and lighter if allowed to stand awhile after mixing. This gives the flour granules time to soften and absorb the liquid.**

CHICKEN PAPRIKA WITH SPÄTZLE

Savory paprika-flavored chicken in sour cream sauce, served with tender home-made dumplings.

Makes 6 servings.

     1 broiler-fryer (3 to 3½ pounds),
       cut up
    ½ cup flour
  1½ teaspoons salt
    ¼ teaspoon pepper
    ½ cup (1 stick) butter or margarine
     1 large onion, chopped (1 cup)
     2 tablespoons paprika
     1 cup chicken broth
     1 cup light cream or half and half
    ½ cup dairy sour cream
       Spätzle (*recipe follows*)

1. Shake chicken in a plastic bag with flour, 1 teaspoon of the salt and the pepper until coated. Reserve 2 tablespoons of the flour mixture.

2. Brown chicken in butter in a large skillet; remove; keep warm. Pour pan fat into a measuring cup. Measure and return 3 tablespoons to the skillet.

3. Sauté onion in fat until tender, about 3 minutes. Add paprika, the remaining ½ teaspoon salt and chicken broth. Bring to boiling; lower heat; return chicken, turning to coat. Simmer, covered, 30 minutes, or until chicken is tender. Remove chicken; keep warm in a heated serving dish.

4. Stir light cream into skillet. Combine 2 tablespoons of the flour mixture and sour cream; slowly stir into skillet. Cook, stirring constantly, over low heat until thickened. Spoon sauce over chicken; serve over Spätzle. Sprinkle with chopped parsley, if you wish.

SPÄTZLE
Makes 6 servings.

     3 cups *sifted* all-purpose flour
     1 teaspoon salt
    ⅛ teaspoon pepper
     3 eggs, slightly beaten
     1 cup water
    ¼ cup (½ stick) butter or margarine,
       melted

1. Combine flour, salt and pepper in a medium-size bowl; make a well in center. Add eggs and water to well, stir briskly until thoroughly mixed.

2. Half fill a large saucepan with water; bring to boiling.

3. Scoop up dough on a spatula and cut off small pieces with a knife, dropping into the boiling salted water. As Spätzle rises to the top, scoop out with a slotted spoon and put into a heated covered bowl until all are made. Toss with melted butter; keep warm.

PAELLA

The Spanish chicken-and-rice classic with an Italian accent.

Bake at 400° for 50 minutes.

Makes 6 servings.

     4 hot or sweet Italian sausages
    ¼ cup olive or vegetable oil
     1 broiler-fryer (about 3 pounds), cut up
     1 large onion, chopped (1 cup)
     1 clove garlic, minced
  1½ cups uncooked long-grain rice
     1 can (8 ounces) tomato sauce
     1 can (13¾ ounces) chicken broth
     2 cups water
     1 teaspoon leaf oregano, crumbled
     1 teaspoon salt
    ¼ teaspoon pepper
    ¼ teaspoon powdered saffron
    ½ pound shelled and deveined fresh
       shrimp
       OR: 1 package (8 ounces) frozen
         shelled and deveined shrimp,
         slightly thawed
     1 package (9 ounces) frozen Italian
       green beans
     1 jar (4 ounces) pimientos, drained and
       slivered

1. Parboil sausages in water to cover in a small saucepan, 10 minutes; drain; cut into ¼-inch slices.

2. Heat oil in a paella pan or a large deep skillet. Brown chicken pieces a few at a time; remove pieces as they brown.

3. Sauté onion and garlic in the same skillet until tender, about 3 minutes. Add rice, tomato sauce, chicken broth, water, oregano, salt, pepper and saffron. Bring to boiling. If using a paella pan, place chicken pieces on top of rice mixture. (If using a skillet, pour mixture into a 13x9x2-inch baking dish.) Cover with aluminum foil.

4. Bake in a hot oven (400°) 30 minutes. Add shrimp and sausages to mixture. Cov-er; bake 20 minutes longer, or until chicken, rice and shrimp are tender.

5. Cook green beans following label directions; drain. Fluff up rice mixture; stir in pimiento; arrange green beans around the edge of the pan.

> Turmeric can be substituted for the more expensive saffron, if you wish. The taste will be different, but the color will be just as golden.

Paella

HULI HULI CHICKEN

Huli—in Hawaiian—means "to turn," and that's how you cook this fantastic chicken —turn it over and over on a grill.

Makes 6 servings.

3 broiler-fryers (about 2½ pounds each) split or quartered
¼ cup catsup
¼ cup soy sauce
¼ cup white wine or chicken broth
3 tablespoons frozen concentrate for pineapple juice
1 tablespoon Worcestershire sauce
1 tablespoon finely chopped gingerroot

1. Wash chicken halves; pat thoroughly dry with paper toweling.
2. Mix catsup, soy sauce, wine, pineapple concentrate, Worcestershire and ginger in a small bowl; brush part over chicken.
3. Grill, 5 to 6 inches from grayed coals, turning and basting often with sauce until chicken is browned and meat is no longer pink near bone, about 40 minutes.

CHICKEN FRICASSEE

Makes 8 servings.

1 roasting chicken (5 pounds)
  OR: 2 broiler-fryers (2½-pounds each), cut up
1 medium-size onion
1 celery stalk, halved
1 carrot
4 cloves
4 peppercorns
1 teaspoon salt
1 bay leaf
12 small white onions (1 pound)
1 pound carrots, pared and cut into 1½-inch pieces
1 package (10 ounces) frozen lima beans
3 tablespoons butter or margarine
1 teaspoon salt
3 tablespoons flour
¼ teaspoon pepper
½ teaspoon leaf thyme, crumbled
3 egg yolks
1 cup light cream or half and half
1 tablespoon lemon juice

1. Place chicken in a kettle or Dutch oven with water to cover. Bring to boiling; skim off foam. Add onion, celery, carrot, cloves, peppercorns, 1 teaspoon of the salt and bay leaf. Lower heat; cover; simmer roaster 45 minutes, broiler-fryers 30 minutes, or until chicken is tender, but does not fall away from bones. Remove to large serving bowl; keep warm.
2. Strain broth; return to kettle; add onions and carrots; cover; cook 20 minutes, or until firm-tender; add lima beans and cook 5 minutes longer. Remove vegetables with slotted spoon; add to serving bowl. Measure out 2 cups chicken broth. (Use remainder for soups and gravies.)
3. Melt butter in a large skillet; add flour, the remaining 1 teaspoon salt, pepper and thyme; cook 1 minute; carefully stir in the 2 cups of broth; cook, stirring constantly, until thick and bubbly. Beat egg yolks with cream; add slowly to gravy in skillet, stirring constantly. Cook over medium-low heat, until bubbly, about 2 minutes; add lemon juice. Spoon over chicken and vegetables. Sprinkle with chopped parsley, if you wish.

EASY OVEN CHICKEN AND VEGETABLES

Bake at 375° for 1½ hours.
Makes 6 servings.

2 cups sliced leeks (white part only)
1 pound mushrooms
2 tablespoons butter or margarine
6 chicken legs (1½ pounds)
6 chicken thighs (1½ pounds)
¼ cup vermouth or dry white wine
1 can condensed cream of mushroom soup
¼ teaspoon pepper

1. Sauté leeks and mushrooms in butter in

a large skillet, stirring frequently until tender, about 5 minutes. Transfer to a 13x9x2-inch baking dish.

2. Arrange chicken pieces, skin-side up, on vegetable mixture.

3. Mix wine, soup and pepper in a 2-cup measure. Pour over chicken.

4. Bake in a moderate oven (375°) for 1½ hours, basting occasionally, or until chicken is lightly browned and tender.

CHICKEN CACCIATORE

Makes 4 servings.

⅓ cup plus 1 tablespoon flour
1 teaspoon salt
½ teaspoon pepper
1 broiler-fryer (about 3 pounds), cut up
3 tablespoons olive or vegetable oil
1 large onion, sliced
3 cloves garlic, minced
½ pound mushrooms, sliced
6 medium-size ripe tomatoes, cored and cut into wedges
¼ cup dry red wine
1½ teaspoons salt
½ teaspoon pepper
1 tablespoon Italian seasoning
1 can (6 ounces) tomato paste
1 sweet green pepper, seeded and sliced

1. Combine the ⅓ cup flour, 1 teaspoon of the salt and ½ teaspoon of the pepper in a plastic bag. Add chicken; shake to coat well.

2. Heat oil in Dutch oven. Brown chicken, part at a time; remove; keep warm.

3. Pour off all but 1 tablespoon oil. Add onion, garlic and mushrooms; cook 1 minute. Add tomatoes, wine, remaining salt and pepper and Italian seasoning. Simmer, stirring often, 15 minutes.

4. Stir in tomato paste; return chicken.

5. Simmer over low heat for 1 hour, or until chicken is tender.

6. Remove chicken to a heated serving platter; keep warm. Blend the remaining 1 tablespoon flour with small amount of

water in cup; stir into sauce. Add green pepper; bring to boiling. Cook and stir until sauce is thickened; spoon over chicken.

CAJUN JAMBALAYA

Makes 8 servings.

1 broiler-fryer (about 3 pounds), cut up
½ teaspoon salt
¼ teaspoon pepper
2 tablespoons bacon fat
2 tablespoons flour
1 pound smoked sausage, sliced
1 large onion, chopped (1 cup)
1 sweet green pepper, halved, seeded and diced
3 cups diced, peeled ripe tomatoes
1 clove garlic, minced
3 cups water
¾ teaspoon leaf thyme, crumbled
½ teaspoon salt
½ teaspoon liquid red-pepper seasoning
2 cups uncooked long-grain rice
1 pound fresh shrimp, shelled and deveined
   OR: 1 package (12 ounces) frozen shelled and deveined shrimp
¼ cup chopped parsley
⅓ cup finely chopped green onions

1. Sprinkle chicken with the ½ teaspoon of the salt and the pepper. Heat bacon fat in a large skillet; brown chicken; remove from skillet.

2. Sprinkle flour into fat remaining in skillet. Cook, stirring constantly, until the mixture (called a "roux") turns light brown.

3. Return chicken to skillet, along with sausage, onion, green pepper, tomatoes and garlic. Cook, stirring, 10 minutes.

4. Stir in the water, thyme, the remaining ½ teaspoon salt, red-pepper seasoning and rice. Bring to boiling; lower heat; cover. Simmer 15 minutes. Stir in shrimp; simmer 15 minutes. Stir in parsley and green onions; simmer 5 minutes longer, or until rice is tender.

JUMBO CHICKEN POPOVER

Bake at 350° for 1 hour.
Makes 4 servings.

 1 broiler-fryer (about 3 pounds)
1¼ cups water
 4 tablespoons plus 1½ cups flour
 1 teaspoon salt
 1 teaspoon paprika
 ¼ teaspoon pepper
 ½ cup vegetable oil
1½ teaspoons baking powder
 1 teaspoon salt
 4 eggs
1½ cups milk
 3 tablespoons melted butter or
 margarine
 Cream Gravy (*recipe follows*)

1. Cut chicken into 8 pieces—2 breasts, 2 wings, 2 thighs, 2 drumsticks. Cut away back and any small bones from breasts. Simmer bones with neck and giblets in water in small saucepan, 1 hour. Strain; reserve 1 cup broth.
2. Shake chicken pieces with the 4 tablespoons flour, 1 teaspoon of the salt, paprika and pepper in a plastic bag to coat lightly.
3. Brown chicken, a few pieces at a time, on both sides, in hot oil in heavy skillet; drain on paper toweling.
4. Sift the 1½ cups flour, baking powder and remaining 1 teaspoon salt into a medium-size bowl.
5. Beat eggs slightly in a bowl; blend in milk and melted butter. Stir into dry ingredients; beat with rotary beater until smooth.
6. Pour batter into a buttered shallow 8-cup baking dish; arrange chicken in batter.
7. Bake in a moderate oven (350°) for 1 hour, or until golden. (Keep oven door closed for full hour.) Serve with Cream Gravy.

CREAM GRAVY: Melt 2 tablespoons butter in a small saucepan; blend in 2 tablespoons flour. Cook until bubbly, 1 minute. Stir in 1 cup half and half and the 1 cup reserved chicken broth. Cook until thickened and bubbly, about 2 minutes. Taste; add salt and pepper, if needed.

ITALIAN CHICKEN ROLL

Bake at 350° for 1 hour.
Makes 8 servings.

 2 sweet Italian sausages, each about
 5 inches long
 3 whole chicken breasts (about
 14 ounces each), skinned
 and boned
 ¼ pound sliced Genoa salami
 ¼ pound sliced prosciutto
 ¼ pound sliced mortadella
 2 cups fresh Italian or French
 bread crumbs (about 4 slices)
 ½ cup grated Parmesan cheese
 ¼ cup chopped parsley
 ⅔ cup olive oil
 2 tablespoons dry white wine
 6 eggs

1. Brown sausages slowly in a small skillet; drain on paper toweling.
2. Arrange chicken breasts in two rows between two long sheets of parchment or wax paper, overlapping slightly to fill spaces.
3. Pound with the side of a wooden meat mallet or a bottle until chicken meat is thin and as even as possible. Lift up the top sheet of paper occasionally and fill the empty spaces by pushing chicken meat together. (It may be necesary to replace the top sheet of paper.) You are aiming for a 10x15-inch solid sheet of chicken meat. Remove the top sheet of paper.
4. Arrange a layer of Genoa salami, then prosciutto, then mortadella over chicken breasts to within 1 inch of the edges.
5. Combine bread crumbs, Parmesan, parsley, 4 tablespoons of the olive oil and wine in a medium-size bowl. Spread mixture over cold cuts to 1 inch of the edges, pressing down firmly.
6. Beat eggs slightly in a medium-size bowl. Heat 2 tablespoons of the olive oil in

a large skillet. Add eggs; scramble softly.

7. Arrange eggs over the bread-crumb mixture at the 10-inch edge closest to you and spread upward 6 inches and to within 1 inch of the edges. Line up sausages end to end in the center of eggs.

8. Carefully roll up like a jelly-roll with the help of the bottom sheet of paper.

9. Cut a double thickness of cheesecloth long enough to cover chicken plus enough on ends to gather and tie. Carefully wrap around chicken roll. Tie ends and tie roll in 4 or 5 places with kitchen twine to keep shape. Brush cheesecloth all over with remaining olive oil. Place chicken roll on a rack in a roasting pan.

10. Bake in moderate oven (350°) for 45 minutes. Remove from oven. Carefully cut twine and remove cheesecloth. Brush chicken roll with pan drippings; return to oven and continue to bake 15 minutes longer until lightly browned.

11. Remove chicken roll to a heated serving platter; let rest 15 minutes before cutting. Garnish with watercress and cherry tomatoes, if you wish.

To serve cold: Remove from refrigerator about 30 minutes before serving.

STIR-FRIED CHICKEN WITH FRESH MUSHROOMS

Makes 4 servings.

      1 whole boneless chicken breast,
          skinned (about 12 ounces)
      2 teaspoons cornstarch
      5 tablespoons water
    ½ teaspoon salt
      2 medium-size zucchini
    ⅓ pound mushrooms
      5 tablespoons vegetable oil
      1 tablespoon dry sherry
      1 carrot, sliced and parboiled
      1 teaspoon salt
    1½ teaspoons cornstarch

1. Slice chicken breast into 2x1x⅛-inch pieces. Combine 2 teaspoons of the corn-

starch with 2 tablespoons of the water and ½ teaspoon of the salt; stir into chicken. (Chicken mixture can be kept in refrigerator for up to 24 hours.)

2. Halve zucchini lengthwise; slice diagonally into ½-inch pieces; slice mushrooms.

3. Heat large skillet or wok until very hot. Pour in 2 tablespoons of oil, then add chicken. Stir-fry quickly until chicken turns white and pieces separate. Sprinkle with sherry; transfer to a plate.

4. Reheat skillet, adding remaining 3 tablespoons of oil. Add vegetables and stir-fry quickly about 2 minutes, until crisp-tender. Sprinkle with the remaining 1 teaspoon salt. Return the chicken to the skillet.

5. Mix the remaining cornstarch and water. Pour into skillet, stirring constantly, until sauce coats chicken and vegetables.

CHICKEN ROSEMARY

Makes 4 servings.

      2 whole chicken breasts (14 ounces
          each), split
      2 tablespoons flour
    ½ teaspoon salt
    ⅛ teaspoon pepper
      1 tablespoon butter or margarine
      1 tablespoon vegetable oil
    ½ cup chopped leek (white part only)
    ¼ pound mushrooms, chopped
    ½ teaspoon leaf rosemary, crumbled
    ½ cup dry white wine or chicken broth

1. Skin and bone chicken. Flatten slightly between sheets of wax paper with a rolling pin or flat side of meat mallet. Combine flour, salt and pepper on wax paper. Turn chicken in flour to coat on both sides; shake off any excess.

2. Heat butter and oil in large skillet. Sauté leeks, mushrooms and rosemary until tender, about 3 minutes. Add chicken to pan. Sauté 3 minutes on one side; turn chicken pieces.

3. Stir in wine; cook 3 more minutes. Taste and add more salt and pepper, if you wish.

WALNUT CHICKEN WITH BROCCOLI
Makes 4 servings.

  2 whole chicken breasts (about 12 ounces each), skinned and boned
    OR: 1 pound boneless chicken breasts
  1 egg white
  1 tablespoon cornstarch
  ½ teaspoon salt
  ½ teaspoon sugar
  ½ bunch broccoli (1 pound)
  ½ bunch green onions
  8 tablespoons vegetable oil
  ¼ cup chicken broth or water
  1 cup walnut halves or pieces
  2 cloves garlic, minced
  3 thin slices pared fresh gingerroot
  1 tablespoon soy sauce
  1 tablespoon dry sherry

1. Cut chicken into 1-inch cubes. Place in bowl; add egg white, cornstarch, salt and suger; toss until mixed.
2. Pare off tough outer layer of broccoli stalks; cut each stalk crosswise in half. Separate top half into flowerets; cut lower half into ½-inch strips. Cut green onions into 1-inch lengths.
3. Heat large deep skillet, Dutch oven or wok over high heat. Add 2 tablespoons of the oil; swirl to coat bottom and side. Add broccoli and onions; stir-fry until coated with oil. Add broth; cover; cook 2 minutes, or until broccoli is crisp-tender. Remove to medium-size bowl; cover; keep warm.
4. Reheat pan. Add remaining oil. Add walnuts; stir-fry until lightly browned; remove to paper toweling to drain. Remove all but about 2 tablespoons oil from pan. Add garlic and ginger; sauté just until browned to flavor the oil and then discard. Add chicken; stir-fry until golden brown. Stir in reserved vegetables, soy sauce and sherry. Taste for salt; add, if needed. Spoon mixture onto warm platter; sprinkle with walnuts. Serve with hot fluffy rice, if you wish.

CHICKEN ATHENA
Makes 8 servings.

  8 boneless chicken breast halves (about 3 pounds)
  ¼ cup (½ stick) butter or margarine
  3 tablespoons lemon juice
  3 tablespoons Worcestershire sauce
  1 teaspoon Dijon-style mustard
  ½ teaspoon salt
  1 teaspoon chopped chives
  2 tablespoons chopped parsley
    Lemon wedges or slices

1. Sauté chicken breasts, 4 at a time, in butter in a large skillet a few minutes on each side, until they feel firm to the touch. Transfer to a serving platter; keep warm.
2. Pour off fat from skillet. Pour any juices that accumulate in serving platter back into skillet. Add lemon juice, Worcestershire, mustard and salt; bring to boiling. Stir in chives and parsley. Pour over chicken breasts. Garnish with lemon.

A boneless chicken breast is called a *suprême*. It is usually sautéed, and cooks very quickly. Learn to cook it by the feel. If you touch an uncooked suprême, it will feel soft and squashy. As it cooks, though, it will turn from pink to almost white and will be springy to the touch.

CHICKEN DIVAN
Makes 6 servings.

  2 packages (10 ounces each) frozen broccoli spears
  6 slices cooked chicken (breasts or thighs)
  ¼ cup (½ stick) butter or margarine
  ¼ cup flour
  2 cups chicken broth
  ½ cup heavy cream
  1 cup grated Parmesan cheese
  4 teaspoons prepared mustard
  2 tablespoons minced onion

2 tablespoons dry sherry
½ teaspoon Worcestershire sauce

1. Cook broccoli, following label directions. Drain; arrange in bottom of 2-quart shallow baking dish. (Cut spears in half for easier serving.) Arrange sliced chicken overlapping, over broccoli.

2. Melt butter in a medium-size saucepan; blend in flour; cook 1 minute; remove from heat. Gradually stir in chicken broth and cream. Cook, stirring constantly, until sauce thickens and bubbles 1 minute. Stir in cheese, mustard, onion, sherry and Worcestershire sauce. Continue cooking and stirring over low heat 1 minute longer. Taste; add salt and pepper if needed. Pour sauce over chicken and broccoli.

3. Bake, uncovered, in hot oven (400°) for 25 minutes or until bubbly-hot.

OLD-FASHIONED CHICKEN PIE

Bake at 400° for 30 minutes.
Makes 8 servings.

    2 broiler-fryers (about 2½ pounds
        each)
      Water
    2 teaspoons salt
    ¼ teaspoon pepper
    2 cups sliced carrots
    1 package (10 ounces) frozen peas
    ¼ cup (½ stick) butter or margarine
    6 tablespoons flour
 1½ cups buttermilk baking mix
    ½ cup dairy sour cream
    1 egg
    2 teaspoons sesame seeds

1. Place chickens in a kettle or Dutch oven; add 2 cups water, salt, pepper and carrots. Heat to boiling; lower heat; cover; simmer 45 minutes. Add peas; simmer 15 minutes longer, or until chickens and peas are tender. Remove chickens to a large bowl to cool.

2. Skim fat from broth-vegetable mixture; reserve 2 tablespoons. Melt butter with the reserved chicken fat in a medium-size saucepan; stir in flour; cook, stirring constantly, until bubbly, 1 minute. Stir broth-vegetable mixture into flour mixture; continue cooking and stirring until gravy thickens and bubbles 1 minute.

3. When chickens are cool enough to handle, skin and bone; cut meat into bite-size pieces; stir into gravy; pour into a 2-quart baking dish.

4. Combine baking mix and sour cream in a small bowl; stir to form a stiff dough; turn out onto a lightly floured surface; knead a few times; roll out dough to ¼-inch thickness; trim to make an 8½-inch square; cut into 8 strips, each about 1-inch wide.

5. Using 4 of the strips, make a lattice design on top of chicken mixture, spacing evenly and attaching ends firmly to the edges of dish. Place remaining strips, one at a time, on edges of dish, pinching dough to make a stand-up rim; flute rim. (Or, roll out dough to a 9-inch square and place over chicken mixture; turn edges under, flush with rim; pinch to make a stand-up edge; flute. Cut slits near center to let steam escape.)

6. Combine egg with 1 tablespoon water in a cup; mix with a fork until well blended. Brush over the pastry; sprinkle evenly with the sesame seeds.

7. Bake in a hot oven (400°) 30 minutes, or until chicken mixture is bubbly-hot and crust is golden.

Chicken pies for the freezer: Prepare individual pies from this recipe, to freeze for future meals, when there is no time to cook. Divide the chicken mixture among foil freezer containers. Divide biscuit topping in portions; roll out; top filling, but do not cut vent holes. Pinch topping to edge of containers. Wrap pies in heavy duty foil. To bake: Cut vent holes; bake pies, frozen, in a hot oven (425°) about 40 minutes, or until browned and bubbly.

> **A broiler-fryer will yield 1 cup of cooked meat for every pound of uncooked bird.**
>
> **Freezing cooked chicken: Cool quickly; wrap in freezer-weight plastic wrap or foil. Label; date; freeze for use in recipes for up to 4 months.**

CHICKEN AND HAM CREPES

An excellent way to use leftovers or make a perfect "from scratch" entree.
Bake at 375° for 20 minutes.
Makes 6 servings.

    3 tablespoons finely chopped shallots
    ½ cup finely chopped celery
    1 carrot, finely chopped
    6 tablespoons butter or margarine
    5 tablespoons flour
    1 can condensed chicken broth
    1 can (4 ounces) mushroom pieces
    ¼ cup Madeira or sherry
    1 cup heavy cream
    1 teaspoon salt
    ¼ teaspoon pepper
    2 cups diced cooked chicken
    1 cup diced cooked ham
    2 tablespoons chopped parsley
    ½ teaspoon leaf thyme, crumbled
      Basic Crepes (*recipe follows*)

1. Sauté shallots, celery and carrot in butter in large saucepan until soft, about 5 minutes; stir in flour and cook 1 minute. Gradually stir in chicken broth and liquid from mushrooms. Cook, stirring constantly, until sauce thickens and bubbles; stir in Madeira. Lower heat and simmer, covered, stirring often, 10 minutes. Stir in ½ cup of the cream, the salt and pepper.
2. Combine chicken, ham, mushrooms, parsley and thyme in a medium-size bowl. Stir in 1½ cups of the sauce.
3. Place about ¼ cup filling on each crepe; roll up. Place filled crepes seam-side down in a lightly buttered 13x9x2-inch baking dish. (Crepes may be refrigerated for one to two hours at this point.)

4. Whip remaining cream until stiff; fold into remaining sauce; spoon over crepes.
5. Bake in a moderate oven (375°) for 20 minutes or until bubbly hot.

BASIC CREPES
Makes 18 five-inch crepes.

    2 eggs
    1 cup milk
    1 cup *sifted* all-purpose flour
    ¼ teaspoon salt
    2 tablespoons melted butter or
      margarine

1. Combine eggs, milk, flour, salt and butter in container of electric blender; whirl at medium speed 1 minute or until batter is smooth. Refrigerate at least 1 hour.
2. Heat a small skillet, 5 or 6 inches, over medium-high heat; butter lightly. Pour in batter, 2 to 3 tablespoons at a time, quickly rotating pan to spread batter evenly.
3. Cook over medium heat to brown lightly, about 1 minute on each side. Slide onto a plate; when cool, stack with wax paper.

DEVILED CHICKEN THIGHS
Makes 4 servings.

    ¼ cup dry sherry
    3 tablespoons soy sauce
    1 large clove garlic, minced
    1 large slice fresh gingerroot
      OR: ½ teaspoon ground ginger
    ⅛ teaspoon cayenne
    ½ cup water
    8 small chicken thighs (about 1½
      pounds)

Combine sherry, soy sauce, garlic, ginger, cayenne and water in a large skillet. Add chicken; turn to coat; bring to boiling; lower heat; cover; simmer 10 minutes. Remove cover, turn chicken; raise heat so liquid boils briskly. Turn chicken occasionally and cook until liquid is evaporated and chicken is golden, about 10 minutes.

SWEET AND PUNGENT CHICKEN WINGS

Small but meaty chicken wings are a good choice for this tasty skillet dish.

Makes 4 servings.

    1 egg
    6 tablespoons water
    ½ cup flour
    1 teaspoon salt
   12 chicken wings (about 2 pounds),
        tips removed
    1 can (8 ounces) pineapple chunks
        in pineapple juice
    ⅓ cup cider vinegar
    2 tablespoons brown sugar
    1 teaspoon soy sauce
    4 tablespoons cornstarch
    2 tablespoons water
    ¾ cup uncooked long-grain rice
    ½ cup vegetable oil
    1 large sweet red pepper, seeded and
        cut into chunks
    1 package (6 ounces) frozen snow peas
    ½ cup sliced canned water chestnuts,
        drained
    2 tablespoons cashews

1. Beat egg slightly in a medium-size bowl. Add 6 tablespoons of the water, flour and salt; mix well Add chicken wings; turn to coat. Let stand 20 to 30 minutes.
2. Drain the juice from pineapple into a 2-cup measure; add water to make 1 cup liquid; stir in vinegar, brown sugar and soy sauce. Combine cornstarch and the remaining 2 tablespoons water in a small cup.
3. Start rice cooking, following label directions.
4. Heat oil in a large skillet. Remove chicken wings from batter. Sauté wings, a few at a time, 10 minutes on each side, or until brown and tender. Remove to paper toweling to drain. Keep warm on a heated serving platter. Pour fat from the skillet.
5. Add red pepper, snow peas and water chestnuts; stir-fry for 3 minutes, or until crisp-tender. Remove and reserve.
6. Pour pineapple juice mixture into skil-

let; heat thoroughly. Return vegetables with pineapple cubes to skillet. Stir cornstarch mixture again; slowly mix into skillet; cook several minutes, until vegetables and pineapple glisten and mixture thickens.
7. Arrange rice on platter; top with chicken wings; spoon vegetables and sauce over wings; sprinkle with cashews.

CHICKEN WINGS, HUNTER'S STYLE

Makes 4 servings.

   12 chicken wings (2 pounds)
    1 teaspoon salt
    ¼ teaspoon pepper
    ¼ cup olive or vegetable oil
    1 large onion, chopped (1 cup)
    1 clove garlic, minced
    1 can (15 ounces) tomato sauce with
        tomato bits
    ½ cup dry red wine
    ¼ teaspoon leaf oregano, crumbled
    ¼ teaspoon leaf basil, crumbled
    ¼ teaspoon leaf rosemary, crumbled
    1 medium-size sweet green pepper,
        seeded and cut into thin strips
      Buttered cooked orzo

1. Rub chicken wings with salt and pepper; brown in oil in a large skillet. Remove when brown; keep warm. Drain off fat; return 3 tablespoons to skillet.
2. Sauté onion and garlic in skillet until tender, about 3 minutes. Stir in tomato sauce, wine, oregano, basil and rosemary; bring to boiling. Return chicken wings and add green pepper to skillet. Lower heat; cover; simmer 20 minutes, or until wings are tender. Serve over buttered orzo.

Money savers: Chicken wings and backs are bony, but have a lot of flavor. Simmered to make soups or stews, and, with the addition of vegetables and rice or pasta, they make a satisfying meal.

SAUTEED CHICKEN LIVERS

An easy and elegant way to prepare the delicate livers.

Makes 6 servings.

1½ pounds chicken livers
⅓ cup flour
½ teaspoon salt
¼ teaspoon pepper
¼ cup (½ stick) butter or margarine
2 tablespoons vegetable oil
½ cup dry white wine
2 tablespoons chopped parsley
    Hot cooked rice

1. Combine flour, salt and pepper in a plastic bag. Add chicken livers; shake until livers are well coated with mixture.

2. Heat butter and oil in a large skillet until foamy. Sauté livers, part at a time, until browned and no pink remains, about 5 minutes. Remove livers to a warm bowl until all are browned.

3. Pour wine into skillet, stirring and scraping all browned bits. Bring pan juices just to boiling; lower heat. Return livers to skillet; simmer 1 minute. Sprinkle with chopped parsley. Serve over rice.

ROAST TURKEY WITH TWO DRESSINGS

Roast at 325° for 3½ to 4½ hours.
Makes 16 servings.

An 8- to 12-pound turkey will make 8 servings with ample for seconds. Stuff body cavity with Cornbread and Sausage Stuffing *(recipe follows)* and the neck with White and Wild Rice Stuffing *(recipe follows)*. Place turkey, breast-side up, on rack in a shallow roasting pan. Brush with melted butter. Roast in a slow oven (325°) for 3½ to 4½ hours, or until drumstick joint moves easily or meat thermometer temperature

registers 185° with bulb in thickest part of thigh, not touching bone. Remove turkey from oven and let stand 20 minutes. After serving, remove remaining stuffing from bird and refrigerate separately.

CORNBREAD AND SAUSAGE STUFFING: Cook 1 pound bulk sausage in a large skillet until no pink remains; drain. Prepare 2 packages (8 ounces each) cornbread stuffing mix, following label directions. Stir in sausage. Stuff body cavity loosely. Close cavity with skewers.

WHITE AND WILD RICE STUFFING: Sauté ¼ pound chopped mushrooms in ¼ cup butter in a large saucepan. Add 1 package (6 ounces) white and wild rice mix; sauté 2 minutes. Blend in 2½ cups boiling water and seasoning packet. Cover; simmer 25 minutes. Stir in ⅓ cup chopped parsley and ¼ cup pine nuts. Stuff neck cavity. Close cavity with skewers. To serve: Spoon stuffing onto heated serving platter; pipe edge with mashed sweet potatoes.

TURKEY FACTS:

How much to buy? Allow 1 pound per person, which will yield some extra for leftovers.

If a meat thermometer is not available, use this method to test for doneness: Protect hand with several layers of paper toweling. Grasp drumstick, which will move up and down easily if turkey is done. The thick part of the thigh meat will feel soft too. If the juices of the bird are pink, roast longer. If yellow or almost colorless, the bird is done.

A meat thermometer is an accurate guide to judge doneness in poultry. Insert the thermometer so the bulb is in the thickest part of the breast meat or in the center of the inside thigh muscle. Be sure bulb is not touching bone, which would give an incorrect reading. Turkey is done when the meat thermometer registers 185°.

Roast Turkey with Two Dressings

TURKEY BREAST TETRAZZINI WITH GREEN NOODLES

A variation of the popular chicken dish named after a famous Italian soprano.

Bake at 350° for 30 minutes.
Makes 8 servings.

  6 tablespoons butter or margarine
½ cup flour
  1 teaspoon salt
¼ teaspoon pepper
¼ teaspoon ground nutmeg
  1 can (13¾ ounces) chicken broth
  1 cup heavy cream
⅔ cup milk
⅔ cup grated Parmesan cheese
⅓ cup dry sherry
  2 packages (8 ounces each) spinach
     noodles

  8 slices (each ¼-inch thick) cooked
     turkey
  1 can (4 ounces) slivered almonds

1. Melt butter in a large saucepan. Stir in flour, salt, pepper and nutmeg; heat, stirring constantly, 1 minute. Gradually add broth, heavy cream and milk. Cook, stirring constantly, until sauce thickens and bubbles. Continue to cook for 1 minute. Remove from heat. Stir in ⅓ cup of the Parmesan and sherry until well blended.
2. Cook noodles, following label directions. Drain. Turn into a well-buttered 8-cup shallow baking dish.
3. Arrange turkey slices on noodles. Pour sauce over slices. Sprinkle the remaining ⅓ cup Parmesan and almonds over the sauce.
4. Bake in a moderate oven (350°) for 30 minutes, until bubbly and lightly browned.

STUFFED TURKEY BREAST

The stuffed breast can be prepared through step 5 early in the day and kept in the refrigerator until 3 hours before serving time. Makes 12 servings.

½ pound mushrooms
4 tablespoons (½ stick) butter or margarine
3 packages (10 ounces each) frozen chopped spinach, thawed
3 eggs, beaten
1 teaspoon leaf thyme, crumbled
1 teaspoon salt
¼ teaspoon pepper
1½ cups fresh bread crumbs (3 slices)
1 whole turkey breast (about 6½ to 7 pounds), thawed if frozen
1 slice cooked ham, cut about ½ inch thick (½ pound)
2 cans (13¾ ounces each) chicken broth
1½ cups dry white wine
1 large onion, quartered
2 stalks celery, cut into 1-inch pieces
2 carrots, cut into 1-inch pieces
6 peppercorns
1 large bay leaf
Creamy Mustard Gravy (recipe follows)

1. Reserve two mushroom caps for garnish; finely chop remaining mushrooms. Sauté chopped mushrooms in butter in a small skillet until just tender and lightly browned, about 5 minutes.

2. Drain thawed spinach thoroughly, pressing out excess liquid against the side of a strainer. Combine sautéed mushrooms, drained spinach, eggs, thyme, salt, pepper and bread crumbs; mix well; reserve.

3. Place turkey breast skin-side down on board. With a sharp thin-bladed knife, carefully remove breastbone and ribs from meat without piercing the skin; reserve bones. Split through thickest part of breast, but not cutting all the way through; fold out; flatten with hand. (This will give you a larger amount of breast meat to enclose stuffing.)

4. Spoon one-third of the spinach mixture down center of boned breast. Cut ham slice into 6 half-inch wide strips. Place 3 strips on dressing. Carefully spoon one-third of dressing over ham strips. Repeat with remaining 3 ham strips and remaining dressing. Fasten overlapped meat with skewers to aid in rolling.

5. Wrap skewered breast tightly in cheese-cloth. Remove skewers. Tie at 1-inch intervals with string.

6. Place rolled and wrapped turkey breast atop the bones in a Dutch oven or roasting pan. Add chicken broth, wine, onion, celery, carrots, peppercorns and bay leaf. Bring to boiling; lower heat; cover. Simmer, turning once, about 2 hours, or until tender and juices from meat run clear with no trace of pink when pierced with a two-tined fork. Cool in broth for 1 hour.

7. Remove turkey breast from broth; unwrap from cheesecloth. Slice and serve with Creamy Mustard Gravy. Serve with buttered broccoli and carrots, if you wish.

CREAMY MUSTARD GRAVY: Melt 4 tablespoons (½ stick) butter or margarine in a medium-size saucepan. Gradually stir in ¼ cup flour. Cook, stirring constantly, over medium heat until bubbly; cook 1 minute longer. Gradually stir in 1 cup milk, 1 cup heavy cream and 2 to 3 tablespoons Dijon-style mustard. Continue to cook over medium heat, stirring constantly, just until sauce thickens and bubbles, about 5 minutes.

Thawing turkey when you have time: Leave bird in original wrapping. Place in a shallow pan or tray. Thaw in refrigerator for 3 to 4 days. (Allow 1 day for each 5 pounds.) A 15-pound bird will thaw in 3 days.

ROAST TURKEY BREAST WITH BARBECUE SAUCE

This easy-to-carve, all white meat is moist and flavorful.
Roast at 325° for 3 to 3½ hours.
Makes 8 servings.

   1 turkey breast, (8 to 9 pounds), thawed if frozen
   3 tablespoons butter or margarine, softened
      Barbecue Sauce (*recipe follows*)

1. Place turkey breast, skin-side up, on a rack in a shallow open roasting pan. Rub skin well with butter. Insert a meat thermometer in the thickest part of the breast, not touching the bone.
2. Roast in a slow oven (325°) for 2½ hours, basting frequently with drippings.
3. Brush with Barbecue Sauce and continue to roast, brushing occasionally with sauce, 1 to 1½ hours longer or until meat thermometer registers 180° and juices run yellow when breast is pierced with a fork.

BARBECUE SAUCE
Makes about 2 cups.

   ⅓ cup chopped onion
   2 cloves garlic, minced
   2 tablespoons vegetable oil
   1 jar (12 ounces) apricot preserves
   ¼ cup chili sauce
   ⅓ cup wine vinegar
   1 teaspoon hickory salt

Sauté onion and garlic in oil in a small saucepan until tender. Stir in preserves, chili sauce, vinegar and salt. Simmer for 20 minutes.

> **Words to the wise: Never stuff a bird the day before. Stuffing ingredients can be prepared, but not assembled until you are ready to stuff and roast the bird. Always remove leftover stuffing from the bird right after the meal. Refrigerate stuffing and bird separately.**

> **Ground turkey is now a supermarket item. It is an excellent high-protein, low-cholesterol product. Use in meatballs, meatloaf, or as any ground meat.**

> **Freezer storage: Leave turkey in original wrapping, if wrapping is intact, as supermarket turkeys are usually frozen and wrapped in a heavy plastic bag. Store at 0° for up to 12 months.**

POJARSKI CUTLETS

Turkey patties fried to a golden crisp.
Makes 4 servings.

   2 pounds white and dark raw turkey meat, well trimmed (about 4 cups)
      OR: 2 pounds ground raw turkey
   1½ cups crumbled, slightly stale white bread, without crusts
   ¾ cup milk
   1 egg
   ⅔ cup heavy cream
   ½ cup (1 stick) butter or margarine, softened
   ¼ teaspoon ground nutmeg
   1 cup packaged bread crumbs
   1 cup (2 sticks) butter or margarine

1. Put turkey meat twice through the fine blade of meat grinder. Soak bread in milk until completely soft, about 10 minutes. Squeeze out excess milk.
2. Combine turkey, soaked bread, egg, cream, softened butter, salt, pepper and nutmeg in a large bowl. Beat with a spoon until smooth, thick and well mixed.
3. Shape into 8 oval patties. Dredge with bread crumbs, gently flattening each patty to a 1-inch thickness.
4. Melt butter in a large skillet; sauté patties slowly until crisp and golden brown, turning once, about 10 minutes. Good with buttered rice and peas.

TURKEY AND HAM FLORENTINE

A delicious casserole that combines favorite holiday meats.

Bake at 350° for 1 hour.

Makes 8 servings.

Spinach Layer:
- 3 packages (10 ounces each) frozen chopped spinach
- 1½ teaspoons salt
- 3 tablespoons butter or margarine
- 1 medium-size onion, chopped (½ cup)
- ¾ cup light cream or half and half
- ½ cup grated Parmesan cheese
- ¼ teaspoon ground nutmeg

Turkey and Ham Layer:
- 1 medium-size onion, chopped (½ cup)
- 2 tablespoons vegetable oil
- 2 pounds ground raw turkey
- 1 pound cooked ham, cut into ½-inch cubes
- ¼ cup (½ stick) butter or margarine
- ¼ cup flour
- 2 teaspoons salt
- ½ teaspoon pepper
- 1¼ cups light cream or half and half
- 2¾ cups milk
- 1½ cups shredded Gruyère cheese (6 ounces)
- ½ cup grated Parmesan cheese
- ½ pound lasagne noodles

1. Prepare spinach layer: Cook spinach, following label directions and using the 1½ teaspoons salt. Drain well, pressing out as much liquid as possible with the back of a spoon against the side of a strainer.

2. Melt the 3 tablespoons butter in a small pan; sauté onion until tender, about 5 minutes. Stir in spinach, cream, Parmesan and nutmeg.

3. Prepare turkey and ham layer: Sauté onion in oil in a large skillet. Cook turkey, breaking up with a fork, until it loses its pink color; stir in ham.

4. Melt the ¼ cup butter in a large saucepan; stir in flour, salt and pepper. Cook, stirring, until smooth and bubbly, about 1 minute. Gradually stir in cream, then the milk. Cook and stir over medium-high heat until thickened and bubbly, about 10 minutes. Stir in 1 cup of the Gruyère cheese and ¼ cup of the Parmesan cheese. Combine the remaining Gruyère and Parmesan in a bowl; reserve.

5. Cook lasagne noodles, following label directions to the al dente stage.

6. To assemble: Preheat the oven to moderate (350°). Line the bottom of a 13x9x2-inch baking dish with one-third of the lasagne noodles. Spoon one-third of the turkey mixture on top. Distribute one-third of the spinach mixture evenly over the turkey mixture; repeat layering two more times. Top with the reserved Gruyère and Parmesan. Cover the baking dish with foil.

7. Bake in a preheated moderate oven (350°) for 50 minutes, or until bubbly-hot; uncover for the last 15 minutes of baking. Let stand 15 minutes before serving.

Stuffed or unstuffed turkey? You can cut an hour off the roasting time if you roast the bird unstuffed. The stuffing can bake right along with the bird in a baking dish for the last hour of roasting.

For a small family, a turkey breast is an ideal choice for a roast. The yield is excellent, the roasting time is shorter, and a small amount of special dressing can be baked under the breastbone.

Another convenient form is the rolled turkey roast, which is all white or a combination of white and dark, boned and rolled, tied in a netting, and ready to thaw and roast in the oven or rotisserie.

> About leftover turkey: Turkey is a very useful bird right down to the bones, which make excellent soup, along with the addition of vegetables and a pasta. Bits and pieces are fine for creamed dishes or hot sandwiches. Any slices, light or dark meat, warmed in a creamy sauce and stretched with pasta or rice make a hearty and satisfying main dish.

TURKEY SAUTÉ
Makes 4 servings.

1¾ pounds fresh turkey thighs
2 cloves garlic, quartered
¼ cup vegetable oil
1 teaspoon salt
　Pinch pepper
2 tablespoons flour
½ teaspoon paprika
⅛ teaspoon ground nutmeg
1 medium-size onion, thinly sliced
½ cup dry white wine
2 cans (4 ounces each) sliced
　　mushrooms, undrained
¼ cup chopped parsley

1. Cut meat from the thigh bones in thin slices.
2. Sauté garlic in oil in a large skillet for 2 minutes; discard garlic.
3. Sprinkle turkey meat with salt and pepper. Sauté in the garlic-flavored oil for about 5 minutes, turning once. Combine flour, paprika and nutmeg; sprinkle over turkey slices.
4. Stir in onion, wine and liquid from mushrooms. Cover; cook 20 minutes, stirring occasionally, until turkey is tender:
5. Stir in mushrooms; heat until thoroughly hot. Sprinkle with parsley. Serve over buttered noodles, if you wish.

TURKEY WITH MUSHROOMS AND SNOW PEAS
Makes 4 servings.

2 tablespoons vegetable oil
1 medium-size onion, cut into 8 wedges
½ pound medium-size mushrooms,
　　quartered
½ cup water chestnuts, sliced
1 teaspoon salt
　Dash pepper
¼ cup dry sherry
½ cup uncooked long-grain rice
½ cup chicken broth
2 teaspoons cornstarch
2 tablespoons soy sauce
1½ cups cooked turkey, cut into
　　2-inch strips
1 package (6 ounces) frozen snow peas,
　　thawed and drained

1. Heat oil in a large skillet over medium-high heat. Add onion; stir-fry about 2 minutes. Add mushrooms, water chestnuts, salt, pepper and sherry to skillet; stir-fry for 1½ minutes.
2. Cook rice, following label directions.
3. While rice is cooking, pour broth over vegetables; bring to simmering. Combine cornstarch and soy sauce in a small cup; stir into broth. Cook 30 seconds until sauce thickens and clears. Add turkey and snow peas. Stir gently 1 minute until heated through. Serve over hot cooked rice.

> When roasting a stuffed turkey, the stuffing temperature should register 165°. Standing time after roasting is a very helpful procedure, since the 2 minutes or so lets the steam created by roasting settle back into the meat, making it easier to carve. It also frees the oven to warm the rolls and the holiday pies, and leaves time to prepare the vegetables.

Roast Duckling with Orange Sauce

ROAST DUCKLING WITH ORANGE SAUCE

Roast at 425° for 20 minutes, then at 350° for 1½ hours.

Makes 4 servings.

1 duckling, (about 5 pounds), thawed if frozen
1 carrot, sliced
1 medium-size onion, sliced
4 tablespoons butter or margarine
1 can (13¾ ounces) chicken broth
1 teaspoon salt
¼ teaspoon pepper
3 oranges
1 lemon
2 tablespoons sugar
3 tablespoons red wine vinegar
2 tablespoons brandy
1 tablespoon cornstarch

1. Remove wing tips and giblets from duckling; cut up giblets; sauté with carrot and onion in 2 tablespoons of the butter in a large saucepan 10 minutes. Stir in chicken broth. Simmer, partially covered, 1 hour. Strain and reserve broth (about 1 cup).

2. Remove any visible fat from cavity of duckling; sprinkle cavity with salt and pepper. Prick skin all over with a 2-tined fork. Truss and place in a roasting pan, breast-side up.

3. Roast in a hot oven (425°) for 20 minutes. Lower heat to 350° and continue roasting 1 hour and 30 minutes, or until duckling is tender.

4. While duckling is roasting, remove the rind from 2 of the oranges and the lemon (colored part only, no white) with a vegetable parer. Cut into julienne strips. Poach in water to cover in a small saucepan 5 minutes; drain, rinse and reserve.

5. Trim all white from the 2 pared oranges; section, removing membranes and seeds. Reserve. Squeeze juice from the remaining orange and reserve.

6. Combine sugar and vinegar in a medium-size saucepan. Cook over medium heat until the mixture comes to boiling and turns a golden amber color. (Watch carefully so it does not burn.) Remove from heat; stir in orange juice. Stir brandy and cornstarch in a small cup; stir into mixture. Heat to boiling, stirring until thickened and clear. Add the remaining 2 tablespoons butter and half of the reserved julienned peel. Cover and keep warm until duckling is done.

7. When duckling is done, remove to a board. Remove strings and cut into quarters with poultry shears. Arrange on a heated serving platter. Spoon sauce over duckling. Sprinkle with the remaining strips of orange and lemon rind and orange sections. Serve with glazed sweet potatoes, apples and pineapple, if you wish.

HONEY ROAST DUCKLING

Roast at 350° for 2¼ hours, then at 400° for 5 minutes.
Makes 4 servings.

> 1 duckling (about 5 pounds), thawed if frozen
> 2 teaspoons salt
> 4 green onions
> 2 cups boiling water
> 2 tablespoons honey
> Spicy Duck Sauce (*recipe follows*)

1. Remove visible fat from cavity of duckling; rub inside and out with salt; stuff onions inside cavity; tie legs together. Place on a rack in a roasting pan. Mix boiling water and honey; pour over duckling, letting water run into the roasting pan. The duckling should not touch the water.

2. Roast in a moderate oven (350°) 1 hour. Prick skin all over with a 2-tined fork to let out excess fat. Continue roasting until duckling is deep brown and juices run clear, 1 to 1¼ hours longer.

3. Increase oven temperature to hot (400°). Brush duckling with Spicy Duck Sauce; return to oven and roast 5 minutes. Serve remaining sauce as a dip for duckling.

SPICY DUCK SAUCE: Combine ½ teaspoon crushed anise seeds, ½ teaspoon ground cinnamon, ½ teaspoon ground ginger, ⅛ teaspoon ground allspice, 2 tablespoons dry sherry, 2 tablespoons honey, 1 tablespoon chili sauce, 1 tablespoon soy sauce and 1 clove garlic, minced. Let stand at least 2 hours for flavors to blend. Makes about ⅓ cup. Reheat before using.

> **Duckling: How much to buy?** Allow ¼ to ½ a bird per person depending on recipe. Cut duckling in halves or quarters with a poultry shears. Since all the duckling meat is dark, and the bird is bony, it is seldom carved.

BRAISED DUCKLING WITH TURNIPS

Moist, tender and well seasoned, this duckling prepared in the French style is easy to serve, since it is quartered before cooking.

Makes 4 servings.

- 1 duckling, (about 5 pounds), thawed if frozen
- 1 tablespoon vegetable oil
- 1 medium-size onion, sliced
- ½ cup sliced celery
- 1 can condensed chicken broth
- ¾ teaspoon salt
- ½ teaspoon leaf thyme, crumbled
- ⅛ teaspoon pepper
- 1 bay leaf
- 1 pound turnips
- 2 tablespoons flour
- 3 tablespoons water

1. Brown duckling quarters slowly in oil in a large skillet or Dutch oven to melt off as much fat as possible, about 20 minutes. Remove and reserve. Drain off all but 1 tablespoon of the fat.

2. Sauté onion and celery in the fat remaining in pan until tender; stir in chicken broth, salt, thyme, pepper and bay leaf. Bring to boiling. Return duckling to skillet; lower heat; cover.

3. Simmer 1 hour and 30 minutes, or until duckling is tender.

4. Meanwhile, pare turnips; cut into 1-inch chunks. Parboil in boiling salted water 5 minutes; drain.

5. Remove duckling to a bowl. Pour liquid from duck through a strainer into a 4-cup measure; skim off fat. Add water, if necessary, to make 1¼ cups liquid. Return liquid and vegetables to pot; bring to boiling. Mix flour and water into a smooth paste; stir into boiling liquid; cook, stirring constantly, until mixture thickens. Add parboiled turnips to sauce; cover; lower heat.

6. Simmer 15 minutes longer, or until turnips are tender; add duckling; simmer 15 minutes longer to heat thoroughly. Spoon into deep heated platter.

ROAST GOOSE WITH PUMPERNICKEL DRESSING

In Germany, Christmas wouldn't be Christmas without roast goose. This one is stuffed with a rich fruited pumpernickel dressing.

Roast at 325° for 3½ hours.
Makes 8 servings.

- 1 young goose, about 10 pounds, thawed if frozen
- 2½ teaspoons salt
- ¾ teaspoon pepper
- 1 package (12 ounces) pitted prunes
- 1 package (8 ounces) dried apricots
- ½ cup dry white wine
- 1 large onion, chopped (1 cup)
- 2 tablespoons butter or margarine
- 4 cups pumpernickel bread crumbs (8 slices)
- 2 medium-size apples, pared, cored and chopped
  Giblet Gravy (*recipe follows*)

1. Remove giblets and any large pieces of fat from goose. Sprinkle goose inside and out with ½ teaspoon of the salt and ¼ teaspoon of the pepper. Reserve giblets.

2. Dice apricots and prunes; place in a large bowl. Heat wine; pour over fruits; let stand 30 minutes.

3. Sauté onion in butter in a small skillet until tender, 3 minutes. Add onion, bread crumbs, apples and the remaining salt and pepper to fruits and wine.

4. Stuff goose lightly; fasten opening with wooden picks or skewers; lace with string; tie legs together. Place, breast-side up, on rack in a roasting pan. Prick skin all over with a 2-tined fork to let fat cook out.

5. Roast in a slow oven (325°) for 3½ hours, or until thick portion of the drumstick is tender when pierced with a fork.

GIBLET GRAVY: Cook reserved giblets in 4 cups salted water until tender, about 2 hours. Measure 2 cups broth, adding water, if needed. Measure ¼ cup goose fat from the roasting pan into a medium-size saucepan. Stir in ¼ cup flour; cook 1 minute. Stir in the 2 cups broth; cook and stir until thickened, 3 minutes. Add giblets and 1 tablespoon chopped parsley. Taste; season with salt and pepper, if needed.

BRAISED CORNISH HENS

Bake at 350° for 1 hour.
Makes 6 servings.

    3 Cornish game hens (2 pounds each),
        fresh or thawed if frozen
    ½ cup chicken broth
    ½ cup (1 stick) butter or margarine,
        softened
    ¼ cup dry white wine
    2 tablespoons thinly sliced green
        onions
    1 teaspoon leaf tarragon, crumbled
    1 teaspoon finely chopped parsley
    1 teaspoon garlic salt
    ½ teaspoon pepper
    1 teaspoon cornstarch
    ¼ cup dry white wine

1. Split hens in half lengthwise and place in single layer in a shallow baking dish. Gently loosen skin from meat on breast of each half to form a pocket. Pour chicken broth over.

2. Whip butter in small bowl with fork until fluffy. Stir in wine, green onions, tarragon, parsley, garlic salt and pepper, mixing well. Place rounded tablespoonful of the butter mixture in the pocket of each half breast.

3. Braise, covered, in moderate oven (350°) for 1 hour, basting with drippings every 15 minutes. Hens are done when tender and juices run clear when thigh is pierced with a fork. Serve hot.

4. Lift hens from roasting pan to a warm platter while making sauce.

5. Stir cornstarch into wine in a small cup. Stir into pan juices. Cook and stir over low heat until sauce is thickened and bubbly. Taste; add additional salt and pepper, if needed. Hens may also be served cold; cool; turn skin-side down; cover; refrigerate.

LEMON-ROASTED CORNISH HENS

The tender little birds are brightly flavored with lemon and mint.
Baket at 400° for 45 minutes.
Makes 4 servings.

    2 lemons
    3 tablespoons butter or margarine,
        softened
    1 teaspoon salt
    ¼ teaspoon pepper
    2 teaspoons chopped fresh mint
        OR: ½ teaspoon dried mint, crumbled
    4 Cornish game hens (¾ to 1 pound
        each), thawed if frozen
    2 tablespoons vegetable oil
    1 small onion, minced
    1 clove garlic, minced
    1 cup chicken broth
    2 teaspoons cornstarch
    1 tablespoon water
        Chopped fresh mint or parsley
        Watercress (*optional*)

1. Grate enough lemon rind from one lemon to make 1 teaspoon. Peel thin yellow rind from the remaining lemon; cut into julienne strips to make about 2 tablespoons; reserve. Squeeze enough lemon juice to make ¼ cup.

2. Combine butter, grated lemon rind, salt, pepper and mint. Rub mixture over hens. Place in a shallow small roasting pan.

3. Roast in a moderate oven (400°), basting often, for about 45 minutes, or until hens are golden and juices run clear when skin is pierced. Arrange on a heated serving platter. Keep hot.

4. While hens cook, prepare lemon sauce: Heat oil in a medium-size saucepan; sauté onion for 5 minutes. Stir in reserved lemon rind and garlic; cook and stir 1 minute. Add chicken broth; bring to boiling. Mix cornstarch with water; stir into boiling sauce; boil 1 minute. Stir in lemon juice.

5. Spoon a little sauce over each hen; sprinkle with additional chopped mint or parsley. Garnish with watercress.

Clockwise, starting lower left: Salmon Florentine (page 208); Planked Flounder Fillets;
Cod Provençale (page 203)

Fish and Shellfish

Discover the healthful properties of fish through these delicious recipes, which include frozen or canned alternatives to fresh.

PLANKED FLOUNDER FILLETS

A glorious party dish.
Bake at 400° for 15 minutes.
Makes 6 servings.

2 packages (1 pound each) frozen flounder fillets, thawed
OR: 2 pounds fresh flounder fillets
¼ cup (½ stick) butter or margarine
2 tablespoons lemon juice
½ teaspoon paprika
Duchess Potatoes (*recipe follows*)
1 package (10 ounces) frozen mixed vegetables, cooked, drained and seasoned
Buttery Cherry Tomatoes (*recipe follows*)
Watercress

1. Separate fish fillets carefully and arrange in a single layer on a cookie sheet.
2. Melt butter in a small saucepan. Stir in lemon juice and paprika. Brush part of mixture over fish fillets.
3. Broil fillets with tops about 4 inches from heat, 5 minutes.
4. Transfer fillets from cookie sheet with a wide spatula, to the center of a seasoned 15x10-inch plank (*see tip*) or a flameproof platter.
5. Fit a large star tube onto a large pastry bag; fill bag with Duchess Potatoes; pipe 6 nests of potatoes around the plank; border plank between nests with remaining potatoes. Brush remaining paprika-butter over fish.

6. Bake in hot oven (400°) 15 minutes, or until potatoes are tipped with golden brown. At serving time, fill potato nests with mixed vegetables. Garnish plank with Buttery Cherry Tomatoes and watercress.

DUCHESS POTATOES
Makes 6 servings.

6 medium-size potatoes, pared
⅓ cup milk
2 eggs
2 tablespoons butter or margarine
1 teaspoon salt

1. Cook potatoes in boiling salted water in a large saucepan 10 to 15 minutes, or until tender; drain. Return to pan and shake over low heat until dry and fluffy.
2. Mash potatoes; beat in milk, eggs, butter and salt until fluffy-light.

BUTTERY CHERRY TOMATOES: Remove stems from 1 cup cherry tomatoes. Melt 2 tablespoons butter in a small skillet. Sauté tomatoes over low heat, stirring gently, just until skins burst. Sprinkle with 1 tablespoon chopped parsley.

> **Plank cookery:** To season a new plank, rub top and sides with vegetable oil; heat on a rack in a very slow oven (275°) for 1 hour; cool; wipe off any excess oil.

FLOUNDER AND SALMON ROULADE

Makes 8 servings.

  1 fresh or frozen salmon steak (about 1 pound)
  4 fresh or frozen thawed flounder or sole fillets (about 8 ounces each)
  2 teaspoons lemon juice
  ¼ teaspoon pepper
  ½ cup water
  ½ cup dry white wine
  2 shallots, chopped
  ½ teaspoon salt
  1 teaspoon leaf tarragon
    Crab Sauce (recipe follows)

1. Skin and bone salmon; halve crosswise; cut each half into 4 strips.
2. Halve each flounder fillet lengthwise; sprinkle with lemon juice and pepper. Place a strip of salmon on the thick end of each fillet. Roll up, jelly-roll fashion; secure with wooden picks.
3. Combine water, wine, shallots and salt in a large skillet. Tie tarragon in a small piece of cheesecloth; drop into skillet. Stand fish rolls in skillet.
4. Bring to boiling; lower heat; cover; simmer 5 minutes, or just until fish becomes white and feels firm, not spongy, to the touch. Remove rolls with a slotted spoon to a warm platter; keep warm.
5. Cook pan liquid rapidly until reduced to ½ cup; reserve.
6. Prepare Crab Sauce; spoon over fish; garnish with fresh dill, if you wish.

CRAB SAUCE: Cook 1½ cups heavy cream rapidly in a large saucepan until reduced to 1 cup. Add reserved fish liquid, ¼ teaspoon salt, ⅛ teaspoon paprika and 1 can (6½ ounces) drained crab with any cartilage removed. Add coarsely shredded crab. Heat, stirring constantly, until piping hot.

ROLLED STUFFED FILLETS OF SOLE PARISIENNE

An elegant dish of tender fillets, pinwheeled with a fish and parsley mousse, poached in a fragrant white wine.
Poach at 350° for 10 minutes.
Makes 6 servings.

  7 fillets of sole or flounder (2½ to 3 pounds)
    OR: 2 packages (1 pound each) frozen flounder or sole fillets, thawed
  2 eggs, separated
  ⅓ cup heavy cream
  ¾ teaspoon salt
  ¼ cup loosely packed parsley sprigs
  4 tablespoons lemon juice
  1½ cups dry white wine
  1 small onion, sliced
  1 small stalk celery, sliced
  1 bay leaf
    Sauce Parisienne (recipe follows)

1. Select 6 fillets; arrange flat on a large cookie sheet, skin-side up. Cut remaining fillet into 1-inch strips (about 1 cup); place in container of electric blender. (With frozen fish, puree smaller pieces of fish.) Add egg whites, cream, ¼ teaspoon of the salt and the parsley. Whirl until mousse is smooth, 1 to 1½ minutes.
2. Drizzle 1 tablespoon of the lemon juice over fillets. Spoon fish mousse mixture onto each, dividing evenly, spreading mixture slightly. Roll up fillets, jelly-roll fashion. Arrange, seam-side down, in an 8x8x2-inch buttered baking dish or shallow ovenproof serving dish. (Recipe can be prepared ahead to this point, then refrigerated.) Drizzle the remaining 3 tablespoons lemon juice over.
3. Combine wine, onion, celery, bay leaf and remaining ½ teaspoon salt in a small saucepan; bring to boiling; lower heat; simmer, covered, 10 minutes. Strain wine mixture over fish. Cover with wax paper.
4. Poach fish in a moderate oven (350°) about 8 minutes, or just until fish becomes white, and feels firm, not spongy, to the

touch. Drain wine stock from fish into a small saucepan; keep fish warm. If you have more than 1½ cups stock, boil rapidly a few minutes until volume is reduced; reserve.
5. Prepare Sauce Parisienne; spoon over fish. Garnish with shrimp, if you wish.

SAUCE PARISIENNE: Melt 2 tablespoons butter or margarine in small saucepan; blend in 1 tablespoon flour. Gradually stir in reserved fish stock. Cook, stirring constantly, until sauce thickens and bubbles, 2 minutes. Beat 2 egg yolks with ¼ cup heavy cream in small bowl; stir in ½ cup hot sauce, then pour mixture back into saucepan. Heat, stirring constantly, just to boiling; remove from heat.

COD PROVENÇALE
A pleasing garlic and herb-scented tomato sauce flavors the fish.

Makes 4 servings.

    1 large onion, chopped (1 cup)
    1 clove garlic, minced
    3 tablespoons olive or vegetable oil
    2 large ripe tomatoes
    1 teaspoon salt
    1 teaspoon leaf thyme, crumbled
    ¼ teaspoon pepper
    1 package (1 pound) frozen cod, not
        thawed
        OR: 1 pound fresh cod fillets
        Boiled potatoes
        Cucumber slices
        Chopped parsley

1. Sauté onion and garlic in olive oil in a large skillet until tender, about 3 minutes.
2. Peel, core and chop tomatoes; stir into onion mixture and cook 2 minutes; add salt, thyme and pepper.
3. Place the block of frozen fish fillets in the sauce in skillet, spooning part of the

sauce over the fish; cover skillet. Simmer 15 minutes, or until fish *just* begins to flake when touched with a fork. Transfer fish with a wide spatula to a heated serving platter; spoon sauce over and around fish. Surround with boiled potatoes and cucumber slices; garnish with parsley.

FISH FACTS:

As this recipe proves, it is possible—and most often preferable—to cook frozen fish without thawing. It takes a little longer but there is no loss of liquid, and therefore texture and flavor are better. If you must thaw fish for a particular recipe let it thaw slowly in the refrigerator.

Cooking fish just right: Fish cooks quickly, so do not overcook and destroy the delicate texture and flavor. In addition to following the timing in the recipe, look for the following signs.
1. Fish will change from a transluscent off-white to a solid opaque-white when cooked.
2. The layers will *just begin* to separate easily when touched with a fork. If the layers flake *easily*, the fish is overdone.

Cooking by the inch: As a rule of thumb for baking or broiling fish, measure thickness of fish at thickest part and cook 10 minutes for every inch measured. For baking, oven temperature should be 400° to 425°. If fish is stuffed, measure after stuffing.

Fish, both freshwater and saltwater, are divided into two groups, lean and fatty. Lean fish (such as flounder or halibut), when broiled or baked, needs to be basted with butter or other fat to keep it moist; while fatty fish (such as bluefish or salmon), needs very little basting.

GERMAN SEAFOOD PIE

This pie is particularly good with fresh fish, although you can substitute frozen.

Bake at 425° for 25 minutes.

Makes 6 servings.

  6 cups water
  1 cup dry white wine
  2 teaspoons salt
  2 medium-size onions, halved
  2 small celery ribs, quartered
  2 medium-size carrots, quartered
  2 sprigs parsley
  1 pound fresh cod
    OR: frozen cod, thawed
  1 pound fresh flounder
    OR: frozen flounder, thawed
  ½ pound shelled and deveined fresh
      shrimp
    OR: frozen shelled and deveined
      shrimp, thawed
  ½ pound small mushrooms, halved
  5 tablespoons butter or margarine
  3 tablespoons flour
  1 egg yolk
  ½ cup heavy cream
  1 tablespoon chopped fresh dill
    OR: 1 teaspoon dillweed
  ½ teaspoon salt
  ¼ teaspoon pepper
  ½ package piecrust mix

1. Combine water, wine, salt, onion, celery, carrots and parsley in a Dutch oven; bring to boiling; lower heat; simmer 15 minutes. Add cod and flounder; simmer 3 minutes. Remove fish from liquid with a slotted spoon; cut into bite-size pieces. Combine with shrimp in a large bowl.

2. Boil fish liquid rapidly until reduced to 2 cups; strain and reserve.

3. Sauté mushrooms in 2 tablespoons of the butter in a medium-size saucepan until crisp-tender, about 3 minutes. Remove from pan; add to fish mixture.

4. Melt remaining butter in same saucepan; add flour, stirring to make a smooth paste. Stir in fish liquid gradually. Cook, stirring constantly, until sauce is smooth and thickened. Preheat oven to hot (425°).

5. Beat egg yolk lightly in a small bowl; blend in cream. Reserve 1 tablespoon of the mixture to brush over crust. Spoon about 3 tablespoons hot sauce into remaining egg mixture, stirring rapidly to blend. Return mixture to sauce. Stir in dill, salt and pepper. Stir sauce into fish mixture. Spoon filling into a 10-inch pie plate.

6. Prepare piecrust mix, following label directions. Roll out on a floured surface to a 13-inch round; cut slits for steam vents. Cover pie; pinch to make a stand-up edge; flute. Brush pastry with reserved egg mixture.

7. Bake in a preheated hot oven (425°) for 25 minutes, or until golden brown.

Whenever you buy fresh fish, choose ones that are clear-eyed, red-gilled, bright-skinned, sweet-smelling and firm and tender. The kinds of fish sold include *whole fish:* fish as it is pulled from the water, which must be cleaned, dressed, scaled and finned before cooking. *Drawn fish* has been eviscerated but still needs to be scaled and finned. *Pan-dressed* is completely cleaned and ready to cook. *Fish fillets* are skinned and boned sides of fish ready to cook. *Fish steaks* are crosscut slices of large fish containing the backbone and vertebrae, ready to cook.

For whole or drawn fish: allow 1 pound per serving. For pan-dressed fish, fillets or steaks: allow ½ pound per serving.

OVEN-FRIED FISH FILLETS

Bake at 525° for 12 minutes

Makes 4 servings

  4 tablespoons (½ stick) butter or
      margarine, melted
  ½ cup milk
  ½ teaspoon salt
  ¾ cup packaged bread crumbs
  2¼ teaspoons leaf tarragon, crumbled

1 teaspoon parsley flakes
1 package (1 pound) frozen fish fillets, thawed
OR: 1 pound fresh fish fillets

1. Brush bottom of a 15x10x1-inch jelly-roll pan or a small cookie sheet with 1 tablespoon of the melted butter. Preheat oven to extremely hot (525°).
2. Combine milk and salt in a shallow dish. Mix bread crumbs with tarragon and parsley on a sheet of wax paper.
3. Dip fillets into milk mixture, then into bread crumbs, coating evenly. Arrange in pan. Drizzle with remaining butter.
4. Bake in a preheated extremely hot oven (525°) for 10 minutes, or until fish is golden brown and crisp. Serve with tartar sauce, if you wish.

BROILED MARINATED WHOLE SNAPPER
Makes 6 servings.

1 whole dressed red snapper, striped bass or haddock (weighing 3 to 4 pounds)
OR: 2 pounds salmon, tuna or swordfish steaks
3 tablespoons soy sauce
3 tablespoons dry sherry
2 tablespoons lemon juice
1 tablespoon vegetable oil
1 teaspoon peeled and finely chopped fresh gingerroot
1 teaspoon sugar
3 green onions, sliced
Lemon slices
Green onions cut into 3-inch lengths

1. Make 3 or 4 shallow slashes on each side of fish. Place fish in a shallow non-metal dish.
2. Combine soy sauce, sherry, lemon juice, oil, ginger, sugar and onions in a cup; pour over fish. Let fish marinate 1 hour at room temperature, turning several times.
3. Place fish on a greased broiler pan. Insert lemon slices and green onion pieces in

slashes in fish. Preheat broiler.
4. Broil fish, 4 inches from heat, in preheated broiler, about 10 minutes on each side, brushing several times with marinade. Fish should just begin to flake when touched with a fork. Transfer to a warm serving platter. Serve with additional lemon and melted butter, if you wish.

POACHED SALMON STEAKS
Makes 4 servings.

1 lemon, sliced
1 medium-size onion, sliced
1 bay leaf
½ teaspoon salt
3 peppercorns
4 salmon steaks (each about 1-inch thick)
Green Mayonnaise Sauce *(recipe follows)*
Cucumber Sour Cream Sauce *(recipe follows*

1. Half fill a large skillet with water. Add lemon and onion slices, bay leaf, salt and peppercorns. Bring to boiling.
2. Lower heat; add salmon steaks to skillet; cover. Simmer about 10 minutes, or until salmon just begins to flake when touched with a fork (don't overcook).
3. Lift steaks from poaching liquid with a slotted pancake turner to a warm serving platter. Serve with Green Mayonnaise Sauce or Cucumber Sour Cream Sauce.

GREEN MAYONNAISE SAUCE: Combine 1 cup mayonnaise, 2 tablespoons lemon juice, ¼ cup finely chopped parsley and 2 tablespoons chopped green onion in a small bowl; mix; refrigerate. Makes 1½ cups.

CUCUMBER SOUR CREAM SAUCE: Pare, halve, seed, dice and finely chop 1 cucumber. Combine with 1 tablespoon lemon juice and 1 cup dairy sour cream. Chill well.
Note: Salmon steaks may be served cold, with sauce, too. Just cool, cover and refrigerate.

> When poaching fish, care should be taken that the liquid never reaches boiling, but rather gently simmers, with almost no movement on the surface. Poaching liquids are flavorful stocks and can be utilized for making sauces and gravies or in stews and casseroles, where the ingredients are from a similar category. A fish poaching liquid can be the basis of a sauce for the fish or fish soup.

QUENELLES GRATINÉED IN MUSHROOM SAUCE

These light-as-a-feather dumplings are one of the most elegant yet easy-to-make French dishes.

Bake at 425° for 10 to 15 minutes.
Makes 6 servings.

- ⅔ cup water
- 3 tablespoons butter or margarine
- ⅔ cup *sifted* all-purpose flour
- 2 eggs, separated
- 1 pound fresh or frozen flounder fillets, partially thawed
- ¾ cup heavy cream
- 1½ teaspoons salt
- ¼ teaspoon pepper
- ¼ teaspoon ground nutmeg
- 2 teaspoons finely chopped parsley
- 1 teaspoon lemon juice
- 3 cups lightly salted boiling water
  Mushroom Sauce (*recipe follows*)
- ½ cup shredded Swiss or Gruyère cheese (2 ounces)
  Watercress (*optional*)

1. Heat water and butter in a small heavy saucepan to a rolling boil. Remove from heat; stir in flour all at once; stir vigorously with a wooden spoon until mixture is smooth. Return to heat; cook, stirring constantly, 1 minute; cool slightly.

2. Add egg yolks, one at a time, beating well after each addition, until shiny and smooth. Cover; refrigerate until completely chilled. (This is called a "panade.")

3. Drain fish well on paper toweling. Cut into 1-inch-wide strips; place a fourth of the fish and 2 to 3 tablespoons cream in container of electric blender. Cover; whirl on high speed for about 30 seconds; stop blender. Scrape down side of container with a rubber scraper; blend and guide mixture into blades with scraper 15 seconds longer, or until smooth. Empty into a large bowl and repeat with remaining fish and cream until all is pureed.

4. Beat fish mixture into chilled panade with a wooden spoon or electric mixer, 1 tablespoon at a time, alternating with egg whites, beating well after each addition until very smooth. Beat in salt, pepper, nutmeg and parsley. Chill mixture 30 minutes, or until stiff enough to hold its shape.

5. Butter a large, deep skillet or 13x9x2-inch baking pan. Using two large dessert or serving spoons dipped into cold water, shape mixture into ovals (about ⅓ cup for each); arrange in prepared pan. Dip spoons in water between shaping of each quenelle. Cover with a piece of buttered wax paper. Mix lemon juice and lightly salted boiling water and pour gently down the side of pan (water should just cover quenelles). Cover and poach over low heat 10 to 15 minutes or just until quenelles feel firm to the touch. With slotted spoon, carefully transfer quenelles to a shallow baking dish. Reserve 2 cups of the poaching liquid for the sauce.

6. Make Mushroom Sauce; pour over quenelles; sprinkle with cheese.

7. Bake in a hot oven (425°) 10 minutes or until bubbly. Place under broiler, about 4 inches from heat, a few minutes to brown. Garnish with watercress.

MUSHROOM SAUCE
Makes about 2½ cups.

- 2 cups poaching liquid
- 1 cup dry white wine
- ½ pound small to medium mushrooms, sliced
- ¼ cup (½ stick) butter or margarine

4 tablespoons flour
¾ cup heavy cream

1. Combine poaching liquid and wine in a small skillet; boil, uncovered, until reduced by half (1½ cups), about 5 minutes.
2. Sauté mushrooms in butter in a medium-size saucepan just until they begin to brown. Sprinkle flour over mushrooms, then stir in. Gradually stir in hot wine mixture. Bring to boiling, stirring constantly; lower heat and simmer 2 minutes. Stir in cream; simmer 5 minutes longer.

CURRIED TUNA AND PEAS WITH BISCUIT TOPPING

Bake at 400° for 20 minutes.
Makes 6 servings.

3 tablespoons butter
1 medium-size onion, chopped (½ cup)
1 stalk celery, chopped (½ cup)
3 tablespoons flour

½ teaspoon salt
½ to 1 teaspoon curry powder
⅛ teaspoon pepper
2 cups milk
1 can (6½ ounces) tuna, drained and flaked
1 cup frozen green peas, slightly thawed
3 tablespoons chopped dill pickle
1 package (7.5 ounces) refrigerated buttermilk biscuits

1. Preheat oven to hot (400°). Melt butter in a medium-size saucepan. Sauté onion and celery until tender, about 3 minutes. Blend in flour, salt, curry powder and pepper; cook and stir 2 minutes.
2. Stir in milk slowly. Cook, stirring constantly, until sauce thickens and bubbles, 2 minutes. Stir in tuna, peas and pickle. Heat, stirring constantly, just to boiling. Pour into a 6-cup baking dish. Top with biscuits.
3. Bake in a preheated hot oven (400°), 20 minutes, or until biscuits are golden brown.

Flounder and Salmon Roulade (page 202)

TUNA-POTATO PIE

Bake at 375° for 55 minutes.
Makes 6 servings.

    1 package piecrust mix
    3 medium-size potatoes
    2 large onions
    1 can (7 ounces) tuna, drained
        and flaked
    6 tablespoons (¾ stick) butter
 1½ teaspoons salt
    ¼ teaspoon pepper
    3 tablespoons chopped parsley
      Milk
      Sesame seeds

1. Preheat oven to moderate (375°). Pre-pare piecrust mix, following label directions. Roll out half the pastry to a 13-inch round on a lightly floured surface; fit into a 9-inch pie plate; trim overhang to 1-inch.
2. Pare potatoes; cut into *very thin* slices. Peel onions; cut into thin slices. Layer potatoes, onions and tuna in pastry, dot each layer with part of the butter and sprinkle with part of the salt, pepper and parsley.
3. Roll out remaining pastry to a 12-inch round. Cut slits near center for steam to escape; cover pie. Trim overhang to 1-inch; turn edge under flush with rim; pinch to make a stand-up edge; flute. Brush pastry with milk; sprinkle with sesame seeds.
4. Bake in a preheated moderate oven (375°) for 55 minutes, or until potatoes are tender and pastry is golden. Cool on wire rack about 10 minutes before serving.

SALMON FLORENTINE

When a recipe has "Florentine" in the name, it means there is spinach among the ingredients.
Makes 4 servings.

    1 package (about 10 to 16 ounces)
        spinach
    1 can (1 pound) salmon
    3 tablespoons butter or margarine
    3 tablespoons flour

    ½ teaspoon salt
    ½ teaspoon dillweed
 1½ cups milk
    1 egg, beaten
    2 tablespoons lemon juice

1. Trim stems and any coarse leaves from spinach. Wash leaves well; place in a large saucepan; cover. (There's no need to add any water.)
2. Cook 1 minute over low heat, or just until spinach wilts; drain well; chop.
3. Drain salmon; remove and discard skin and bones; break salmon into small pieces.
4. Melt butter in a small saucepan; stir in flour, salt and dillweed. Cook, stirring constantly, just until bubbly. Stir in milk; continue cooking and stirring until sauce thickens and bubbles, 1 minute. Stir half of the hot mixture into beaten egg in a small bowl; return to saucepan; cook, stirring constantly, 1 minute, or until sauce thickens; do not boil.
5. Fold 1 cup of the hot sauce into salmon. Line 4 scallop shells or 4 individual heat-proof baking dishes with chopped spinach. Spoon salmon mixture onto center of spinach. Spoon remaining sauce over salmon.
6. Broil, about 4 inches from heat, 3 minutes, or until tops are lightly browned and bubbly. Garnish with a slice of lemon and a sprig of parsley, if you wish.

SALMON LOAF WITH CREAMY DILL SAUCE

Bake at 350° for 40 minutes.
Makes 6 servings.

    1 can (1 pound) salmon
    ¼ cup (½ stick) butter or margarine
    ¼ cup milk
    1 cup coarsely crumbled soda crackers
        (12 crackers)
    3 eggs, separated
    2 tablespoons chopped parsley
    1 tablespoon grated onion
    1 tablespoon lemon juice
    ½ teaspoon Worcestershire sauce

½ teaspoon salt
⅛ teaspoon pepper
Creamy Dill Sauce (*recipe follows*)
Sour Cream Herb Sauce
(*recipe follows*)

1. Grease a 9x5x3-inch loaf pan. Line bottom and ends with a strip of aluminum foil, leaving a 1-inch overhang; grease foil.

2. Drain liquid from salmon into a medium-size saucepan; stir in butter and milk; heat until butter is melted. Stir in crackers; let stand 5 minutes.

3. Flake salmon; remove bones and dark skin; fold into cracker mixture. Beat egg yolks in a small bowl until foamy; blend into salmon mixture along with parsley, onion, lemon juice, Worcestershire, salt and pepper.

4. Beat egg whites in a medium-size bowl until soft peaks form; fold into salmon mixture; pour into prepared pan. Put filled loaf pan in a shallow baking pan, then place on oven shelf. Pour boiling water into outer pan to a 1-inch depth.

5. Bake in a moderate oven (350°) for 40 minutes, or until a thin-bladed knife inserted into the center comes out clean.

6. Remove pan from water to a wire rack. Let stand 5 minutes. Loosen loaf from pan; lift out with foil strips onto a warm serving platter; remove strips. Keep warm while making sauce. Serve with Creamy Dill Sauce or Sour Cream Herb Sauce.

CREAMY DILL SAUCE: Melt 2 tablespoons butter in a medium-size saucepan. Stir in 2 tablespoons flour, 1 teaspoon dillweed, ½ teaspoon salt and ⅛ teaspoon pepper. Cook, stirring constantly, 1 minute. Stir in 1½ cups milk slowly; continue cooking and stirring until sauce thickens and bubbles, 3 minutes. Makes 1½ cups.

SOUR CREAM HERB SAUCE: Blend 1 cup dairy sour cream with 1 teaspoon crumbled leaf tarragon, 1 tablespoon chopped parsley, ¼ teaspoon salt and ⅛ teaspoon pepper in a small bowl. Chill well. Makes 1 cup.

SCALLOPED OYSTERS

A traditional favorite at Thanksgiving.
Bake at 350° for 20 minutes.
Makes 8 servings.

4 cans (8 ounces each) oysters
   OR: 2 pints shucked fresh oysters
      with liquid
1 cup light cream or half and half
¼ cup (½ stick) butter or margarine
1 package (5 ounces) oyster
   crackers, crushed
¼ cup chopped parsley
½ teaspoon salt
1 teaspoon Worcestershire sauce
   Dash of liquid red-pepper
      seasoning
   Paprika

1. Drain oysters, reserving ½ cup liquid. Combine with light cream in a 2-cup measure.

2. Melt butter in a medium-size saucepan; stir in crushed oyster crackers, parsley and salt; mix well.

3. Spread half the buttered crackers in a shallow 1½-quart baking dish; spoon drained oysters over; cover with the remaining crackers.

4. Stir Worcestershire sauce and red-pepper seasoning into cream mixture; pour over oysters.

5. Bake in moderate oven (350°) for 20 minutes or until top is golden; sprinkle with paprika before serving.

SCALLOP FACTS:
The large muscle that opens and closes the handsome fluted scallop shell is the only edible portion of this shellfish. Scallops are of two varieties, the large ocean or sea variety, and the small bay variety. Generally, sea scallops are more readily available, but should a recipe call for bay scallops, sea scallops can be cut into several smaller pieces. They are easy to cook: Sauté in butter 2 or 3 minutes and add a squeeze of lemon.

Coquilles St. Jacques Mornay

COQUILLES ST. JACQUES MORNAY

A subtle wine sauce enhances the delicate scallop flavor in this classic French seafood recipe.

Makes 4 servings.

- 1 cup dry white wine
- ½ teaspoon salt
- 1 pound fresh or frozen sea scallops
- 2 tablespoons finely chopped onion
- ¼ pound small mushrooms, sliced
- ¼ cup (½ stick) butter or margarine
- ¼ cup flour
- ½ cup heavy cream
- 2 teaspoons lemon juice
- ⅓ cup shredded Swiss cheese
- 1 tablespoon chopped parsley
- ½ cup soft bread crumbs (1 slice)
- 1 tablespoon butter or margarine melted

  Parsley
  Lemon wedges

1. Bring wine to boiling in a small saucepan; lower heat. Add the salt and scallops; cover. Simmer until just tender, 5 to 6 minutes. Drain, reserving liquid (1 cup).

2. Sauté onion and mushrooms in the ¼ cup butter in a medium-size saucepan until

210

tender, about 3 minutes. Stir in flour until smooth; gradually stir in reserved liquid. Return to heat; cook, stirring constantly, until sauce thickens and bubbles, 1 minute. Add cream and lemon juice. Heat to boiling; remove from heat. If sauce is too thick, add a little more cream or wine, 1 tablespoon at a time. Taste; add more salt if needed.

3. Add scallops, cheese and parsley to sauce; spoon into 4 buttered scallop shells or 1-cup baking dishes, dividing evenly.

4. Toss bread crumbs with the 1 tablespoon melted butter; sprinkle crumbs around edges of the shells. Broil, 4 to 6 inches from heat, 4 minutes, or until crumbs are brown and sauce is bubbly. Garnish with parsley and lemon wedges.

SHRIMPS TEMPURA

Makes 8 servings.

  2 pounds large shrimp
     OR: 1½ pounds frozen shelled and
        deveined shrimp, thawed
  2 cups *sifted* all-purpose flour
  2 teaspoons salt
  2 teaspoons sugar
  1 teaspoon ground ginger
  4 eggs
  1 cup ice water
     Vegetable oil for deep frying
     Spicy Plum Sauce (*recipe follows*)

1. Shell shrimp, leaving tails intact; devein. Pat fresh shrimp or thawed frozen shrimp with paper toweling to dry.

2. Combine flour, salt, sugar, ginger and eggs in a medium-size bowl; beat until smooth. Stir in water; batter will be thin. Refrigerate at least 2 hours.

3. Pour oil into a large heavy skillet or deep-fat fryer to a 2-inch depth. Heat to 380° on a deep-fat frying thermometer.

4. Holding each shrimp by the tail, dip into batter, then drop into hot oil. Fry, turning once, about 3 minutes, or until golden brown; drain on paper toweling. Keep

shrimp warm until all are fried. Serve with Spicy Plum Sauce for dipping.

SPICY PLUM SAUCE: Combine 1 cup plum jam or preserves, 1 tablespoon cider vinegar, 1 teaspoon grated onion, ½ teaspoon ground allspice, ¼ teaspoon ground ginger and a dash cayenne in a small saucepan. Bring to boiling, stirring constantly; cool. Makes 1 cup.

QUICK SHRIMP CURRY

A colorful curry that is not too hot.
Makes 6 servings.

  2 tablespoons butter
  1 tablespoon vegetable oil
  1 large onion, chopped (1 cup)
  4 teaspoons curry powder
  1 can condensed chicken broth
  ½ teaspon salt
  2 pounds medium-size shrimp, shelled
        and deveined
     OR: 1½ pounds frozen shelled and
        deveined shrimp
  2 tablespoons cornstarch
  ½ teaspoon ground ginger
  2 tablespoons water
  1 tablespoon lime juice
  1 ripe tomato, cut into wedges
     Hot cooked rice

1. Heat butter and oil in a large skillet; sauté onion until tender, about 3 minutes. Stir in curry powder; cook, stirring constantly, 2 minutes. Stir in chicken broth, salt and shrimp. Bring to boiling; lower heat; cover. Simmer 6 minutes.

2. Blend cornstarch, ginger, water and lime juice in a small bowl until smooth. Stir into shrimp mixture; continue cooking and stirring until mixture thickens and bubbles, about 3 minutes.

3. Stir in tomato wedges; cover. Simmer until tomatoes are hot, but still firm. Serve over hot cooked rice, with accompaniments of chutney, shredded coconut, peanuts and chopped sweet green pepper, if you wish.

BROILED SHRIMP WITH GARLIC SAUCE

Succulent shrimp simply prepared.

Makes 2 servings (double ingredients for 4 servings).

- 1 pound medium-size fresh shrimp
  OR: ½ pound frozen, shelled and deveined shrimp
- ¼ cup (½ stick) butter or margarine
- ¼ cup vegetable oil
- 1 tablespoon lemon juice
- ¼ cup chopped shallots or onion
- 2 cloves garlic, minced
- ½ teaspoon salt
  Dash pepper
- ¼ cup chopped parsley

1. Shell fresh shrimp; devein. Rinse; dry on paper toweling. Preheat broiler. (Thaw frozen shrimp just enough to separate.)
2. Melt butter in a shallow broiler pan large enough to hold shrimp in one layer; do not let it brown. Stir in oil, lemon juice, shallots, garlic, salt and pepper. Add shrimp and turn them in the mixture until well coated.
3. Broil, 3 inches from heat, about 5 minutes; turn and broil 3 to 5 minutes longer until slightly browned and tender but firm. Do not overcook. Transfer shrimp to heated serving dish; pour sauce over and sprinkle with parsley. Serve with steamed rice, if you wish.

SHRIMP AU GRATIN

A nice way to help a little shrimp go a long way.

Bake at 400° for 10 minutes.

Makes 4 servings.

- 4 tablespoons (½ stick) butter or margarine
- 3 tablespoons chopped onion
- ¼ cup flour
- ½ teaspoon salt
- ¼ teaspoon dry mustard
  Pinch pepper

> There are many sizes of shrimp, from the tiny North Pacific variety to the large Gulf prawns. They are available all year round fresh or frozen, in or out of the shell, cooked or uncooked. One pound of unshelled raw shrimp yields ½ pound cooked and shelled, and makes 2 servings.

- 1½ cups milk
- 1 cup shredded Swiss cheese (4 ounces)
- 1 pound frozen, shelled and deveined shrimp, cooked and drained
- 1 can (4 ounces) whole mushrooms, drained
- ¼ cup packaged bread crumbs

1. Melt 3 tablespoons of the butter in a medium-size saucepan. Sauté onion until tender but not brown, about 5 minutes.
2. Stir in flour, salt, mustard and pepper. Cook, stirring constantly, until mixture is bubbly. Add milk. Cook, stirring constantly, until sauce thickens and bubbles. Add ¾ cup of the cheese; stir until melted.
3. Add shrimp and mushrooms to sauce. Turn into a buttered 1½-quart shallow baking dish. Combine crumbs and the remaining ¼ cup cheese; sprinkle over top of shrimp. Dot with the remaining 1 tablespoon butter.
4. Bake in a hot oven (400°) 10 minutes, or until sauce is bubbly and top is lightly browned.

SZECHUAN SHRIMP

Makes 4 servings.

- ¼ cup catsup
- 2 tablespoons soy sauce
- 1 tablespoon dry sherry
- ½ teaspoon sugar
- ½ teaspoon ground ginger
- ¼ teaspoon crushed red pepper flakes
- 2 tablespoons vegetable oil
- 1 pound fresh or frozen shelled and deveined shrimp

4 cloves garlic, chopped
½ cup sliced green onions

1. Combine catsup, soy sauce, sherry, sugar, ginger and red pepper in a small cup.

2. Heat the oil in a wok or large skillet over high heat. Stir-fry shrimp until pink and firm, about 2 minutes. Remove shrimp with a slotted spoon to a heated bowl. Add garlic to wok; stir-fry 1 minute. Add catsup mixture. Cook, stirring constantly until bubbly. Return shrimp to wok, heat 1 minute more. Serve with hot cooked rice, if you wish.

SHRIMP SCAMPI
Makes 4 servings.

1 pound large shrimp
   OR: 1 pound frozen shelled and
     deveined shrimp, thawed
½ cup (1 stick) butter
½ cup olive or vegetable oil
3 cloves garlic, finely chopped
2 tablespoons chopped parsley
1 lemon, cut in thin wedges

1. Cut shrimp down the back lengthwise with kitchen shears, being careful not to cut all the way through. With shells intact, remove black vein; rinse and pat dry.

2. If using frozen shrimp, start with this step. Melt butter with oil in a large skillet. Add garlic; sauté just until garlic is lightly golden.

3. Add shrimp; sauté, shaking skillet and stirring, 2 to 3 minutes or just until shrimp is pink and firm. Garnish with chopped parsley and lemon wedges.

> Olive oil is the classic oil used in the cuisines of Mediterranean countries. One of its greatest advantages when used in recipes, is the distinctive flavor it imparts to the dish. It can be kept at room temperature, if tightly capped, or stored in the refrigerator. If refrigerated, it can be warmed up quickly under running water, until it flows easily.

> To shell shrimp, hold the fan end of the tail and give it a slight twist to release the meat but not break it off. Holding the tail by the narrow part, unwind the shell starting at the widest part and pulling when you get to the tail to remove the shell.

SHRIMP, GRECIAN STYLE
Makes 6 servings.

1½ pounds medium-size shrimp
   OR: 1 pound frozen shelled and
     deveined shrimp, thawed
2 tablespoons lemon juice
4 small ripe tomatoes
¼ cup chopped green onions
1 clove garlic, crushed
2 tablespoons olive or vegetable oil
½ cup dry white wine
1 tablespoon chopped fresh basil
   OR: 1 teaspoon leaf basil, crumbled
2 tablespoons chopped parsley
1 teaspoon salt
⅛ teaspoon pepper
3 ounces feta cheese, cubed (¾ cup)

1. Wash and shell shrimp, leaving tail section intact; devein. Place in a medium-size bowl. If using frozen shrimp, start recipe here. Sprinkle with lemon juice.

2. Peel, seed and chop tomatoes to make 1½ cups.

3. Sauté onion and garlic in oil in a large skillet until tender, about 3 minutes. Stir in the chopped tomatoes, wine, basil, 1 tablespoon of the parsley, the salt and pepper. Lower heat; simmer, uncovered, 15 minutes, or until mixture thickens slightly.

4. Stir in shrimp with lemon juice. Cook just until shrimp turns pink and feels firm, about 5 minutes. Add cheese. Taste; add additional seasoning, if needed. Sprinkle with remaining parsley. Serve with hot cooked rice, if you wish.

BASIC BOILED LOBSTER

For the glorious moment when you are given or can afford live lobsters.

Makes 4 servings.

    4 small live lobsters (about 1 pound
        each)
      Boiling salted water
    ½ cup (1 stick) butter or margarine,
        melted

1. Drop live lobsters head-first into a very large kettle of boiling salted water. Cover kettle; bring back to boiling and begin timing. Cook 10 to 15 minutes; lobsters will turn bright red. Remove at once with tongs and drain.

2. With a sharp knife, split lobsters down the center (underside) and brush liberally with melted butter. Or, if you prefer, simply place 1 lobster and a small ramekin of melted butter on each of 4 plates. Put out the lobster crackers and picks for getting every last bit of meat. Each person can then crack his own lobster, twist out the meat and dip it into melted butter.

SEAFOOD GUMBO

Pride of Creole cooking and one of its great gifts to American cuisine. This one is based on crabmeat and oysters.

Makes 8 servings.

    4 tablespoons (½ stick) butter or
        margarine
    3 tablespoons flour
    2 large onions, chopped (2 cups)
    1 clove garlic, minced
    1 can (1 pound, 12 ounces) tomatoes
    1 can condensed chicken broth
    2 cups water
    1 teaspoon salt
    1 tablespoon Worcestershire sauce
    ¼ teaspoon liquid red-pepper
        seasoning
    1 pound fresh or frozen crabmeat
      OR: 2 cans (7½ ounces each)
        crabmeat

    1 pint shucked oysters with liquid
      OR: 3 cans (7 ounces each) oysters
    2 tablespoons file powder (*optional*)
      Hot cooked rice

1. Make a roux by melting butter in a heavy kettle; stir in flour. Cook, stirring constantly, over low heat, until flour turns a rich brown, about 15 minutes.
2. Stir in onion and garlic. Cook, stirring often, until soft, about 10 minutes. Add tomatoes, chicken broth, water, salt, Worcestershire and red-pepper seasoning. Cover.
3. Simmer 15 minutes to develop flavors. Add crabmeat and oysters with their liquid. Continue cooking just until oysters are curled, about 5 minuters.
4. Remove from heat; stir file powder into gumbo to thicken. Ladle into deep soup bowls over hot rice.

File powder is made from the leaves of the sassafras tree. It is used extensively in Creole cooking to thicken soups and stews. It should be added at the end, though, since reheating and stirring tends to make the soup or stew stringy.

A *roux* is used mainly to thicken soups or stews. It is the French name for a butter-flour mixture that is cooked over low heat to several stages. As a white roux, it is used for cream sauces. Cooked a little longer, it becomes pale beige, which is just right for thickening meat sauces and gravies. The longest cooking, the brown roux stage, adds color as well as flavor to brown gravies and sauces, and is a standard in making gumbos. Care must be taken with a brown roux, and stirring is essential to keep it from scorching.

Okra, a large podded green vegetable, favored in Southern cooking, is often used to thicken and flavor gumbos and soups. It is used as an alternate to file powder, not usually with it.

CAPE COD CLAM PIE

Scalloped clams in a crisp-crusted pie.

Bake at 450° for 15 minutes, then at 350° for 30 minutes.

Makes 6 servings.

1 package piecrust mix
2 eggs
2 cans (7 to 8 ounces each) minced clams
¾ cup milk
½ cup coarsely crumbled unsalted soda crackers (6 crackers)
1 teaspoon salt
¼ teaspoon pepper
2 tablespoons butter or margarine
1 teaspoon water

1. Prepare piecrust mix, following label directions. Roll out half to a 13-inch round on a lightly floured surface; fit into a 9-inch pie plate. Preheat oven to very hot (450°).
2. Beat eggs well in a medium-size bowl. Measure and reserve 1 tablespoon.
3. Drain liquid from clams; measure ¾ cup and stir into eggs with the clams, milk, cracker crumbs, salt and pepper. Spoon mixture into pastry-lined plate; dot filling evenly with butter.
4. Roll out remaining pastry to a 12-inch round; cut several slits near center to let steam escape; cover pie. Trim overhang to 1 inch; fold edge under, flush with rim; pinch to make a stand-up edge; flute. Stir water into reserved egg in a cup; brush evenly over pastry.
5. Bake in a preheated very hot oven (450°) for 15 minutes; lower oven temperature to moderate (350°). Bake 30 minutes longer, or until crust is golden brown. Cool on wire rack for 15 minutes before cutting.

MARYLAND CRAB CAKES

Makes 6 servings.

2 cans (7½ ounces each) crabmeat
½ teaspoon salt
½ cup soft white bread crumbs (1 slice)
2 eggs, well beaten
1 teaspoon Worcestershire sauce
⅛ teaspoon liquid red-pepper seasoning
¼ cup (½ stick) butter or margarine
Lemon wedges
Tartar sauce

1. Drain crabmeat; pick over and remove any bones and cartilage; flake. Combine with salt, bread crumbs, eggs, Worcestershire and red-pepper seasoning in a large bowl; mix well.
2. Shape mixture into 6 cakes. Refrigerate about 30 minutes to stiffen mixture.
3. Heat butter in a large skillet; add cakes and sauté about 5 minutes on each side, or until golden brown. Transfer to a heated serving platter; serve with lemon wedges and tartar sauce.

CRABMEAT AND TUNA PUFF

Bake at 350° for 50 minutes.
Makes 6 servings.

1 can (6½ ounces) crabmeat
1 can (3½ ounces) tuna
8 slices dry white bread, cubed
½ pound Swiss cheese, cubed
4 eggs
3 cups milk
1 teaspoon dry mustard

1. Drain, flake and remove any cartilage from crabmeat. Drain and flake tuna. Combine in a medium-size bowl.
2. Arrange alternate layers of bread cubes, crabmeat mixture and cheese in a buttered deep 6 cup baking dish.
3. Beat eggs in a medium-size bowl until foamy; stir in milk. Pour over layers; let stand 1 hour.
4. Bake in a preheated moderate oven (350°) for 50 minutes, or until puffy.

Sausage and Pepper Pizza

Quick and Easy

A special collection of delicious no-fuss recipes, carefully tested and timed to help the busy working woman get a good dinner on the table.

Everyone is busy, so we've planned our main dishes with fast cooking techniques, easier cleanup, fewer ingredients and the kinds of recipes most families like. Our recipes are all prepared in less than one hour, and many in less than one-half hour. Each recipe is timed, and the method of cooking is noted. Each main dish has a suggested menu, with each item on the menu a convenience food from the freezer, refrigerator or supermarket shelf and easily prepared within the time limit of the main dish. These are recipes that will impress your guests, as well as please your family. And, if you should have a little extra time, you will find some fast and fabulous dessert recipes, timed to the table in less than one hour, that will satisfy all the sweet-toothed members of the family.

SAUSAGE AND PEPPER PIZZA

Skillet and Oven: 40 minutes.
Bake at 375° for 30 minutes.
Makes 6 servings.

- 2 packages (8 ounces each) refrigerated crescent rolls
- ½ pound sweet Italian sausage
- 2 cans (8 ounces each) tomato sauce
- ½ teaspoon leaf basil, crumbled
- ¼ cup grated Parmesan cheese
- 1 sweet green pepper, halved, seeded and cut into strips
- 1 sweet red pepper, halved, seeded and cut into strips
- 1 large onion, sliced
- 1 package (8 ounces) shredded mozzarella cheese

1. Preheat oven to moderate (375°). Unroll crescent rolls. Arrange the triangles evenly in a 14-inch pizza pan. Press dough together with fingers to make a solid lining for pan.
2. Bake crust in a preheated moderate oven (375°) for 10 minutes. Remove to wire rack.
3. Remove sausage from casing; cook in a large skillet, breaking up with a spoon, until meat loses its pink color. Add tomato sauce and basil; cook, stirring constantly, until juice has almost evaporated and mixture is thick, about 5 minutes. Remove from heat; cool slightly.
4. Spread tomato mixture over partially baked crust; sprinkle with Parmesan cheese. Arrange peppers and onion over sauce; sprinkle with shredded cheese.
5. Bake 20 minutes longer, or until crust is golden brown and cheese is melted and bubbly.

Quick Menu Makers
Cucumber and Romaine Salad with Onion Dressing
Lemon Sherbet with Strawberries

Freeze very soft cheese 15 minutes, or until firm (but not frozen), to make shredding easier.

SOUTH OF THE BORDER PIZZA

Skillet and Oven: 30 minutes.
Bake at 450° for 15 minutes.
Makes 8 servings.

    ¾ pound ground chuck
    1 can (7½ ounces) taco sauce
    1¼ cups buttermilk baking mix
    ½ cup yellow cornmeal
    ½ cup milk
    1 can (4 ounces) green chilies, drained
    1 package (8 ounces) sliced Monterey
        Jack cheese
      Sliced green onions
      Shredded lettuce
      Pickled cherry peppers

1. Brown meat lightly in large skillet; stir in taco sauce; cook, uncovered, 5 minutes, or until almost dry. Remove from heat; cool. Preheat oven to very hot (450°).
2. Combine baking mix and cornmeal in a large bowl; add milk; mix with a fork until moistened; press, with floured hands, on a lightly greased cookie sheet to a 12-inch round. Spread meat mixture over dough to edge. Arrange chili peppers and cheese over meat.
3. Bake in a preheated very hot oven (450°) for 15 minutes, or until edges are brown and cheese is melted. Sprinkle with green onions and shredded lettuce; garnish with pickled red cherry peppers.

Quick Menu Makers
Avocado and Tomato Salad with Cucumber Dressing
Strawberry Ice Cream with Strawberry Sauce

HUNTER'S STYLE CHICKEN

Take the ingredients right out of the freezer and off the pantry shelf to make chicken that tastes the delicious Old World way.
Skillet: 45 minutes.
Makes 6 servings.

    2 pounds chicken legs
      OR: 1 broiler-fryer, cut up (about
        3 pounds)

    2 tablespoons olive or vegetable oil
    1 cup frozen chopped onion
    1 jar (about 14 ounces) spaghetti sauce
        with mushrooms
    ½ cup dry red wine

1. Brown chicken quickly in oil in a large skillet; push to one side; sauté onion until tender, about 3 minutes.
2. Stir in spaghetti sauce and wine until well-blended; cover skillet. Simmer 25 minutes, or until chicken is tender.

Quick Menu Makers
Hot Spaghetti   Buttered Green Peas
Marble Pound Cake

CHICKEN LIVERS WITH BACON AND GREEN BEANS

Skillet: 30 minutes.
Makes 4 servings.

    4 slices bacon
    1 pound chicken livers
    2 tablespoons flour
    1 package (9 ounces) frozen Italian
        green beans

1. Cook bacon in a large skillet; remove to paper toweling; crumble and reserve. Pour bacon fat into a cup; measure and return 2 tablespoons to skillet.
2. Roll chicken livers in flour to coat. Brown on all sides in bacon fat (10 minutes). Stir in ¼ cup water, scraping up browned bits in skillet. Add beans; cover and cook 10 minutes, or until beans are tender. Livers should be brown outside and slightly pink inside. Taste; add salt and pepper, if you wish. Sprinkle with crumbled bacon.

Quick Menu Makers
Chilled Tomato Juice   Buttered Orzo
Frozen Vanilla Yogurt with Fresh Fruit

> **If chicken livers are frozen, remember to move them from freezer to refrigerator the morning you plan to use them.**

CHICKEN RISOTTO
Skillet: 45 minutes.

Makes 4 servings.

- 1 broiler-fryer, cut up (2½ pounds)
- 1 package (7½ ounces) risotto rice mix
- 1 can condensed chicken broth
- 1 jar (3 ounces) pimiento-stuffed olives, drained

1. Place chicken pieces, skin-side down, in a large skillet over very low heat. (Do not add fat.) Cook chicken slowly in its own fat until skin side is a rich brown, about 10 minutes; turn; brown other side. Remove chicken from skillet with tongs.
2. Add rice and seasoning packet from mix to pan fat; stir to coat rice with fat.
3. Pour chicken broth into a 4-cup measure; add water to make 2½ cups. Stir into rice mixture; bring to boiling. Arrange chicken pieces over mixture. Lower heat; cover. Simmer 20 minutes, or until chicken is tender and liquid is absorbed. Stir in olives; fluff up rice.

Quick Menu Makers
Buttered Asparagus Spears
Fresh Apples with Cheddar Cheese

STIR-FRIED CHICKEN AND VEGETABLES
Wok or Skillet: 25 minutes.

Makes 2 servings.

- 3 teaspoons vegetable oil
- 1 package (10 ounces) frozen Chinese-style stir-fry vegetables with seasoning
- 1 whole boneless chicken breast (about 8 ounces), cut into ¼-inch slices
- ¼ cup water
- Soy sauce

1. Heat 2 teaspoons of the oil in a wok or heavy skillet. Remove and reserve seasoning envelope from vegetables. Add frozen vegetables to hot oil and stir to break up pieces. Cover and let cook 2 minutes. Re-

move to a small bowl; keep warm.
2. Heat remaining 1 teaspoon oil in wok. Add chicken; cook, stirring constantly with wooden spoon, 5 minutes. (There should be no pink left in the chicken.)
3. Return vegetables to wok; sprinkle seasoning over and stir in water until sauce thickens (about 1 minute). Taste; season with soy sauce.

Quick Menu Makers
Buttered rice
Boston Lettuce with French Dressing
Mandaran Orange Slices with Shortbread Cookies

WALNUT CHICKEN
Wok or Skillet: 30 minutes.

Makes 4 servings.

- 4 tablespoons soy sauce
- 1 tablespoon dry sherry
- ½ teaspoon ground ginger
- 1 pound boneless chicken breasts, cut into 1-inch pieces
- 3 tablespoons vegetable oil
- ⅓ cup sliced green onions
- 1 garlic clove, cut in half
- 1 cup walnuts, coarsely chopped

1. Combine 3 tablespoons of the soy sauce, sherry and ginger in a medium-size bowl; add chicken pieces; let stand 15 minutes.
2. Meanwhile, heat wok or a large skillet; add 2 tablespoons of the oil; heat until almost smoking; add green onions, garlic and walnuts. Cook 3 minutes, tossing mixture with slotted spoon; remove garlic; remove walnut-onion mixture to a small bowl.
3. Add remaining 1 tablespoon oil to wok; heat; add chicken pieces and soy mixture. Stir-fry until chicken is done and soy mixture begins to coat chicken, about 5 minutes. Add walnuts-onion mixture; toss.

Quick Menu Makers
Buttered Rice   Buttered Snow Peas
Chilled Grapefruit Sections

TURKEY SCALLOPINE

Skillet: 20 minutes.

Makes 4 servings.

1½ pounds cooked turkey breast in one
    piece (from deli counter)
¼ cup flour
1 egg, slightly beaten
⅓ to ½ cup packaged bread crumbs
2½ tablespoons butter or margarine
½ teaspoon dry mustard
¼ teaspoon salt
⅛ teaspoon pepper
½ teaspoon Worcestershire sauce
½ cup beef broth or dry white wine
1 tablespoon chopped parsley

1. Cut turkey into ¼-inch slices. Dip in flour and then in beaten egg; coat with bread crumbs. Let stand a few minutes for coating to set.

2. Brown breaded slices quickly in the 2½ tablespoons butter in a large skillet, about 2 minutes on each side. Remove from skillet; keep warm.

3. Add mustard, salt, pepper, Worcestershire and beef broth to skillet. Stir to loosen browned bits on bottom of pan. Heat to boiling. Spoon sauce over hot turkey; sprinkle with parsley.

Quick Menu Makers

Buttered Green and White Noodles
Green Bean and Radish Salad
Fresh Sugared Strawberries

> This is an excellent recipe for any leftover roast turkey. It may not be possible to cut large slices, but the smaller pieces of both light and dark meat can be dipped, coated and sautéed the same way as the large slices.

> About toasting nuts: Blanched nuts like almonds and pine nuts, and nuts with a thin outer coat, like walnuts and pecans, may be toasted easily in the oven. Spread nuts out in a jelly-roll or other shallow pan. Preheat oven to slow (300°), and toast nuts, stirring often, about 20 minutes, or until browned.

QUICK TURKEY AND RICE CASSEROLE

Skillet and oven: 30 minutes.
Bake at 400° for 10 minutes.
Makes 4 servings.

1 package (8 ounces) chicken-flavored
    rice and vermicelli mix
4 green onions, sliced
¼ cup (½ stick) butter or margarine
2¾ cups boiling water
1 teaspoon salt
¼ teaspoon pepper
2 cups cubed cooked turkey
1 cup dairy sour cream
¼ cup shredded Cheddar cheese
    (2 ounces)
½ teaspoon salt
½ teaspon dillweed
¼ cup toasted slivered almonds

1. Sauté rice and vermicelli mixture and onions in butter in a large skillet, stirring frequently until vermicelli is light brown.

2. Add boiling water, the 1 teaspoon salt and pepper. Stir once. Lower heat; cover; simmer 15 minutes, until no liquid remains.

3. Add turkey, sour cream, cheese, the remaining ½ teaspoon salt and dillweed.

4. Spread cooked rice mixture over bottom of an 8-cup shallow baking dish. Top with turkey mixture. Sprinkle with nuts.

5. Bake in a hot oven (400°) about 10 minutes, or until heated through.

Quick Menu Makers

Marinated Artichoke Hearts with Romaine Salad
Raspberry Sherbet with Sliced Pears

Turkey Scallopine

Chicken Suprêmes with Sherry Sauce

CHICKEN SUPRÊMES WITH SHERRY SAUCE

Skillet: 20 minutes.

Makes 6 servings.

 3 whole boneless chicken breasts
   (about 1½ pounds)
 ½ teaspoon leaf thyme, crumbled
 ½ teaspoon salt
 ¼ teaspoon pepper
 4 tablespoons (½ stick) butter
   or margarine
 ¼ pound small mushrooms, sliced
 ¼ cup dry sherry
 1 cup light cream or half and half

1. Cut chicken breasts in half. Rub with a mixture of thyme, salt and pepper. Sauté in 3 tablespoons of the butter in a large skillet about 4 minutes on each side; don't over-cook. Remove to a heated serving platter; keep warm.

2. Sauté mushrooms in the remaining 1 tablespoon butter, stirring rapidly, about 3 minutes. Spoon mushrooms over chicken.
3. Deglaze skillet with the sherry, stirring and scraping up browned bits. Add cream; cook rapidly just until sauce is thickened, about 2 minutes. Spoon over chicken; sprinkle with parsley, if you wish.

Quick Menu Makers

Spinach and Onion Salad with Herb Dressing
Buttered Hot Rolls
Warm Cherry Pie à la mode

SHRIMP MARINARA

Saucepan: 35 minutes.

Makes 4 servings.

 1 tablespoon vegetable oil
 1 clove garlic, minced
 1 can (1 pound, 12 ounces) Italian-style
   tomatoes

1 bay leaf
1 package (1 pound) frozen, shelled and deveined shrimp

1. Heat oil in a large saucepan. Sauté garlic just until tender. Add tomatoes; crushing with a spoon. Add bay leaf. Cook, stirring frequently until sauce thickens and tomatoes break up, about 25 minutes.
2. Add shrimp. Continue cooking for 5 minutes or just until shrimp turn pink.

Quick Menu Makers
Lettuce Wedges with Russian Dressing
Buttered Green Peas
Coconut Layer Cake

FISH AND POTATO CHOWDER

A warming and hearty meal-in-one soup.
Dutch oven: 30 minutes.
Makes 4 servings.

½ cup diced salt pork
1½ cups frozen chopped onions
2 cans (1 pound each) potatoes, drained and sliced (can liquid reserved)
1 bay leaf
½ teaspoon salt
½ teaspoon leaf savory, crumbled
¼ teaspoon white pepper
⅛ teaspoon leaf thyme, crumbled
1 package (1 pound) frozen cod fillets, partially defrosted
OR: 1 pound fresh cod fillets
1½ cups milk

1. Place salt pork and onions in a Dutch oven or large kettle. Cook over high heat until pork has begun to brown and liquid has evaporated from onions.
2. Add potatoes with can liquid, bay leaf, salt, savory, pepper and thyme. Cover; cook over high heat 5 minutes.
3. Meanwhile, pat fish between sheets of paper toweling to remove excess liquid.

Cut into 1-inch cubes. Add to Dutch oven; lower heat; cover; cook gently 3 minutes. Add milk; heat just until piping-hot.

Quick Menu Maker
Hot Baking Powder Biscuits with Butter
Cole Slaw with Blue Cheese Dressing
Apple Pie with Cheddar Cheese

BASQUE PIPERADE

A colorful, open-face omelet with sautéed vegetables, that is a specialty of the Basque country between France and Spain.
Skillet: 30 minutes.
Makes 6 servings.

1 medium-size onion, sliced
1 sweet green pepper, halved, seeded and cut into strips
1 clove garlic, halved
¼ cup olive or vegetable oil
2 medium-size ripe tomatoes, cut into wedges
1½ teaspoons salt
¼ teaspoon leaf oregano, crumbled
¼ teaspoon leaf basil, crumbled
¼ teaspoon pepper
8 eggs
2 tablespoons butter or margarine

1. Sauté onion, pepper and garlic in oil in a large skillet until tender, about 3 minutes. Remove and discard garlic. Add tomatoes, ½ teaspoon of the salt, the oregano, basil and pepper. Simmer 3 minutes. Remove vegetables to a small bowl. Wipe out skillet.
2. Beat eggs with the remaining 1 teaspoon salt in a large bowl until foamy. Heat butter in skillet until bubbles die down. Add eggs, stirring quickly with a fork until they are almost set. Pour warm vegetable mixture into soft top layer of eggs; do not stir. Cook 1 minute longer. Cut into wedges.

Quick Menu Makers
Mixed Green Salad with Creamy Garlic Dressing
Hot French Bread with Butter
Fresh Pears with Roquefort Cheese Wedges

SZECHUAN BEEF
Wok or skillet: 25 minutes.

Makes 4 servings.

    1 flank steak (about 1 pound)
    ¼ cup bottled chili sauce
    2 tablespoons soy sauce
    1 tablespoons dry sherry
    1 teaspoon cornstarch
    ½ teaspoon ground ginger
    ¼ teaspoon crushed red pepper flakes
    3 tablespoons peanut or vegetable oil
    3 cloves garlic, minced
    1 small bunch green onions, cut into
        1-inch pieces

1. Cut steak in half lengthwise; cut each half into ⅛-inch slices. Prepare remaining ingredients before cooking beef.

2. Mix chili sauce, soy sauce, sherry, cornstarch, ginger and red pepper flakes in a small bowl; reserve.

3. Heat 1 tablespoon of the oil in a wok or large skillet. Add garlic and green onions; stir-fry 1 minute. Remove to a bowl with slotted spoon.

4. Add remaining 2 tablespoons oil to wok. Add steak slices, a third at a time, and stir-fry quickly until no pink remains. Add meat to bowl with green onions.

5. Add chili sauce mixture to wok; heat until bubbly-hot. Stir in meat and green onions; cook and stir until chili sauce mixture coasts meat and green onions.

Quick Menu Makers
Won Ton Soup
Buttered Rice
Pineapple Chunks with Yogurt and Brown Sugar

A flank steak is a tasty buy, but a long-fibered cut of beef. To carve it for best eating: Hold the carving knife almost parallel to the surface of the steak on the cutting board. Cut into very thin slices. This technique cuts the long, chewy fibers into short, manageable lengths.

Shorten cooking time by cutting up, or portioning foods individually before cooking. For instance, cut boneless beef or chicken breasts into narrow strips for stir-frying or to make individual servings instead of one large serving.

BEEF PEPPER STEAK
Skillet or Wok: 25 minutes

Makes 6 servings.

    1 boneless top round steak, cut 1-inch
        thick (about 1 pound)
    ⅓ cup cornstarch
    ½ cup vegetable oil
    3 medium-size sweet green peppers,
        halved, seeded, and cut into strips
    3 medium-size onions, sliced
    2 cloves garlic, minced
    ½ cup soy sauce
    1 cup water

1. Cut meat into ¼-inch slices. Toss with cornstarch in a large bowl until coated.

2. Sauté beef, a few slices at a time, in ¼ cup of the oil in a wok until no pink remains, about 3 minutes. Remove meat as it cooks to a warm platter.

3. Sauté peppers, onions and garlic in remaining oil until tender, about 3 minutes. Return meat to wok.

4. Stir in soy sauce and water. Continue cooking, stirring and scraping browned bits in wok, until sauce thickens.

Quick Menu Makers
Buttered Rice or Orzo
Broccoli Spears in Butter Sauce
Warm Blueberry Turnovers

PICADILLO
Skillet: 20 minutes

Makes 4 servings.

    1 large onion, chopped (1 cup)
    1 small sweet green pepper, seeded and
        chopped (½ cup)
    1 clove garlic, minced

3 tablespoons olive or vegetable oil
1 pound ground chuck
1 can condensed tomato soup
2 tablespoons wine vinegar
¼ cup raisins
2 teaspoons drained capers (*optional*)
⅛ teaspoon ground cinnamon
¼ teaspoon leaf oregano, crumbled
1 teaspoon salt
⅛ teaspoon red pepper flakes

1. Sauté onion, pepper and garlic in oil in a large skillet 5 minutes or until tender. Stir in beef; cook 5 minutes, stirring frequently, until meat loses its pink color.
2. Add soup, vinegar, raisins, capers, cinnamon, oregano, salt and red pepper to meat mixture; bring to boiling; simmer 5 minutes.

Quick Menu Makers
Red Kidney Beans
Lettuce Salad with Thousand Island Dressing
Toasted Corn Muffins and Butter
Apricot Halves in Syrup

BROILED STEAKS PERSILLADE
Broiler and skillet: 20 minutes.
Makes 6 servings.

4 tablespoons vegetable oil
1 teaspoon salt
½ teaspoon pepper
6 individual beef steaks, ¾-inch thick
2 large sweet green peppers, halved, seeded and cut into ¼-inch strips
2 large sweet red peppers, halved, seeded and cut into ¼-inch strips
2 tablespoons butter or margarine
2 large cloves garlic, minced
½ cup finely chopped parsley

1. Preheat the broiler; trim and slash the fat edges of the steaks.
2. Rub the steaks on both sides with 1 tablespoon of the oil. Place on a broiler pan, with tops 4 inches from the heat. Broil 3 minutes on one side; sprinkle with half the salt and pepper; turn. Broil on other side 4 more minutes; sprinkle with remaining salt and pepper. Remove to hot platter; keep warm.
3. While steaks broil, heat 2 tablespoons of the oil in a skillet. Quickly cook the peppers, stirring often, until they are heated through, about 5 minutes. They should remain very crisp. Remove to warm platter with steaks.
4. Heat the remaining tablespoon oil and butter in the skillet. Add the garlic and parsley; stir until both are light brown. Spoon over the steaks and peppers; serve immediately.

Quick Menu Makers
Mashed Potatoes   Buttered Green Beans
Lemon Layer Cake

BEEF STROGANOFF
Skillet: 30 minutes.
Serve this favorite over hot noodles.
Makes 6 servings.

1½ pounds boneless round steak
½ envelope (2 tablespoons) onion soup mix
1 can (6 ounces) sliced mushrooms
1 cup dairy sour cream

1. Cut meat into ¼-inch strips, 2 to 3 inches long, for quick cooking. Add a quarter of the meat to skillet; brown quickly. Remove with slotted spoon to bowl. Repeat until all meat is cooked, then return meat to skillet.
2. Stir in onion soup mix and mushrooms with liquid; heat until bubbly. Slowly stir in sour cream until thoroughly blended. Cook, stirring constantly, until heated thoroughly.

Quick Menu Makers
Buttered Noodles
Carrots in Butter Sauce
Cherry Cheese Pie

BEEF SAUTÉ BORDELAISE

Ground beef is treated to red wine and mushrooms for a special dish in minutes.
Skillet: 20 minutes.

Makes 4 servings.

1½ pounds ground chuck
1 tablespoon dry red wine
1 envelope ground-beef seasoning mix
¼ pound mushrooms, quartered
½ cup dry red wine
1 can (15 ounces) beef gravy

1. Divide meat into 4 portions. Shape each gently into a thick oval patty. Sprinkle with the 1 tablespoon wine on both sides, then with seasoning mix.
2. Heat a large skillet over medium heat. Sauté patties 4 minutes on each side; remove from skillet.
3. Sauté quartered mushrooms briefly in the same skillet. Stir in the ½ cup wine; simmer 1 minute.
4. Add canned beef gravy; heat to boiling. Return beef patties to skillet for 1 minute. Garnish with watercress and tomatoes, if you wish.

Quick Menu Makers

French Fried Potatoes
Tomato and Romaine Salad with French Dressing
Chocolate Ice Cream and Sugar Cookies

For the most tender beef patties and hamburgers, handle the ground beef as little as possible. The meat can be divided easily into portions right in the tray as it comes from the supermarket. Scoop out each portion, press it down gently, then turn and shape with the palms of the hands on a flat surface to form a rough oval or round.

LINGUINE WITH SAUSAGE SAUCE

Skillet: 45 minutes.

Makes 6 servings.

1 pound sweet Italian sausage
  OR: ½ pound each sweet and hot sausage
1 small onion, chopped (¼ cup)
1 sweet green pepper, halved, seeded and chopped
1 jar (21 ounces) Italian cooking sauce
1 pound linguine or spaghetti
  Grated Parmesan cheese

1. Remove casing from sausage; cut into 1-inch pieces. Cook in large skillet until browned, about 15 minutes. Add onion and pepper, sauté until tender, 3 minutes.
2. Add sauce; bring to boiling; lower heat; cover. Simmer 25 minutes, stirring once or twice.
3. While sauce cooks, start pasta cooking, following label directions. Drain; return to kettle.
4. Spoon sauce over drained spaghetti in kettle; toss gently. Spoon onto hot plates. Serve with Parmesan cheese to sprinkle over.

Quick Menu Makers

Romaine, Green Onion and Cucumber Salad
with Creamy Italian Dressing
Orange Sherbet with Butter Cookies

HAM AND POTATOES AU GRATIN

No need to pare potatoes or make a sauce for this creamy all-in-one skillet meal.
Skillet: 40 minutes.

Makes 6 servings.

1 medium-size onion, sliced
2 tablespoons vegetable oil
1 package (5.5 ounces) Au Gratin Potatoes
2 cups boiling water
⅔ cup milk

Beef Sauté Bordelaise

1 ham steak, cut about ½-inch thick
(about 1¾ pounds)

1. Sauté onion in oil in a large skillet until tender, about 3 minutes.

2. Stir in potato slices, sauce mix, water and milk. Cut ham into cubes; add to potatoes. Bring to boiling, stirring frequently; lower heat cover. Simmer 30 minutes, or until potatoes are tender and ham is piping hot.

Quick Menu Makers

Buttered Broccoli with Almonds
Corn Muffins with Butter
Sliced Fresh Fruit

3. GINGERED PORK CHOPS

Skillet: 25 minutes.

Makes 4 servings.

4 loin pork chops (about ½-inch thick)
½ teaspoon salt
¼ teaspoon pepper
¼ teaspoon ground sage
¼ cup (½ stick) butter or margarine
½ pound mushrooms, slices
1 clove garlic, minced
1 teaspoon grated fresh gingerroot
OR: ¼ teaspoon ground ginger
¼ cup orange juice

1. Sprinkle pork chops evenly with salt, pepper and sage. Sauté chops in butter in a large skillet, about 10 minutes on each side, or until well browned. Remove chops to a warm platter.

2. Add mushrooms, garlic and ginger to skillet. Sauté until mushrooms are tender, about 3 minutes. Stir in orange juice; cook 5 minutes longer. Return chops to skillet; heat just until chops are piping-hot.

Quick Menu Makers

Buttered Mashed Sweet Potatoes
Spinach in Butter Sauce
Sliced Bananas in Sour Cream

PORK CHOPS WITH RED CABBAGE

A hearty dish for man-size appetites.
Skillet: 45 minutes.

Makes 4 servings.

- 4 loin pork chops, cut 1-inch thick (1¾ pounds)
- 1 large onion, chopped (1 cup)
- 1 jar (15 ounces) sweet/sour red cabbage
- 1 apple, quartered, cored and sliced

1. Sauté chops slowly in oil in a large skillet until brown; turn; brown other side. Remove to warm platter. Sauté onion in oil remaining in skillet until tender, about 3 minutes. Arrange pork chops over onion. Lower heat; cover. Cook 30 minutes, turning once. Remove cover; cook, turning chops until glazed and most of the liquid has evaporated. Remove chops; keep warm.
3. Drain liquid from cabbage; stir cabbage into skillet with apple slices; cook until heated thoroughly. Arrange pork chops over mixture and serve.

Quick Menu Makers
*Carrot, Cabbage and Pepper Salad
with Garlic French Dressing
Buttered Poppyseed Rolls
Cheesecake*

REUBEN DOGS

Broiler: 12 minutes.

Makes 4 to 5 servings.

- Spicy brown mustard
- 8 to 10 slices Swiss cheese
- 1 can (8 ounces) sauerkraut, drained
- 1 package (1 pound) frankfurters (8 to 10)
- 8 to 10 split frankfurter buns

1. Spread mustard lightly on one side of Swiss cheese slices; divide sauerkraut equally over cheese slices. Put frankfurter at one end of cheese; roll up. Place, seamside down, on split frankfurter roll. Arrange on a cookie sheet.

2. Broil, 6 to 8 inches from heat, until cheese is melted and frankfurter is hot. Garnish with olives if you wish.

Quick Menu Makers
*Bean and Bacon Soup
Dill Pickles, Corn Chips, Potato Sticks
Chocolate Chip Cookies*

PEPPER AND ONION DOGS

Skillet and saucepan: 15 minutes.

Makes 4 to 5 servings.

- 2 medium-size sweet red peppers, halved, seeded and cut into strips
- 2 medium-size sweet green peppers, halved, seeded and cut into strips
- 1 large onion, cut into thin rounds
- ¼ cup olive or vegetable oil
- ½ teaspoon salt
- ½ teaspoon leaf oregano, crumbled
- ½ teaspoon leaf basil, crumbled
- 1 package (1 pound) frankfurters (8 to 10)
- 8 to 10 split frankfurter buns, toasted

1. Sauté peppers and onion in oil in a large skillet until crisp-tender; drain off any excess oil. Add salt, oregano and basil; toss gently; heat 1 minute longer.
2. Drop frankfurters in boiling water in a medium-size saucepan for 5 minutes; drain. Place frankfurters in toasted rolls; top with pepper-onion mixture.

Quick Menu Makers
*Deli Cole Slaw and Garlic Dill Pickles
Buttered Corn on the Cob
Strawberries and Cream*

ALL-AMERICAN DOGS

Skillet and broiler: 15 minutes.

Makes 4 to 5 servings.

- 4 slices bacon
- 16 to 20 slices American cheese
- 1 package (1 pound) frankfurters (8 to 10)

8 to 10 split frankfurter rolls
8 to 10 thin dill pickle strips

1. Cook bacon until crisp in a large skillet; remove and drain on paper toweling; crumble. Reserve.

2. Line each frankfurter roll with 2 slices of the cheese. Place one frankfurter in the center of each roll. Place the rolls on cookie sheet.

3. Broil, 6 to 8 inches from heat, until frankfurter is hot and cheese is melted. Garnish with pickle strips and bacon.

Quick Menu Makers

Tomato Soup
Deli German Potato Salad
Sugared Doughnuts and Fresh Fruit

BAVARIAN-STYLE KNACKWURST AND RED CABBAGE

Skillet: 40 minutes.

Makes 4 servings.

4 slices bacon
1 medium-size onion, chopped (½ cup)
½ medium-size head red cabbage, shredded (4 cups)
1 tart apple, pared, quartered, cored and chopped (1 cup)
1 tablespoon sugar
½ teaspoon salt
⅛ teaspoon pepper
¼ teaspoon caraway seeds
3 tablespoons cider vinegar
4 knackwurst (1 pound)
Chopped parsley

1. Cook bacon in a large skillet until crisp; remove and drain on paper toweling; crumble; reserve. Pour fat into a 1-cup measure; measure 2 tablespoons and return to skillet.

2. Add onion; sauté until tender, about 3 minutes. Add cabbage, apple, sugar, salt, pepper and caraway seeds; stir to coat with pan fat. Cover; cook over low heat, 10 minutes. Add vinegar.

3. Remove casings from knackwurst; place on top of cabbage. Cover; cook 15 minutes, or until knackwurst is hot and cabbage is crisp-tender.

4. To serve: Place cabbage on heated serving platter; arrange knackwurst on top; sprinkle with crumbled bacon and parsley.

Quick Menu Makers

Buttered Boiled Potatoes
Deep-Dish Apple Pie

Cook extra potatoes when preparing dinner. If they are whole, they can be sliced and cooked with onions for Lyonnaise Potatoes, or if mashed, can be combined with sour cream, chives and cubes of Cheddar or Swiss cheese to be heated in the toaster oven until golden brown.

HAM MADEIRA

Instant soup with a measure of wine makes a great sauce for a ham steak.

Skillet: 25 minutes.

Makes 6 servings.

1 ready-to-eat ham steak (about 1½ pounds)
2 tablespoons vegetable oil
¾ cup Madeira
1 envelope (1 cup size) instant cream of mushroom soup mix
2 tablespoons prepared mustard with horseradish

1. Trim excess fat from ham edge; score edge at 2-inch intervals

2. Brown steak in oil in a large skillet for 3 minutes on each side; stir in Madeira and heat to bubbling. Stir in instant mushroom soup and mustard with horseradish until sauce is very smooth; cover skillet. Simmer 10 minutes longer.

Quick Menu Makers

Buttered Green Beans   *Buttered Kernel Corn*
Pound Cake with Chilled Peaches in Syrup

HERBED LAMB KEBOBS

Broiler: 40 minutes.

Makes 6 servings.

- 2 pounds boneless leg of lamb, trimmed of fat
- 1 bottle (8 ounces) herb and garlic salad dressing
- ¼ teaspoon pepper
- 1 teaspoon dillweed
- ½ teaspoon garlic salt

1. Cut meat into 1-inch cubes. Place in a nonmetal bowl. Pour salad dressing over meat. Sprinkle with pepper and ½ teaspoon of the dillweed. Let meat marinate for 15 minutes, stirring frequently.
2. Preheat broiler.
3. Thread meat onto 6 skewers. Broil, about 5 inches from heat, basting frequently with marinade, for 8 minutes. Turn skewers, continue broiling and basting for another 8 minutes, or until lamb is done as you like it. During last 5 minutes of broiling time, sprinkle remaining ½ teaspoon dill weed and garlic salt over meat.

Quick Menu Makers
Rice Pilaf
Cauliflower in Cheese Sauce
Apple Turnovers

GREEK-STYLE LAMB CHOPS

Skillet: 45 minutes.

Makes 4 servings.

- 4 shoulder lamb chops, cut ½-inch thick (about 1½ pounds)
- 2 tablespoons olive or vegetable oil
- 1 package (6 ounces) Greek-style rice pilaf
- 2 cups water
- ¼ cup raisins
- 4 thin slices lemon

1. Brown chops slowly in oil in a large skillet, turning once. Drain off all but 1 tablespoon fat from skillet.
2. Add contents of rice packet to skillet; sauté 3 minutes; add water, seasoning mix-

ture and raisins; bring to boiling.
3. Arrange lamb chops over rice with lemon slices. Cover; lower heat; simmer 30 minutes, or until liquid is absorbed and lamb chops are tender. Fluff up rice.

Quick Menu Makers
Tomato and Red Onion Salad
Oil and Vinegar
Warm Pita Bread with Butter
Chilled Green Grapes

LINGUINE WITH CREAMY ZUCCHINI SAUCE

The sauce of finely shredded zucchini and mozzarella flavors this pasta dish.

Kettle: 20 minutes.

- 1 pound linguine, fusilli or macaroni
- ⅓ cup olive or vegetable oil
- 3 large cloves garlic, minced
- 1 package (8 ounces) whole-milk mozzarella cheese, shredded
- ½ cup grated Parmesan cheese
- 1 pound zucchini, scrubbed and coarsely grated (about 3 cups)
- ½ cup chopped fresh parsley
- ½ teaspoon salt
- ¼ teaspoon pepper

1. Cook lingine in boiling salted water in a kettle, following label directions; drain.
2. Heat oil in pasta kettle over moderate heat. Add garlic and cook 30 seconds. Return pasta to kettle and toss to coat with oil and garlic.
3. Add cheeses and toss again. Add zucchini, parsley, salt and pepper; continue to toss over moderate heat until cheese and moisture from zucchini coat pasta with a light sauce. Serve immediately with additional Parmesan cheese, if you wish.

Quick Menu Makers
Antipasto of Marinated Artichoke Hearts,
Olive Condite, Chick-Peas with Oil and Vinegar
Warm Italian Bread with Butter
Lemon Ice with Macaroons

APRICOT CHARLOTTE BOMBE

A spectacular dessert with five ingredients that go together like a breeze.

Time to table: 30 minutes.

Makes 6 servings.

1 can (1 pound) whole apricots
⅓ cup apricot preserves
1 pint ice cream (vanilla, chocolate or your favorite flavor)
7 to 8 ladyfingers, split
Frozen whipped topping

1. Drain apricots, reserving 1 tablespoon syrup. Heat preserves with reserved syrup in a small saucepan until melted.

2. Unmold ice cream from carton in one piece onto a chilled serving plate. Press ladyfingers onto side and top of ice cream to cover completely, cutting to fit where necessary. Brush melted preserves mixture over ladyfingers until absorbed. Return to freezer about 10 minutes.

3. Just before serving, arrange apricots on plate and decorate with whipped topping.

TROPICAL QUEEN OF PUDDINGS

Three favorite tropical flavors topped with fluffy meringue.

Time to table: 50 minutes.

Bake at 400° for 3 minutes.

Makes 6 servings.

1 package banana cream flavor instant pudding and pie filling
2 cups milk
6 slices pound cake (frozen or from bakery)
1 can (8 ounces) crushed pineapple in pineapple juice
2 egg whites
2 tablespoons sugar
2 tablespoons flaked coconut

1. Prepare pudding with milk, following label directions.

2. Layer cake, pineapple and pudding in a 4-cup baking dish. Chill 30 minutes.

3. Just before serving, beat egg whites until foamy; gradually beat in sugar until soft peaks form. Spread over pudding, making swirls with spoon. Sprinkle coconut around edge.

4. Bake in a hot oven (400°) for 3 minutes or just until lightly browned.

COCONUT CREAM CAKES

Time to table: 45 minutes.

Makes 4 servings.

1 package (3¾ ounces) vanilla flavor instant pudding and pie filling
2 cups milk
½ cup flaked coconut
1 cup frozen whipped topping
4 individual dessert sponge shells

1. Prepare pudding with milk, following label directions; refrigerate.

2. Toast 3 tablespoons of the coconut on a cookie sheet in a moderate oven (350°) for 8 minutes. Cool.

3. Spread whipped topping around side and top edges of dessert shells. Sprinkle with toasted coconut. Stir remaining coconut into vanilla pudding; spoon mixture into shells. Garnish with whipped topping.

If individual sponge cakes are not available, substitute ready-to-use individual pastry or graham cracker crumb tart shells, available in most supermarkets year-round.

For toasting coconut: Use the toaster oven instead of your regular oven. You'll save time and money!

PINEAPPLE CREAM

Time to table: 30 minutes.

Makes 6 servings.

    2 envelopes unflavored gelatin
    ⅓ cup sugar
    1 can (8¼ ounces) crushed pineapple
       in heavy syrup, undrained
    1 can (6 ounces) frozen lemonade
       concentrate
    1 cup heavy cream
    1 cup crushed ice

1. Combine gelatin and sugar in container of electric blender. Heat pineapple with syrup to boiling; add to blender all at once. Whirl on high speed until smooth.
2. Add frozen lemonade concentrate, cream, then crushed ice. Blend until smooth. Pour into 6 serving glasses. Chill until ready to serve, about 15 minutes.

STRAWBERRY PINEAPPLE CREAM: Substitute 1 package (10 ounces) quick-thaw frozen strawberries for the lemonade concentrate.

CAFÉ GRANITE

A cooling meal-ender that's a favorite in Italian cuisine.

Time to table: 25 minutes.

Makes 4 servings.

    ⅓ cup cold water
    ⅓ cup granulated or firmly packed light
       brown sugar
    2 tablespoons instant espresso coffee
   12 ice cubes (regular size)
    4 strips lemon rind (no white)

1. Measure water, sugar and coffee in container of electric blender; whirl on low speed until sugar is dissolved. Chill 4 sherbet glasses in freezer 10 minutes.
2. Just before serving: Turn blender to high and add ice cubes to coffee mixture, one at a time. Keep blending until mixture is a complete mush. Spoon into chilled glasses. Add a twist of lemon and serve at once with crisp butter cookies, if you wish.

STRAWBERRY-BANANA COUPE

Time to table: 15 minutes.

Makes 4 servings.

    ⅓ cup firmly packed light brown sugar
    3 tablespoons butter or margarine
    ½ pint strawberries, halved
    1 ripe banana, sliced
    ⅓ cup light rum
    8 dry almond macaroons (amaretti)
    1 pint strawberry ice cream

1. Melt sugar and butter in a small skillet or chafing dish, stirring often. Stir in strawberries and bananas.
2. Heat rum slightly in small saucepan, just until warm. Ignite with match; pour over fruits in chafing dish; shake pan until flames die.
3. Crumble macaroons into 4 dessert dishes; scoop ice cream on top. Spoon hot fruit sauce over and serve immediately.

> **For a non-alcoholic version, substitute orange juice for the rum, and omit the flaming.**

BLACK FOREST TARTLETS

Time to table: 40 minutes.

Makes 6 servings.

    1 cup canned cherry pie filling
    1 package (4 ounces) graham cracker
       tart shells (6 shells)
    1 container (8 ounces) vanilla flavor
       yogurt
    ¾ cup milk
    1 package (3¾ ounces) chocolate
       flavor instant pudding and pie filling

1. Spoon pie filling into tart shells.
2. Combine yogurt, milk and pudding in medium-size bowl; beat until smooth and thickened, about 1 minute. Spoon over cherries; chill until serving time. Garnish with whipped cream, if you wish.

Strawberry-Banana Coupe

ORANGE-CHEESE PARFAITS
Time to table: 45 minutes.
Use a cheesecake mix to make a no-bake parfait.

Makes 8 servings.

- 1 package (10¾ ounces) cheesecake mix
- 2 tablespoons sugar
- 2 tablespoons butter or margarine, melted
- 1 orange
- 2 cups milk

1. Mix crumbs from cheesecake mix with sugar and butter. Spoon about half into bottoms of 8 sherbet or parfait glasses, dividing evenly. Reserve remaining.
2. Grate 2 teaspoons rind from orange. Remove white membrane from orange with a sharp knife; section orange; halve sections.
3. Prepare cheesecake with milk, following label directions. Stir in orange rind and orange. Layer with reserved crumb mixture in glasses. Serve at once or chill. Garnish with whipped cream and additional orange, if you wish.

> For quick cake or dessert decorating, fill a plastic sandwich bag with frosting, whipped topping or whipped cream; snip off a tiny corner and squeeze out icing in decorative swirls.

DOUBLE BANANA-SPLIT CAKE
An ice cream parlor classic in a cake.
Time to table: 15 minutes.
Makes 8 servings.

- 1 package (13¾ ounces) frozen banana cake, thawed
- 3 ripe bananas
- 1 pint vanilla or strawberry ice cream
- 2 tablespoons bottled chocolate fudge sauce

- 2 tablespoons broken walnuts
- Whipped topping

1. Split cake horizontally into two layers. Place bottom layer on serving plate.
2. Split 2 bananas; arrange over cake. Spoon ice cream over in an even layer; top with frosted layer.
3. Slice remaining banana; arrange slices on top. Drizzle with fudge sauce; sprinkle with nuts; decorate with whipped topping.

> For an instant garnish for pies, puddings and shortcakes, whip half a pint of heavy cream and spoon into little mounds on a cookie sheet; freeze. When frozen, transfer to a plastic bag. Defrost for 20 minutes before using.

SICILIAN APRICOT-CHEESE CAKES
These individual desserts go together easily.
Time to table: 20 minutes.
Makes 6 servings.

- 1 package (5 ounces) dessert sponge shells (6)
- ¼ cup rum
- ¾ cup apricot preserves
- 1 square semisweet chocolate, chopped
- 1 container (15 ounces) ricotta cheese
- ¼ cup 10X (confectioners') sugar
- 1 tablespoon chopped red candied cherries
- 1 tablespoon chopped candied orange peel
- ½ teaspoon vanilla
- 1 can (1 pound, 13 ounces) apricot halves, drained
- Candied cherries for garnish

1. Brush inside of dessert shells with rum.
2. Melt apricot preserves in a small saucepan over low heat; press through a strainer. Brush shell sides with part of strained preserves.

3. Blend chocolate, ricotta cheese, 10X sugar, cherries, orange peel and vanilla in a medium-size bowl. Divide mixture equally among shells.

4. Place 3 apricot halves on top of cheese mixture. Brush with remaining apricot preserves. Garnish with candied cherries. Refrigerate until ready to serve.

QUICK BLUEBERRY COBBLER

Time to table: 40 minutes.

Makes 4 servings.

    2 containers (9 ounces each) frozen,
        drypack blueberries
    ⅓ cup sugar
    1 tablespoon flour
    1 tablespoon butter or margarine
    1 tablespoon water
    1 teaspoon grated lemon rind
        (*optional*)
    ⅛ teaspoon ground cinnamon
    1¾ cups buttermilk biscuit mix
    ⅔ cup half and half

1. Preheat oven to hot (425°).

2. Combine blueberries, sugar, flour, butter, water, lemon rind and cinnamon in a medium-size saucepan. Bring to boiling, stirring, for 5 minutes.

3. Meanwhile, combine biscuit mix and half and half in a medium-size bowl.

4. Pour hot berries into a 9-inch pie plate. Drop heaping teaspoons of batter over top, leaving room between each.

5. Bake in a hot oven (400°) for 20 minutes, or until biscuits are lightly browned. Serve warm with ice cream or heavy cream.

> **For an even *quicker* dessert, substitute blueberry pie filling for the blueberries, sugar, flour, butter, water, lemon rind and cinnamon. Heat to boiling and pour into pie plate just before dropping the biscuit batter on top.**

FAST AND FABULOUS BANANA-STRAWBERRY ICE CREAM

Keep frozen bananas on hand for a quick ice cream treat. Peel, cut into ½-inch slices; seal in plastic freezer bags; freeze.

Time to table: 15 minutes.

Makes 4 servings.

    ½ cup heavy cream
    1 cup fresh strawberries or frozen,
        thawed strawberries, drained
    1 teaspoon honey
    1 teaspoon vanilla
    4 large frozen sliced bananas

Whirl cream, strawberries, honey and vanilla in container of electric blender until smooth. Add frozen banana slices. Whirl until pureed. The frozen bananas will blend the ingredients into a smooth soft ice cream to be enjoyed immediately.

> **The Apricot Cream recipe, below, will make a wonderful trifle, if you have a little time. (The extra time is needed for chilling, which is essential.) Layer the same ingredients in a bowl with cubes or crumbs of plain cake. Chill overnight.**

QUICK APRICOT CREAM

Time to table: 45 minutes.

Makes 4 servings.

    1 package 3¾ ounces) vanilla-flavor
        instant pudding and pie filling
    1 cup milk
    1 cup heavy cream
    1 can (1 pound) apricot halves, drained
    ½ cup dairy sour cream

1. Prepare pudding mix with milk and cream, following label directions. Spoon into serving dish.

2. Layer the drained apricot halves over the pudding. Spoon dollops of sour cream over apricots. Refrigerate until ready to serve.

Clockwise, from lower left: Orange Cream Torte, Hazelnut Torte (page 240), Sacher Torte (page 238), Swiss Almond Meringue Torte (page 240), Dobos Torte (page 238)

Cakes and Cookies

Special occasions and holidays demand more elaborate cakes and cookies,
but we also include recipes for enjoying any time.

ORANGE CREAM TORTE

Bake at 350° for 20 minutes.
Makes 12 servings.

  3 eggs
  ¾ cup granulated sugar
  1 tablespoon grated orange rind
  ⅓ cup orange juice
  1 cup *sifted* cake flour
  1 teaspoon baking powder
  ¼ teaspoon salt
    Candied Orange Peel (*recipe follows*)
  6 tablespoons orange juice
  3 cups heavy cream
  ½ cup 10X (confectioners') sugar
    Easy Orange Fondant (*recipe follows*)

1. Lightly grease two 9x1½-inch layer-cake pans; line bottoms with wax paper; grease paper. Preheat oven to moderate (350°).
2. Beat eggs and granulated sugar in a small bowl with electric mixer at high speed until light and fluffy; this will take about 5 minutes. Beat in orange rind and the ⅓ cup orange juice.
3. Sift flour, baking powder and salt over egg mixture; fold in until well blended. Pour into prepared pans, spreading evenly.
4. Bake in a preheated moderate oven (350°) for 20 minutes, or until centers spring back when lightly pressed with fingertip. Cool in pans on wire racks 5 minutes; loosen around the edges; turn out onto racks; peel off wax paper. Cool completely.
5. Prepare Candied Orange Peel.
6. Combine reserved syrup from Candied Orange Peel with the 6 tablespoons orange juice; drizzle over layers. Beat cream with 10X sugar in a small bowl until stiff. Place one layer on a serving plate; spread with 1 cup whipped cream. Top with second layer.
7. Prepare Easy Orange Fondant and pour over top; spread with a spatula just to the edge; let set. Pipe remaining whipped cream onto the side of torte. Chill 2 hours before serving. Decorate with Candied Orange Peel.

CANDIED ORANGE PEEL: Remove the bright orange part (zest) from the skin of 1 navel orange with a vegetable peeler; cut into julienne strips (about ⅓ cup). Simmer in water in a small saucepan 10 minutes. Drain; rinse in cold water; dry on paper toweling. Combine ¼ cup sugar, 2 tablespoons light corn syrup and ¼ cup water in a small saucepan; bring to boiling; lower heat. Cover; simmer 5 minutes. Uncover and boil 5 minutes longer. Add orange peel; boil 5 minutes. Remove from heat; let stand at least 30 minutes. Drain when ready to use. Reserve 3 tablespoons of syrup to drizzle over layers.

EASY ORANGE FONDANT: Blend 2 tablespoons orange juice, 1 tablespoon light corn syrup and 1 cup 10X (confectioners') sugar in a small bowl. Set bowl over simmering water, stirring often, just until mixture is thin enough to pour over cake.

SACHER TORTE

This is an adaptation of the classic cake from the Hotel Sacher in Vienna. Our version is a rich chocolate cake, split and filled with apricot preserves and gilded with a satiny chocolate glaze. Serve it with whipped cream.

Bake at 325° for 1 hour and 15 minutes.
Makes 12 servings.

    Almond Crunch (*recipe follows*)
  6 eggs, separated
  ½ cup sugar
  ½ cup (1 stick) butter or margarine,
      softened
  1 package (6 ounces) semisweet
      chocolate pieces, melted
      and cooled
  ¾ cup *sifted* cake flour
  1 teaspoon baking powder
  1 jar (12 ounces) apricot preserves
    Chocolate Glaze (*recipe follows*)

1. Prepare Almond Crunch. Grease an 8-inch springform pan that is 2½ to 3 inches deep. Preheat oven to slow (325°).
2. Beat egg whites in a large bowl with electric mixer at high speed until foamy-white. Sprinkle in ⅓ cup of the sugar, 1 tablespoon at a time, beating constantly, until meringue forms soft peaks.
3. With the same beaters, beat butter until softened in a small bowl; add the remaining sugar and the egg yolks; beat until light and fluffy, about 3 minutes. Beat in chocolate and ½ cup of the Almond Crunch at low speed; gently fold into egg whites. Sift flour and baking powder over the bowl; fold in just until blended. Pour into prepared pan.
4. Bake in a preheated slow oven (325°), for 1 hour and 15 minutes, or until center springs back when lightly pressed with fingertip. Cool in pan on wire rack 10 minutes. Loosen around edge; loosen and remove side of pan; cool completely.
5. Even off top, then split cake horizontally into 2 layers. Spread about half the preserves on the bottom layer; replace top.

Brush or spread the remaining preserves on top and side of cake. Let stand at least 2 hours for preserves to soak in and partially dry.
6. Prepare Chocolate Glaze and pour over top of cake, letting it drip down the side, smoothing with a warm spatula. (Reserve about 2 tablespoons glaze to drizzle over top.) Sprinkle top with remaining Almond Crunch. Drizzle reserved glaze from a wax paper cone over Almond Crunch. Serve with whipped cream, if you wish.

ALMOND CRUNCH: Heat ⅓ cup sugar in a small skillet just until melted and starting to turn golden in color. Add ⅓ cup slivered almonds. Continue heating over medium heat until almonds start to "pop" and mixture is deep golden. Pour onto buttered cookie sheet. Cool completely. Break into smaller pieces and crush finely in blender or with a rolling pin. Makes about ¾ cup.

CHOCOLATE GLAZE: Blend 2 tablespoons water, 2 tablespoons light corn syrup and 1½ cups 10X (confectioners') sugar in a medium-size bowl; stir in 1½ squares unsweetened chocolate. Set the bowl over hot, not boiling, water; heat, stirring often, until chocolate melts and glaze has a good pouring consistency to cover cake completely. Makes about 1 cup.

DOBOS TORTE

The original was created by Hungarian pastry chef Josef Dobos 100 years ago. Our version is a close cousin.

Bake at 350° for 12 minutes.
Makes 12 servings.

  5 eggs, separated
  ⅔ cup granulated sugar
  1 teaspoon vanilla
  ⅔ cup *sifted* cake flour
  4 squares unsweetened chocolate
  1 cup (2 sticks) butter or margarine,
      softened
  2 egg yolks

2½ to 3 cups *sifted* 10X (confectioners')
    sugar
½ cup light cream or half and half
1 tablespoon vanilla
    Lace Cookies (*recipe follows*)
    Brandy Cream (*recipe follows*)

1. Grease and line two 15x10x1-inch jelly-roll pans with wax paper; grease paper. Preheat oven to moderate (350°).

2. Beat egg whites in a large bowl with electric mixer at high speed until foamy-white. Sprinkle with ⅓ cup of the granulated sugar, 1 tablespoon at a time, until meringue forms soft peaks.

3. With the same beaters, beat egg yolks with the remaining granulated sugar and vanilla in a medium-size bowl until thick; fold in flour. Stir in one-third of the meringue; fold yolk mixture into remaining meringue. Spread batter into prepared pans, dividing evenly; smooth tops.

4. Bake in a preheated moderate oven (350°) for 12 minutes, or until centers spring back when lightly pressed with fingertip. Invert onto wire racks or clean towels; peel off wax paper; cool completely. Cut each cake crosswise into 4 strips, about 10x4 inches each.

5. Melt chocolate in the top of a double boiler over hot, not boiling, water. Remove from heat; beat in butter and egg yolks until well blended. Beat in 10X sugar alternately with cream until filling is smooth and spreadable. Stir in the remaining 1 tablespoon vanilla. Chill briefly if too soft to spread.

6. Trim layers, if necessary, and stack (8 in all) on a serving plate, using a slightly rounded ¼ cup of filling between each layer. Smooth remaining filling on sides and top.

7. Prepare Lace Cookies. Arrange about 12 on top of torte. Pipe Brandy Cream into ends of cookies and in small rosettes around base of torte. Chill several hours; overnight would be best.

LACE COOKIES
Bake at 375° for 5 minutes.
Makes about 15.

¼ cup ground blanched almonds
¼ cup sugar
¼ cup (½ stick) butter or margarine
1 tablespoon flour
1 tablespoon milk

1. Combine almonds, sugar, butter, flour and milk in a small saucepan. Heat, stirring constantly, just until butter is melted and mixture is smooth. Drop by teaspoonful, 4 inches apart, onto buttered and floured cookie sheets. Work with only 4 or 5 of the cookies at a time.

2. Bake in a moderate oven (375°) for 5 minutes, or until lacy and golden brown. Cool briefly on a wire rack, then, working quickly, turn upside down with a spatula and quickly roll cookie around the handle of a wooden spoon. (If the cookies cool too quickly or are too brittle to work with, return to a warm oven for a few minutes.) Slide off the handle onto a wire rack.

BRANDY CREAM: Beat ¼ cup (½ stick) softened butter with ⅔ cup sifted 10X (confectioners') sugar and 2 teaspoons brandy in a small bowl until smooth. Spoon into a pastry bag fitted with a small notched tip.

ALTERNATE PAN CHART:

If your recipe calls for:	You may use:
Three 8x1½-inch layers	Two 9x9x2-inch layers
Two 9x1½-inch layers	Two 8x8x2-inch layers
One 9x5x2-inch loaf	One 9x9x2-inch layer
One 9x3½-inch angel cake tube pan	One 10x3¾-inch Bundt pan or 9x3½-inch fancy tube pan

HAZELNUT TORTE

This torte typifies the cakes found in European pâtisseries, with ground nuts and bread crumbs instead of flour.

Bake at 375° for 25 minutes.
Makes 12 servings.

  7 eggs, separated
  ¼ teaspoon salt
  ¾ cup granulated sugar
  2 teaspoons grated lemon rind
  1 teaspoon vanilla
  2 cups ground blanched hazelnuts
      or pecans
  ⅓ cup packaged bread crumbs
  1 teaspoon baking powder
  1 cup heavy cream
  ¼ cup 10X (confectioners') sugar
      Mocha Butter Cream (*recipe follows*)
  2 tablespoons unsweetened
      cocoa powder
      Whole hazelnuts (*optional*)

1. Line the bottoms of three 8x1½-inch layer-cake pans with wax paper. Preheat oven to moderate (375°).
2. Beat egg whites with salt in a large bowl with electric mixer at high speed until foamy-white. Beat in ½ cup of the granulated sugar, 1 tablespoon at a time, until meringue forms soft peaks.
3. With the same beaters, beat egg yolks with the remaining sugar until very thick and fluffy. Beat in lemon rind and vanilla. Fold yolk mixture into meringue. Combine nuts, bread crumbs and baking powder; gently fold into egg mixture. Pour into prepared pans, dividing evenly; smooth tops.
4. Bake in a preheated moderate oven (375°) for 25 minutes, or until the centers spring back when lightly pressed with fingertip. Turn pans upside down on a wire rack; cool completely.
5. Loosen cakes from the edges with a knife; turn out of pans; peel off wax paper.
6. Beat cream with 10X sugar in a medium-size bowl until stiff. Stack layers on a serving plate with whipped cream between layers. Refrigerate while making

Mocha Butter Cream.
7. Spread Mocha Butter Cream on the side and top of the torte, reserving about 1 cup. Add 2 tablespoons unsweetened cocoa powder to the reserved butter cream and pipe through a decorating tube onto top and around base of cake. Decorate with whole hazelnuts, if you wish. Refrigerate 3 hours before serving.

MOCHA BUTTER CREAM
Makes about 1½ cups.

  ½ cup (1 stick) butter or margarine
  1 egg yolk
  2¾ cups 10X (confectioners') sugar
  3 tablespoons unsweetened
      cocoa powder
  3 teaspoons instant coffee powder
  ⅓ cup water

Beat butter in a medium-size bowl until softened; beat in egg yolk, 1 cup of the sugar and cocoa. Dissolve coffee in water. Beat in alternately with remaining sugar until smooth and spreadable.

Shelled hazelnuts, filberts, pistachios and peanuts can be skinned easily in the oven. Heat them in a single layer on a jelly-roll pan in a moderate oven for 20 minutes. Turn the hot nuts into a clean towel and rub them vigorously until the skins flake off.

SWISS ALMOND MERINGUE TORTE

A famous Swiss cake with alternating layers of nutted meringue, butter cream, sponge cake and cherry preserves.

Bake at 275° for 30 minutes.
Makes 12 to 16 servings.

  4 egg whites
  ⅛ teaspoon cream of tartar
  1 cup granulated sugar
  ⅓ cup ground blanched almonds
  1 tablespoon cornstarch

Almond Butter Cream
(*recipe follows*)
- 16 ladyfingers, split
- ¼ cup cherry brandy or dry sherry
- ½ cup cherry preserves
- ½ cup toasted sliced blanched almonds
- 10X (confectioners') sugar

1. Butter and flour 2 cookie sheets. Outline an 8-inch circle on each. Preheat oven to slow (275°).

2. Beat egg whites with cream of tartar in a small bowl with electric mixer at high speed until foamy. Beat in ⅓ cup of the granulated sugar, 1 tablespoon at a time, until meringue forms soft peaks. Gradually beat in another ⅓ cup of the granulated sugar until meringue is very stiff and dull.

3. Mix the remaining ⅓ cup granulated sugar with almonds and cornstarch; fold into meringue. Spoon meringue into a pastry bag with a large plain tip (about ½-inch opening), or no tip. Starting in the center of one of the circles, pipe small puffs touching each other in neat circles with the last circle just inside the outline. This will be the top layer. For a second layer, pipe remaining meringue in a continuing spiral until outline is filled in. Or, use a spatula to spread meringue ½ inch thick.

4. Bake in a preheated slow oven (275°) for 30 minutes, or until crisp and light golden. Turn off the oven and let meringues cool in the oven. Loosen carefully from the cookie sheets with a wide spatula.

5. Sprinkle split ladyfingers with cherry brandy; let stand 10 minutes.

6. Cover the plain meringue layer with about one-third of the Almond Butter Cream. Arrange half of the ladyfingers, cut-side up, on butter cream, cutting to fit if necessary. Spoon cherry preserves over; top with the remaining ladyfingers. Spread half the remaining butter cream over ladyfingers. Gently place second meringue layer on top. Smooth remaining butter cream around side of torte. Press toasted almonds onto side. Chill overnight.

Sprinkle top with 10X sugar.

ALMOND BUTTER CREAM
Makes about 3 cups

- ¾ cup sugar
- ½ cup water
- ¼ cup light corn syrup
- 1 cup (2 sticks) butter or margarine
- 2 egg yolks
- ½ teaspoon almond extract

1. Bring sugar, water and corn syrup to boiling in a small saucepan; lower heat; cook, covered, 5 minutes. Uncover and boil 5 minutes longer without stirring. There should be about ¾ cup. Cool.

2. Beat butter in a medium-size bowl with electric mixer until softened; beat in egg yolks. Gradually beat in cooled syrup until light and fluffy. Beat in almond extract. Chill briefly if too soft to spread.

> **Chiffon, sponge and angel food cakes** have a special method for cooling. They should be suspended, inverted, either over a bottle or inverted funnel until they are cold. This simple step will keep all the high fragile structure of the cake from collapsing until it has cooled enough to become self-supporting. The best way to cut a sponge cake or chiffon cake is to use a cake breaker, or a long serrated knife. If using the knife, cut with a gentle sawing motion. Left over sponge or plain butter cakes will make super desserts. Cut in cubes; drizzle the cubes with a liqueur, or fruit juice, then combine with a prepared and cooled packaged vanilla pudding. Chill well, then spoon into dessert dishes and garnish with whipped cream.

> **If you plan to keep a decorated cake longer than a day, freeze if firm and wrap in plastic wrap or foil.**

STRAWBERRY ICE-CREAM CAKE

Makes 12 to 16 servings.

    3 pints strawberry ice cream
    1 cup heavy cream
  12 dry Italian almond macaroons
    3 tablespoons cream sherry
      Easy Chiffon Cake Layer
      (*recipe follows*)
    1 jar (8 ounces) strawberry ice cream
      topping
    1 cup heavy cream
  ¼ cup strawberry or red currant jelly
      (optional)
    1 pint strawberries

1. Soften ice cream in a chilled large bowl; whip 1 cup of the heavy cream in a small bowl; fold into ice cream. Spread into two 8x8x2-inch layer-cake pans lined with plastic wrap; freeze 1 hour, or until almost firm.
2. Crumble macaroons into a small bowl; sprinkle with sherry; let stand 15 minutes.
3. Split cake layer horizontally to make 2 layers. Place 1 layer, cut-side up, on a small cookie sheet; spread with about one-third of the strawberry topping. Top with one ice-cream layer. Sprinkle macaroon crumbs evenly over; spoon another one-third of strawberry topping over. Top with remaining ice-cream layer, strawberry topping and cake layer, cut-side down, in that order; press lightly together. Freeze several hours or overnight.
4. To decorate: Whip the remaining 1 cup cream in a medium-size bowl. Spread or pipe whipped cream onto sides of cake. Just before serving, melt jelly in small saucepan over low heat. Wash, dry, hull and halve strawberries; arrange over top of cake; brush with melted jelly, if you wish.

EASY CHIFFON CAKE LAYER
Bake at 350° for 30 to 35 minutes.
Makes one 8-inch square cake.

    1 egg, separated
  ¾ cup sugar

    1 cup plus 2 tablespoons *sifted* cake
      flour
  1½ teaspoons baking powder
  ¼ teaspoon salt
    3 tablespoons vegetable oil
  ½ cup milk
    1 teaspoon vanilla

1. Preheat oven to moderate (350°). Grease and flour an 8x8x2-inch pan.
2. Beat egg white in a small bowl with electric mixer until foamy; add 4 tablespoons of the sugar, 1 tablespoon at a time. Beat 1 minute after each addition. Beat until stiff and glossy.
3. Sift the remaining sugar, flour, baking powder and salt into a large bowl. Add oil, then ¼ cup of the milk, then vanilla. Beat 1 minute, scraping bowl occasionally. Add the remaining milk and the egg yolk; beat 1 minute, scraping bowl. Fold in meringue; pour into prepared pan.
4. Bake in preheated moderate oven (350°) for 30 minutes, or until center springs back when lightly pressed with fingertip. Cool on wire rack 10 minutes. Remove from pan.

HOW TO WORK WITH ICE CREAM:
Chill bowl and beaters well. Make sure you have adequate freezer space before you start. Pans of ice cream should rest directly on freezer surface. Beat ice cream with electric mixer or work with a wooden spoon to soften. Do not allow melting, or ice crystals will form when ice cream refreezes. Fill ice cream cake layers in either of two ways:
1. Spoon the softened ice cream over cake, then spread evenly and gently with a spatula to keep from lifting crumbs from cake. Return to freezer until firm.
2. Smooth softened ice cream into foil-lined layer-cake pans the same size as the cake layers. Freeze until firm, then turn out onto cake layers, all the while peeling off pieces of foil as you go.
Plan to make ice cream cake a day or two before serving, so it has plenty of time to freeze firm. Wrap in foil.

Strawberry Ice Cream Cake

ORANGE CHIFFON CAKE

Truly an all-American variety, the chiffon cake was created in the 1930s.

Bake at 325° for 1 hour and 10 minutes.
Makes 16 servings.

2⅓ cups *sifted* cake flour
1⅓ cups sugar
  3 teaspoons baking powder
 ¼ teaspoon salt
 ½ cup vegetable oil
  5 egg yolks
 ½ cup water
  2 tablespoons grated orange rind
 ¼ cup orange juice
  1 cup egg whites (7 to 8)
 ½ teaspoon cream of tartar
    Orange Glaze (*recipe follows*)

1. Preheat oven to slow (325°).
2. Sift flour, 1 cup of the sugar, the baking powder and salt into a medium-size bowl. Make a well in the center and add in order: oil, egg yolks, water, orange rind and orange juice; beat with a spoon until smooth.
3. Beat egg whites with cream of tartar in a large bowl with electric mixer at high speed until foamy. Beat in remaining sugar, 1 tablespoon at a time, until meringue forms soft peaks.
4. Pour egg-yolk mixture over beaten egg-white mixture; fold gently until no streaks of white remain. Pour into an ungreased 10-inch angel-cake tube pan.
5. Bake in a preheated slow oven (325°) for 1 hour and 10 minutes, or until top springs back when lightly pressed with fingertip.
6. Invert pan on a funnel or bottle to keep top of cake off counter; let cake cool completely upside down. When cool, loosen cake around tube and down side with a spatula. Remove from pan. Drizzle with Orange Glaze, or sprinkle with 10X (confectioners') sugar and serve with fruit.

ORANGE GLAZE: Combine 1 cup 10X (confectioners') sugar with 2 tablespoons orange juice in a small bowl, stirring until smooth.

> Chiffon, sponge and angel cakes are baked in ungreased pans to let the batter cling to the side and the cake rise to its full height. The batter is so light and air-filled, a greased pan would provide no support and the cake would collapse.

OLD-FASHIONED SPONGE CAKE

Bake at 325° for 1 hour.
Makes 12 servings.

  1 cup *sifted* cake flour
  1 teaspoon baking powder
 ½ teaspoon salt
  6 eggs, separated
  1 cup sugar
  1 teaspoon grated lemon rind

1. Sift flour, baking powder and salt onto wax paper. Preheat oven to slow (325°).
2. Beat egg whites in a large bowl with electric mixer at high speed, until foamy. Gradually beat in ½ cup of the sugar, until meringue forms soft peaks. Do not underbeat.
3. Beat egg yolks in a small bowl with electric mixer at high speed until thick and lemon-colored. Gradually beat in the remaining ½ cup sugar until mixture is very thick and fluffy. Beat in lemon rind.
4. Fold flour mixture, one-third at a time, into egg-yolk mixture with a rubber scraper until completed blended.
5. Fold flour-egg yolk mixture into meringue until no streaks of white remain. Pour into an ungreased 9-inch angel-cake tube pan.
6. Bake in preheated slow oven (325°) for 1 hour, or until top springs back when lightly pressed with fingertip.
7. Invert pan, placing tube over a funnel or bottle to let air circulate all around; let cake cool completely. Loosen cake around the tube and down the side with a spatula. Remove from pan. Sift 10X (confectioners') sugar over top, if you wish.

STRAWBERRIES AND CREAM ROLL

Bake 375° for 12 minutes.
Makes 8 servings.

1 cup *sifted* cake flour
1 teaspoon baking powder
¼ teaspoon salt
3 eggs
¾ cup granulated sugar
⅓ cup water
1 teaspoon vanilla
  10X (confectioners') sugar
1 cup heavy cream, whipped
1 cup sliced strawberries

1. Grease a 15x10x1-inch jelly-roll pan; line bottom with wax paper; grease paper.
2. Sift flour, baking powder and salt onto a second piece of wax paper. Preheat oven to moderate (375°).
3. Beat eggs in a medium-size bowl with electric mixer until thick and creamy. Gradually add sugar, beating constantly, until mixture is very thick. Stir in water and vanilla. Fold in flour mixture. Spread batter evenly in prepared pan.
4. Bake in a preheated moderate oven (375°) for 12 minutes, or until cake is golden and center springs back when lightly pressed with fingertip.
5. Loosen cake around edges with a knife; invert pan onto clean towel dusted with 10X sugar; peel off wax paper. Trim ¼ inch from all 4 sides for easy rolling. Starting at short end, *roll up cake and towel together.* Place roll, seam-side down, on wire rack; cool completely. When cool, unroll carefully. Spread with whipped cream. Spoon strawberries evenly over cream. Lift end of cake with towel to start re-rolling. Place roll, seam-side down on a serving plate. Sprinkle with 10X sugar. Refrigerate until ready to serve.

CHOCOLATE CREAM ROLL

Bake at 375° for 12 minutes.
Makes 8 servings.

1 cup *sifted* cake flour
¼ cup unsweetened cocoa powder
1 teaspoon baking powder
¼ teaspoon salt
3 eggs
1 cup granulated sugar
⅓ cup strong cold coffee
  10X (confectioners') sugar
1 cup heavy cream, whipped

1. Grease a 15x10x1-inch jelly-roll pan; line bottom with wax paper; grease paper. Preheat oven to moderate (375°).
2. Sift flour, cocoa, baking powder and salt onto a second piece of wax paper.
3. Beat eggs in a medium-size bowl with electric mixer until fluffy. Gradually add sugar, beating constantly until mixture is *very thick* (about 5 minutes). Do not underbeat. Stir in coffee; fold in flour mixture. Spread batter evenly in prepared pan.
4. Bake in a preheated moderate oven (375°) for 12 minutes, or until center springs back when lightly pressed with fingertip.
5. Loosen cake around edge with a knife; invert on clean towel dusted with 10X sugar; peel off paper. Trim ¼ inch from all sides. Roll up cake and towel together, starting with one of the short ends; turn seam-side down; cool completely on wire rack.
6. Unroll cooled cake; spread with whipped cream; reroll. Refrigerate until serving time. Sprinkle with additional 10X sugar, if you wish.

Time saver: If you bake a lot, make your own quick pan-coat. Blend equal parts vegetable shortening and flour; keep in a covered container at room temperature. To use: Scoop out a tablespoon with paper toweling wrapped around your fingers and rub on pan.

Banana-Nut Cake

BANANA-NUT CAKE

The cake layers have nuts baked inside. The finished, frosted cake has nuts outside; and there is banana through and through!

Bake at 350° for 30 minutes.

Makes 12 servings.

2⅓ cups *sifted* cake flour
2½ teaspoons baking powder
½ teaspoon baking soda
½ teaspoon salt
½ teaspoon ground cinnamon
1 cup mashed ripe bananas (2 medium-size)
½ cup buttermilk
½ cup (1 stick) butter or margarine
1¼ cups sugar
2 eggs
¼ teaspoon vanilla
¾ cup chopped walnuts
  Rum Butter Cream Frosting
    (*recipe follows*)

1. Grease two 9x1½-inch layer-cake pans; dust lightly with flour; tap out excess flour.
2. Sift flour, baking powder, baking soda, salt and cinnamon onto wax paper. Stir buttermilk into mashed bananas in a small bowl. Preheat oven to moderate (350°).
3. Beat butter, sugar and eggs in a large bowl with electric mixer, 3 minutes. (Finish mixing cake by hand.)
4. Stir in flour mixture alternately with banana-milk mixture, beating after each addition, until batter is smooth. Stir in vanilla and ¼ cup of the chopped nuts; pour batter into prepared pans, smoothing with spatula.
5. Bake in a preheated moderate oven (350°) for 30 minutes, or until centers spring back when lightly pressed with fingertip.
6. Cool layers in pans on wire racks 10 minutes; loosen around edges with a knife; turn out onto wire racks; cool completely.

7. Put layers together with Rum Butter Cream Frosting and top with remaining frosting. Press remaining ½ cup chopped nuts on side of cake. Garnish top of cake with banana slices, if you wish. (Dip slices in orange or pineapple juice to keep them white.)

RUM BUTTER CREAM FROSTING: Beat ½ cup (1 stick) softened butter in a medium-size bowl with electric mixer until fluffy. Beat in 1 package (1 pound) 10X (confectioners') sugar alternately with 2 tablespoons rum and 2 tablespoons milk until smooth and spreadable. (Or substitute 1½ teaspoons rum extract, 1½ teaspoons vanilla and 3 tablespoons milk for the rum and milk.)

When cake is done: The best of ovens sometimes vary in temperature. Therefore, you need some way of knowing when a cake is done. Here are four clues:
1. Follow time given in recipe, plus your own good judgment.
2. Notice that a baked cake shrinks slightly from side of pan, except for sponge and chiffon cakes, which cling tightly to the pan.
3. Press top of cake lightly with fingertip. If baked, the top will spring back to shape; if not baked, imprint will remain.
4. For a loaf, Bundt and tube-pan cake, as an alternate to pressing the top: Insert a wooden pick in center. If done, there will be no batter or moist cake crumbs clinging to the pick.

Most butter cakes will make between 24 and 36 medium-size cupcakes. Line muffin pan cups with pleated liners or grease and flour cups. Fill each two-thirds full. The baking time will vary, but it is usually about 5 minutes less than the cake recipe requires.

Storing cakes: Cover cut surfaces with plastic wrap to keep moist. Put in a cake keeper, or invert a large bowl over the cake plate. Cake may be kept several days this way.
Freezing cakes: Wrap cooled cake in foil or freezer-weight plastic wrap. If frosted, freeze an hour or so until frosting is firm, then wrap. Store cakes up to 2 months at 0°. Cakes will defrost in 1 to 2 hours at room temperature.

LEMON-YOGURT CAKE
Bake at 350° for 50 minutes.
Makes 12 servings.

2¾ cups *sifted* all-purpose flour
  2 teaspoons baking powder
  1 teaspoon baking soda
  ½ teaspoon salt
  ½ cup (1 stick) butter or
      margarine, melted
  1 cup granulated sugar
  2 eggs
1½ cups plain yogurt
  1 tablespoon grated lemon rind
     10X (confectioners') sugar

1. Grease a 9-inch kugelhopf or angel-cake tube pan. Preheat oven to moderate (350°).
2. Sift flour, baking powder, baking soda and salt onto wax paper.
3. Beat butter and sugar in a large bowl with electric mixer until light and fluffy, about 3 minutes. Beat in eggs one at a time.
4. Add flour mixture alternately with yogurt, beating after each addition, until batter is smooth. (Use low speed on mixer.) Pour into prepared pan.
5. Bake in a preheated moderate oven (350°) for 50 minutes, or until the top springs back when lightly pressed with fingertip. Cool in pan on wire rack 5 minutes; loosen around the edge with a knife; turn out onto rack; cool completely. Sprinkle top with 10X sugar.

Lady Baltimore Cake

LADY BALTIMORE CAKE
Bake at 350° for 30 minutes.
Makes 12 servings.

2⅔ cups *sifted* cake flour
1½ cups sugar
 4 teaspoons baking powder
 ½ teaspoon salt
 ⅔ cup vegetable shortening
1¼ cups milk
 1 teaspoon vanilla
 4 egg whites
    Lady Baltimore Frosting and Filling
      (*recipes follow*)

1. Grease two 9x1½-inch layer-cake pans. Line bottoms with wax paper; grease paper. Preheat oven to moderate (350°).
2. Combine flour, sugar, baking powder, salt, shortening, ¾ cup of the milk and the vanilla in a large bowl. Beat at low speed with electric mixer until blended, then at high speed for 2 minutes. Add the remaining milk and the egg whites; beat 2 minutes longer. Pour into prepared pans.
3. Bake in a preheated moderate oven (350°) for 30 minutes, or until centers spring back when lightly pressed with fingertip. Cool on wire rack 10 minutes; invert; peel off paper; cool completely.
4. Fill layers with Lady Baltimore Filling; frost with Lady Baltimore Frosting. Decorate with additional fruits and nuts, if you wish.

LADY BALTIMORE FROSTING: Combine 1 cup sugar, ⅓ cup light corn syrup, ¼ cup water and ¼ teaspoon salt in a small saucepan. Cook until mixture registers 242° on a candy thermometer. Meanwhile, beat 4 egg whites with ⅛ teaspoon cream of tartar in a large bowl until stiff peaks form. Pour hot syrup into whites in a thin stream, beating until frosting is stiff.

LADY BALTIMORE FILLING: Combine 2 tablespoons grated orange rind; ½ cup chopped pecans, ⅓ cup snipped dried figs, ⅓ cup raisins and 2 tablespoons chopped maraschino cherries. Stir into 1½ cups of the Lady Baltimore Frosting.

> **When frosting a cake, it is helpful to turn the cake as you work. If you do not have a turntable, put the cake on its plate over a canister (with lid removed), then turn as you frost.**
> **Do you have trouble with cakes layers scooting apart as you try to frost them smoothly? Just pin them together with metal or bamboo skewers, thrusting them straight down through the layers. When cake is frosted, pull them out and smooth over the tiny holes.**

CHOCOLATE CREAM CAKE
Bake at 350° for 35 minutes.
Makes 12 servings.

 3 squares unsweetened chocolate
2¼ cups *sifted* cake flour
 2 teaspoons baking soda
 ½ teaspoon salt
 ½ cup (1 stick) butter or margarine, softened
2¼ cups firmly packed light brown sugar
 3 eggs
1½ teaspoons vanilla
 1 cup dairy sour cream
 1 cup boiling water
    Whipped Cocoa Cream
      (*recipe follows*)

Chocolate Cream Cake

Chocolate Fudge Cake

1. Melt chocolate in a small bowl over hot, not boiling, water; cool.

2. Grease and flour two 9x1½-inch layer-cake pans; tap out excess flour.

3. Sift flour, baking soda and salt onto wax paper. Preheat oven to moderate (350°).

4. Beat butter, sugar and eggs in a large bowl with electric mixer at high speed until light and fluffy. Beat in vanilla and cooled chocolate.

5. Stir in dry ingredients, alternating with sour cream, beating well with a spoon, until smooth. Stir in water. (Batter will be thin.) Pour into prepared pans.

6. Bake in a preheated moderate oven (350°) for 35 minutes, or until centers spring back when lightly pressed with fingertip. Cool in pans 10 minutes; turn out on wire racks; cool completely. Split each layer horizontally to make 4 thin layers.

7. Fill and frost with Whipped Cocoa Cream. Refrigerate.

WHIPPED COCOA CREAM: Whip 2 cups heavy cream, ⅔ cup 10X sugar, ½ cup unsweetened cocoa powder and 1 teaspoon vanilla in a medium-size bowl until stiff. *Variation:* For CHOCOLATE FUDGE CAKE, leave layers in chocolate cream cake unsplit; fill and frost with Chocolate Fudge Frosting (*recipe follows*).

CHOCOLATE FUDGE FROSTING:
Makes enough to fill and frost two 9-inch layers.

   4 squares unsweetened chocolate
   ½ cup (1 stick) butter or margarine
   1 package (1 pound) 10X
       (confectioners') sugar
   ½ cup milk
   2 teaspoons vanilla

1. Combine chocolate and butter in a small heavy saucepan. Place over very low heat just until melted; remove from heat.

2. Combine 10X sugar, milk and vanilla in a medium-size bowl; stir until smooth; stir in the chocolate mixture. Set bowl in a pan of ice and water; beat with a wooden spoon until the frosting is thick enough to spread and hold its shape.

> **Good circulation is important when baking more than one cake layer at a time. Stagger pans on oven racks so they do not block the heat circulation from one another.**
> **To keep cocoa and chocolate cakes brown on the outside, grease pans and dust with unsweetened cocoa powder instead of flour.**

CARROT-NUT CAKE

Bake at 350° for 1 hour.
Makes 8 servings.

- 1 cup *sifted* all-purpose flour
- 2 teaspoons baking powder
- ⅛ teaspoon salt
- ½ cup vegetable shortening
- 1 cup sugar
- 3 eggs, separated
- 1 cup shredded carrots
- ½ cup finely chopped walnuts
- 2 tablespoons rum, brandy or orange juice
- 1 teaspoon lemon juice
  Apricot Glaze (*recipe follows*)
  Walnut halves

1. Grease an 8-cup fancy tube pan (or you can use a 9-inch angel-cake tube pan but cake will not be as high). Dust lightly with flour; tap out excess. Preheat oven to moderate (350°).
2. Sift flour, baking powder and salt onto wax paper.
3. Beat shortening, sugar and egg yolks in a large bowl with electric mixer at high speed for 3 minutes, scraping down side of bowl and beaters occasionally. (Finish mixing cake by hand.)
4. Stir in carrots, walnuts, rum and lemon juice. Stir in flour mixture a little at a time until batter is smooth.
5. Beat egg whites in a small bowl with electric mixer until soft peaks form; fold into cake batter. Spoon into prepared pan, smoothing top evenly.
6. Bake in a preheated moderate oven (350°) for 1 hour, or until top springs back when lightly pressed with fingertip. Cool in pan on wire rack 10 minutes; loosen cake around edge with a metal spatula; turn out onto a wire rack; cool completely. Brush with Apricot Glaze; garnish with walnut halves

APRICOT GLAZE: Heat ⅓ cup apricot preserves in a small saucepan; press through a sieve into a small bowl. Brush glaze over top and side of cake.

ALMOND POUND CAKE

Crumbled almond paste provides the nutty flavor in this smooth pound cake.
Bake at 325° for 45 minutes.
Makes 12 servings.

- 2½ cups *sifted* cake flour
- 1 teaspoon baking powder
- ½ cup almond paste, from an 8-ounce can or package (not almond filling)
- ⅔ cup butter or margarine, softened
- 1¼ cups sugar
- 4 eggs
- ½ cup milk

1. Grease a 10-inch Bundt or a 9-inch angel-cake tube pan. Dust lightly with flour; tap out excess.
2. Sift flour and baking powder onto wax paper. Preheat oven to slow (325°).
3. Crumble almond paste into butter in a large bowl. Beat with electric mixer until creamy and smooth. Slowly add sugar, beating until fluffy. Add eggs, one at a time, beating well.
4. Add the flour mixture alternately with milk, beating after each addition, until batter is smooth. (Use low speed on mixer.) Pour into prepared pan.
5. Bake in a preheated slow oven (325°) for 45 minutes, or until top springs back when lightly pressed with fingertip. Cool in pan on wire rack 10 minutes; loosen around edge with a knife; turn out onto wire rack; cool completely. Serve with ice cream, if you wish.

GINGERBREAD

Dark, spicy gingerbread — a treat for all seasons!
Bake at 350° for 30 minutes.
Makes 12 servings.

- 2½ cups *sifted* all-purpose flour
- 1½ teaspoons baking soda
- 1 teaspoon ground ginger
- 1 teaspoon ground cinnamon
- ½ teaspoon salt

½ cup vegetable shortening
½ cup sugar
¾ cup molasses
1 egg
1 cup hot water

1. Sift flour, baking soda, ginger, cinnamon and salt onto wax paper. Grease a 13x9x2-inch baking pan. Preheat oven to moderate (350°).
2. Beat shortening with sugar in a large bowl until fluffy; beat in molasses and egg.
3. Stir in flour mixture, half at a time, just until blended; beat in hot water until smooth. Pour into prepared pan.
4. Bake in a preheated moderate oven (350°) for 30 minutes, or until center springs back when lightly pressed with fingertip.
5. Leave in pan to cool on a wire rack, or let cool 10 minutes, then loosen around edge with a knife and turn out onto rack. Serve with whipped cream, applesauce or lemon sauce, if you wish.

CHOCOLATE-NUT UPSIDE-DOWN CAKE

Fudgy and crunchy and topped with nuts. So good when served warm with either whipped or heavy cream.
Bake at 350° for 45 minutes.
Makes 12 servings.

10 tablespoons (1¼ sticks) butter or margarine
¼ cup firmly packed light brown sugar
⅔ cup light corn syrup
¼ cup heavy cream
1 cup broken walnuts
1¾ cups *sifted* cake flour
2 teaspoons baking powder
¼ teaspoon salt
1½ cups granulated sugar
2 eggs, separated
3 squares unsweetened chocolate, melted
1 teaspoon vanilla
1 cup milk

Chocolate-Nut Upside-Down Cake

1. Melt 4 tablespoons of the butter in a small saucepan; stir in brown sugar; heat until bubbly. Stir in corn syrup and cream; heat, stirring constantly, just to boiling. Add nuts; pour into a generously greased 10-inch Bundt pan. (Mixture will be thin.) Let stand while preparing cake batter.
2. Sift flour, baking powder and salt onto wax paper. Preheat oven to moderate (350°).
3. Beat the remaining butter in a large bowl until softened. Gradually beat in granulated sugar until well blended. Beat in egg yolks, chocolate and vanilla until thoroughly blended.
4. Add flour mixture alternately with milk, beginning and ending with flour. Beat egg whites in a small bowl until soft peaks form; fold into cake batter until no streaks of white remain. Spoon batter evenly over nut mixture in pan.
5. Bake in a preheated moderate oven (350°) for 45 minutes, or until a wooden pick inserted in the center comes out clean.
6. Loosen cake from edge of pan with a small knife; cover pan with serving plate; invert; shake gently, then lift off pan. Scoop out any nuts and syrup clinging to pan onto cake with a rubber scraper.

PINEAPPLE-APRICOT UPSIDE-DOWN CAKE

Apricot joins pineapple in our version of the granddaddy of all upside-down cakes.
Bake at 350° for 45 minutes.
Makes 8 servings.

- ¼ cup (½ stick) butter or margarine
- ¼ cup firmly packed brown sugar
- 6 pineapple slices packed in juice (from a 1-pound, 4-ounce can), drained
- 1 can (8 ounces) apricot halves, drained Maraschino cherries
- 1¼ cups *sifted* all-purpose flour
- 2 teaspoons baking powder
- ¼ teaspoon salt
- 1 cup sugar
- ¼ cup vegetable shortening
- ¾ cup milk
- 1 teaspoon vanilla
- 1 egg

1. Melt butter; pour into a 9x9x2-inch baking pan. Sprinkle brown sugar over butter. Arrange pineapple slices and apricot halves in butter-sugar mixture; fill centers of pineapple slices with cherries. Preheat oven to moderate (350°).

2. Sift flour, baking powder, salt and sugar into a large bowl. Add shortening and milk. Beat 2 minutes at medium speed with electric mixer, scraping down side of bowl several times. Add vanilla and egg; beat 2 minutes longer. Pour over fruit in baking pan.

3. Bake in a preheated moderate oven (350°) for 45 minutes, or until center springs back when lightly pressed with fingertip.

4. Invert cake onto a serving plate; leave baking pan in place 2 minutes. Lift off pan. Serve warm with whipped cream or dessert topping, if you wish.

BOURBON FRUIT CAKE

Light, moist and not too heavy with fruit.
Bake at 300° for 2 hours and 10 minutes.
Makes 12 servings.

- 1½ cups raisins
- 1 container (8 ounces) mixed candied fruits
- ⅓ cup bourbon
- 3½ cups *sifted* all-purpose flour
- 1½ teaspoons baking powder
- ¾ teaspoon ground nutmeg
- 1½ cups (3 sticks) butter or margarine
- 1¾ cups sugar
- 6 eggs
- ⅓ cup milk
- 1½ cups pecans or walnuts, coarsely chopped
- Bourbon

1. Combine raisins, candied fruits and bourbon in a medium-size bowl. Let stand at room temperature several hours.

2. Grease a 10-inch angel-cake tube pan. Dust with flour; tap out excess. Sift flour, baking powder and nutmeg onto wax paper. Preheat oven to slow (300°).

3. Beat butter in a large bowl with electric mixer until softened; add sugar and beat on high speed until smooth and fluffy. Add eggs, one at a time, beating after each addition until light and fluffy.

4. Stir in flour mixture alternately with

Bourbon Fruitcake

Sugar Cookie Leaves (page 254); Spritz Fingers

milk, beating after each addition until smooth. Stir in fruits and nuts. Turn into prepared pan.

5. Bake in a preheated slow oven (300°) for 2 hours and 10 minutes, or until top springs back when lightly pressed with fingertip. Cool in pan on wire rack 20 minutes. Loosen around tube and edge with a small spatula; turn out of pan onto wire rack; cool completely.

6. Wrap cake in cheesecloth that has been soaked in about ⅓ cup bourbon; then wrap tightly in foil. Store in refrigerator. Resoak cheesecloth as it dries out, about once a week. Store cake 3 to 4 weeks to develop flavors. To serve, brush top of cake with heated corn syrup, and decorate with candied fruits and nuts, if you wish.

> **Oven geography: When you are baking cookies, pound cakes, layer cakes, etc., keep in mind this oven placement guide for even browning: thick things on the bottom (lowest rack), thin things on the top (top rack).**

SPRITZ FINGERS

Bake at 375° for 8 minutes.
Makes 6 dozen cookies.

1½ cups (3 sticks) butter or margarine, softened
 1 cup sugar
 3 egg yolks
 1 teaspoon vanilla
 ¼ teaspoon salt
3½ cups *sifted* all-purpose flour
 4 squares semisweet chocolate, melted
 ½ cup chopped pistachio nuts or almonds

1. Preheat oven to moderate (375°).

2. Beat butter, sugar, egg yolks, vanilla and salt in a large bowl with electric mixer until fluffy. Stir in flour, blending well.

3. Fit a pastry bag with a star tip; fill bag with dough. Pipe out dough into 3-inch lengths about 1 inch apart on ungreased large cookie sheets.

4. Bake in a preheated moderate oven (375°) for 8 minutes, or until set and lightly golden. Cool on wire racks. Dip ends of cooled cookies into melted chocolate, then in nuts. Leave on wire racks until coating is set.

THIMBLE COOKIES

Delicate little cookies with raspberry or strawberry preserves spooned into the center. Why not try different flavors the next time you bake them and make your own interesting variations?

Bake at 350° for 12 minutes.
Makes 3 dozen cookies.

2¼ cups *sifted* all-purpose flour
　1 cup (2 sticks) butter or margarine, softened
　½ cup firmly packed brown sugar
　2 eggs, separated
1½ teaspoons vanilla
1½ cups finely chopped walnuts
　　Raspberry or strawberry preserves

1. Sift flour onto wax paper.
2. Beat butter with brown sugar in a medium-size bowl until fluffy and light; beat in egg yolks and vanilla. Stir in flour, half at a time, blending well to make a stiff dough.
3. Beat egg whites in a pie plate until foamy; sprinkle walnuts on wax paper.
4. Preheat oven to moderate (350°).
5. Roll dough, 1 teaspoonful at a time, into balls between palms of hands; roll each in egg white, then into walnuts to coat all over. Place, 2 inches apart, on large cookie sheets. Press center of each cookie with fingertip or thimble to make a little hollow.
6. Bake in a preheated moderate oven (350°) for 12 minutes, or until firm and lightly golden. Remove from cookie sheets to wire racks; cool completely. Spoon preserves into each hollow.

SUGAR COOKIE LEAVES

Crispy vanilla cookies with a shiny icing.
Bake at 350° for 8 minutes.
Makes 4 dozen cookies.

1½ cups *sifted* all-purpose flour
　1 teaspoon baking powder
　½ teaspoon baking soda
　½ teaspoon ground nutmeg

　½ cup (1 stick) butter or margarine, softened
　1 egg
　½ cup sugar
1½ tablespoons milk
　1 teaspoon vanilla
　　Sugar Icing (*recipe follows*)
　2 squares semisweet chocolate, melted

1. Sift flour, baking powder, baking soda and nutmeg onto wax paper.
2. Beat butter, egg and granulated sugar in a large bowl with electric mixer until fluffy, about 3 minutes. Stir in milk and vanilla.
3. Stir in sifted dry ingredients until mixture is blended and smooth. Chill several hours or overnight until firm.
4. Preheat oven to moderate (350°).
5. Roll out dough a quarter at a time on a floured surface to a ¼-inch thickness. Cut out with a floured leaf-shape cookie cutter (or cut out with a plain 3-inch cutter). Arrange on ungreased cookie sheets, 1½ inches apart.
6. Bake in a preheated moderate oven (350°) for 8 minutes, or until set and lightly golden. Cool on wire racks. Ice with Sugar Icing. Decorate with "veins" of cooled melted semisweet chocolate.

Sugar Icing: Blend 1 package (1 pound) 10X (confectioners') sugar in a medium-size bowl with ⅓ cup water, 1 teaspoon vanilla and a few drops of food coloring to tint pale yellow or orange.

ISCHL TARTLETS

A favorite in Viennese pastry shops; we share our version of these two-layer jam-filled cookies with you.

Bake at 350° for 8 minutes.
Makes about 3½ dozen cookies.

2¾ cups *sifted* all-purpose flour
　½ teaspoon baking powder
　1 cup (2 sticks) butter or margarine, softened

1 package (3 ounces) cream cheese, softened
1 cup granulated sugar
1 egg
½ cup almonds, ground
1 tablespoon grated lemon rind
1 jar (12 ounces) raspberry preserves or jam
10X (confectioners') sugar

1. Sift flour and baking powder onto wax paper.

2. Beat butter, cream cheese, sugar and egg in a large bowl until light and fluffy.

3. Add flour mixture, blending thoroughly. Stir in ground almonds and lemon rind. Turn dough out onto wax paper (mixture will be sticky). Shape into a ball. Chill several hours, or overnight.

4. Preheat oven to moderate (350°).

5. Cut dough in half. (Refrigerate other half.) Roll out dough on a lightly floured surface with a lightly floured rolling pin to a ⅛-inch thickness. With a 3-inch round cookie cutter, cut out as many circles from the dough as you can. Place circles on ungreased cookie sheets. Refrigerate scraps of dough for second rolling.

6. Repeat with other half of dough, cutting out an equal number of 3-inch circles as the first batch. Place on ungreased cookie sheets. With a ½-inch cookie cutter or thimble, cut out center of each of the second batch of circles. Use any scraps of dough for second rolling; cut out an equal number of solid circles, and circles with open centers.

7. Bake in a preheated moderate oven (350°) for 8 minutes, or until edges of cookies are lightly browned. Remove cookie sheets from oven; let stand 1 minute. Remove cookies with a spatula to wire racks. Cool.

8. Heat raspberry preserves in a small saucepan. Spread each of the solid cookies completely with a thin layer of hot preserves. Top each with cut out cookie; press together gently to make a "sandwich." Place on wire rack. Sprinkle tops of cookies with 10X sugar. Spoon a dab of preserves into the opening of each cookie; let preserves set slightly. To keep cookies fresh, store between wax paper-lined layers in a tightly covered container.

HERMITS

A spicy, fruity drop cookie from New England.
Bake at 375° for 12 minutes.
Makes 4 dozen cookies.

¾ cup *sifted* all-purpose flour
½ teaspoon baking soda
¼ teaspoon salt
½ teaspoon ground cinnamon
¼ teaspoon ground nutmeg
⅛ teaspoon ground cloves
½ cup vegetable shortening
1 cup firmly packed brown sugar
1 egg
¼ cup cold coffee
1 container (4 ounces) candied lemon peel
1 cup raisins
¾ cup coarsely chopped walnuts

1. Sift flour, baking soda, salt, cinnamon, nutmeg and cloves onto wax paper.

2. Beat shortening, sugar, egg and coffee in a large bowl with electric mixer until fluffy-light.

3. Stir in flour mixture, blending well. Stir in candied lemon peel, raisins and walnuts until mixture is thoroughly blended.

4. Preheat oven to moderate (375°).

5. Drop mixture by heaping teaspoonsful, 1 inch apart, onto greased cookie sheets.

6. Bake in a preheated moderate oven (375°) for 12 minutes, or until lightly browned. Remove from cookie sheets to wire racks; cool completely. Store in a tightly covered container to mellow.

ALMOND-FILLED PASTRY CRESCENTS

Called "Gazelle Horns" in Morocco.
Bake at 400° for 12 minutes.
Makes about 4 dozen cookies.

2¼ cups *sifted* all-purpose flour
½ teaspoon salt
1 cup (2 sticks) butter or margarine
4 tablespoons ice water
1 can (8 ounces) almond paste
    (not almond filling)
1 egg
2 tablespoons granulated sugar
⅓ cup blanched almonds, ground
⅔ cup 10X (confectioners') sugar

1. Combine flour and salt in a medium-size bowl. Cut in butter with a pastry blender until mixture is crumbly. Add ice water, 1 tablespoon at a time; combine with a fork until mixture is thoroughly moistened.
2. Shape pastry into a ball; divide into 3 equal pieces; shape each piece into a round; flatten slightly. Wrap each piece in wax paper. Refrigerate at least 1 hour.
3. Place almond paste in a small bowl, breaking up with a fork. Beat in egg, sugar and ground almonds until thoroughly combined. (Mixture will be sticky.)
4. Turn almond mixture out onto a lightly floured surface. Shape into a ball with floured hands. Divide into thirds. Shape each third into a rope ½ inch in diameter and 16 inches long. (If mixture sticks, flour hands and surface lightly.) Cut each rope into sixteen 1-inch pieces. Reserve.
5. Roll out pastry, a third at a time, on a lightly floured surface to a 12-inch square (⅛ inch thick). Trim off rough edges. Using a ruler and a sharp knife or pastry wheel, cut into 16 three-inch squares.
6. Preheat oven to hot (400°).
7. Place one piece of almond paste diagon-ally across one corner of pastry square. Lift the point over paste and roll jelly-roll fashion. Pinch ends, enclosing almond filling. Curve pastry into a crescent. Repeat with remaining pastry and almond paste.
8. Place, 1 inch apart, on ungreased cookie sheets. Bake in a preheated hot oven (400°) for 12 minutes, or until cookie edges begin to brown.
9. Place 10X sugar on a pie plate or on a large sheet of wax paper. Place cookies, while still warm, a few at a time, into sugar and coat, turning twice.
10. Place cookies on wire racks to cool thoroughly. Store in a tightly covered container with wax paper separating layers. Sprinkle with additional 10X sugar.

LEMON SQUARES

Bake at 325° for 45 minutes.
Makes about 2 dozen squares.

1 cup *sifted* all-purpose flour
½ cup (1 stick) butter or margarine
1¼ cups sugar
2 eggs, lightly beaten
1 teaspoon grated lemon rind
3 tablespoons lemon juice
¼ teaspoon salt
2 tablespoons flour
½ teaspoon baking soda

1. Preheat oven to slow (325°).
2. Blend the 1 cup flour, butter and ¼ cup of the sugar in a small bowl until smooth. Press crust mixture firmly into an 11x7x1½-inch baking pan.
3. Bake shortbread crust in a preheated slow oven (325°) for 20 minutes, or until lightly browned.
4. Combine the remaining 1 cup sugar, eggs, lemon rind, lemon juice, salt, the 2 tablespoons flour and baking soda in a medium-size bowl. Beat until well blended. Spread mixture over the hot baked shortbread crust. Return to oven.
5. Bake an additional 25 minutes. Remove from oven; cool in pan. Cut into squares.

Top: Hermits (page 255); center: Almond-Filled Pastry Crescents; bottom: Ischl Tartlets (page 254)

CINNAMON STARS

An unusual nutty-cinnamon flavored cookie that has its own baked-on frosting.

Bake at 350° for 20 minutes.
Makes 2 dozen cookies.

3¼ cups very finely ground hazelnuts
    or almonds
1¼ cups superfine granulated sugar
  7 tablespoons 10X (confectioners')
    sugar
1½ teaspoons ground cinnamon
  3 egg whites
    Royal Icing (*recipe follows*)

1. Combine hazelnuts, superfine sugar, 10X sugar and cinnamon in a large bowl; beat in egg whites, blending well to make a stiff dough; wrap in wax paper; chill several hours or overnight. (Mixture will be sticky.)
2. Roll out dough between sheets of wax paper to a ½-inch thickness. Remove top sheet of wax paper. With a 2½-inch star cookie cutter, cut out as many stars as you can. Carefully remove dough from the bottom sheet of wax paper. Place dough on greased cookie sheets. Reroll scraps of dough and cut out as many stars as you can. Let stand 3 hours to dry.
3. Prepare Royal Icing. Preheat oven to moderate (350°). Spread tops of cookies evenly with Royal Icing, using a metal spatula; let stand 15 minutes, or until icing is dry to the touch.
4. Bake in a preheated moderate oven (350°) for 20 minutes, or until icing is a light brown. Remove cookies from oven; let stand on cookie sheets 1 minute, then remove with a wide spatula to wire racks to cool thoroughly.

ROYAL ICING: Beat 1 egg white and a pinch of cream of tartar in a small bowl until foamy. Slowly beat in 1½ cups *sifted* 10X (confectioners') sugar until the icing forms firm peaks. Keep icing covered with damp toweling while working.

DANISH BUTTER COOKIES

Bake at 400° for 7 minutes.
Makes about 7 dozen cookies.

  1 cup (2 sticks) butter or margarine,
    softened
1½ cups 10X (confectioners') sugar
  1 egg
  1 teaspoon vanilla
2½ cups *sifted* all-purpose flour
  ¼ teaspoon salt
    Milk
    Coarse sugar crystals*

1. Beat butter, sugar, egg and vanilla in a large bowl with electric mixer until fluffy.
2. Sift flour and salt into the butter mixture. Stir with a wooden spoon until mixture forms a soft dough.
3. Shape dough into 4 rolls, 1½ inches in diameter. Roll each in foil or plastic wrap; refrigerate 2 hours or until firm.
4. Preheat oven to hot (400°).
5. Slice dough ¼ inch thick and place slices 1 inch apart on ungreased cookie sheets. Brush cookies with milk and sprinkle with sugar crystals.
6. Bake in top third of a preheated hot oven (400°) for 7 minutes, or until golden brown. Remove with spatula to wire racks; cool completely. Store in a container with a tight-fitting lid. Cookies can be stored in freezer for up to 3 months.
If coarse sugar crystals are not available, crush sugar cubes with a hammer or rolling pin.

DATE-PECAN CHEWS

Sugar-topped logs with dates and pecans rolled inside.

Bake at 350° for 25 minutes.
Makes about 6 dozen cookies.

  ¾ cup *sifted* all-purpose flour
  ½ teaspoon baking powder
  ¼ teaspoon salt
  3 eggs
  1 cup sugar

2 tablespoons orange juice
1 package (8 ounces) pitted dates, chopped
1 cup pecans, chopped
¼ cup candied orange peel, chopped
Sugar (for coating)

1. Sift flour, baking powder and salt onto wax paper. Grease a 13x9x2-inch baking pan. Preheat oven to moderate (350°).
2. Beat eggs in a large bowl until light and foamy; slowly beat in the 1 cup sugar; continue beating until mixture is thick and fluffy. Stir in orange juice.
3. Fold in flour mixture, dates, pecans and orange peel. Spread mixture evenly in prepared pan.
4. Bake in a preheated moderate oven (350°) for 25 minutes, or until golden and top springs back when pressed with fingertip. Cool in pan on wire rack 15 minutes.
5. Cut lengthwise into 9 strips and crosswise into 8 to make 72 pieces, about 1x1½ inches each. Roll each in sugar in a pie plate to coat generously. (Cookies are soft and will roll into a log shape.)

SHORTBREAD

A lovely buttery cookie, originating in Scotland. They are sometimes known as "petticoat tails."
Bake at 325° for 25 minutes.
Makes 2 dozen cookies.

1 cup (2 sticks) butter or margarine, softened
½ cup sugar
2½ cups *sifted* all-purpose flour

1. Beat butter and sugar in a large bowl until creamy and smooth. Work in flour, part at a time, with a wooden spoon until a stiff dough forms.
2. Preheat oven to slow (325°).
3. Divide dough into 3 parts. Working with one part at a time, roll out to about a 5-inch circle on an ungreased cookie sheet. Place a 5-inch saucer or small plate on dough and cut around to make an even circle. Score

circle with a knife into 8 equal triangles. Mark entire top of dough with the tines of a fork. Repeat with remaining dough.
4. Bake in a preheated slow oven (325°) for 25 minutes, or until circles are faintly golden brown. They should be quite pale.
5. Remove from oven. Cut all the way through at score lines. Remove cookies to wire racks to cool. Store in tightly covered containers. These cookies keep well.

RASPBERRY MERINGUE BARS

Bake at 350° for 15 minutes, then an additional 25 minutes.
Makes 2 dozen bars.

¾ cup (1½ sticks) butter or margarine
¾ cup sugar
2 eggs, separated
1½ cups *sifted* all-purpose flour
1 cup chopped walnuts
1 cup raspberry preserves
½ cup flaked coconut

1. Preheat oven to moderate (350°). Beat butter with ¼ cup of the sugar and the egg yolks in a medium-size bowl until mixture is light and fluffy.
2. Stir in flour until blended. Spread evenly in a 13x9x2-inch baking pan.
3. Bake in a preheated moderate oven (350°) for 15 minutes, or until golden; remove from oven.
4. While layer bakes, beat egg whites in a small bowl until foamy-white; gradually beat in the remaining ½ cup sugar until meringue forms firm peaks; fold in walnuts.
5. Spread raspberry preserves over baked layer in pan; sprinkle with coconut. Spread meringue over raspberry-coconut layer.
6. Bake in a moderate oven (350°) 25 minutes, or until lightly golden. Cool completely in pan on wire rack. Cut into bars. Carefully lift the cookies out of pan with a wide spatula. Store in tightly covered container, with wax paper between layers.

Top: Profiteroles with Espresso Sauce (page 262); center: Strawberry Cream Puffs (page 262); bottom: Chocolate Eclairs and Mocha Eclairs

Desserts

Old favorites with new twists that will establish any cook's reputation.
Every step is carefully explained for guaranteed success.

CHOCOLATE ECLAIRS

Bake at 400° for 40 minutes.
Makes 12 servings.

> Basic Cream Puff Paste
> (*recipe, page 263*)
> Vanilla Custard Filling
> (*recipe, page 262*)
> Chocolate Glaze (*recipe follows*)

1. Prepare Basic Cream Puff Paste.
2. Preheat oven to hot (400°).
3. Attach large plain tip to pastry bag (or use pastry bag without a tip); spoon paste into bag. Press paste out into 4 or 5-inch strips, 1 inch wide, 1½ inches apart, on ungreased cookie sheets. OR: Shape with spoon into 1x4-inch strips, smoothing with spatula. Makes 12 strips.
4. Bake in a preheated hot oven (400°) for 40 minutes, or until puffed and golden brown. Remove from cookie sheets to wire rack; cool completely.
5. To fill: Make a small hole in one end of each eclair with the tip of a knife. Fit pastry bag with small tip. Fill bag with Vanilla Custard Filling. Press filling through hole into eclairs. OR: Split eclairs lengthwise, then spoon filling in and replace tops.

CHOCOLATE GLAZE: Combine 1 square unsweetened chocolate, 1 tablespoon butter and 2 tablespoons water in a small bowl. Place in pan of barely simmering water, stirring often, until chocolate is melted. Remove from heat; stir in 1 cup 10X (confectioners') sugar and 1 teaspoon vanilla. Spread over tops of eclairs while still warm.

To decorate: Mix ½ cup 10X sugar with 2 teaspoons strong brewed coffee until smooth; drizzle over eclairs.

MOCHA ECLAIRS

A variation of the classic eclair.
Bake at 400° for 40 minutes.
Makes 12 servings.

> Basic Cream Puff Paste
> (*recipe, page 263*)
> Chocolate Custard Filling
> (*recipe, page 262*)
> Coffee Glaze (*recipe follows*)

1. Follow directions for Chocolate Eclairs through step 4.
2. Fill with Chocolate Custard Filling.

COFFEE GLAZE: Dissolve 1 teaspoon instant coffee in 2 tablespoons water in small bowl; stir in 2 cups 10X (confectioners') sugar until smooth. If too thick, add a few more drops of water. Spread over tops of eclairs to glaze.

To decorate: Melt 1 square semisweet chocolate in small bowl over hot water; drizzle over eclairs.

> A no-fail clue to the "thoroughly-baked" stage for eclairs, cream puffs or profiteroles is to check for the presence of tiny bubbles on the surface of the pastry, close to the end of the baking time. When the bubbles disappear, the puffs are dry and will hold their shapes.

VANILLA CUSTARD FILLING

Makes about 3½ cups.

2½ cups milk
5 egg yolks
¾ cup sugar
⅔ cup *sifted* all-purpose flour
2 tablespoons butter or margarine
3 teaspoons vanilla

1. Heat milk in large heavy saucepan until bubbles appear around edge.
2. Beat egg yolks and sugar in large bowl with electric mixer until pale yellow and thick. Beat in flour until well mixed. Gradually beat in hot milk; pour all back into saucepan. Cook, stirring constantly, over moderately high heat until mixture thickens and comes to boiling; lower heat. (Mixture will be lumpy in the beginning, but lumps disappear during cooking and stirring.) Continue cooking 2 to 3 minutes, stirring constantly. Mixture will be quite thick. Remove from heat.
3. Stir in butter and vanilla. Place a piece of plastic wrap directly on surface of filling to prevent skin from forming. Chill at least 2 hours. If filling becomes too stiff after it is chilled, gradually stir in 2 to 4 tablespoons cream or milk, 1 tablespoon at a time.

CHOCOLATE CUSTARD FILLING: Follow the directions for Vanilla Custard Filling, adding 3 squares unsweetened chocolate to milk in step 1, stirring often until melted.

Flour-based dessert fillings and sauces need to be cooked a few minutes after they have thickened and come to boiling. This step cooks off the raw starchy taste that would affect the smooth silkiness of the filling. When cooking these fillings and sauces, press a piece of plastic wrap directly on the hot surface to keep the air from forming a "skin" on the cooling surface, which, unless skimmed off, would form lumps in the otherwise smooth texture.

STRAWBERRY CREAM PUFFS

Cloud-light puffs filled with juicy berries and snowy cream.
Bake at 400° for 40 minutes.
Makes 12 servings.

Basic Cream Puff Paste
(*recipe, page 263*)
2 pints strawberries
4 tablespoons 10X (confectioners') sugar
2 cups heavy cream

1. Preheat oven to hot (400°).
2. Prepare Basic Cream Puff Paste. Drop by rounded tablespoonsful into 12 even mounds, 2 inches apart, on an ungreased large cookie sheet.
3. Bake in a preheated hot oven (400°) for 40 minutes, or until puffed and golden brown. Remove to wire rack; cool.
4. Make filling: Wash strawberries; let dry on paper toweling. Reserve a few for garnish; hull remainder. Slice into a medium-size bowl; stir in 2 tablespoons of the 10X sugar. Chill 30 minutes.
5. Beat cream with the remaining 2 tablespoons 10X sugar in a medium-size bowl until stiff. Chill.
6. Just before serving, cut slice from top of each puff; remove any filaments of soft dough. Fold berries into cream; spoon into puffs, dividing evenly; replace tops. Sieve additional 10X sugar over tops; garnish with reserved strawberries, if you wish.

PROFITEROLES WITH ESPRESSO SAUCE

Bake at 400° for 35 minutes.
Makes 12 servings.

Basic Cream Puff Paste
(*recipe, page 263*)
1 quart vanilla, butter pecan or chocolate ice cream
1¼ cups firmly packed light brown sugar
1 tablespoon instant espresso coffee
¼ cup light corn syrup

½ cup water
2 tablespoons butter or margarine
1 to 2 tablespoons brandy or whisky

1. Prepare Basic Cream Puff Paste. Preheat oven to hot (400°).
2. Drop paste by slightly rounded teaspoonful into 36 even mounds, 1 inch apart, on an ungreased large cookie sheet.
3. Bake in a preheated hot oven (400°) for 35 minutes, or until puffed and golden brown. Remove to wire rack; cool.
4. Cut a slice from top of each puff; remove any filaments of soft dough. Fill puffs with small scoops of ice cream of your choice; replace tops. Freeze until serving time.
5. Make Espresso Sauce: Combine sugar, coffee, corn syrup and water in a large saucepan. Heat to boiling, stirring constantly. Lower heat; simmer 5 minutes, stirring often. Remove from heat; stir in butter until melted. Stir in brandy. Cool, stirring several times.
6. To serve: Mound filled profiteroles in compote dish or deep serving plate. Spoon Espresso Sauce over and serve.

BASIC CREAM PUFF PASTE

Makes 12 large cream puffs or 12 eclairs or 36 profiteroles (miniature cream puffs).

1 cup water
½ cup (1 stick) butter or margarine
1 teaspoon sugar
¼ teaspoon salt
1 cup *sifted* all-purpose flour
4 eggs

1. Heat water, butter, sugar and salt to a full rolling boil in a large saucepan.
2. Add flour all at once. Stir vigorously with a wooden spoon until mixture forms a thick, smooth ball that leaves side of the pan clean. Remove from heat.
3. Add eggs, one at a time, beating well after each addition with a wooden spoon or electric hand mixer until paste is shiny and

smooth. Follow recipe directions for shaping.

VIENNESE CHOCOLATE-ALMOND RING

Bake at 400° for 40 minutes.
Makes 6 servings.

½ recipe Basic Cream Puff Paste (*recipe this page*)
½ cup granulated sugar
⅛ teaspoon cream of tartar
2 tablespoons water
½ cup blanched almonds, toasted
Chocolate Glaze (*recipe page 261*)
2 cups heavy cream
3 tablespoons unsweetened cocoa powder
¼ cup 10X (confectioners') sugar

1. Preheat oven to hot (400°). Prepare Basic Cream Puff Paste.
2. Mark a 7-inch circle on an ungreased cookie sheet with a very thin line of vegetable shortening. Spoon paste into 6 even mounds just inside circle; puffs should almost touch.
3. Bake in a hot oven (400°) for 40 minutes, or until puffed and golden. Make several slits in the side of the ring to let the steam escape. Turn off heat; leave ring in oven 5 minutes longer. Cool on wire rack.
4. Combine sugar, cream of tartar and water in a small skillet. Cook over low heat until sugar mixture caramelizes to a golden brown. Stir in almonds. Pour out on a lightly buttered cookie sheet; cool. Break up almond praline into small pieces. Whirl, part at a time, in container of electric blender until pulverized.
5. Prepare Chocolate Glaze; cool. Split puff ring in half horizontally. Scoop out any filaments of soft dough.
6. Beat cream in a medium-size bowl until stiff. Fold in almond praline powder, cocoa and 10X sugar. Spoon filling into bottom of ring; return top half of ring. Spoon Chocolate Glaze over top.

Date-Apricot Steamed Pudding

DATE-APRICOT STEAMED PUDDING

Makes 6 servings.

  1 package (6 ounces) dried apricots, chopped
  ½ cup pitted dates, chopped
  2 cups *sifted* all-purpose flour
1½ teaspoons baking powder
  ½ teaspoon baking soda
  ½ teaspoon salt
  ¾ teaspoon ground cinnamon
  ¼ teaspoon ground nutmeg
  ½ cup vegetable shortening
  1 cup firmly packed light brown sugar
  2 eggs
  ⅓ cup orange juice
    Orange Custard Sauce
    (*recipe follows*)

1. Grease an 8-cup tube pan or pudding mold; dust with sugar.
2. Simmer apricots in boiling water 5 minutes; drain. Combine apricots and dates in a small bowl.
3. Sift flour, baking powder, soda, salt, cinnamon and nutmeg onto wax paper.
4. Beat shortening, sugar and eggs in a large bowl until fluffy. Stir in flour and orange juice until mixture is smooth. Fold in apricots and dates. Spoon batter into mold and cover with aluminum foil, securing tightly with string.
5. Place mold on a rack in steamer. Pour in boiling water to a depth of 2 inches. Cover; simmer for 2 hours, replenishing water if necessary, or until a wooden skewer inserted near center comes out clean.
6. Cool in mold on wire rack 5 minutes; remove from mold. Serve warm with Orange Custard Sauce.

ORANGE CUSTARD SAUCE: Combine 1 package (3¾ ounces) vanilla flavor instant pudding and pie filling, ¼ cup 10X (confectioners') sugar, 2 cups milk, 2 tablespoons grated orange rind and 1 cup orange juice in a medium-size bowl; beat 1 minute with rotary beater. Beat ½ cup heavy cream until stiff; fold into orange mixture; cover; chill 1 hour. Makes 4 cups.

QUEEN'S PUDDING

A regal bread pudding indeed, with its crown of golden-tipped meringue.
Bake at 350° for 50 minutes.
Makes 6 servings.

    3 cups very dry bread cubes (about 4
        slices)
    4 cups milk
    ¼ cup (½ stick) butter or margarine
    ¾ cup sugar
    ½ teaspoon salt
    ½ teaspoon ground cinnamon
    6 eggs
    2 teaspoons vanilla
    ⅛ teaspoon cream of tartar
    ½ cup apricot preserves

1. Place bread in a buttered 6-cup baking dish.
2. Heat milk, butter, ½ cup of the sugar, salt and cinnamon in a large saucepan, stirring, until butter is melted.
3. Combine 3 whole eggs and 3 egg yolks in a medium-size bowl. Place the 3 egg whites in a small bowl; reserve. Beat eggs and egg yolks with rotary beater just until frothy. Stir in vanilla. Stir in hot milk slowly. Pour over bread cubes. Let stand 30 minutes.
4. Set baking dish in larger pan; place on oven shelf. Pour boiling water into pan to come halfway up side of baking dish.
5. Bake in a preheated moderate oven (350°) for 40 minutes, or until a knife blade inserted 1 inch from edge comes out clean. Remove from water.
6. Beat reserved egg whites and cream of tartar until foamy. Beat in the remaining ¼ cup sugar, 1 tablespoon at a time, until meringue forms stiff, glossy peaks.
7. Spoon apricot preserves evenly over pudding. Spoon meringue over preserves.
8. Bake in a moderate oven (350°) for 10

minutes, or until meringue is golden. Cool slightly. Serve warm or cold.

> Bread puddings and savory main-dish stratas and fondues should be allowed to stand at least 15 minutes before baking. This standing time lets the custard become completely absorbed by the bread, thus forming a custardy, smooth texture when baked.

OLD-FASHIONED CHOCOLATE BREAD PUDDING

Pour a little cream over this delicious chocolate custard for extra richness.
Bake at 350° for 40 minutes.
Makes 6 servings.

    2 cups milk
    2 squares unsweetened chocolate
    ¼ cup (½ stick) butter or margarine
    2 eggs
    ½ cup sugar
    ¼ teaspoon salt
    1 teaspoon ground cinnamon
    3 cups very dry bread cubes (about
        4 slices)

1. Heat milk, chocolate and butter in a medium-size saucepan over low heat, stirring, until chocolate is melted.
2. Beat eggs, sugar, salt and cinnamon in a medium-size bowl just until blended. Pour chocolate mixture slowly into egg mixture, stirring constantly.
3. Place bread cubes in a greased 6-cup baking dish. Pour chocolate mixture over. Let stand 30 minutes. Stir well; set baking dish in a larger pan. Place on oven shelf. Pour boiling water into pan to come halfway up side of baking dish.
4. Bake in a preheated moderate oven (350°) for 40 minutes, or until a knife blade inserted 1 inch from edge comes out clean.

ORANGE UPSIDE-DOWN PUDDING

A feathery spongecake topping over a soft orange custard.

Bake at 325° for 30 minutes.
Makes 6 servings.

2 eggs, separated
½ cup sugar
¼ cup (½ stick) butter or margarine, softened
¼ cup thawed undiluted frozen orange juice concentrate
½ teaspoon vanilla
2 tablespoons flour
¼ teaspoon salt
1 cup milk

1. Beat egg whites in a small bowl until foamy-white; beat in 2 tablespoons of the sugar, 1 tablespoon at a time, until meringue forms soft peaks.
2. Preheat oven to slow (325°).
3. Beat butter with the remaining sugar in a medium-size bowl until fluffy; beat in egg yolks, thawed orange juice and vanilla.
4. Stir in flour and salt, then slowly stir in milk. Gently fold in meringue until no streaks of white remain. Spoon into 6 buttered 6-ounce custard cups.
5. Set cups in a large shallow pan; place on oven shelf; pour boiling water into pan to a depth of 1 inch.
6. Bake in a preheated slow oven (325°) for ˙30 minutes, or until tops spring back when lightly pressed with fingertip. Remove cups from pan of water; cool.
7. To unmold, loosen puddings around edge with a knife; invert into serving dishes. Serve warm or cold.

Custards and bread puddings need an even, moderate heat to bake smooth and velvety. To assure this, these desserts are baked in a container of hot water, which insulates them from the heat and keeps temperature uniform.

RICE CUSTARD PUDDING

Old-fashioned, light and custardy. Serve warm or chilled, plain or with Raspberry Sauce.

Bake at 350° for 45 minutes.
Makes 8 servings.

3 cups milk
1 cup heavy cream
½ cup uncooked long-grain rice
3 eggs, separated
¾ cup sugar
¼ teaspoon salt
1 teaspoon vanilla
Ground nutmeg
Raspberry Sauce (*recipe follows*)

1. Combine milk and cream in the top of a double boiler over simmering water. Stir in rice; cover. Cook, stirring occasionally, until rice is tender and creamy and all the liquid is absorbed, about 1½ to 2 hours. (Check occasionally to prevent sticking.) Remove from heat.
2. Generously butter a deep 8-cup glass or ceramic baking dish.
3. Beat egg yolks in a large bowl until frothy. Gradually beat in sugar, salt and vanilla. Stir in the hot rice, a small portion at a time.
4. Beat egg whites in a small bowl until soft peaks form. Fold into rice mixture. Turn mixture into prepared baking dish; sprinkle top with nutmeg. Place baking dish in a shallow pan, then put pan on oven shelf. Pour boiling water into pan to a depth of 2 inches.
5. Bake in a moderate oven (350°) for 45 minutes. Remove baking dish from water and allow pudding to cool to room temperature on wire rack before serving or refrigerating. Serve with Raspberry Sauce.

RASPBERRY SAUCE: Drain two 10-ounce packages frozen thawed raspberries, reserving the syrup. Combine syrup and 2 tablespoons sugar in a small saucepan. Bring to boiling. Combine 1½ teaspoons cornstarch with ¼ cup water in a cup. Stir mixture into raspberry syrup; lower heat; simmer, stirring constantly, until mixture thickens and clears. Remove from heat; stir in the raspberries. Cool; refrigerate. Makes 2 cups.

> **Twice-cooked rice makes a smoother creamier dessert, and one that will not form hard grains when chilled.**

FLAN (BAKED CUSTARD)

Spanish in origin, this dessert has a French cousin called *Crème Renversée au Caramel*. It is delicious in any language.
Bake at 325° for 30 minutes.
Makes 6 servings.

⅔ cup sugar
1 cup light cream or half and half
1½ cups milk
1 four-inch piece stick cinnamon
4 eggs
2 teaspoons vanilla

1. Preheat oven to slow (325°). Place a 4 to 5-cup ring mold in the oven to warm. (Caramelized sugar coats a warm mold more evenly.)
2. Heat ⅓ cup of the sugar in a large skillet over medium heat until sugar melts and turns golden. Remove mold from oven; immediately pour caramelized sugar into warm mold. Hold mold with pot holder and tilt from side to side to cover bottom and side with the sugar.
3. Combine cream, milk, the remaining sugar and cinnamon in a medium-size saucepan; heat just until bubbles form around edge, but do not boil.
4. Beat eggs slightly with vanilla in a medium-size bowl; gradually add hot milk mixture, stirring constantly; strain into prepared mold. Place mold in a large shallow pan; place on oven shelf; pour boiling water into pan to depth of about ½ inch.
5. Bake in a preheated slow oven (325°) for 30 minutes, or until almost set. Remove from pan of water; cool, then chill several hours or overnight.
6. To unmold, loosen custard around edge with small spatula. Cover mold with serving dish or plate; turn upside down, shaking gently to release custard; lift off mold. Spoon onto serving dishes with the caramel syrup spooned over each serving. Garnish with whipped cream, if you wish.

> **About caramelizing sugar: A thin layer of granulated sugar when heated in a skillet will melt to a colorless liquid (barley sugar), and as it is heated further, will turn to an amber liquid. It should be watched carefully as the liquid approaches the caramel stage, so it doesn't overcook and burn.**

ZABAGLIONE

This light frothy custard dessert is the Italian version of the French *Sabayon*.
Makes about 4 servings.

⅔ cup dry white wine
⅓ cup sugar
4 egg yolks

1. Pour wine over sugar in a large metal bowl set over a saucepan of simmering water. Bottom should not touch the water. (Or, use a metal double boiler with a wide top.) Add egg yolks.
2. Cook over simmering water, beating constantly with an electric mixer at low speed, 5 minutes, or just until mixture mounds slightly; remove bowl from pan of water at once.
3. Continue beating at low speed 5 minutes longer, or until mixture has cooled to room temperature. Serve in stemmed glasses, or cover and chill to serve over fruit. Chill no longer than 3 hours so sauce holds its airy lightness.

NO-BAKE LEMON CHEESECAKE

A cool, creamy, not-too-sweet cheesecake that's quick to mix and needs no baking. Makes 12 servings.

    1 cup brown-edge lemon wafer crumbs
       (about 18 wafers)
    ¼ cup (½ stick) butter or margarine,
       melted
    2 tablespoons sugar
    2 envelopes unflavored gelatin
    ¾ cup sugar
    3 eggs, separated
    1 cup milk
    1 pound creamed cottage cheese
    2 teaspoons grated lemon rind
    ⅓ cup lemon juice
    1 cup heavy cream

1. Combine crumbs, butter and the 2 tablespoons sugar in a small bowl. Press onto the bottom of a 9-inch springform pan, reserving 2 tablespoons of the mixture to sprinkle on the top.
2. Combine gelatin, ½ cup of the remaining sugar and egg yolks in a medium-size saucepan. Beat with a rotary beater until well mixed. Stir in milk until well blended. Cook over medium heat, stirring constantly, until sugar and gelatin are dissolved and mixture is slightly thickened, about 5 minutes. Cool.
3. Press cheese through a sieve or food mill into a large bowl. Stir in cooled gelatin mixture, lemon rind and juice.
4. Beat egg whites until foamy-white in a small bowl. Beat in the remaining ¼ cup sugar gradually, until meringue forms soft peaks. Beat cream in a small bowl until stiff.
5. Fold cream, then meringue, into cheese mixture. Spoon into prepared pan. Sprinkle top with reserved crumbs. Chill 4 hours or until set. Carefully remove the side of springform pan to serve.

WELSH CHEDDAR CHEESECAKE

Bake at 475° for 12 minutes, then at 250° for 1½ hours.

Makes 16 servings.

    1 package (6 ounces) zwieback,
       crushed (1½ cups)
    3 tablespoons sugar
    6 tablespoons (¾ stick) butter or
       margarine, melted
    4 packages (8 ounces each) cream
       cheese, softened
    2 cups shredded Cheddar cheese (8
       ounces)
 1¾ cups sugar
    3 tablespoons flour
    5 eggs
    3 egg yolks
    ¼ cup beer

1. Blend zwieback crumbs, the 3 tablespoons sugar and butter in a small bowl. Press firmly over the bottom and partly up the side of a lightly buttered 9-inch springform pan. Refrigerate until ready to fill.
2. Preheat oven to very hot (475°).
3. Beat cream cheese with Cheddar cheese in a large bowl with electric mixer just until smooth. (Cheeses will beat smoother if they are at room temperature.) Add the remaining 1¾ cups sugar and flour. Beat until light and fluffy. Add eggs and egg yolks, one at a time, beating well after each addition; stir in beer; pour into crumb crust.
4. Bake in a preheated very hot oven (475°) 12 minutes; lower temperature to slow (250°) and bake 1½ hours longer. Turn off oven; let cake remain in oven for an hour.
5. Remove from oven; cool completely on a wire rack; loosen around edge with a knife; release spring and remove side of pan, leaving cake in pan bottom.
Note: It is the nature of this cake to crack on top. However, this cracking will not affect its flavor.

No-Bake Lemon Cheesecake

Welsh Cheddar Cheesecake

PUMPKIN-WALNUT CHEESECAKE

Bake at 325° for 1 hour, 45 minutes.
Makes 16 servings.

    1 package (6 ounces) zwieback,
        crushed (1½ cups)
    ¼ cup granulated sugar
    6 tablespoons butter or margarine,
        melted
    3 packages (8 ounces each) cream
        cheese, softened
    ¾ cup granulated sugar
    ¾ cup firmly packed light brown sugar
    5 eggs
    1 can (16 ounces) pumpkin
    1¾ teaspoons pumpkin pie spice
    ¼ cup heavy cream
        Walnut Topping (*recipe follows*)

1. Blend zwieback crumbs, the ¼ cup sugar and butter in a medium-size bowl. Press firmly over bottom and up side of a lightly buttered 9-inch springform pan. Chill until ready to fill.
2. Preheat oven to slow (325°).
3. Beat cream cheese in a large bowl with electric mixer at medium speed until smooth. Add remaining ¾ cup granulated sugar and the brown sugar gradually, beating until well mixed. Beat in eggs, one at a time, until mixture is light and fluffy. Beat in pumpkin, pumpkin pie spice and heavy cream at low speed. Pour into prepared pan.
4. Bake in a preheated slow oven (325°) for 1 hour and 35 minutes. Remove cake from oven; sprinkle with Walnut Topping; bake an additional 10 minutes. Cool cake on wire rack; refrigerate several hours, or overnight. Beat cream in a small bowl until stiff. Garnish pie with dollops of whipped cream and additional walnut pieces, if you wish.

WALNUT TOPPING: Combine 6 tablespoons softened butter with 1 cup firmly packed light brown sugar in a small bowl; mix well until crumbly. Blend in 1 cup coarsely chopped walnuts.

ORANGE SHERBET

Makes 1½ quarts (about 8 servings).

    1¼ cups sugar
    1 envelope unflavored gelatin
    2¼ cups water
    1 tablespoon grated orange rind
    1 can (6 ounces) frozen concentrated
        orange juice
    1 cup milk
    2 egg whites
    ¼ cup sugar

1. Combine the 1¼ cups sugar and gelatin in a medium-size saucepan; stir in water and orange rind.
2. Heat, stirring often, until mixture comes to boiling; lower heat; simmer 5 minutes. Remove saucepan from heat; stir in frozen orange juice until thawed. Strain mixture into a 13x9x2-inch metal pan.
3. Cool at room temperature 30 minutes. Stir in milk. Freeze mixture, stirring several times for even freezing until almost frozen, approximately four hours.
4. Beat egg whites in a small bowl until foamy. Beat in the remaining ¼ cup sugar, a tablespoon at a time, until meringue forms soft peaks.
5. Spoon frozen mixture into a chilled large bowl. Beat with electric mixer until very smooth.
6. Fold in meringue quickly. Spoon into a 6-cup mold or bowl; cover with foil or plastic wrap.
7. Freeze about 6 hours, or overnight.

LEMON VELVET ICE CREAM

Makes 3 quarts (about 16 servings).

    2 cups sugar
    ¼ teaspoon salt
    3 tablespoons flour
    3½ cups milk
    6 egg yolks, slightly beaten
    2 tablespoons grated lemon rind
    ⅔ cup lemon juice
    3 cups heavy cream

1. Combine sugar, salt and flour in a large saucepan; stir in milk gradually. Cook over medium heat, stirring constantly, until mixture thickens and bubbles. Remove saucepan from heat.

2. Stir half the mixture slowly into beaten egg yolks; stir back into remaining mixture in saucepan. Cook, stirring constantly, 1 minute. Remove from heat; pour into a large bowl; cool. Add lemon rind and lemon juice. Stir in cream; chill.

3. Pour mixture into a 4 to 6-quart freezer can; freeze, following manufacturer's directions.

4. Pack in containers; freeze until firm.

PRALINE ICE CREAM CAKE

All ice cream with a fantastic praline between layers.

Makes 20 servings.

Almond Praline (*recipe follows*)
1 quart pistachio ice cream
1 quart lemon sherbet
1 quart orange sherbet

Praline Ice Cream Cake

> Almost any ice cream recipe that specifies a hand- or electric-crank freezer can be still-frozen in the home freezer. It will not be quite as smooth, but the flavor will be unaffected. To still-freeze: Omit the cream from the recipe until the mixture is frozen in a shallow pan in the freezer. Then, beat the frozen mixture in a chilled bowl with chilled beaters. Whip the cream and fold in.

1 quart strawberry ice cream
1½ cups heavy cream
½ cup 10X (confectioners') sugar
½ cup chopped pistachio nuts
Fruit for garnish (*optional*)

1. Prepare Almond Praline. Sprinkle ¾ cup of the praline powder over the bottom of a 10x2¾-inch springform pan.

2. Soften the ice creams and the sherbets, one flavor at a time, in a chilled large bowl, starting with pistachio. Layer each flavor of ice cream or sherbet, with ¾ cup praline powder for each layer, topping the lemon and orange sherbets with strawberry ice cream. Freeze each layer about 1 hour before adding praline and next flavor. Freeze layers at least 4 hours or overnight. Remove side of pan.

3. Beat cream with sugar in a medium-size bowl until stiff. Spread side of layers, then decorate with a ring of cream pressed through a pastry bag. Sprinkle with pistachio nuts and garnish with fresh fruits, if you wish.

ALMOND PRALINE: Combine 1 cup sugar, ¼ cup water and ¼ teaspoon cream of tartar in a large skillet. Cook over low heat until mixture caramelizes to a golden brown; stir in 1 cup toasted blanched almonds. Pour out on a lightly buttered cookie sheet; cool; break up into small pieces; whirl, part at a time, in container of electric blender until pulverized. (Makes 3 cups.)

FRENCH CHOCOLATE ICE CREAM

Rich, smooth and supremely chocolate!
Makes about 2 quarts.

 1 three-inch piece vanilla bean
   OR: 2 teaspoons vanilla
 2 cups milk
 6 egg yolks
 1 cup sugar
 1 tablespoon cornstarch
 ¼ teaspoon salt
 6 squares unsweetened chocolate
 3 cups heavy cream

1. Split vanilla bean pod with a small sharp knife; scrape seeds into milk in a medium-size saucepan; drop in bean pod. Heat until bubbles appear around edge of pan.
2. Beat egg yolks in a large bowl until frothy; beat in sugar, cornstarch and salt. Gradually stir in hot milk. Return to saucepan; cook, stirring constantly, over medium heat until mixture thickens and just comes to boiling. Remove from heat; add the 2 teaspoons vanilla, if using, and chocolate, stirring until melted. Stir in cream. Cool completely. Strain into 4-quart freezer can of an electric- or hand-crank ice cream freezer.
3. Freeze, following manufacturer's directions.
4. Serve immediately or spoon into freezer container; place in freezer.
Note: If your freezer is very cold, remove ice cream to refrigerator about 30 minutes before serving.

FROZEN PLUM SOUFFLÉ

Makes 10 servings.

 2 pounds ripe red or purple
   plums, halved, pitted and sliced
 ¾ cup granulated sugar
 2 teaspoons grated lemon rind
 2 teaspoons lemon juice
 4 egg yolks
 1¾ cups 10X (confectioners') sugar

 ½ cup Curaçao or Cointreau
 2 cups heavy cream

1. Prepare a collar for a 5-cup soufflé dish: Measure off a length of wax paper or foil long enough to encircle dish. Fold in half lengthwise (collar should be about 2½ inches higher than rim of dish.) Fasten collar to dish with string or tape.
2. Combine sliced plums and granulated sugar in a large saucepan; let stand about 20 minutes until plums yield some of their liquid and sugar is partly dissolved. Bring to boiling; lower heat; simmer until tender, about 15 minutes. Puree through a sieve; cool; stir in lemon rind and juice.
3. Beat egg yolks with 10X sugar in a medium-size bowl with electric mixer until very thick. Add orange liqueur in a slow, steady stream, while continuing to beat. Beat 5 minutes longer. (Do not underbeat.) Stir in plum mixture.
4. Beat cream in a medium-size bowl until stiff; fold into plum-egg mixture. Pour into prepared soufflé dish. Freeze until firm, about 4 hours.
5. Remove soufflé from freezer to refrigerator about 30 minutes before serving, to allow for softening. Garnish top with whipped cream and lemon, if you wish.

MOUSSE AU CHOCOLAT

Makes 8 servings.

 1 package (6 ounces) semisweet
   chocolate pieces
 ⅓ cup strong hot coffee
 4 egg yolks
 2 tablespoons apricot brandy, or any
   fruit-flavored brandy
 4 egg whites
 3 tablespoons sugar

1. Combine chocolate pieces and hot coffee in container of electric blender; cover. Whirl for 30 seconds, or until smooth.
2. Add egg yolks and brandy; cover. Whirl at high speed 30 seconds.
3. Beat egg whites in a medium-size bowl

until foamy; gradually beat in sugar until well-blended. Fold in chocolate mixture until no streaks of white remain. Spoon mousse into 8 parfait glasses or a shallow serving bowl.

4. Chill at least 1 hour. Garnish with whipped cream, if you wish.

> You can usually substitute fruit juice in equal quantity in a recipe that calls for a small amount of liqueur, without an appreciable change in taste.

COOL LEMON SOUFFLÉ

Elegant and creamy, this fabulous no-bake soufflé is lively with the flavor of fresh lemons. It whips up in only 20 minutes, then lets your refrigerator take over to chill it perfectly for dinner.

Makes 8 servings.

2 envelopes unflavored gelatin
½ cup water
6 eggs
1½ cups sugar
2 cups heavy cream
1 tablespoon grated lemon rind
⅔ cup lemon juice

Cool Lemon Soufflé

Candied violets or grapes
Lemon wedges
Mint leaves

1. Prepare a collar for a 4-cup soufflé dish: Measure off a length of foil long enough to encircle dish, fold in half lengthwise (collar should be about 2 inches higher than rim of dish). Fasten with tape or string.

2. Sprinkle gelatin over water in a small saucepan. Let stand 10 minutes to soften. Place saucepan over very low heat, stirring until gelatin is dissolved (mixture will be clear). Remove from heat; cool.

3. Combine eggs and sugar in a large bowl; beat with electric mixer at high speed until very thick and light. (This will take 7 to 8 minutes.)

4. Beat 1½ cups of the cream in a small bowl until stiff; refrigerate.

5. Combine lemon rind and juice with cooled gelatin; pour into egg-sugar mixture. Continue beating until well blended. Chill briefly (5 minutes), either in the refrigerator or by placing bowl in a large pan partly filled with ice and water. Stir frequently, just until mixture is thick enough to mound when spooned.

6. Fold in whipped cream until no streaks of white remain. Pour into prepared dish. Refrigerate at least 3 hours, or until set. Remove collar gently, freeing soufflé from foil, if necessary, with a small paring knife.

7. Beat the remaining ½ cup cream in a small bowl until stiff. Garnish soufflé with cream, grapes or candied violets, thin lemon wedges and mint leaves.

> It's a cinch to retrieve all the grated citrus rind from the pores of the grater if you brush it out with a pastry brush.

STRAWBERRY MOUSSE

Served in a soufflé dish, this mousse is an elegant yet simple way to savor the season's bounty of luscious red berries.

Makes 8 servings.

    2 pints (4 cups) strawberries
      OR: 1 package (1 pound) frozen
        unsugared strawberries, thawed
    1 envelope unflavored gelatin
    ½ cup sugar
    ½ cup water
    2 egg whites
      Pinch cream of tartar
    1 cup heavy cream

1. Prepare a collar for a 5-cup soufflé dish: Measure off a length of wax paper or foil long enough to encircle the dish. Fold in half lengthwise (collar should be about 2 inches higher than rim of dish). Fasten collar to dish with tape or string.

2. Wash, hull and pat strawberries dry on paper toweling. Puree berries, a cup at a time, in container of electric blender; repeat until all are pureed. Pour into a large bowl as pureed.

3. Combine gelatin and ¼ cup of the sugar in a small saucepan; stir in water. Place over very low heat and stir constantly until gelatin and sugar are dissolved; cool.

4. Stir cooled gelatin mixture into pureed strawberries. Put bowl in a pan partly filled with ice and water to speed setting.

5. Beat egg whites with cream of tartar in a small bowl with electric mixer until foamy-white. Beat in the remaining ¼ cup sugar, a tablespoon at a time, until meringue forms soft peaks. Beat cream in another small bowl until stiff.

6. Fold whipped cream, then meringue, into strawberry mixture until no streaks of white remain. Pour into prepared dish. Refrigerate 4 hours, or until set. Remove collar gently, freeing soufflé from wax paper, if necessary, with a small knife. Garnish with additional whipped cream and strawberries, if you wish.

HOT CHOCOLATE SOUFFLÉ

An impressive and delightful finale for a special dinner. Have it ready to go in the oven as dinner begins.

Bake at 350° for 50 minutes.
Makes 6 servings.

    2 tablespoons butter or margarine,
        softened
    2 tablespoons sugar
    3 tablespoons flour
    ¼ teaspoon salt
    8 tablespoons sugar
    1 cup milk
    3 squares unsweetened chocolate
    2 tablespoons butter or margarine
    1 teaspoon vanilla
    6 eggs
      Sugar

1. Preheat oven to moderate (350°).

2. Coat a 6-cup soufflé dish with softened butter; sprinkle evenly with 1 tablespoon of the sugar, tapping out excess. Fold a 24-inch piece of foil in thirds lengthwise; butter on one side; wrap around the dish, buttered-side in, to make a 2-inch collar. Tie with string. Sprinkle paper with remaining 1 tablespoon sugar.

3. Blend flour and salt with 6 tablespoons of the remaining sugar in a small saucepan. Gradually stir in milk; add chocolate. Cook over medium heat, stirring constantly, until chocolate is melted and mixture thickens and bubbles 2 minutes. Remove from heat; stir in butter and vanilla. Cool slightly.

4. Separate eggs; put 4 yolks into a small bowl (reserve remaining yolks to add to breakfast scrambled eggs). Put whites into a large bowl.

5. Beat egg yolks until light; stir in slightly cooled chocolate mixture.

6. Beat egg whites with electric mixer until foamy. Add the remaining 2 tablespoons sugar, 1 tablespoon at a time, beating until meringue forms soft peaks.

7. Stir about ¼ of the meringue into chocolate mixture, then add to remaining meringue and gently fold in until no streaks of white remain. Pour mixture into prepared dish; sprinkle top lightly with sugar. Place dish in a baking pan on oven rack; pour boiling water into pan to a depth of 1 inch.

8. Bake in a preheated moderate oven (350°) for 50 minutes, or until light and puffy. To serve: Remove the collar; serve immediately with heavy cream, custard sauce or warm chocolate sauce.

STRAWBERRY SHORTCAKE

The all-American dessert favorite is certainly strawberry shortcake. This mouthwatering version is made with soft sponge cake and whipped cream.

Bake at 350° for 25 minutes.
Makes 8 servings.

Strawberry Shortcake

    1 cup *sifted* all-purpose flour
    1 teaspoon baking powder
    ¼ teaspoon salt
    ⅓ cup milk
    2 tablespoons butter or margarine
    3 eggs
    1 cup sugar
    1 teaspoon vanilla
    2 pints (4 cups) strawberries
      OR: 1 package (1 pound) frozen
          unsugared strawberries, thawed
    ½ to ¾ cup sugar
    1 cup heavy cream

1. Sift flour, baking powder and salt onto wax paper.

2. Heat milk with butter in a small saucepan just to scalding; cool slightly.

3. Preheat oven to moderate (350°).

4. Beat eggs in a small bowl with electric mixer until foamy. Beat in the 1 cup sugar gradually until mixture is very thick and fluffy. Add vanilla.

5. Sprinkle flour mixture, a third at a time, over eggs, alternating with warmed milk mixture, beginning and ending with flour. Pour into two greased and floured 8x1½-inch layer-cake pans (or one 8-inch springform pan).

6. Bake in a preheated moderate oven (350°) for 25 minutes (35 minutes for springform pan), or until tops spring back when lightly pressed with fingertip. Cool layers on wire racks for 10 minutes; loosen around the edges with a knife; turn out; cool completely.

7. Reserve 1 cup of whole berries for garnish, wash, hull and slice remaining berries into a large bowl. (For frozen berries, sprinkle with sugar and let stand while defrosting.) Add sugar; stir lightly, crushing a few of the berries. Let stand 30 minutes or until juices run freely.

8. Beat cream in a small bowl until stiff.

9. Place one cake layer on a serving plate (split cake in half if using a springform pan). Top with half of the cream and the sliced strawberries. Top with remaining cake layer and cream. Place one whole strawberry in center of cake; cut remaining reserved strawberries in half. Arrange halved strawberries cut-side up in a rosette pattern over cake.

> It is a good practice to whip heavy cream over ice and water, and it is especially desirable in the warm summer months when cream can curdle so easily.

CHERRIES JUBILEE

Makes 6 servings.

- 1 can (1 pound, 14 ounces) pitted sweet cherries
- 3 tablespoons sugar
- 2 tablespoons cornstarch
- 1 tablespoon grated orange rind
- ½ cup Grand Marnier or Cointreau, heated
- 1 quart vanilla ice cream

1. Drain cherry liquid into a 2-cup measure; add water to make 1½ cups; reserve cherries.

2. Combine sugar and cornstarch in a chafing dish or medium-size skillet; stir in cherry liquid until smooth; add orange rind.

3. Cook, stirring constantly, until mixture thickens and bubbles 1 minute. Add reserved cherries and heat until very warm.

4. Pour warmed orange liqueur over cherries and ignite. Stir cherries until flames die down, then ladle over ice cream in individual serving dishes .

STRAWBERRIES ON THE HALF-SHELL

These strawberry tarts have a new shape, but the same delicious flavor.

Makes 8 servings.

- 3 ounces cream cheese, softened
- 3 tablespoons cream or milk
- 2 to 3 teaspoons honey
- ½ cup red currant jelly
- 8 baked Sweet Pastry Tart Shells (recipe, this page)
- 2 pints (4 cups) strawberries

1. Combine cream cheese, cream and honey in a small bowl; beat until smooth. Melt jelly in a small saucepan; cool.

2. Just before serving, arrange tart shells on serving plates; spoon a little cheese filling into each. Arrange strawberries on top (cut berries in half if they are large). Brush with melted jelly. Arrange a second unfilled shell over each tart, if you wish.

SWEET PASTRY TART SHELLS

These buttery sweet pastry tart shells are so nice to have on hand to fill with fresh and sweetened berries and cream.

Bake at 400° for 10 minutes.

Makes about twenty 2½-inch shells.

- 2¼ cups *sifted* all-purpose flour
- ¼ cup sugar
- 1 cup (2 sticks) butter or margarine
- 1 egg
- 1 teaspoon vanilla

1. Mix flour and sugar in a large bowl; cut in butter with a pastry blender until mixture is crumbly. Add egg and vanilla; mix with a fork just until pastry holds together.. Turn out onto a lightly floured surface; knead a few times; chill 1 hour, or until ready to use.

2. Roll out pastry, half at a time, on a floured surface to ⅛-inch thickness; cut into 3½ to 4-inch rounds. Mold each round on the outside of 3-inch scallop shells (available in department and cookware stores), or press against outside of fluted tart pans or 5-ounce custard cups, pinching edge of pastry into pleats to fit snugly.

3. Bake shells on a large cookie sheet in a hot oven (400°) for 10 minutes, or until golden brown. Cool slightly on wire racks; carefully ease pastry from shells or pans. Cool completely on wire racks. Store in tightly covered container in a cool place. *Note:* Baked shells are fragile. Do not stack more than 2 to 3 or crowd in a tightly covered container.

BANANAS FOSTER

A recipe that is said to be the invention of a South Pacific island plantation owner.

Makes 4 servings.

- ½ cup firmly packed brown sugar
- ¼ cup (½ stick) butter or margarine
- 4 ripe bananas, peeled and quartered
  Dash of ground cinnamon

½ cup light rum
¼ cup banana liqueur
1 pint vanilla ice cream

1. Melt brown sugar and butter in a chafing dish or skillet, stirring often, just until bubbly.

2. Add bananas and heat just until soft (don't overcook). Sprinkle cinnamon evenly over bananas.

3. Heat rum and banana liqueur in a small saucepan. Pour over bananas, but do not stir into sauce. Carefully ignite mixture and keep spooning sauce over bananas until flames die.

4. Scoop ice cream into 4 large dessert dishes. Spoon bananas and sauce over cream, dividing evenly.

STRAWBERRY FOOL

From the 19th century comes a dessert so simple to make that it was considered to be a "little nothing," hence "foolish."

Makes 8 servings.

2 packages (10 ounces each) frozen
    strawberries in quick-thaw pouch
1 cup dry almond macaroons, crumbled
2 cups heavy cream, whipped

1. Thaw strawberries, following label directions, 5 to 10 minutes. Puree in contain-

Strawberry Fool

er of electric blender on low speed, just until smooth, or press through sieve. Turn into serving bowl; refrigerate.

2. Just before serving, fold macaroons into cream; spoon on top of strawberry puree, then gently fold together, leaving streaks of red and white.

FROZEN VANILLA YOGURT

Although fairly new on the American scene, frozen yogurt already has millions of fans. Ours is a basic to which you can add any fruit or nut topping.

Makes about 1½ quarts.

1 cup sugar
½ cup water
3 egg whites
⅛ teaspoon cream of tartar
1 package (3 ounces) cream cheese
3 cups plain yogurt
1 tablespoon vanilla
1 teaspoon grated lemon rind

1. Combine sugar and water in a small saucepan; bring to boiling, stirring until sugar is dissolved. Boil rapidly, without stirring, 5 minutes, or until syrup registers 236°(soft ball) on a candy thermometer.

2. Beat egg whites with cream of tartar in a small bowl with electric mixer until soft peaks form; pour hot syrup in a thin stream over egg whites while beating constantly. Continue beating until very stiff peaks form and mixture cools (it will take about 15 minutes altogether).

3. Soften cream cheese in a large mixing bowl; gradually blend in yogurt; stir in vanilla and lemon rind. Beat one-fourth of the meringue into the yogurt mixture. Fold in the remaining meringue.

4. Pack in freezer containers and freeze until firm, 4 to 6 hours.

Variation: Add 2 cups crushed fruit; mix well; freeze.

Cheese Blintzes

CHEESE BLINTZES

We like these little packages of cheese as a dessert, although they can be served with cinnamon and sugar (instead of cherry sauce) as a main dish.

Makes 6 servings.

    2 eggs
1¼ cups milk
    1 cup *sifted* all-purpose flour
    ½ teaspoon salt
    2 tablespoons butter or margarine, melted
    2 packages (3 ounces each) cream cheese, softened
    1 container (12 ounces) uncreamed cottage or pot cheese
    1 egg
    2 tablespoons sugar
    1 teaspoon grated lemon rind
       Butter or margarine
    1 can (1 pound, 5 ounces) cherry pie filling
       Dairy sour cream

1. Beat eggs and milk in medium-size bowl just until blended; add flour and salt; beat just until smooth. Stir in butter; chill at least 1 hour.
2. Meanwhile, beat cream cheese and cottage cheese in small bowl until smooth. Stir in egg, sugar and lemon rind until well blended; refrigerate while preparing blintz wrappers.
3. Heat a 7-inch skillet over medium heat. Grease lightly with butter or margarine. Pour in 3 tablespoons batter, rotating pan quickly to spread batter evenly. Cook until lightly browned on underside and dry on top. Remove from pan to a plate. Repeat with remaining batter to make 12 blintzes; stack on plate.
4. Place about 3 tablespoons filling on browned side of each blintz. Fold opposite sides over filling, then overlap ends envelope-style to cover filling completely.
5. Melt 2 tablespoons butter in a large skillet; add 5 or 6 blintzes, seam-side down. Cook over low to medium heat until lightly

browned on underside; carefully turn and brown other side, cooking about 5 minutes on each side. Keep warm in a low oven until all blintzes are browned.
6. Heat cherry pie filling in a small saucepan. Serve with blintzes along with extra sour cream.

Filled blintzes can be frozen. Place seam-side down on a cookie sheet or in foil pans; cover with freezer wrap. To cook: Follow step 5, but cook 10 minutes on each side, or until heated through.

CRANBERRY-GLAZED BAKED APPLES

The rosy cranberry juice adds flavor as well as a warm glowing color.

Bake at 350° for 50 minutes.
Makes 6 servings.

    6 large Rome Beauty or other baking apples
1¼ cups sugar
    ¾ cup cranberry juice cocktail
    ½ cup water
    2 tablespoons sugar

1. Wash apples; core. Pare one-third down from top; reserve parings.
2. Place apples in an 8-cup shallow baking dish that will hold them without crowding.
3. Combine the 1¼ cups sugar with cranberry juice and water in a medium-size saucepan. Add apple parings. Bring to boiling; lower heat; simmer 10 minutes. Remove apple parings; spoon syrup over apples.
4. Bake in a moderate oven (350°) 50 minutes, or until apples are tender. Remove from oven.
5. Sprinkle tops of apples with the remaining 2 tablespoons sugar. Place under broiler, watching carefully, until sugar is bubbly and apples are glazed. Serve with cream, if you wish.

Top: Open Plum Tart (page 282); center: Frozen Plum Soufflé (page 272); bottom: Deep-Dish Plum and Peach Pie

Pies, Tarts and Pastries

Who can resist a sparkling glazed fruit tart, a deep-dish pie or pastry to end a meal or nibble on at a kaffeklaatsch?

DEEP-DISH PLUM AND PEACH PIE

Bake at 425° for 35 minutes.
Makes 6 servings.

  Flaky Pastry (*recipe follows*)
2 pounds ripe red or purple plums
    (about 12 plums)
5 large peaches
1 cup sugar
2 tablespoons quick-cooking tapioca
2 teaspoons grated lemon rind
1 teaspoon ground cinnamon
1 teaspoon ground mace
¼ teaspoon salt

1. Prepare Flaky Pastry. Preheat oven to hot (425°).
2. Pit and slice plums and peaches; combine with sugar, tapioca, lemon rind, cinnamon, mace and salt; let stand 15 minutes. Pour into a 9-inch deep-dish pie plate.
3. Roll Flaky Pastry out on a floured surface. Cut into 1-inch strips and cover pie with lattice top (OR: roll to a 13-inch circle, cut steam vent in crust and cover pie with plain crust); flute edge.
4. Bake in a preheated hot oven (425°) for 35 minutes, or until filling is bubbly and crust is browned. Check pie during baking; if it is browning too fast, cover edge with foil.

FLAKY PASTRY
Makes one 9-inch crust.
  ⅓ cup + 1 tablespoon butter or
    margarine
  1 cup *sifted* all-purpose flour

½ teaspoon salt
2 tablespoons cold water

Cut butter into flour and salt in a medium-size bowl; mix with fingers until butter is blended. Stir in water and mix with fingers until dough forms a ball. Cover and refrigerate while preparing filling.

PLUM FACTS:
Plums can be grouped into two categories: *Japanese,* **which include the popular Santa Rosa and Late Santa Rosa types, with purplish-red skin, yellow juicy flesh and rich tart flavor. Also included in this variety are Nubiana plums, with black-red skins and light amber flesh.** *European* **plums include President (oval, dark purple color, yellow flesh) and Italian Prune plums (small, oval, purple, with greenish-yellow flesh). President, Nubiana and Italian Prune plums are especially good for pies, cakes and tarts. Santa Rosa, Nubiana and Italian Prune plums are good for canning.**

Plums are high in pectin, and, therefore, good for making jam (especially the Santa Rosa variety). If a recipe calls for pitted plums, cut along the seam and twist in half. You should be able to cut the pit out easily. (Some varieties have pits that simply pop out when opened.) If a recipe calls for peeled plums, hold the plum with a fork in boiling water until skin cracks; then, peel as a tomato. For more flavor when cooking, leave the skins on.

OPEN PLUM TART

Bake at 450° for 10 minutes, then at 350° for
35 minutes.
Makes 6 servings.

Short and Tender Pastry
(*recipe follows*)
½ cup graham cracker crumbs
2 pounds ripe purple plums
(about 12 plums)
½ cup sugar
⅛ teaspoon ground cinnamon
2 tablespoons sugar

1. Prepare Short and Tender Pastry. Preheat oven to very hot (450°).
2. Roll out chilled dough on a lightly
floured surface to a 13-inch round; fit into
a 9-inch fluted tart pan with removable bottom or a 9-inch pie plate.
3. Sprinkle graham cracker crumbs on the
bottom of pastry shell. Cut plums in half;
remove pits. Place plums snugly in shell,
skin-side down, in concentric circles.
Sprinkle the ½ cup sugar evenly over the
top; shake down gently.
4. Bake in a preheated very hot oven
(450°) for 10 minutes. Lower temperature
to moderate (350°) and continue baking
for 35 minutes longer, or until skins of
plums are soft. Remove from oven. Combine the cinnamon and the 2 tablespoons
sugar; sprinkle over tart. Garnish with
whipped cream, toasted slivered almonds
and mint sprigs, if you wish. Serve warm.

SHORT AND TENDER PASTRY
Makes one 9-inch pastry shell.

½ cup (1 stick) butter or margarine,
cut into ½-inch slices
3 tablespoons vegetable shortening
2 cups sifted all-purpose flour
½ teaspoon salt
5 to 6 tablespoons cold water

Work butter and shortening into flour and
salt with fingers or a pastry blender until
mixture is crumbly. Gradually add water
and work until dough is soft enough to
gather into a ball but will not stick to fingers or bowl. Cover and allow dough to
rest in refrigerator for at least 2 hours.

> **Golden rule for tender pastry: Always
> measure pastry ingredients with an ac-
> curate hand, and mix with a light hand.**

BEST APPLE PIE

Bake at 425° for 40 minutes.
Makes 6 servings.

6 medium-size tart cooking apples
⅓ cup firmly packed light brown
sugar
⅓ cup granulated sugar
1 tablespoon cornstarch
1 teaspoon ground cinnamon
¼ teaspoon ground nutmeg
¼ teaspoon ground mace
1 package piecrust mix
2 tablespoons butter or margarine
Milk
Sugar

1. Wash, pare, quarter, core and slice apples thinly. (You should have 7 to 8 cups.)
Place in a large bowl. Mix brown and granulated sugars, cornstarch, cinnamon, nutmeg and mace; sprinkle over apples; toss
gently to mix. Let stand about 10 minutes.
Preheat oven to hot (425°).
2. Prepare piecrust mix, following label directions for a 9-inch double-crust pie. Cut
vents in top crust for steam to escape.
3. Spoon apples and any accumulated
juice into pastry-lined plate. Dot with butter. Arrange top pastry over apples; turn
edge under; pinch to make a stand-up
edge; flute. Brush top with milk; sprinkle
with sugar.
4. Bake in a preheated hot oven (425°) for
40 minutes, or until juices bubble through
the slits and pastry is golden brown. Cool
on a wire rack. Serve warm with ice cream
or Cheddar cheese, if you wish.

Best Apple Pie

SOUR CREAM APPLE PIE

Bake at 400° for 15 minutes, then at 350° for 30 minutes, then at 400° again for 10 minutes.
Makes 6 servings.

½ package piecrust mix
2 tablespoons flour
¾ cup sugar
¼ teaspoon salt
¼ teaspoon ground nutmeg
1 egg, slightly beaten
1 cup dairy sour cream
1 teaspoon vanilla
3 medium-size Golden Delicious or Winesap apples
Crumb Topping (*recipe follows*)

1. Preheat oven to hot (400°). Prepare pie-crust mix, following label directions for a 9-inch pastry shell with a high fluted edge.
2. Sift flour, sugar, salt and nutmeg into a large bowl. Stir in beaten egg, sour cream and vanilla. Wash, pare, quarter, core and slice apples thinly (you should have about 2 cups). Fold into sour cream mixture; spoon into unbaked pastry shell. Bake in a preheated hot oven (400°) for 15 minutes. Lower heat to moderate (350°); bake 30 minutes longer.
4. Prepare Crumb Topping. Remove pie from oven; reset oven to hot (400°); sprinkle pie with topping; and return to oven.
5. Bake pie 10 minutes longer, or until

topping is nicely browned. Cool slightly on wire rack, and serve barely warm.

CRUMB TOPPING: Mix ½ cup sugar, ⅓ cup flour, 1 teaspoon ground cinnamon and ¼ cup (½ stick) butter, melted, in a small bowl until crumbly.

CINNAMON-APPLE CUSTARD PIE

Bake at 400° for 40 minutes.
Makes 6 servings.

½ package piecrust mix
4 medium-size tart cooking apples, pared, quartered, cored and thinly sliced
1 tablespoon lemon juice
½ cup sugar
2 eggs
1¼ cups light cream or half and half
2 tablespoons butter or margarine, melted
¼ teaspoon ground nutmeg
2 tablespoons sugar
½ teaspoon ground cinnamon

1. Preheat oven to hot (400°). Prepare pie-crust mix, following label directions for a 9-inch pastry shell with a high fluted edge.
2. Wash, pare, quarter, core and slice apples thinly (you should have about 2¾ cups). Toss sliced apples with lemon juice and the ½ cup sugar in large bowl. Arrange slices in overlapping circles in pastry shell; cover loosely with foil.
3. Bake in a preheated hot oven (400°) for 20 minutes; remove foil.
4. Beat eggs slightly in small bowl; beat in cream, melted butter and nutmeg; pour over apples.
5. Continue baking 10 minutes; mix the remaining 2 tablespoons sugar and cinnamon; sprinkle over top of pie. Bake 10 minutes longer, or until pastry is golden and custard is almost set. Cool on wire rack at least 2 hours before cutting.

DEEP-DISH CHERRY PIE

Bake at 425° for 30 minutes.
Makes 6 servings.

    3 cans (1 pound, 5 ounces each)
        cherry pie filling
    ½ package piecrust mix
    1 egg yolk
    2 tablespoons water
    2 teaspoons ground almonds
    2 teaspoons sugar

1. Turn pie filling into a 6-cup shallow baking dish or deep-dish pie plate. Preheat oven to hot (425°).
2. Prepare pastry, following label directions for a 9-inch single-crust pie. Cut pastry into 1-inch strips. Weave over filling in a lattice design. (Pastry should be inside the dish.) Pinch to make a stand-up edge; flute.
3. Brush pastry with egg yolk mixed with water. Mix almonds with sugar; sprinkle evenly over pastry.
4. Bake in a preheated hot oven (425°) for 30 minutes, or until pastry is golden brown and filling is bubbly. Cool at least 1 hour on a wire rack. Serve with sour cream or vanilla ice cream, if you wish.

A stand-up edge is very attractive and allows you to add more filling to a pie. You can slip the server between the pieplate and the pie without losing this handsome edging.

SHAKER LEMON PIE

Bake at 450° for 15 minutes, then at 350° for 30 minutes.
Makes 6 servings.

    3 lemons
    2½ cups sugar
    1 package piecrust mix
    5 eggs
        Cream or milk
        Sugar

1. Slice lemons *paper thin*, rind and all; seed. Combine with sugar in a medium-size bowl; mix gently; cover. Let stand in refrigerator overnight.
2. Prepare piecrust mix, following label directions for a 9-inch double-crust pie. Preheat oven to very hot (450°).
3. Beat eggs in a medium-size bowl until frothy. Stir gently into lemon-sugar mixture. Spoon into pastry-lined pie plate.
4. Cut an X in center of top crust to allow steam to escape. Fit over filling, turning back corners of the X. Trim overhang to 1 inch. Pinch to make a stand-up edge; flute. Brush with cream; sprinkle with sugar.
5. Bake in a preheated very hot oven (450°) for 15 minutes. Lower heat to moderate (350°). Bake 30 minutes longer, or until pastry is golden brown.

To freshen a baked pie: Wrap loosely in aluminum foil. Heat in a moderate oven (350°) for 10 minutes.

LEMON MERINGUE PIE

The easy meringue top is prepared in a special way.

Bake crust at 450° for 8 minutes.
Makes 6 servings.

    ½ package piecrust mix
    1½ cups sugar
    ½ cup cornstarch
    ¼ teaspoon salt
    2½ cups water
    4 eggs, separated
    3 tablespoons butter or margarine
    1 tablespoon grated lemon rind
    ½ cup lemon juice
    ¼ teaspoon cream of tartar
    ½ cup sugar

1. Preheat oven to very hot (450°). Prepare piecrust mix, following label directions for a 9-inch pastry shell with a high fluted edge. Prick shell all over with a fork.

2. Bake in a preheated very hot oven (450°) for 8 minutes, or until pastry is golden brown. Cool on wire rack.

3. Combine 1½ cups of the sugar, cornstarch and salt in a large saucepan; gradually add water, stirring constantly.

4. Cook over medium heat, stirring constantly, until mixture thickens and bubbles. Cook 1 minute and remove from heat.

5. Beat egg yolks slightly in a small bowl; slowly blend in about ½ cup of the hot cornstarch mixture; stir back into remaining mixture in saucepan. Cook over low heat, stirring constantly, 2 minutes; remove from heat. (Do not overcook.)

6. Stir in butter, lemon rind and juice; pour into cooled pastry shell. Press a piece of plastic wrap directly on filling to prevent skin from forming. (Remove before topping pie.) Refrigerate for at least 4 hours.

7. Beat egg whites with cream of tartar in a medium-size bowl until foamy. Slowly add the remaining ½ cup sugar, a tablespoon at a time, beating at high speed until the meringue forms firm peaks.

8. Grease and lightly flour a small cookie sheet. Shape meringue into 6 to 8 small mounds on the cookie sheet, swirling with the back of a teaspoon to form peaks.

9. Bake in a moderate oven (350°) 15 minutes, or until meringues are golden. Cool on cookie sheet. When the puffs are cool, carefully place on chilled pie with a small spatula.

If you have had slipping and weeping problems with a meringue spread over a lemon pie and browned in the oven, you will appreciate our alternate method in the Lemon Meringue Pie. However, if you prefer the traditional finish, make sure that the meringue is spread to touch the edge of the pastry all around. It should be spread over a cool, but not chilled, filling. Bake in a preheated hot oven (425°) for 5 to 6 minutes, or until peaks of meringue are golden brown. Allow to cool to room temperature before refrigerating.

The secret to good meringue is having as much sugar dissolve as possible. For best results, add sugar *only* after egg whites are foamy-white.

Shaker Lemon Pie

FRESH BLUEBERRY PIE

Bake at 425° for 15 minutes, then at 350° for 35 minutes.
Makes 6 servings.

- 1 cup sugar
- ¼ cup flour
- ¼ teaspoon salt
- ¼ teaspoon ground cloves
- ¼ teaspoon ground cinnamon
- 2 pints blueberries
- 1 package piecrust mix
- 3 tablespoons butter or margarine
  Milk
  Sugar

1. Combine sugar, flour, salt, cloves and cinnamon in a small bowl; mix well.

2. Pick over blueberries; wash gently; drain on paper toweling. Combine with sugar mixture in a large bowl; toss gently. Preheat oven to hot (425°).

3. Prepare piecrust mix, following label directions for a 9-inch double-crust pie. Cut vents in top crust for steam to escape.

4. Spoon blueberry filling into pastry-lined pie plate; dot with butter. Fit top over filling. Trim overhang to 1 inch; fold under, flush with rim; pinch to make a stand-up edge; flute. Brush pastry with milk; sprinkle with sugar.

5. Bake in a preheated hot oven (425°) for 15 minutes, then lower oven temperature to moderate (350°) and continue to bake 35 minutes longer, or until juices bubble up and pastry is golden brown. Cool on wire rack. Serve warm or at room temperature.

> **To help transfer the rolled-out pie pastry to the pie plate, just use your rolling pin! Put pin on edge of pastry circle, roll up pastry around pin, transfer, then unroll into the plate. Be sure to fit the pastry loosely in the plate. If the pastry is stretched, it will shrink during baking.**

> **When rolling pie pastry, invert the empty pie plate on the pastry to judge approximately how much more to roll.**

FRESH PEACH PIE

Bake at 425° for 15 minutes, then at 350° for 30 minutes.
Makes 6 servings.

- ½ cup sugar
- 2 tablespoons flour
- ½ teaspoon ground cinnamon
- ¼ teaspoon salt
- 2½ pounds peaches
- 1 tablespoon lemon juice
- ¼ teaspoon almond extract
- 1 package piecrust mix
- 2 tablespoons butter or margarine
  Milk
  Sugar

1. Combine sugar, flour, cinnamon and salt in a small bowl; mix well.

2. Drop peaches, a few at a time, into boiling water; let stand 15 seconds; lift out with a slotted spoon. Peel off skins; halve, pit and slice into a large bowl. (You should have about 5 cups.) Sprinkle with lemon juice and almond extract; toss gently. (Lemon juice sharpens flavor and keeps peaches from browning.) Add sugar mixture; stir to coat. Preheat oven to hot (425°).

3. Prepare piecrust mix, following label directions for a 9-inch double-crust pie.

4. Spoon filling into pastry-lined pie plate; dot with butter. Cut top crust into 1-inch strips. Weave over filling in a lattice design. Trim overhang to 1 inch; fold under, flush with rim. Pinch to make a stand-up edge; flute. Brush pastry with milk; sprinkle with sugar.

5. Bake in a preheated hot oven (425°) for 15 minutes, then lower oven temperature to moderate (350°) and continue to bake 30 minutes longer, or until the juices bubble up and pastry is golden brown. Cool on a wire rack.

Clockwise from lower left: Deep-Dish Rhubarb-Strawberry Pie (page 290); Fresh Peach Pie; Nectarine Streusel Pie (page 288); Fresh Blueberry Pie

> To make a high fluted edge on a pie: Fit pastry gently into pie plate without stretching. Roll the pastry large enough to extend at least 1 inch over the rim. Trim edges neatly to 1 inch. Fold pastry under, flush with rim. Pinch with fingers to make a stand-up edge. Flute with fingers into whatever edging you wish—scallop, rope or plain flute.

NECTARINE STREUSEL PIE

Bake at 425° for 45 minutes.
Makes 6 servings.

- ¾ cup granulated sugar
- 3 tablespoons quick-cooking tapioca
- 1 teaspoon grated lemon rind
- ¼ teaspoon ground cinnamon
- 2½ pounds nectarines
- 1 teaspoon lemon juice
- ½ package piecrust mix
- ⅔ cup quick oats
- ⅓ cup firmly packed brown sugar
- ¼ cup *sifted* all-purpose flour
- ¼ cup chopped walnuts or pecans
- 6 tablespoons butter or margarine

1. Combine sugar, tapioca, lemon rind and cinnamon in a small bowl; mix well.
2. Drop nectarines, a few at a time, into boiling water; let stand 15 seconds; lift out with a slotted spoon. Peel off skins; halve, pit and slice into a large bowl. (You should have about 5 cups.) Sprinkle with lemon juice; toss gently. Add sugar mixture; stirring gently to coat.
3. Prepare piecrust mix, following label directions for a 9-inch pastry shell with a high fluted edge.
4. Preheat oven to hot (425°).
5. For streusel topping: Combine oats, brown sugar, flour and nuts in a small bowl. Work in butter with fingertips until mixture is crumbly and thoroughly mixed.
6. Spoon nectarine filling into pastry-lined pie plate. Sprinkle evenly with streusel topping. Put a piece of aluminum foil loosely over pie to cover top.

7. Bake in a preheated hot oven (425°) for 30 minutes. Remove foil; continue baking 15 minutes longer, or until juices bubble up and streusel is set. Cool on wire rack at least 1 hour.

CARAMEL CUSTARD AND PEAR TART

A drizzle of caramel syrup and a cloud of spun sugar top this pretty pie.
Bake at 400° for 45 minutes.
Makes 6 servings.

- ½ package piecrust mix
- 4 firm pears
- 1 tablespoon lemon juice
- 1 tablespoon coarsely shredded lemon rind
- 2 teaspoons finely chopped preserved ginger (in syrup)
- ½ cup firmly packed light brown sugar
- 2 eggs
- 1 cup light cream or half and half
- 4 tablespoons granulated sugar

1. Prepare piecrust mix, following label directions for a 9-inch pastry shell with a high fluted edge. Preheat oven to hot (425°).
2. Pare pears; quarter, core and cut into eighths. Toss pear pieces with lemon juice in a large bowl. Arrange petal fashion, starting at outside edge, in 2 circles in bottom of pastry shell. Sprinkle lemon rind, ginger and brown sugar evenly over pears; cover loosely with foil.
3. Bake in a preheated hot oven (400°) for 30 minutes, or until pears are almost tender.
4. Beat eggs slightly in a small bowl; beat in cream; pour over pears.
5. Continue baking 15 minutes, or until custard is almost set in center. Cool on a wire rack 2 hours before serving.
6. Shortly before serving, heat the 4 tablespoons sugar in a small heavy skillet until melted; continue heating until mixture is

light brown; cool slightly. Drizzle from the tip of a spoon in a back-and-forth motion over the pie. If you wish to make the "spun-sugar" top, let the last tablespoon of syrup cool until syrupy-thick; wave the spoon in a circular motion over center of pie to "spin" sugar in threads.

Note: If the syrup hardens, place over low heat until melted again.

> **Baked custard mixtures should be tested for doneness by inserting a knife blade 1 inch from the edge. The blade should come out clean. Custards continue to cook slightly after they have been removed from the oven. If the edge test is positive, yet the center ripples softly when the plate is gently moved, it is safe to remove the custard from the oven, as the center will set as it cools.**

Caramel Custard and Pear Tart

PUMPKIN-NUT PIE

A dessert that's always in demand, even more appealing with golden candy-like topping. This recipe makes a very full pie!
Bake at 425° for 15 minutes, then at 375° for 30 minutes.
Makes 6 servings.

- ½ package piecrust mix
- 2 eggs
- 1 can (1 pound) pumpkin
- ½ cup granulated sugar
- ½ cup firmly packed brown sugar
- 1 teaspoon salt
- 1 teaspoon ground cinnamon
- ¼ teaspoon ground cloves
- ¼ teaspoon ground nutmeg
- 1 tall can (1⅔ cups) evaporated milk
  Nut Topping (*recipe follows*)

1. Prepare piecrust mix, following label directions for a 9-inch pastry shell with a high fluted edge. Preheat oven to hot (425°).
2. Beat eggs slightly in a large bowl; stir in pumpkin, granulated and brown sugars, salt, cinnamon, cloves and nutmeg; stir in evaporated milk.
3. Pour pumpkin filling into shell. Place pastry shell on middle shelf of oven.
4. Bake in a preheated hot oven (425°) 15 minutes; lower oven temperature to moderate (375°). Continue baking 20 minutes.
5. Spoon Nut Topping around edge of pie. Bake 10 minutes longer, or until custard is almost set, but still soft in center. (Do not overbake.) Cool pie on a wire rack. Leave plain or garnish with whipped cream, if you wish.

NUT TOPPING: Beat 3 tablespoons butter or margarine with ⅔ cup firmly packed brown sugar in a small bowl; stir in ⅔ cup coarsely chopped pecans until blended.

> **A frozen *deep* 9-inch pastry shell may be substituted for any recipe calling for a 9-inch pastry shell. Follow directions on label.**

PECAN PIE

Bake at 350° for 45 minutes.
Makes 8 servings.

½ package piecrust mix
4 eggs
1 cup sugar
¼ cup flour
½ teaspoon salt
1½ cups dark corn syrup
1 teaspoon vanilla
1 cup pecan halves

1. Prepare piecrust mix, following label directions for a 9-inch pastry shell with a high fluted edge. Preheat oven to moderate (350°).
2. Beat eggs lightly in a medium-size bowl. Stir in sugar, flour, salt, corn syrup and vanilla. Pour into prepared shell; arrange pecan halves on top. OR: Chop pecans coarsely; sprinkle inside shell before adding filling.
3. Bake in a preheated moderate oven (350°) for 45 minutes, or until the center is almost set but still soft. (Do not overbake.) Cool on a wire rack. Serve with whipped cream, if you wish.

PINEAPPLE PIE

Bake at 425° for 35 minutes.
Makes 6 servings.

1 package piecrust mix
1 teaspoon grated lemon rind
¾ cup sugar
3 tablespoons cornstarch
1 can (1 pound, 4 ounces) crushed pineapple in pineapple juice
1 tablespoon lemon juice

1. Prepare piecrust mix, following label directions for a 9-inch double-crust pie, adding the lemon rind with the liquid called for in the directions. Cut vents in top crust for steam to escape.
2. Combine sugar, cornstarch, pineapple and juice and lemon juice in a medium-size saucepan. Cook over medium heat, stirring

constantly, until mixture thickens and bubbles 1 minute. Remove from heat. Pour into pastry-lined plate.
3. Preheat oven to hot (425°).
4. Place top crust over filling; trim overhang to 1 inch; fold under, flush with rim. Pinch to make a stand-up edge; flute. Brush crust with milk and sprinkle with sugar, if you wish.
5. Bake in a preheated hot oven (425°) for 35 minutes, or until pastry is golden brown. Serve cool with ice cream, if you wish.

> **Pie browning too fast?** Cover top loosely with a piece of aluminum foil. Start out baking with the aluminum foil in place and remove it approximately 10 minutes before the end of baking time. This should allow the pastry to brown to the perfect shade.

DEEP-DISH RHUBARB-STRAWBERRY PIE

Bake at 425° for 40 minutes.
Makes 6 servings.

¾ cup sugar
⅓ cup flour
1 teaspoon ground cinnamon
½ teaspoon ground cloves
1 pound rhubarb
1 pint strawberries
2 tablespoons butter or margarine
½ package piecrust mix

1. Combine sugar, flour, cinnamon and cloves in a small bowl; mix well.
2. Wash rhubarb; trim ends; cut into 1-inch pieces. (You should have about 6 cups.) Wash strawberries; hull and halve. (You should have about 2 cups.) Combine fruit with sugar mixture in a large bowl; toss to mix. Let stand 15 minutes; toss again.
3. Spoon filling evenly into an 8x8x2-inch baking dish; dot with butter. Preheat oven to hot (425°).
4. Prepare piecrust mix, following label di-

Lemon Angel Pie

rections. Roll out on a lightly floured surface a little larger than an 10-inch square; trim evenly to a 10-inch square. Cut into 1-inch strips. Weave strips in a lattice design over filling. Trim overhang to 1 inch. Use pastry trimmings to join lattice strips around edge of the dish. Press pastry to inside edge of the dish; crimp with a fork.

5. Bake in a preheated hot oven (425°) for 40 minutes, or until juices bubble up and pastry is golden brown. Cool on wire rack. Serve warm with vanilla ice cream, if you wish.

PIE FACTS:
Pastry for deep-dish pies is usually pinched and fluted *inside* the rim of the baking dish to make it easier to serve the pie without breaking off all the crust.

Easy lattice work: You may find it easier to weave the lattice top for a pie on a piece of wax paper, then flip the completed design over the filling. A pastry wheel will make professional-looking strips for the lattice topping.

For a sparkling, extra-flaky top crust on fruit pies, brush with milk or cream, then sprinkle with sugar before baking.

To keep your oven clean, especially when baking a juicy fruit pie, put a piece of foil directly below the pie. Crimp all four edges to hold any bubble-over.

LEMON ANGEL PIE
Bake at 275° for 1 hour.
Makes 8 servings.

  3 egg whites
¼ teaspoon cream of tartar
  1 cup sugar
  5 egg yolks
⅔ cup sugar
  1 tablespoon grated lemon rind
⅓ cup lemon juice
  1 cup heavy cream, whipped

1. Preheat oven to slow (275°).
2. Make meringue shell: Beat egg whites with cream of tartar in a medium-size bowl until foamy. Beat in 1 cup of the sugar, a tablespoon at a time, until the meringue forms stiff glossy peaks.
3. Lightly butter a 9-inch pie plate. Spoon meringue over bottom and up side to form a shell about 1 inch thick.
4. Bake in a preheated slow oven (275°) for 1 hour. Turn off oven; leave meringue in oven until cool.
5. Make lemon filling: Beat egg yolks in top of a double boiler until frothy. Beat in the remaining ⅔ cup sugar slowly until mixture is thick and light. Stir in lemon rind and juice. Cook, stirring constantly, over hot, not boiling, water until filling is thick, about 13 minutes; remove from heat; cool.
6. Spoon cooled filling into meringue shell; cover loosely; refrigerate *at least* 12 hours for meringue to soften. Top with whipped cream; decorate with orange and lemon slices and mint, if you wish.

FROZEN MINCEMEAT-ICE CREAM PIE

The traditional mincemeat pie sporting a spicy ice-cream topper and a buttery nut crust has a brand-new look. You can make it up to 2 weeks ahead and freeze.

Bake crust at 350° for 10 minutes.
Makes 8 servings.

1½ cups pecan halves, finely chopped (about 6 ounces)
  3 tablespoons sugar
  2 tablespoons butter or margarine, melted
  1 cup prepared bottled mincemeat
  1 quart vanilla ice cream
  ½ teaspoon ground cinnamon
  ½ teaspoon ground ginger
  ¼ teaspoon ground allspice
  1 tablespoon grated orange rind
  ½ pint heavy cream, whipped
    Candied red cherries
    Pecan halves

1. Preheat oven to moderate (350°).
2. Combine pecans, sugar and melted butter in a medium-size bowl; mix well. Press firmly and evenly onto the bottom and side of a well-greased 9-inch pie plate.
3. Bake in a preheated moderate oven (350°) for 10 minutes. Cool thoroughly on wire rack.
4. Spread prepared mincemeat evenly onto bottom of cooled prepared shell.
5. Soften ice cream in a chilled medium-size bowl; blend in cinnamon, ginger, allspice and grated orange rind. Spread ice cream evenly over mincemeat layer. Freeze until firm, several hours or overnight.
6. To serve, remove pie from freezer 20 minutes before serving. Garnish with whipped cream; decorate with candied cherries and pecan halves.

Top: Cinnamon-Apple Custard Pie (page 283), center: Double Fudge Brownie Pie; bottom: Coconut Cream Pie (page 297)

DOUBLE FUDGE BROWNIE PIE

Bake at 350° for 40 minutes.
Makes 12 servings.

½ package piecrust mix
½ cup (1 stick) butter or margarine
4 squares semisweet chocolate
¼ cup water
¾ cup firmly packed light brown sugar
2 eggs, separated
1 teaspoon vanilla
⅓ cup flour
¼ teaspoon salt
¾ cup broken walnuts
12 walnut halves
  Coffee ice cream or whipped cream
  Bottled fudge topping

1. Prepare piecrust mix, following label directions for a 9-inch pastry shell with a high fluted edge; chill while preparing filling.
2. Preheat oven to moderate (350°).
3. Melt butter and chocolate in a medium-size saucepan; cool slightly. Stir in water and sugar until blended; beat in egg yolks and vanilla. Fold in flour and salt.
4. Beat egg whites in a medium-size bowl until soft peaks form; fold into chocolate mixture; add broken walnuts until well blended. Spread evenly in pastry shell. Arrange walnut halves around edge.
5. Bake in a preheated moderate oven (350°) for 40 minutes. Cool completely on wire rack. Serve with coffee ice cream or whipped cream and fudge topping.

MAI TAI PIE

The official happy hour drink of the Islands inspired this pie.

Bake crust at 300° for 25 minutes.
Makes 6 servings.

Coconut Crust*:
1 package (7 ounces) flaked coconut
6 tablespoons butter or margarine, melted

Mai Tai Filling:
1 envelope unflavored gelatin
½ cup sugar
4 eggs, separated
1 can (6 ounces) unsweetened pineapple juice
½ cup fresh lime juice
⅓ cup light or golden rum
2 tablespoons orange-flavored liqueur
¼ cup sugar
½ cup heavy cream, whipped

1. Preheat oven to slow (300°). Blend coconut and butter in a medium-size bowl. Press evenly and firmly onto bottom and up side of a 9-inch pie plate.
2. Bake in a preheated slow oven (300°) for 25 minutes, or until golden brown. Cool on wire rack.
3. Mix gelatin and ¼ cup of the sugar in a small saucepan; beat in egg yolks until well blended. Gradually add pineapple juice, blending well.
4. Cook, stirring constantly, until gelatin dissolves and mixture is slightly thickened. (Do not boil.) Remove from heat. Stir in lime juice, rum and orange-flavored liqueur. Pour into a large bowl. Place bowl in pan of ice and water to speed setting; chill, stirring often, until mixture begins to thicken and mounds when spooned.
5. While gelatin mixture chills, beat egg whites in a medium-size bowl until foamy; slowly beat in the remaining ¼ cup sugar until meringue forms soft peaks. Fold whipped cream into gelatin, then meringue mixture until no streaks of white remain. Spoon into cooled coconut shell. Chill at least 3 hours, or until set.
*You may substitute a graham-cracker shell, if you wish.

Unless otherwise indicated, our pies are made in 9x1½-inch pie plates, and will hold all the fillings. The capacity is 4 cups. Measure if in doubt.

LUSCIOUS LIME CHIFFON PIE

Makes 6 servings.

14 to 15 shortbread cookies
 2 tablespoons butter or margarine
½ cup chopped pecans or walnuts
 1 envelope unflavored gelatin
¼ cup cold water
 4 eggs, separated
½ cup sugar
 1 tablespoon grated lime rind
½ cup lime juice
   Green food coloring (*optional*)
½ cup sugar
½ cup heavy cream, whipped

1. Crush cookies in a plastic bag with rolling pin. (You should have about 1 cup.) Melt butter in a medium-size heavy skillet; stir in pecans and cookie crumbs. Stir over low heat 1 minute. Press firmly over bottom and side of a 9-inch pie plate. Chill while preparing filling.
2. Sprinkle gelatin over water in a small cup to soften, 5 minutes. Set cup in pan of simmering water, stirring often, until gelatin is dissolved. Remove from heat.
3. Beat egg yolks with ½ cup of the sugar in a large bowl until light and fluffy; stir in lime rind, lime juice and gelatin. Place bowl in pan of ice and water to speed setting; chill, stirring often, until mixture begins to thicken. Tint pale green with a few drops of green food coloring, if you wish.
4. While gelatin mixture chills, beat egg whites until foamy; gradually beat in the remaining ½ cup sugar until meringue forms soft peaks.
5. Fold whipped cream, then meringue into gelatin mixture until no streaks of white remain. Spoon into chilled pie crust. Chill 4 hours, or until firm.
6. Garnish with lime slices and sprigs of mint, if you wish.

PEPPERMINT CHIFFON PIE

Makes 6 servings.

14 chocolate sandwich cookies
 3 tablespoons butter or margarine
 1 envelope unflavored gelatin
 1 cup milk
¾ cup finely crushed peppermint hard candy
 4 egg whites
 2 tablespoons sugar
 1 cup heavy cream, whipped

1. Crush cookies in plastic bag with rolling pin. (You should have about 1¼ cups.) If fillings from cookies stick to inside of bag, scrape off with rubber spatula and blend with crumbs. Melt butter in a medium-size skillet; stir in cookie crumbs; remove from heat and stir 1 minute. Press crumb mixture against side and bottom of a 9-inch pie plate. Chill while preparing filling.
2. Sprinkle gelatin over milk in a small heavy saucepan; let stand a few minutes to soften. Add ½ cup of the crushed candy. Cook, stirring constantly, over medium heat until gelatin is completely dissolved. Place pan in bowl of ice and water to speed setting; chill, stirring often, until mixture begins to thicken.
3. While gelatin mixture chills, beat egg whites in a medium-size bowl until foamy; gradually beat in sugar until meringue stands in soft peaks.
4. Fold whipped cream, 2 tablespoons of the crushed candy and meringue into gelatin mixture until no streaks of white remain; spoon into chilled pie crust. Chill 4 hours, or until firm.
5. Just before serving, sprinkle remaining candy over top and decorate with additional whipped cream, if you wish.

Unflavored gelatin should always be softened first in liquid before heating. The only exception is in a Bavarian cream mixture, where the gelatin is "dry diluted" by the sugar.

Top: Luscious Lime Chiffon Pie; center: Tropical Pineapple Chiffon Pie (page 296); bottom: Peppermint Chiffon Pie

TROPICAL PINEAPPLE CHIFFON PIE

Makes 6 servings.

20 brown-edge vanilla wafers
½ cup flaked coconut
¼ cup (½ stick) butter or margarine
1 envelope unflavored gelatin
⅓ cup sugar
4 eggs, separated
1 medium-size lemon
1 can (1 pound, 4 ounces) crushed pineapple in pineapple juice
½ cup heavy cream, whipped

1. Crush cookies in plastic bag with rolling pin. (You should have about 1 cup.) Heat coconut in a medium-size heavy skillet over medium heat, stirring constantly, until golden brown. Stir in butter until melted; remove from heat; stir in cookie crumbs. Press crumb mixture against side and bottom of a 9-inch pie plate. Chill while preparing filling.

2. Mix gelatin and 3 tablespoons of the sugar in medium-size heavy saucepan; add egg yolks; beat with a wooden spoon until well blended. Grate rind from lemon; measure and reserve 2 teaspoons. Squeeze lemon; measure 2 tablespoons juice. Drain juice from pineapple, (½ to ¾ cup); stir into gelatin mixture along with lemon juice until smooth.

3. Cook gelatin mixture over low heat, stirring constantly, 8 to 10 minutes, or until gelatin is completely dissolved and mixture thickens slightly and coats a spoon. Cool slightly; stir in lemon rind and pineapple. (For a smoother pie, puree pineapple in container of electric blender until smooth before adding to gelatin mixture.) Place pan in a bowl of ice water to speed setting; chill, stirring often, until mixture begins to thicken.

4. While pineapple mixture chills, beat egg whites in medium-size bowl until foamy; gradually beat in remaining sugar until meringue forms soft peaks.

5. Fold whipped cream, then meringue into gelatin mixture until no streaks of white remain. Spoon into chilled pie crust, mounding high. Chill 4 hours, or until firm. Garnish with additional cream, pineapple and toasted coconut, if you wish.

To hasten the chilling of chiffon pies, place saucepan of filling in a large bowl partially filled with ice cubes and water. Stir often until mixture begins to thicken, and will mound when spooned. Remove from ice at once, fold in remaining ingredients. This method is also helpful to thicken the fillings sufficiently to allow them to be swirled and mounded high in the pastry shell.

LEMON CHIFFON PIE

Feathery light, tangy and refreshing!
Bake crust at 450° for 8 minutes.
Makes 6 servings.

½ package piecrust mix
2 lemons
1 envelope unflavored gelatin
½ cup sugar
¼ teaspoon salt
6 eggs, separated
¼ cup water
½ cup sugar
½ cup heavy cream, whipped
1 lemon, sliced (*optional*)

1. Preheat oven to very hot (450°).
2. Prepare piecrust mix, following label directions for a 9-inch pastry shell with a high fluted edge. Prick shell all over with a fork.
3. Bake in a preheated very hot oven (450°) for 8 minutes, or until golden brown. Cool on wire rack.
4. Grate 1 teaspoon lemon rind; squeeze ½ cup lemon juice; reserve.
5. Combine gelatin, ½ cup of the sugar,

salt and egg yolks in a medium-size saucepan. Beat with a rotary beater until well blended. Stir in reserved lemon juice and water. Cook over low heat, stirring constantly, until gelatin is dissolved and mixture is slightly thickened. Place pan in a bowl of ice and water to speed setting; chill, stirring often, until mixture begins to thicken and will mound when spooned.

6. Beat egg whites in a large bowl until foamy-white. Slowly beat in remaining ½ cup sugar, 1 tablespoon at a time, until soft peaks form. Fold into gelatin mixture.

7. Spoon into cooled pastry shell; refrigerate until set, about 3 hours. Garnish with whipped cream and decorate with lemon slices, if you wish.

Lemon Chiffon Pie

COCONUT CREAM PIE

Bake crust at 450° for 8 minutes.
Makes 6 servings.

½ package piecrust mix
½ cup sugar
⅓ cup flour
¼ teaspoon salt
2 cups milk
4 egg yolks
2 teaspoons vanilla
2 tablespoons butter or margarine
1 can (4 ounces) flaked coconut
½ cup heavy cream, whipped

1. Preheat oven to very hot (450°). Prepare piecrust mix, following label directions for a 9-inch pastry shell with a high fluted edge. Prick shell all over with a fork.

2. Bake in a preheated very hot oven (450°) for 8 minutes, or until golden brown; cool on wire rack.

3. Mix sugar, flour and salt in a medium-size saucepan; gradually stir in milk. Cook, stirring constantly, until mixture thickens and bubbles 2 minutes.

4. Beat egg yolks slightly in a small bowl; slowly stir in about half of the hot mixture; pour back into saucepan; cook, stirring constantly, over low heat, 1 minute; remove from heat; stir in vanilla and butter; press a piece of plastic wrap directly on hot surface of filling to prevent skin from forming; cool.

5. Chop half the coconut finely; stir into cream filling. Spoon mixture into baked pastry shell. Press a piece of wax paper or plastic wrap directly on surface to prevent skin from forming. Chill 4 hours, or until firm enough to cut.

6. Meanwhile, spread remaining coconut on a small cookie sheet. Toast in a slow oven (300°) for 8 to 10 minutes. Reserve.

7. Just before serving, remove the plastic wrap from top of pie. Spread or pipe whipped cream decoratively on top of pie. Garnish with the reserved toasted coconut.

MACADAMIA NUT CREAM PIE

This pie of creamy lightness is a perfect setting for the exotic macadamia nut.

Bake crust at 450° for 8 minutes.

Makes 8 servings.

½ package piecrust mix
½ cup sugar
¼ cup cornstarch
   Pinch salt
3 egg yolks
2 cups milk
1 tablespoon butter
1½ cups heavy cream
2 tablespoons coffee-flavored liqueur
½ cup chopped macadamia nuts
   Whole macadamia nuts

1. Preheat oven to very hot (450°). Prepare piecrust mix, following label directions for a 9-inch pastry shell with a high fluted edge. Prick shell all over with a fork.
2. Bake in a preheated very hot oven (450°) for 8 minutes, or until golden brown; cool on wire rack.
3. Beat sugar, cornstarch, salt and egg yolks in a small bowl until very well mixed.
4. Heat milk in a medium-size saucepan just to boiling, but do not boil. Stir sugar mixture into hot milk. Put mixture back over heat. Cook, stirring constantly, until mixture thickens and bubbles, about 3 minutes. Remove from heat; stir in butter. Press a piece of plastic wrap directly on surface of filling to keep skin from forming; cool.
5. Beat ½ cup of the heavy cream in a small bowl until stiff; fold into cooled mixture along with coffee liqueur and all but 1 tablespoon of the chopped nuts. Spoon into pastry shell; chill several hours or overnight.
6. To serve: Beat remaining 1 cup heavy cream in a small bowl. Spread part of the cream over top of pie. Sprinkle with reserved chopped nuts. Decorate with whole nuts and remaining whipped cream.

> Bake pastry shells the professional way: Fit a piece of foil or wax paper into pastry-lined plate. Fill the shell with rice or beans, which will keep the pastry flat. Bake 5 minutes or as soon as pastry is "set" but not brown. Remove rice or beans and foil. Pierce any bubbles that might form; continue to bake until crust is golden brown. You can cool the rice or beans; keep them in a jar with a tight-fitting lid and reuse.

BANANA CREAM PIE

Creamy smooth, and oh, so delicious!

Bake crust at 450° for 8 minutes.

Makes 6 servings.

½ package piecrust mix
⅔ cup sugar
3 tablespoons flour
2 tablespoons cornstarch
¼ teaspoon salt
3 cups milk
3 eggs
2 teaspoons vanilla
3 medium-size ripe bananas
1 cup heavy cream, whipped

1. Preheat oven to very hot (450°). Prepare piecrust mix, following label directions for a 9-inch pastry shell with a high fluted edge. Prick shell all over with a fork.
2. Bake pastry shell in a preheated very hot oven (450°) for 8 minutes, or until golden brown; cool on wire rack.
3. Combine sugar, flour, cornstarch and salt in a large saucepan. Stir in milk slowly.
4. Cook, stirring constantly, over moderate heat, until mixture thickens and bubbles. Continue cooking and stirring until mixture is very thick, about 6 minutes longer.
5. Beat eggs in a medium-size bowl until frothy. Stir in half the cooked mixture until blended. Return to saucepan, blending into mixture. Cook 2 minutes more over low heat, stirring constantly.
6. Remove from heat; stir in vanilla. Place a piece of plastic wrap directly on surface of

the filling to keep skin from forming; cool.
7. Slice bananas into pie shell. Pour cooled cream filling over bananas; chill several hours. Just before serving, spread or pipe whipped cream decoratively on top of pie.

CHOCOLATE CREAM PIE
Rich and smooth, the luscious chocolate filling is topped with fluffy whipped cream.
Bake crust at 450° for 8 minutes.
Makes 6 servings.

½ package piecrust mix
2 squares unsweetened chocolate
3¼ cups milk
1⅓ cups sugar
⅓ cup cornstarch
½ teaspoon salt
4 egg yolks
3 teaspoons vanilla
1 cup heavy cream, whipped

1. Preheat oven to very hot (450°). Prepare piecrust mix, following label directions for a 9-inch pastry shell with a high fluted edge. Prick shell all over with a fork.
2. Bake in a preheated very hot oven (450°) for 8 minutes, or until golden brown; cool on wire rack.
3. Heat chocolate and ½ cup of the milk in a small saucepan over low heat, stirring constantly, until chocolate is melted.
4. Combine sugar, cornstarch, salt, the remaining 2¾ cups milk and egg yolks in a large saucepan. Beat with a rotary beater or wire whisk until mixture is well blended. Stir in chocolate mixture.
5. Cook over medium heat, stirring constantly, until mixture thickens and comes to boiling. Cook 1 minute. Remove from heat; stir in vanilla. Pour into prepared shell.

Don't overcook fillings with a cornstarch base because the cornstarch may break down and thin the filling.

Place a piece of plastic wrap directly on surface of hot filling to keep skin from forming. Refrigerate at least 3 hours.
6. Just before serving: Remove plastic from pie. Spread whipped cream over top of pie in a smooth layer.

PEACH DUMPLINGS
Luscious peaches, wrapped in flaky, light pastry. An old-fashioned dessert your family will love.
Bake at 425° for 30 minutes.
Makes 6 servings.

¾ cup water
½ cup granulated sugar
½ cup grenadine syrup
1 package piecrust mix
¼ cup firmly packed brown sugar
¼ teaspoon ground cinnamon
1 tablespoon butter or margarine
6 large peaches, peeled, halved and pitted
Milk or cream
Granulated sugar

1. Combine water, granulated sugar and grenadine in a medium-size saucepan. Heat to boiling; lower heat; simmer 5 minutes; remove from heat.
2. Prepare piecrust mix, following label directions. Roll out on a lightly floured surface to a 18x12-inch rectangle. Cut into six 6-inch squares. Preheat oven to hot (425°).
3. Blend brown sugar, cinnamon and butter in a small bowl. Spoon mixture into hollows of peaches; press the halves back together.
4. Place a filled peach on each of the pastry squares; bring pastry up around peaches, pinching seams to seal. Place in a 13x9x2-inch baking pan. Pour syrup into pan. Brush dumplings with milk; sprinkle with granulated sugar.
5. Bake in a preheated hot oven (425°) for 30 minutes, or until pastry is golden and peaches are tender. Serve warm with cream, if you wish.

GLAZED FRUIT TARTS

Bake tart shells at 450° for 10 minutes.
Makes 36 tarts.

   2 packages piecrust mix
  ¼ cup sugar
   2 eggs, slightly beaten
     Pastry Cream (*recipe follows*)
     Fresh fruits for garnish: strawberries,
      bananas, grapes, kiwi, mandarin
      orange, pineapple slices, etc.
  ⅔ cup apple jelly
   2 teaspoons sugar

1. Preheat oven to very hot (450°).
2. Combine piecrust mix and the ¼ cup
sugar in a medium-size bowl; blend in eggs
with a fork until pastry is moistened and
leaves side of bowl clean. Press about 1
tablespoon of the dough into tiny 2 to 3-
inch fluted tart pans.* Prick shells all over
with a fork. Place on cookie sheets; chill 15
minutes.

3. Bake in a preheated very hot oven
(450°) for 10 minutes, or until golden
brown. Cool on wire racks.
4. Spoon a small amount of Pastry Cream
into each cooled shell. Decorate with fruits.
5. Melt jelly with the remaining 2 teaspoons sugar in a small skillet over low heat;
cool slightly; brush over fruits. Chill.

PASTRY CREAM: Prepare 1 package French vanilla flavor instant pudding with 1 cup milk,
following label directions; beat 1 cup heavy
cream in a small bowl until stiff; fold into
pudding; cover with plastic wrap; chill.
Note: If you don't have enough tart pans,
fill those you have, bake, and refill.

**Tiny bite-size muffin tins can be used in
place of the fluted tart pans.**

Glazed Fruit Tarts

Maple-Walnut Tarts

MAPLE-WALNUT TARTS

Maple sugar was a favorite sweetener in the Early American kitchen.

Bake at 425° for 15 minutes.
Makes 18 tarts.

    1 package piecrust mix
    2 eggs
    ¼ cup firmly packed brown sugar
    1 teaspoon salt
    ½ cup maple syrup
    ⅓ cup butter or margarine, melted and slightly cooled
    ½ cup chopped walnuts
      Whipped cream

1. Prepare piecrust mix, following label directions. Roll out pastry on a lightly floured surface slightly larger than a 16x12-inch rectangle. Trim to 16x12 inches. Using a ruler as a guide, cut into 4-inch squares. Line twelve 2½-inch fluted tart pans with pastry; trim excess pastry and reserve. Re-roll trimmings to a 12x8-inch rectangle; cut into 4-inch squares. Line 6 additional tart pans and trim. Preheat oven to hot (425°).
2. Beat eggs with brown sugar and salt. Beat in maple syrup and butter until creamy smooth. Stir in walnuts.
3. Fill tart pans two-thirds full. Place on cookie sheets.
4. Bake in preheated hot oven (425°) 15 minutes. (Filling will puff up during baking but will flatten when cooled.) Remove tarts to wire racks to cool. Garnish with whipped cream and additional chopped walnuts, if you wish.

STRAWBERRY-CHEESE TARTS

Bake tart shells at 450° for 10 minutes.
Makes 12 servings.

    1 package piecrust mix
    2 tablespoons sugar
    1 egg, beaten
    1 package (8 ounces) cream cheese, softened
    1 cup dairy sour cream
    1 pint strawberries
    ½ cup strawberry jelly, melted and cooled
    ½ cup heavy cream, whipped
      Blanched sliced almonds

1. Preheat oven to very hot (450°).
2. Combine piecrust mix with sugar in a medium-size bowl. Blend in egg with a fork until pastry is moistened and leaves side of bowl clean. Divide into 12 portions; press evenly into twelve 2½ to 3-inch fluted tart pans. Prick shells all over with a fork. Place on cookie sheets.
3. Bake in a preheated very hot oven (450°) for 10 minutes, or until lightly browned. Cool on wire rack.
4. Blend cheese and sour cream in a small bowl until smooth. Divide among cooled pastry shells. Wash, hull and halve strawberries. Dip in strawberry jelly; arrange on tarts. Refrigerate. Just before serving, decorate with whipped cream and almonds.

> **For best results, don't remove cooled tarts from their pans until you're ready to serve them. For easy removal, gently hold the edge of each tart with one hand. With the other hand, use a small paring knife to very carefully lift the tart from the pan.**

DOUBLE APPLE TURNOVERS

Preheat oven to 400°; bake at 375° for 25 minutes.
Makes 12 turnovers.

> Sour Cream Pastry (*recipe follows*)
> 2 cups pared, cored and chopped apples (about 2)
> ¾ cup applesauce
> ¼ cup firmly packed light brown sugar
> ½ teaspoon ground cinnamon
> ¼ teaspoon ground mace
> 2 tablespoons raisins
> Granulated sugar

1. Prepare pastry; chill as directed.
2. Combine apples, applesauce, sugar, cinnamon, mace and raisins in a small bowl. Mix with a fork. Preheat oven to hot (400°).
3. Divide dough in half. Keep one half refrigerated until ready to use. Roll out the other half on a lightly floured surface to a 15x10-inch rectangle; trim edges evenly with a pastry wheel or sharp knife. Cut into six 5-inch squares. Place about 2 tablespoons filling on each square; moisten edges with water; fold over to make triangles. Crimp edges with a fork to seal. Lift onto ungreased cookie sheets. Repeat with remaining pastry and filling.
4. Reroll trimmings; cut into small leaves and rounds with a truffle cutter or pastry wheel. Brush tops of pastries with water; decorate with pastry cutouts; make 1 or 2 small gashes in top of each turnover to let steam escape. Sprinkle with granulated sugar.
5. Lower oven temperature to moderate (375°) as soon as you put turnovers in. Bake 25 minutes, or until puffed and rich brown in color; remove to wire rack to cool. Serve warm.

SOUR CREAM PASTRY FOR TURNOVERS
Makes enough for 12 turnovers.

> 3 cups *sifted* all-purpose flour
> 2 tablespoons sugar
> 1 cup (2 sticks) butter or margarine
> 1 cup dairy sour cream

1. Measure flour and sugar into a medium-size bowl.
2. Cut butter or margarine into flour mixture with a pastry blender until mixture is crumbly. Add sour cream.
3. Mix lightly with a fork until dough clings together and starts to leave side of bowl clean. Gather dough together with hands and knead a few times.
4. Wrap dough in plastic wrap or wax paper; chill several hours or overnight.

MINCEFRUIT PASTRY SQUARES

Bake at 400° for 25 minutes.
Makes 16 servings.

> 2½ cups *sifted* all-purpose flour
> 1 tablespoon granulated sugar
> 1 teaspoon salt
> 1 cup lard or margarine
> 1 egg, separated
> Milk
> 3 cups Mincefruit Filling (*recipe follows*)
> 1 cup 10X (confectioners') sugar
> 2 tablespoons lemon juice

1. Sift flour, granulated sugar and salt into a large bowl. Cut in lard with a pastry blender until it resembles a coarse meal.
2. Put egg yolk in a measuring cup; add milk to make ½ cup; beat with a fork until blended. Add to bowl; stir until dough clings together and forms a ball. Preheat oven to hot (400°).
3. Roll out half dough on a lightly floured surface to a 15x11-inch rectangle; transfer to a cookie sheet. Spread Mincefruit Filling evenly over dough to within ¾ inch of the edges of pastry.
4. Roll out remaining half of dough; cut vents for steam to escape; place over filling. Pinch edges together; crimp.

5. Bake in a preheated hot oven (400°) for 25 minutes, or until golden brown. Remove to wire rack.

7. Combine 10X sugar and lemon juice in a small bowl; drizzle over warm pastry.

MINCEFRUIT FILLING

    4 pounds fresh pears
    3 pounds apples
    4 medium-size oranges
    2 packages (15 ounces each) raisins
    5 cups sugar
    3 teaspoons salt
    4 teaspoons ground cinnamon
    1 teaspoon ground cloves

1. Cut unpared pears, apples and oranges into quarters or eighths. Remove cores and seeds. Run through food grinder, using medium blade.

2. Combine with raisins, sugar, salt, cinnamon and cloves in a kettle or Dutch oven. Bring to boiling, stirring to dissolve sugar. Lower heat; simmer, uncovered, stirring frequently, about 1 hour, or until thick.

3. Pack into 8 clean hot canning jars. Seal jars; process in boiling water bath for 25 minutes. Remove from water bath; complete seal unless closures are self-sealing; cool jars on wire racks. Check seals of 2-piece domed lids if using. Label; store in a cool dry place.

> **This wonderful fruit filling is economical when apples and pears are plentiful and is worth making in this quantity. It can be used for pies, added to oatmeal cookies or used as a sauce over ice cream. It also makes a fabulous gift to keep on hand.**

BAKLAVA

Bake at 325° for 50 minutes.
Makes about 36 servings.

    Honey Syrup (*recipe follows*)
    3 cups shelled walnuts
    ½ cup sugar
    1½ teaspoons ground cinnamon
    1 package (1 pound) phyllo dough
    ½ cup (1 stick) unsalted butter or margarine, melted
    1 tablespoon water

1. Prepare Honey Syrup; cool. Spread walnuts in a jelly-roll pan. Toast in a moderate oven (350°) for 10 minutes. Whirl, while still warm, a small amount at a time, in container of electric blender until finely ground. Remove to a medium-size bowl. Blend in sugar and cinnamon. Lower oven temperature to 325°.

2. Brush bottom of a 13x9x2-inch baking pan with melted butter. Fold two phyllo leaves in half; place on bottom of pan; brush with butter. Add two more leaves; brush with butter.

3. Sprinkle with ½ cup nut mixture. Add two more folded leaves; brush with butter.

4. Repeat Step 3 five more times. Stack remaining pastry leaves, brushing every other one. Brush top leaf with remaining butter; sprinkle with water.

5. With a sharp knife, mark off the Baklava. Cut through the top layer only of the phyllo, making 5 lengthwise cuts, 1½ inches apart. Then cut diagonally at 1½-inches apart, making the traditional diamond shape of the Baklava.

6. Bake in a preheated slow oven (325°) for 50 minutes, or until golden and crisp. Remove pan to wire rack; cut diamonds all the way through. Pour cooled Honey Syrup over. Cool; cover; let stand overnight for syrup to be absorbed.

HONEY SYRUP: Remove the thin yellow rind of 1 lemon. Combine with 1 cup sugar, 1 cup water, 1 two-inch piece stick cinnamon and 2 whole cloves in a medium-size saucepan. Cook without stirring until syrup registers 230° on a candy thermometer. Stir in 1 cup honey and 1½ teaspoons lemon juice; strain.

Cooking Terms

A

À la in the manner of: à *la maison,* in the style of the house— "the house specialty."

Al dente An Italian phrase meaning "to the tooth," used to describe spaghetti or other pasta at the perfect stage of doneness— tender, but with enough firmness to be felt between the teeth.

Antipasto Another Italian word, this one meaning "before the meal." Antipasto is a selection of hors d'oeuvres such as salami, marinated mushrooms, tuna or anchovies.

Aspic A jelly made from the cooking liquids of beef or poultry, principally. It will jell by itself, but is often strengthened with additional gelatin and used for coating and garnishing cold foods.

Au gratin Usually a creamed mixture topped with bread crumbs and/or cheese and browned in the oven or broiler.

B

Bake To cook cakes, pies, cookies, breads and other pastries and doughs in the oven by dry heat.

Barbecue To roast meat, poultry or fish over hot coals or other heat, basting with a highly seasoned sauce. Also the food so cooked, and the social gathering.

Baste To ladle pan fat, marinade or other liquid over food as it roasts in order to add flavor and prevent dryness.

Batter A flour-liquid mixture as for pancakes, thin enough to pour.

Beat To stir vigorously with a spoon, eggbeater or electric mixer.

Blanch To plunge foods (such as tomatoes and peaches) quickly into boiling water, then into cold water, to loosen skins for easy removal. Also, a preliminary step to freezing vegetables.

Blend To mix two or more ingredients until smooth.

Boil To cook in boiling liquid.

Bouillon A clear stock made of poultry, beef or veal, vegetables and seasonings.

Bouquet garni A small herb bouquet, most often sprigs of fresh parsley and thyme plus a bay leaf, tied in cheesecloth. Dried herbs can be used in place of the fresh. The *bouquet garni* is dropped into stocks, stews, sauces and soups as a seasoner and is removed before serving—usually as soon as it has flavored the dish.

Braise To brown in fat, then to cook, covered, in a small amount of liquid.

Bread To coat with bread crumbs, usually after dipping in beaten egg or milk.

Broil To cook under a broiler or on a grill by direct dry heat.

Broth A clear meat, fish, poultry or vegetable stock made of a combination of them.

C

Chantilly Heavy cream whipped until soft, not stiff; it may be sweetened or not.

Chop To cut into small pieces.

Coat To cover with flour, crumbs or other dry mixture before frying.

Coat the spoon A term used to describe egg-thickened sauces when cooked to perfect degree of doneness; when a custard coats a metal spoon; it leaves a thin, somewhat jellylike film.

Combine To mix together two or more ingredients.

Crimp To press edges of piecrust together with the tines of a fork.

Croutons Small, fried bread cubes.

Crumb To coat with bread or cracker crumbs. So that the crumbs will stick, the food should first be dipped in milk or beaten egg.

Crumble To break between the fingers into small, irregular pieces.

Crush To pulverize food with a rolling pin or whirl in a blender until it is granular or powdered.

Cube To cut into cubes.

Cut in To work shortening or other solid fat into a flour mixture with a pastry blender or two knives until the texture resembles coarse meal.

Cutlet A small, thin, boneless piece of meat—usually stew veal, chicken or turkey breast.

D

Dash A very small amount—less than 1/16 teaspoon.

Deep-Fry To cook in hot, deep temperature-controlled fat.

Deglaze To loosen the browned bits in a skillet or roasting pan by adding liquid while stirring and heating. Glaze is used as a flavor base for sauces and gravies.

Demitasse French for "half cup," it refers to small cups used for after-dinner coffee and also to the strong, black coffee served in them.

Devil To season with mustard, pepper and other spicy condiments.

Dice To cut into small, uniform pieces.

Dissolve To stir a powder or solid ingredient into a liquid to make a solution.

Dot To scatter bits of butter or margarine or other seasoning over the surface of a food to be cooked.

Dough A mixture of flour, liquid and other ingredients stiff enough to knead.

Drain To pour off liquid. Also, to place fried foods on paper toweling to soak up the excess fat.

Drawn butter Melted, clarified butter or margarine; often served with boiled shellfish.

Dredge To coat with flour prior to frying.

Drizzle To pour melted butter or margarine, marinade or other liquid over food in a thin stream.

Duchess Mashed potatoes mixed with egg, butter or margarine and cream, piped around meat, poultry or fish dishes as a decorative border, then browned in the oven or broiler just before serving.

Dust To cover lightly with flour, confectioners' sugar or other dry ingredient.

Dutch oven A large, heavy, metal cooking pot with a tight-fitting cover; used for cooking pot roasts and stews and for braising large cuts of meat and poultry.

E

Espresso Robust, dark, Italian coffee brewed under steam pressure. It is traditionally served in small cups and, in this country (though usually not in Italy), accompanied by twists of lemon rind.

F

Fillet A thin, boneless piece of meat or fish.

Fines herbes A mixture of minced fresh or dried parsley, chervil, tarragon and sometimes chives, used to season salads, omelets and other dishes.

Flake To break up food (salmon or tuna, for example) into smaller pieces with a fork.

Flambé, flambéed French words meaning "flaming." In the culinary sense, the verb *flamber* means to pour warm brandy over a food and to set afire with a match.

Florentine In the style of Florence, Italy, which usually means served on a bed of spinach, topped with a delicate cheese sauce and browned in the oven. Fish and eggs are two foods often served Florentine style.

Flour To coat with flour.

Flute To form a fluted edge with the fingers, on a piecrust edging.

Fold in To mix a light, fluffy ingredient such as beaten egg white into a thicker mixture, using a gentle over-and-over motion.

Fondue Switzerland's gift to good eating: a silky concoction of melted cheese, white wine and kirsch served in an earthenware crock set over a burner. To eat the fondue, chunks of bread are speared with special, long-handled fondue forks and then twirled in the semiliquid cheese mixture. *Fondue Bour-*

guignonne is a convivial Swiss version of a French dish: Cubes of raw steak are speared with the fondue forks, fried at table in a pot of piping hot oil, then dipped into assorted sauces.

Frappé A mushy, frozen dessert.

Fricassee To simmer a chicken covered in water with vegetables, and often wine. The chicken may be browned in butter first. A gravy is made from the broth, and served with the chicken.

Fritter A crisp, golden, deep-fried batter bread, often containing corn or minced fruits or vegetables. Also, pieces of fruit or vegetable, batter-dipped and deep-fried.

G

Garnish To decorate with colorful and/or fancily-cut pieces of food.

Glaze To coat food with honey, syrup or other liquid so it glistens.

Gluten The protein of wheat flour that form the framework of cakes, breads, cookies and pastries.

Goulash A beef stew, flavored with paprika.

Grate To cut into small pieces with a grater.

Grease To rub butter, margarine or other fat over a food or container.

Grill To cook on a grill, usually over charcoal.

Grind To put through a food grinder.

H

Hors d'oeuvres Bite-size appetizers served with cocktails.

Hull To remove caps and stems from berries.

I

Ice To cover with icing. Also, a frozen, water-based, fruit-flavored dessert.

Italienne, à la Served Italian style with a garnish of pasta.

J

Julienne To cut food in uniformly long, thin slivers (1½x¼-inches).

K

Kebob Cubes of meat, fish or poultry and/or vegetables threaded on long skewers and grilled over coals or under the broiler.

Kasha Buckwheat groats braised or cooked in liquid and served in place of rice, potatoes or another starch.

Knead To work dough with the hands until it is springy. Necessary for yeast breads to develop gluten for framework and volume.

L

Lard Creamy-white rendered pork fat.

Line To cover the bottom, and sometimes sides, of a pan with paper, or thin slices of food.

Lyonnaise Seasoned in the style of Lyons, France, meaning with parsley and onions.

M

Macédoine A mixture of vegetables or fruits.

Macerate To let food, principally fruits, steep in wine or spirits (usually kirsch or rum).

Maître d'hôtel Simply cooked dishes seasoned with minced parsley, butter and lemon, *Maître d'hôtel* butter is a mixture of butter (or margarine), parsley, lemon juice and salt. It is most often used to season broiled fish, grilled steaks or chops, or boiled carrots.

Marinade The liquid in which food is marinated.

Marinate To let food, principally meats, steep in a piquant sauce prior to cooking. The marinade serves to tenderize and add flavor.

Marzipan A confection made from almond paste, sugar and egg whites—often colored and shaped into tiny fruit and vegetable forms.

Mash To reduce to pulp.

Mask To coat with sauce or aspic.

Melt To heat a solid such as chocolate or butter until liquid.

Meringue A stiffly beaten mixture of sugar and egg white.

Mince To cut into fine pieces.

Mix To stir together.

Mocha A flavoring for desserts, usually made from coffee or a mixture of coffee and chocolate.

Mold To shape in a mold.

Mousse A rich, creamy, frozen dessert; also, a velvety hot or cold savory dish, rich with cream, bound with eggs or—if cold—with gelatin.

Mull To heat a liquid, such as wine or cider, with whole spices.

N

Niçoise Prepared in the manner of Nice, France—with tomatoes, garlic, olive oil and ripe olives.

O

Oil To rub a pan or mold with cooking oil.

P

Panbroil To cook in a skillet in a small amount of fat; drippings are poured off as they accumulate.

Parboil To cook in water until about half done; vegetables to be cooked *en casserole* are usually parboiled.

Pare To remove the skin of a fruit or vegetable.

Pasta The all-inclusive Italian word for all kinds of macaroni, spaghetti and noodles.

Pastry A stiff dough, made from flour, water and shortening, used for piecrusts, turnovers and other dishes; it is also a rich cookie-type dough used for desserts.

Pâté A well-seasoned mixture of finely minced or ground meats and/or liver. *Pâté de foie gras* is made of goose livers and truffles.

Petits fours Tiny, fancily-frosted cakes.

Pilaf Rice cooked in a savory broth, often with small bits of meat or vegetables, herbs and spices.

Pinch The amount of a dry ingredient that can be taken up between the thumb and index finger—less than ¼ teaspoon.

Pipe To press frosting, whipped cream, mashed potatoes or other soft mixture through a pastry bag fitted with a decorative tube to make a fancy garnish or edging.

Plank A well-seasoned (oiled) hardwood plank used to serve a broiled steak or chop, usually edged with Duchess potatoes.

Plump To soak raisins or other dried fruits in liquid until they plump up.

Poach To cook in simmering liquid, as fish fillets for example.

Polenta A cornmeal porridge popular in Italy. Usually cooled, sliced or cubed, then baked or fried with butter and Parmesan cheese.

Pound To flatten by pounding.

Preheat To bring an oven or broiler to the recommended temperature before cooking food.

Puree To reduce food to a smooth, velvety texture by whirling in an electric blender or pressing through a sieve or food grinder. Also, the food so reduced.

R

Ragôut A stew.

Ramekin A small, individual-size baking dish.

Reduce To boil a liquid, uncovered, until the quantity is concentrated.

Render To melt solid fat.

Rice To press food through a container with small holes. The food then resembles rice grains.

Risotto An Italian dish made with rice browned in fat and combined with tomatoes, mushrooms, onions or truffles. It is usually thick and topped with grated cheese.

Roast To cook meat or poultry in the oven by dry heat.

Roe The eggs of fish: sturgeon, salmon (caviar) or shad; considered delicacies.

Roll To press and shape dough or pastry with a rolling pin.

Roux A cooked, fat-flour mixture used to thicken sauces and gravies.

S

Sauté To cook food quickly in a small amount of hot fat in a skillet.

Scald To heat a liquid just until bubbles form around edge of pan, but liquid does not boil.

Scallop To bake small pieces of food *en casserole,* usually in a cream sauce. Also a thin, boneless slice of meat, such as veal.

Score To make shallow, crisscross cuts over the surface of a food with a knife.

Scrape To remove fruit or vegetable skin by scraping with a knife.

Shirr To cook whole eggs in ramekins with cream and crumbs.

Short An adjective used to describe a bread, cake or pastry that has a high proportion of fat and is ultra-tender or crisp.

Shortening A solid fat, usually of vegetable origin, used to add tenderness to pastry, bread, cookies.

Shred To cut in small, thin slivers by rubbing food such as Cheddar cheese over the holes in a shredder-grater.

Sift To put flour or other dry ingredient through a sifter. (*Note*: In this cookbook, all recipes that call for *sifted*, all-purpose flour require that you sift the flour and then measure it, even if you use a flour that says "sifted" on the bag.)

Simmer To cook in liquid just below the boiling point.

Skewer To thread food on a long metal or wooden pin before it is cooked. Also, the pin itself.

Skim To remove fat or scum from the surface of a liquid or sauce.

Silver To cut in long, thin pieces.

Soak To let stand in liquid.

Spit To thread food on a long rod and roast over glowing coals or under a broiler; also the rod itself.

Steam To cook, covered, on a trivet over a small amount of boiling water so that the steam circulates freely around the food.

Steep To let food soak in liquid until the liquid absorbs its flavor, as in steeping tea in hot water.

Stew To cook, covered, in simmering liquid.

Stir To mix with a spoon using a circular motion.

Stock A liquid flavor base for soups and sauces made by long, slow cooking of meat, poultry or fish with their bones. Stock may be brown or white, depending on whether the meat and bones are browned first.

Stud To press whole cloves, slivers of garlic or other seasoning into the surface of a food to be cooked.

T

Thicken To make a liquid thicker, usually by adding flour, cornstarch or egg.

Thin To make a liquid thinner by adding liquid.

Timbale A savory meat, fish, poultry or vegetable custard, baked in a small mold. Also, pastry shells made on special iron molds— Swedish Rosettes, for example.

Torte A very rich, many-layered cake made with eggs and, often, grated nuts. Usually it is filled, but frequently it is not frosted.

Toss To mix, as a salad, by gently turning ingredients over and over in a bowl, either with the hands or with a large fork and spoon.

Truss To tie down into a compact shape before roasting.

Turnover A folded pastry usually made by cutting a circle or square, adding a dollop of sweet or savory filling, folding into a semicircle or triangle, then crimping the edges with the tines of a fork. Most turnovers are baked, but some are deep-fat fried.

Tutti-Frutti A mixture of minced fruits used as a dessert topping.

V

Véronique A dish garnished with seedless green grapes.

Vinaigrette A sauce, French in origin, made from oil, vinegar, salt, pepper and herbs; usually served on cold meat, fish or vegetables.

W

Whip To beat until frothy or stiff with an eggbeater or in an electric mixer.

Wok A round-bottomed, bowl-shaped Chinese cooking utensil used for stir-frying.

Z

Zest The oily, aromatic, colored part of the rind of citrus fruits.

Index

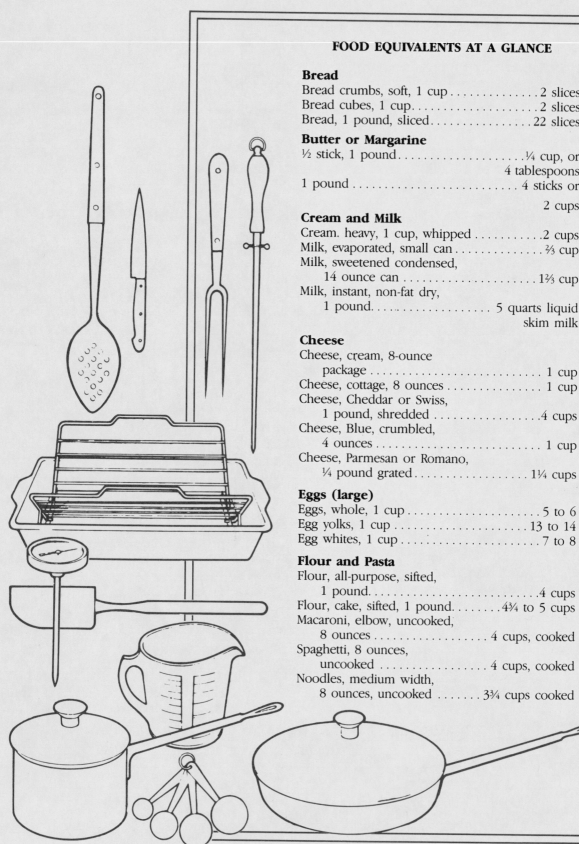

FOOD EQUIVALENTS AT A GLANCE

Bread
Bread crumbs, soft, 1 cup . . . . 2 slices
Bread cubes, 1 cup . . . . 2 slices
Bread, 1 pound, sliced . . . . 22 slices

Butter or Margarine
½ stick, 1 pound . . . . ¼ cup, or
4 tablespoons
1 pound . . . . 4 sticks or

2 cups

Cream and Milk
Cream. heavy, 1 cup, whipped . . . . 2 cups
Milk, evaporated, small can . . . . ⅔ cup
Milk, sweetened condensed,
   14 ounce can . . . . 1⅔ cup
Milk, instant, non-fat dry,
   1 pound . . . . 5 quarts liquid
skim milk

Cheese
Cheese, cream, 8-ounce
   package . . . . 1 cup
Cheese, cottage, 8 ounces . . . . 1 cup
Cheese, Cheddar or Swiss,
   1 pound, shredded . . . . 4 cups
Cheese, Blue, crumbled,
   4 ounces . . . . 1 cup
Cheese, Parmesan or Romano,
   ¼ pound grated . . . . 1¼ cups

Eggs (large)
Eggs, whole, 1 cup . . . . 5 to 6
Egg yolks, 1 cup . . . . 13 to 14
Egg whites, 1 cup . . . . 7 to 8

Flour and Pasta
Flour, all-purpose, sifted,
   1 pound . . . . 4 cups
Flour, cake, sifted, 1 pound . . . . 4¾ to 5 cups
Macaroni, elbow, uncooked,
   8 ounces . . . . 4 cups, cooked
Spaghetti, 8 ounces,
   uncooked . . . . 4 cups, cooked
Noodles, medium width,
   8 ounces, uncooked . . . . 3¾ cups cooked